Annual Editions

FOCUS:
Urban Society

Jacqueline Scherer, Editor

ANNUAL EDITIONS

the dushkin publishing group, inc.
Sluice Dock, Guilford, Ct. 06437

Volumes in the Annual Editions Series

Abnormal Psychology
- Aging
- American Government
- American History Pre-Civil War
- American History Post-Civil War
- Anthropology

Astronomy
- Biology
- Business

Comparative Government
- Criminal Justice

Death and Dying
- Deviance
- Early Childhood Education

Earth Science
- Economics
- Education

Educational Psychology

Energy

Environment

Ethnic Studies

Foreign Policy

Geography

Geology
- Health
- Human Development
- Human Sexuality
- Macroeconomics

Management
- Marketing
- Marriage and Family
- Microeconomics
- Personality and Adjustment

Philosophy

Political Science
- Psychology

Religion
- Social Problems
- Social Psychology
- Sociology
- Urban Society

Western Civilization

Women's Studies

World History

● *Indicates currently available*

CONTENTS

1 Urbanization

2 Varieties of Urban Experiences

3

Urban Problems

4

Urban Social Policies

5

Urban Futures

PREFACE

Today, magazines and newspapers are concerned with the problems of cities and the pathology of urban life. Many of our cities are characterized as dead or dying and specific cases of urban plight, with all the painful details of metropolitan life, are continually discussed in depth. It is very difficult to find comprehensive and balanced discussions of the urban condition in popular journals, and there are relatively few good assessments of social policies to provide guidelines for resolving urban problems. For this reason, the student of urban society utilizing contemporary sources reflects a hard search for intelligent and comprehensive perspectives on urban phenomena.

Today's society is dominated by urban social structures and modes of thinking. In the United States over 70% of Americans live in standard metropolitan areas. The problems of urbanization affect everyone. By urbanization, we refer to the movements of populations from farms and rural areas to cities and metropolitan regions, and to the changes in living which accompany such movement. Industrialization accelerated the pace of urbanization and this rate of change had an effect on our basic social institutions, our economic arrangements, our political organizations, and our values and system of beliefs. The impact of urbanization is an important area of social scientific study. It includes psychology, sociology, anthropology, political science, history, and geography. The many ways of adapting to urban life, and the forms of social organization that evolve provide a rich stage for research and investigation.

The selections in this reader reflect a broad approach to urban study. The process of urbanization is interpreted within the framework utilized by scholars currently working in the field of urban studies. An understanding of urbanization is important for everyone if we are to find solutions to our urban problems.

The articles in this book were selected for their clearity, currency in the sense of addressing relevant concerns for 1978-1979, understanding of urbanization and usefulness as a teaching aid, and finally, ability to stimulate interest in students to pursue the study of urban society.

We think ANNUAL EDITIONS is one of the most useful, up-to-date books available, but we would like to know what you think. Please fill out the Reader Response card on the last page of this book and let us know your opinions. Any anthology can be improved. This one will continue to be—annually.

Jacqueline Scherer, *Editor*

1. ▪ Urbanization

Urbanization is a complex continuous process. It is both the movement of people from rural to urban areas and the spread of urban cultural patterns to rural areas. Historically the city has been the center of economic and cultural activity.

Rapid growth of the cities was largely a consequence of developments in agriculture and industry. As society became more sophisticated in the growing and distribution of food, labor needs for farming lessened. The development of the factory system led to a concentration of labor and services in urban areas. Before 1800 only 3 percent of the world's population lived in towns of more than 5,000 inhabitants. Today over 25 percent of the world's population lives in urban communities of more than 20,000.

Social scientists have been fascinated with the processes of urbanization for many reasons. Historically, a study of the dynamics of urban growth could illustrate the ways in which entire cultures and nations changed over time. Sociologically, the very nature of urbanization was thought to determine social arrangements and transform social structures.

Psychologically, the individual had to learn to cope with new opportunities for and threats of survival. Economically, the city, and recently the suburbs, were viewed as important units for generating wealth and for allocating resources. Political scientists too, studied these issues to gain a better understanding of the ways in which order and change were maintained in these dynamic units. Anthropologists gradually turned from their fascination with distant cultures to those cultural units located within cosmopolitan centers and systematically observed subcultural groups within the urban culture.

It is clear that the experience of living in urban areas has become the dominant mode of life for a large percentage of people in the world. The classic sociological essay of Simmel begins our examination of urbanization. Many of the key themes of Simmel's analysis will be found in articles throughout the section. How does urbanization influence social life? How is the individual affected by this phenomenon? What historical factors contributed to urbanization and continue to operate in the world today? Has urbanization enhanced the quality of human life?

The Metropolis and Mental Life

Georg Simmel

*Georg Simmel was a German sociologist
and conflict theorist who proposed that a
number of stable forms of interaction
underlie the superficial diversity of
manifest social occurrences.*

The deepest problems of modern life derive from the claim of the
individual to preserve the autonomy and individuality of his existence
in the face of overwhelming social forces, of historical heritage, of
external culture, and of the technique of life. The fight with nature
which primitive man has to wage for his *bodily* existence attains in this
modern man its latest transformation. The eighteenth century called
upon man to free himself of all the historical bonds in the state and in
religion, in morals and in economics. Man's nature, originally good and
common to all, should develop unhampered. In addition to more liberty,
the nineteenth century demanded the functional specialization of man
and his work; this specialization makes one individual incomparable to
another, and each of them indispensable to the highest possible extent.
However, this specialization makes each man the more directly dependent upon the supplementary activities of all others. Nietzsche sees the
full development of the individual conditioned by the most ruthless
struggle of individuals; socialism believes in the suppression of all competition for the same reason. Be that is it may, in all these positions the
same basic motive is at work: the person resists to being leveled down
and worn out by a social-technological mechanism. An inquiry into the
inner meaning of specifically modern life and its products, into the soul
of the cultural body, so to speak, must seek to solve the equation which
structures like the metropolis set up between the individual and the
superindividual contents of life. Such an inquiry must answer the question of how the personality accommodates itself in the adjustments to
external forces. This will be my task today.

The psychological basis of the metropolitan type of individuality
consists in the *intensification of nervous stimulation* which results from the
swift and uninterrupted change of outer and inner stimuli. Man is a
differentiating creature. His mind is stimulated by the difference between a momentary impression and the one which preceded it. Lasting
impressions, impressions which differ only slightly from one another,
impressions which take a regular and habitual course and show regular
and habitual contrasts—all these use up, so to speak, less consciousness
than does the rapid crowding of changing images, the sharp discontinu-
ity in the grasp of a single glance, and the unexpectedness of onrushing
impressions. These are the psychological conditions which the metropolis creates. With each crossing of the street, with the tempo and multiplicity of economic, occupational and social life, the city sets up a deep
contrast with small town and rural life with reference to the sensory
foundations of psychic life. The metropolis exacts from man as a dis-
criminating creature a different amount of consciousness than does rural
life. Here the rhythm of life and sensory mental imagery flows more
slowly, more habitually, and more evenly. Precisely in this connection
the sophisticated character of metropolitan psychic life becomes under-

standable—as over against small town life which rests more upon deeply felt and emotional relationships. These latter are rooted in the more unconscious layers of the psyche and grow most readily in the steady rhythm of uninterrupted habituations. The intellect, however, has its locus in the transparent, conscious, higher layers of the psyche; it is the most adaptable of our inner forces. In order to accommodate to change and to the contrast of phenomena, the intellect does not require any shocks and inner upheavals; it is only through such upheavals that the more conservative mind could accommodate to the metropolitan rhythm of events. Thus the metropolitan type of man—which, of course, exists in a thousand individual variants—develops an organ protecting him against the threatening currents and discrepancies of his external environment which would uproot him. He reacts with his head instead of his heart. In this an increased awareness assumes the psychic prerogative. Metropolitan life, thus, underlies a heightened awareness and a predominance of intelligence in metropolitan man. The reaction to metropolitan phenomena is shifted to that organ which is least sensitive and quite remote from the depth of the personality. Intellectuality is thus seen to preserve subjective life against the overwhelming power of metropolitan life, and intellectuality branches out in many directions and is integrated with numerous discrete phenomena.

The metropolis has always been the seat of the money economy. Here the multiplicity and concentration of economic exchange gives an importance to the means of exchange which the scantiness of rural commerce would not have allowed. Money economy and the dominance of the intellect are intrinsically connected. They share a matter-of-fact attitude in dealing with men and with things; and, in this attitude, a formal justice is often coupled with an inconsiderate hardness. The intellectually sophisticated person is indifferent to all genuine individuality, because relationships and reactions result from it which cannot be exhausted with logical operations. In the same manner, the individuality of phenomena is not commensurate with the pecuniary principle. Money is concerned only with what is common to all: it asks for the exchange value, it reduces all quality and individuality to the question: How much? All intimate emotional relations between persons are founded in their individuality, whereas in rational relations man is reckoned with like a number, like an element which is in itself indifferent. Only the objective measurable achievement is of interest. Thus metropolitan man reckons with his merchants and customers, his domestic servants and often even with persons with whom he is obliged to have social intercourse. These features of intellectuality contrast with the nature of the small circle in which the inevitable knowledge of individuality as inevitably produces a warmer tone of behavior, a behavior which is beyond a mere objective balancing of service and return. In the sphere of the economic psychology of the small group it is of importance that under primitive conditions production serves the customer who orders the good, so that the producer and the consumer are acquainted. The modern metropolis, however, is supplied almost entirely by production for the market, that is, for entirely unknown purchasers who never personally enter the producer's actual field of vision. Through this anonymity the interests of each party acquire an unmerciful matter-of-factness; and the intellectually calculating economic egoisms of both parties need not fear any deflection because of the imponderables of personal relationships. The money economy dominates the metropolis; it has displaced the last survivals of domestic production and the direct barter of goods; it minimizes from day to day the amount of work ordered by customers. The matter-of-fact attitude is obviously so intimately interrelated with the money economy, which is dominant in the metropolis, that nobody can say whether the intellectualistic mentality first promoted the money economy or whether the latter determined the former. The metropolitan way of life is certainly the most fertile soil for this reciprocity, a point which I shall document merely by citing the dictum of the most eminent English constitutional historian: throughout the whole course of English history, London has never acted as England's heart but often as England's intellect and always as her moneybag!

In certain seemingly insignificant traits, which lie upon the surface of life, the same psychic currents characteristically unite. Modern mind has become more and more calculating. The calculative exactness of practical life which the money economy has brought about corresponds to the ideal of natural science: to transform the world into an arithmetic problem, to fix every part of the world by mathematical formulas. Only money economy has filled the days of so many people with weighing, calculating, with numerical determinations, with a reduction of qualitative values to quantitative ones. Through the calculative nature of money a new precision, a certainty in the definition of identities and differences, an unambiguousness in agreements and arrangements has been brought about in the relations of life-elements—just as externally this precision has been effected by the universal diffusion of pocket watches. However, the conditions of metropolitan life are at once cause and effect of this trait. The relationships and affairs of the typical metropolitan usually are so varied and complex that without the strictest punctuality in promises and services the whole structure would break down into an inextricable chaos. Above all, this necessity is brought about by the aggregation of so many people with such differentiated interests, who must integrate their relations and activities into a highly complex organism. If all clocks and watches in Berlin would suddenly go wrong in different ways, even if only by one hour, all economic life and communication of the city would be disrupted for a long time. In addition an apparently mere external factor, long distances, would make all waiting and broken appointments result in an ill-afforded waste of time. Thus, the technique of metropolitan life is unimaginable without the most punctual integration of all activities and mutual relations into a stable and impersonal time schedule. Here again the general conclusions of this entire task of reflection become obvious, namely, that from each point on the surface of existence—however closely attached to the surface alone—one may drop a sounding into the depth of the psyche so that all the most banal externalities of life finally are connected with the ultimate decisions concerning the meaning and style of life. Punctuality, calculability, exactness are forced upon life by the complexity and extension of metropolitan existence and are not only most intimately connected with its money economy and intellectualistic character. These traits must also color the contents of life and favor the exclusion of those irrational, instinctive, sovereign traits and impulses which aim at determining the mode of life from within, instead of receiving the general and precisely schematized form of life from without. Even though sovereign types of personality, characterized by irrational impulses, are by no means impossible in the city, they are, nevertheless, opposed to typical city life. The passionate hatred of men like Ruskin and Nietzsche for the metropolis is understandable in these terms. Their natures discovered the value of life alone in the unschematized existence which cannot be defined with precision for all alike. From the same source of this hatred of the metropolis surged their hatred of money economy and of the intellectualism of modern existence.

The same factors which have thus coalesced into the exactness and minute precision of the form of life have coalesced into a structure of the highest impersonality; on the other hand, they have promoted a highly personal subjectivity. There is perhaps no psychic phenomenon which has been so unconditionally reserved to the metropolis as has the blasé attitude. The blasé attitude results first from the rapidly changing and closely compressed contrasting stimulations of the nerves. From this the enhancement of metropolitan intellectuality, also, seems originally to stem. Therefore, stupid people who are not intellectually alive in the first place usually are not exactly blasé. A life in boundless pursuit of pleasure makes one blasé because it agitates the nerves to their strongest reactivity for such a long time that they finally cease to react at all. In the same way, through the rapidity and contradictoriness of their changes, more harmless impressions force such violent responses, tearing the nerves so brutally hither and thither, that their last reserves of strength are spent; and if one remains in the same milieu they have no time to gather new strength. An incapacity thus emerges to react to new sensations with the appropriate energy. This constitutes that blasé attitude which, in fact, every metropolitan child shows when compared with children of quieter and less changeable milieus.

This physiological source of the metropolitan blasé attitude is joined by another source which flows from the money economy. The essence of the blasé attitude consists in the blunting of discrimination. This does not mean that the objects are not perceived, as is the case with the half-wit, but rather that the meaning and differing values of things, and thereby the things themselves, are experienced as insubstantial. They appear to the blasé person in an evenly flat and gray tone; no one object deserves preference over any other. This mood is the faithful subjective reflection of the completely internalized money economy. By being the equivalent to all the manifold things in one and the same way, money becomes the most frightful leveler. For money expresses all qualitative differences of things in terms of "how much?" Money, with all its colorlessness and indifference, becomes the common denominator of all values; irreparably it hollows out the core of things, their individuality, their specific value, and their incomparability. All things float with equal specific gravity in the constantly moving stream of money. All things lie on the same level and differ from one another only in the size of the area which they cover. In the individual case this coloration, or rather discoloration, of things through their money equivalence may be unnoticeably minute. However, through the relations of the rich to the objects to be had for money, perhaps even through the total character which the mentality of the contemporary public everywhere imparts to these objects, the exclusively pecuniary evaluation of objects has become quite considerable. The large cities, the main seats of the money exchange, bring the purchasability of things to the fore much more impressively than do smaller localities. That is why cities are also the genuine locale of the blasé attitude. In the blasé attitude the concentration of men and things stimulate the nervous system of the individual to its highest achievement so that it attains its peak. Through the mere quantitative intensification of the same conditioning factors this achievement is transformed into its opposite and appears in the peculiar adjustment of the blasé attitude. In this phenomenon the nerves find in the refusal to react to their stimulation the last possibility of accommodating to the contents and forms of metropolitan life. The self-preservation of certain personalities is bought at the price of devaluating the whole objective world, a devaluation which in the end unavoidably drags one's own personality down into a feeling of the same worthlessness.

Whereas the subject of this form of existence has to come to terms with it entirely for himself, his self-preservation in the face of the large city demands from him a no less negative behavior of a social nature. This mental attitude of metropolitans toward one another we may designate, from a formal point of view, as reserve. If so many inner reactions were responses to the continuous external contacts with innumerable people as are those in the small town, where one knows almost everybody one meets and where one has a positive relation to almost everyone, one would be completely atomized internally and come to an unimaginable psychic state. Partly this psychological fact, partly the right to distrust which men have in the face of the touch-and-go elements of metropolitan life, necessitates our reserve. As a result of this reserve we frequently do not even know by sight those who have been our neighbors for years. And it is this reserve which in the eyes of the small-town people makes us appear to be cold and heartless. Indeed, if I do not deceive myself, the inner aspect of this outer reserve is not only indifference but, more often than we are aware, it is a slight aversion, a mutual strangeness and repulsion, which will break into hatred and fight at the moment of a closer contact, however caused. The whole inner organization of such an extensive communicative life rests upon an extremely varied hierarchy of sympathies, indifferences, and aversions of the briefest as well as of the most permanent nature. The sphere of indifference in this hierarchy is not as large as might appear on the surface. Our psychic activity still responds to almost every impression of somebody else with a somewhat distinct feeling. The unconscious, fluid and changing character of this impression seems to result in a state of indifference. Actually this indifference would be just as unnatural as the diffusion of indiscriminate mutual suggestion would be unbearable. From both these typical dangers of the metropolis, indifference and indiscriminate suggestibility, antipathy protects us. A latent antipathy and the preparatory stage of practical antagonism effect the distances and aversions without which this mode of life could not at all be led. The extent and the mixture of this style of life, the rhythm of its emergence and disappearance, the forms in which it is satisfied—all these, with the unifying motives in the narrower sense, form the inseparable whole of the metropolitan style of life. What appears in the metropolitan style of life directly as dissociation is in reality only one of its elemental forms of socialization.

This reserve with its overtone of hidden aversion appears in turn as the form or the cloak of a more general mental phenomenon of the metropolis: it grants to the individual a kind and an amount of personal freedom which has no analogy whatsoever under other conditions. The metropolis goes back to one of the large developmental tendencies of social life as such, to one of the few tendencies for which an approximately universal formula can be discovered. The earliest phase of social formations found in historical as well as in contemporary social structures is this: a relatively small circle firmly closed against neighboring, strange, or in some way antagonistic circles. However, this circle is closely coherent and allows its individual members only a narrow field for the development of unique qualities and free, self-responsible movements. Political and kinship groups, parties and religious associations begin in this way. The self-preservation of very young associations requires the establishment of strict boundaries and a centripetal unity. Therefore they cannot allow the individual freedom and unique inner and outer development. From this stage social development proceeds at once in two different, yet corresponding, directions. To the extent to which the group grows—numerically, spatially, in significance and in content of life—to the same degree the group's direct, inner unity loosens, and the rigidity of the original demarcation against others is softened through mutual relations and connections. At the same time, the individual gains freedom of movement, far beyond the first jealous delimitation. The individual also gains a specific individuality to which the division of labor in the enlarged group gives both occasion and necessity. The state and Christianity, guilds and political parties, and innumerable other groups have developed according to this formula, however much, of course, the special conditions and forces of the respective groups have modified the general scheme. This scheme seems to me distinctly recognizable also in the evolution of individuality within urban life. The small-town life in Antiquity and in the Middle Ages set barriers against movement and relations of the individual toward the outside, and it set up barriers against individual independence and differentiation within the individual self. These barriers were such that under them modern man could not have breathed. Even today a metropolitan man who is placed in a small town feels a restriction similar, at least, in kind. The smaller the circle which forms our milieu is, and the more restricted those relations to others are which dissolve the boundaries of the individual, the more anxiously the circle guards the achievements, the conduct of life, and the outlook of the individual, and the more readily a quantitative and qualitative specialization would break up the framework of the whole little circle.

The ancient *polis* is this respect seems to have had the very character of a small town. The constant threat to its existence at the hands of enemies from near and afar effected strict coherence in political and military respects, a supervision of the citizen by the citizen, a jealousy of the whole against the individual whose particular life was suppressed to such a degree that he could compensate only by acting as a despot in his own household. The tremendous agitation and excitement, the unique colorfulness of Athenian life, can perhaps be understood in terms of the fact that a people of incomparably individualized personalities struggled against the constant inner and outer pressure of a deindividualizing small town. This produced a tense atmosphere in which the weaker individuals were suppressed and those of stronger natures were incited to prove themselves in the most passionate manner. This is precisely why it was that there blossomed in Athens what must be called, without defining it exactly, "the general human character" in the intellectual development of our species. For we maintain factual as well as historical validity for the following connection: the most extensive and the most general contents and forms of life are most intimately connected with the most individual ones. They have a preparatory stage in common, that is, they find their enemy in narrow formations and groupings the maintenance of which places both of them into a state of defense against expanse and generality lying without and the freely moving individuality within. Just as in the feudal age, the "free" man was the one who derived his right merely from the narrow circle of a feudal association and was excluded from the larger social orbit—so today metropolitan man is "free" in a spiritualized and refined sense, in contrast to the pettiness and prejudices which hem in the small-town man. For the reciprocal reserve and indifference and the intellectual life conditions of large circles are never felt more strongly by the individual in their impact upon his independence than in the thickest crowd of the big city. This is because the bodily proximity and the narrowness of space makes the mental distance only the more visible. It is obviously only the obverse of this freedom if, under certain circumstances, one nowhere feels as lonely and lost as in the metropolitan crowd. For here as elsewhere it is by no means necessary that the freedom of man be reflected in his emotional life as comfort.

It is not only the immediate size of the area and the number of persons which, because of the universal historical correlation between the enlargement of the circle and the personal inner and outer freedom, has made the metropolis the locale of freedom. It is rather in transcending this visible expanse that any given city expands in a manner comparable to the way in which wealth develops; a certain amount of property increases in a quasiautomatical way in ever more rapid progression. As soon as a certain limit has been passed, the economic, personal, and intellectual relations of the citizenry, the sphere of intellectual predominance of the city over its hinterland, grow as in geometrical progression. Every gain in dynamic extension becomes a step, not for an equal, but for a new and larger extension. From every thread spinning out of the city, ever new threads grow as if by themselves, just as within the city the unearned increment of ground rent, through the mere increase in communication, brings the owner automatically increasing profits. At this point, the quantitative aspect of life is transformed directly into qualitative traits of character. The sphere of life of the small town is, in the main, self-contained and autarchic. For it is the decisive nature of the metropolis that its inner life overflows by waves into a farflung national or international area. Weimar is not an example to the contrary, since its significance was hinged upon individual personalities and died with them; whereas the metropolis is indeed characterized by its essential independence even from the most eminent individual personalities. This is the counterpart to the independence; and it is the price the individual pays for the independence, which he enjoys in the metropolis. The most significant characteristic of the metropolis is this functional extension beyond its physical boundaries. And this efficacy reacts in turn and gives weight, importance, and responsibility to metropolitan life. Man does not end with the limits of his body or the area comprising his immediate activity. Rather is the range of the person constituted by the sum of effects emanating from him temporarily and spatially. In the same way, a city consists of its total effects which extend beyond its immediate confines. Only this range is the city's actual extent in which its existence is expressed. This fact makes it obvious that individual freedom, the logical and historical complement of such extension, is not to be understood only in the negative sense of mere freedom of mobility and elimination of prejudices and petty philistinism. The essential point is that the particularity and incomparability, which ultimately every human being possesses, be somehow expressed in the working-out of a way of life. That we follow the laws of our own nature—and this after all is freedom—becomes obvious and convincing to ourselves and to others only if the expressions of this nature differ from the expressions of others. Only our unmistakability proves that our way of life has not been superimposed by others.

Cities are, first of all, seats of the highest economic division of labor. They produce thereby such extreme phenomena as in Paris the remunerative occupation of the *quatorzième.* They are persons who identify themselves by signs on their residences and who are ready at the dinner hour in correct attire, so that they can be quickly called upon if a dinner party should consist of thirteen persons. In the measure of expansion, the city offers more and more the decisive conditions of the division of labor. It offers a circle which through its size can absorb a highly diverse variety of services. At the same time, the concentration of individuals and their struggle for customers compel the individual to specialize in a function from which he cannot be readily displaced by another. It is decisive that city life has transformed the struggle with nature for livelihood into an inter-human struggle for gain, which here is not granted by nature but by other men. For specialization does not flow only from the competition for gain but also from the underlying fact that the seller must always seek to call forth new and differentiated needs of the lured customer. In order to find a source of income which is not yet exhausted, and to find a function which cannot readily be displaced, it is necessary to specialize in one's services. This process promotes differentiation, refinement, and the enrichment of the public's needs, which obviously must lead to growing personal differences within this public.

All this forms the transition to the individualization of mental and psychic traits which the city occasions in proportion to its size. There is a whole series of obvious causes underlying this process. First, one must meet the difficulty of asserting his own personality within the dimensions of metropolitan life. Where the quantitative increase in importance and the expense of energy reach their limits, one seizes upon qualitative differentiation by playing upon its sensitivity for differences. Finally, man is tempted to adopt the most tendentious peculiarities, that is, the specifically metropolitan extravagances of mannerism, caprice, and preciousness. Now, the meaning of these extravagances does not at all lie in the contents of such behavior, but rather in its form of "being different," of standing out in a striking manner and thereby attracting attention. For many character types, ultimately the only means of saving for themselves some modicum of self-esteem and the sense of filling a position is indirect, through the awareness of others. In the same sense a seemingly insignificant factor is operating, the cumulative effects of which are, however, still noticeable. I refer to the brevity and scarcity of the inter-human contacts granted to the metropolitan man, as compared with social intercourse in the small town. The temptation to appear "to the point," to appear concentrated and strikingly characteristic, lies much closer to the individual in brief metropolitan contacts than in an atmosphere in which frequent and prolonged association assures the personality of an unambiguous image of himself in the eyes of the other.

The most profound reason, however, why the metropolis conduces to the urge for the most individual personal existence—no matter whether justified and successful—appears to me to be the following: the development of modern culture is characterized by the preponderance of what one may call the "objective spirit" over the "subjective spirit."

This is to say, in language as well as in law, in the technique of production as well as in art, in science as well as in the objects of the domestic environment, there is embodied a sum of spirit. The individual in his intellectual development follows the growth of this spirt very imperfectly and at an ever increasing distance. If, for instance, we view the immense culture which for the last hundred years has been embodied in things and in knowledge, in institutions and in comforts, and if we compare all this with the cultural progress of the individual during the same period—at least in high status groups—a frightful disproportion in growth between the two becomes evident. Indeed, at some points we notice a retrogression in the culture of the individual with reference to spirituality, delicacy, and idealism. This descrepancy results essentially from the growing division of labor. For the division of labor demands from the individual an ever more one-sided accomplishment, and the greatest advance in a one-sided pursuit only too frequently means death to the personality of the individual. In any case, he can cope less and less with the overgrowth of objective culture. The individual is reduced to a negligible quantity, perhaps less in his consciousness than in his practice and in the totality of his obscure emotional states that are derived from this practice. The individual has become a mere cog in an enormous organization of things and powers which tear from his hands all progress, spirituality, and value in order to transform them from their subjective form into the form of of purely objective life. It needs merely to be pointed out that the metropolis is the genuine arena of this culture which outgrows all personal life. Here in buildings and educational institutions, in the wonders and comforts of space-conquering technology, in the formations of community life, and in the visible institutions of the state, is offered such an overwhelming fullness of crystalized and impersonalized spirit that the personality, so to speak, cannot maintain itself under its impact. On the one hand, life is made infinitely easy for the personality in that stimulations, interests, uses of time and consciousness are offered to it from all sides. They carry the person as if in a stream, and one needs hardly to swim for oneself. On the other hand, however, life is composed more and more of these impersonal contents and offerings which tend to displace the genuine personal colorations and incomparabilities. This results in the individual's summoning the utmost in uniqueness and particularization, in order to preserve his most personal core. He has to exaggerate this personal element in order to remain audible even to himself. The atrophy of individual culture through the hypertrophy of objective culture is one reason for the bitter hatred which the preachers of the most extreme individualism, above all Nietzsche, harbor against the metropolis. But it is, indeed, also a reason why these preachers are so passionately loved in the metropolis and why they appear to the metropolitan man as the prophets and saviors of his most unsatisfied yearnings.

If one asks for the historical position of these two forms of individualism which are nourished by the quantitative relation of the metropolis, namely, individual independence and the elaboration of individuality itself, then the metropolis assumes an entirely new rank order in the world history of the spirit. The eighteenth century found the individual in oppressive bonds which had become meaningless—bonds of a political, agrarian, guild, and religious character. They were restraints which, so to speak, force upon man an unnatural form and outmoded, unjust inequalities. In this situation the cry for liberty and equality arose, the belief in the individual's full freedom of movement in all social and intellectual relationships. Freedom would at once permit the noble substance common to all to come to the fore, a substance which nature had deposited in every man and which society and history had only deformed. Besides this eighteenth-century ideal of liberalism, in the nineteenth century, through Goethe and Romanticism, on the one hand, and through the economic division of labor, on the other hand, another ideal arose: individuals liberated from historical bonds now wished to distinguish themselves from one another. The carrier of man's values is no longer the "general human being" in every individual, but rather man's qualitative uniqueness and irreplaceability. The external and internal history of our time takes its course within the struggle and in the changing entanglements of these two ways of defining the individual's role in the whole of society. It is the function of the metropolis to provide the arena for this struggle and its reconciliation. For the metropolis presents the peculiar conditions which are revealed to us as the opportunities and the stimuli for the development of both these ways of allocating roles to men. Therewith these conditions gain a unique place, pregnant with inestimable meanings for the development of psychic existence. The metropolis reveals itself as one of those great historical formations in which opposing streams which enclose life unfold, as well as join one another with equal right. However, in this process the currents of life, whether their individual phenomena touch us sympathetically or antipathetically, entirely transcend the sphere for which the judge's attitude is appropriate. Since such forces of life have grown into the roots and into the crown of the whole of the historical life in which we, in our fleeting existence, as a cell, belong only as a part, it is not our task either to accuse or to pardon, but only to understand.[1]

_____

1. The content of this lecture by its very nature does not derive from a citable literature. Argument and elaboration of its major cultural-historical ideas are contained in my *Philosophie des Geldes* [The Philosophy of Money; München and Leipzig: Duncker und Humblot, 1900].

Rural-Urban Differences in Attitudes and Behavior in the United States

Norval D. Glenn and Lester Hill, Jr.

Norval D. Glenn is Professor of Sociology at the University of Texas at Austin. Formerly on the faculties of Miami University and the University of Illinois at Urbana, his publications include four books and more than 80 journal articles and book chapters, primarily on social stratification, political sociology, the family, aging and the life cycle, and urban sociology. He is author of a forthcoming monograph on the methodology of cohort analysis.

Lester Hill, Jr., a doctoral candidate in the Department of Sociology at the University of Texas at Austin, is writing a dissertation on the relationship between attitudes and behavior.

ABSTRACT: Recent American data reveal moderate to substantial farm-nonfarm differences on a few kinds of attitudes and behavior, but since farm people now are only about 4 percent of the population, the farm-nonfarm distinction cannot account for much of the total variation of any kind of attitudes or behavior. The kinds of attitudes and behavior which differ substantially between farm and non-farm people usually differ monotonically by community size; hence, "ruralism" seems to some extent to characterize residents of the smaller dense settlements and, to a lesser extent, those of intermediate-sized cities. Furthermore, city residents with rural backgrounds tend to retain rural attitudes and behavior characteristics, size of community of origin being a

stronger predictor of some attitudes than size of community of current residence. Although the association of community size with a more or less representative list of attitudinal variables is weak, such correlates of community size as age and socio-economic status do not largely account for the larger associations, which probably reflect a tendency for social and cultural change to occur earlier in the larger communities. The explanatory utility of size of community of origin and of residence seems less than that of age and education but at least as great as that of several other explanatory variables favored by social scientists, such as family income and occupational prestige.

THERE is considerable disagreement among social scientists concerning the importance of the rural-urban distinction in modern societies. At least three rather distinctive viewpoints have some prominence. The first, exemplified in Louis Wirth's classic essay on "Urbanism as a Way of Life," posits direct, universal effects of population size, density, and heterogeneity on important aspects of social structure, culture, and personality.[1] According to this view, the concentration of people of diverse characteristics and backgrounds into large, dense settlements necessarily produces social isolation, individualism, social disorganization, and a number of other phenomena.

A second major viewpoint, exemplified in the writings of Richard

Dewey[2] and Herbert Gans,[3] among others, is that few if any social, cultural, and personality characteristics are necessarily and invariably associated with the size, density, and heterogeneity of settlements. Critics of the Wirth thesis also often point out that population size, density, and heterogeneity are imperfectly correlated with one another and that the effects of each may not be the same as the effects of the other two. According to this view, the correlates of urbanization vary from society to society and from time to time in any one society and are often little more than the results of historical accident. For instance, it is pointed out that many present rural-urban differences in the United States result from inclusion among the later immigrants—who arrived after the closing of the frontier and thus generally settled in the industrial cities—of a relatively large percentage of Catholics, Jews, and persons from southern and eastern Europe. Hence, rural-urban differences tend to reflect religious and ethnic differences.

Related to this second view is the thesis that rural-urban differences, whatever their source, tend to disappear during the advanced stages of urbanization and industrialization.[4]

1. Louis Wirth, "Urbanism as a Way of Life," *American Journal of Sociology*, vol. 44 (July 1938), pp. 3–24.

2. Richard Dewey, "The Rural-Urban Continuum: Real but Relatively Unimportant," *American Journal of Sociology*, vol. 66 (July 1960), pp. 60–6.

3. Herbert J. Gans, "Urbanism and Suburbanism as Ways of Life: A Re-Evaluation of Definitions," in Arnold M. Rose, ed., *Human Behavior and Social Processes* (Boston: Houghton-Mifflin, 1962), pp. 625–28.

4. For instance, see Kenneth Boulding, "The Death of the City: A Frightened Look at Post-Civilization," in Oscar Handlin and John Burchard, eds., *The Historian and the City* (Cambridge, Mass.: MIT and Harvard University Press, 1963), p. 143.

From the *Annals of the Political Science Society*, January, 1977. Copyright © 1977, by The American Academy of Political and Social Science. All rights reserved.

This view, which the senior author has called the "massification thesis,"[5] is that due to such influences as standardized education, improved means of transportation which break down rural isolation, and saturation of small towns and the countryside with stimuli from the mass media, urban culture and lifestyles are diffused to the hinterland—that rural people become almost indistinguishable from their city cousins. So far as we know, no social scientist has denied that considerable urban-to-rural cultural diffusion has occurred in modern societies, but the extent to which this diffusion has obliterated rural-urban differences remains an issue of debate.

An intermediate viewpoint—articulated most completely and clearly in a recent essay by Claude Fischer[6] but presented in at least embryonic form in several earlier publications—is that whereas population size, density, and heterogeneity do not have all of the effects attributed to them by Wirth, they are conducive to innovation and unconventional behavior. According to Fischer, population concentration "produces a diversity of subcultures, strengthens them, and fosters diffusion among them. . . ." Presumably, the concentration of diverse people into dense settlements is conducive to a cross-fertilization of ideas, to an awareness of and tolerance of diverse values and lifestyles, and thus to innovation and unconventionality.

If in each society the cities tend to be the sources of innovation and to be in the vanguard of social and cultural change, appreciable rural-urban differences are likely to exist even if much urban-to-rural diffusion of culture has occurred and is occurring. During the initial phases of any particular process of change, the urban population will tend to change more rapidly, leading to rural-urban divergence. Later, "ceiling effects" will tend to limit the rate of change in the urban population, and urban-to-rural diffusion will lead

to more rapid change in the rural population and to rural-urban convergence. Thus, as older rural-urban differences diminish or disappear, new ones will appear. Whereas no particular culture traits, aside from those closely associated with receptivity to change, will invariably be associated with rural or urban communities, important rural-urban differences of some kind will tend to persist even in the most highly urbanized and industrialized societies.

The social scientific literature does not provide the evidence (at least not in a systematic fashion) which would allow a definitive choice among the differing viewpoints. Although the preponderance of evidence seems to suggest that the Wirth thesis is not correct without important qualifications, survey data from virtually all modern societies reveal remaining rural-urban differences in regard to a variety of kinds of attitudes and behavior. There is evidence that in the United States some rural-urban differences have recently increased rather than diminished,[7] but the evidence does not allow any conclusion about the magnitude or direction of the overall change. The evidence that social and cultural change typically originates in cities and proceeds more rapidly among urban than rural people is convincing but not definitive. It is easy to demonstrate that change often has occurred in this fashion, but we do not know that it has always done so, even in modern societies, or that it usually has done so in most societies.

Even though the Fischer thesis is not undeniably correct, presently available evidence, as we assess it, makes it more credible than any competing theoretical perspective. We suspect that it (or some slight variant) will soon become the most widely accepted view among students of rural-urban differences (if it is not already), and we provisionally accept it. However, even a developing consensus on the basic sources of rural-urban cultural and behavioral differences will not still debate

concerning the practical and theoretical importance of these differences in modern societies. For instance, the importance of differences created by any differing receptivity to change depends in large measure on whether the receptivity varies in a more or less linear fashion with community size or whether the main difference is a disjunctive one between the most truly rural people (those who both live and work in the open countryside) and the remainder of the population. If the latter should be correct, the resulting rural-urban differences would be of rapidly diminishing practical importance in most modern societies as the rural-farm population becomes a very small proportion of the total. Furthermore, as Fischer is careful to point out, if his theory is correct, it does not necessarily follow that rural-urban differences are usually large enough to be of much practical importance or that the rural-urban distinction accounts for a large proportion of the variation in attitudes, behavior, and lifestyles in any society. To those who would understand, or who would utilize knowledge of, variations in attitudes and behavior in the United States, an important question remains unanswered: does the rural-urban distinction make enough difference to warrant serious attention? Our purpose here is to provide a provisional answer to that question.

THE MAGNITUDE AND NATURE OF
CONTEMPORARY RURAL-URBAN
DIFFERENCES

The magnitude of rural-urban differences in attitudes and behavior shown by American national surveys varies according to kind of attitudes and behavior and according to the way the rural-urban distinction is made. Usually, although not always, the largest differences appear when farmers (and their families), or rural-farm people, are compared with the rest of the population. Although students of rural and urban society and culture do not agree on just how the rural-urban distinction should be made (or whether it should be conceived of as a continuum rather than a dichotomous distinction), there are compelling reasons for considering rural-farm people the most truly

5. Norval D. Glenn, "Massification versus Differentiation: Some Trend Data from National Surveys," *Social Forces*, vol. 46 (December 1967), pp. 172–80.

6. Claude Fischer, "Toward a Subcultural Theory of Urbanism," *American Journal of Sociology*, vol. 80 (May 1975), pp. 1319–41.

7. Glenn, "Massification versus Differentiation," and Norval D. Glenn, "Recent Trends in Intercategory Differences in Attitudes," *Social Forces*, vol. 52 (March 1974), pp. 395–401.

1. URBANIZATION

TABLE 1
RESPONSES (IN PERCENT) TO SELECTED ATTITUDINAL QUESTIONS ASKED ON AMERICAN GALLUP POLLS, BY OCCUPATION OF HEAD OF HOUSEHOLD

	PROFESSIONAL AND BUSINESS	WHITE COLLAR	FARM	MANUAL
Religious beliefs				
believe in the Devil (1968)	57	56	75	61
believe in life after death (1968)	76	66	86	71
believe in hell (1968)	60	56	86	68
believe in heaven (1968)	77	81	93	89
Issues concerning personal morals and vices				
think that birth control information should be available to anyone who wants it (1968)	86	81	64	76
think use of marijuana should be made legal (1969)	18	22	5	10
would like to see stricter state laws concerning sale of obscene literature on newsstands (1969)	71	69	81	79
would find pictures of nudes in magazines objectionable (1969)	64	64	89	76
have smoked cigarettes in past week (1972)	48	54	29	48
Minority-majority issues				
would vote for a well-qualified Jew for president (1969)	95	92	73	87
would vote for a well-qualified Catholic for president (1969)	95	93	80	91
would vote for a well-qualified Negro for president (1969)	76	74	56	70
would vote for a well-qualified woman for president (1969)	55	58	47	54
think the U.S. would be governed better if women had more say in politics (1969)	21	21	13	25
would vote for a well-qualified woman for Congress (1970)	90	90	71	82
approve of marriage between Catholics and Protestants (1969)	73	67	46	62
approve of marriage between Jews and non-Jews (1968)	71	69	34	59
approve of marriage between whites and nonwhites (1968)	28	24	9	20
Political issues				
consider themselves conservative (1972)	37	34	41	41
favor lowering voting age to 18 (1969)	60	62	72	67
think law enforcement agencies should be tougher in dealing with crime and lawlessness (1972)	80	81	93	84
would favor a law requiring a police permit to buy a gun (1971)	76	69	47	71
think college students should have a greater say in the running of colleges (1969)	29	33	16	27
have favorable view of Red China (1972)	30	20	17	22
have favorable view of Russia (1972)	54	40	35	38

SOURCE: Various issues of the *Gallup Opinion Index.*

rural segment of the population and for considering the farm-nonfarm distinction the most theoretically meaningful of any dichotomous rural-urban distinction. As an aggregate, the farm population differs to an important degree in many demographic characteristics from even the residents of the smaller dense settlements, and farmers are the only major segment of the population for which both place of work and place of residence are usually in the open countryside. Residents of the open countryside who are in nonfarm occupations often (perhaps usually) both work and maintain most of their social relations in dense settlements of some size. Therefore, it is useful to begin a treatment of rural-urban differences with a farm-nonfarm comparison.

Recent national survey data show that farmers (and their families) do not differ substantially from other occupational categories in a large proportion of the kinds of attitudes and behavior covered by the surveys. However, differences not likely to have resulted from sampling error appear in responses to at least a large minority of the questions. For instance, Norval Glenn and Jon Alston drew on data from 92 questions asked on American opinion polls from 1953 to 1965 and found farmers, as a whole, to be relatively prejudiced, ethnocentric, isolationist, intolerant of deviance, opposed to civil liberties, distrustful of people, traditionally religious, ascetic, work-oriented, Puritanical, uninformed, and favorable to early marriage and high fertility.[8] These differences existed not only in the adult population as a whole but also among young nonsouthern Protestants. Although these differences tend to confirm popular stereotypes of rural-farm people, most of them were fairly small, and in many cases only a small minority of farmers exhibited the characteristics which were more prevalent among farmers than among persons in other occupations.

Rural-farm people have become such a small proportion of the total population that the most recent national surveys do not give reliable estimates of the characteristics of the remaining farmers. For instance, the American Institute of Public Opinion (the American Gallup Poll) stopped reporting separate data for the farm respondents late in 1973. However, data from the late 1960s and early 1970s show that farmers were still the most distinctive (and usually the most conservative) segment of the population in regard to many kinds of attitudes (see table 1). For

8. Norval D. Glenn and Jon P. Alston, "Rural-Urban Differences in Reported Attitudes and Behavior," *Southwestern Social Science Quarterly*, vol. 47 (March 1967), pp. 381–400. See, also, Norval D. Glenn and Jon P. Alston, "Cultural Distances among Occupational Categories," *American Sociological Review*, vol. 33 (June 1968), pp. 365–82.

TABLE 2

RESPONSES (IN PERCENT) TO SELECTED ATTITUDINAL QUESTIONS ASKED ON
AMERICAN GALLUP POLLS, BY SIZE OF COMMUNITY*

	UNDER 2,500, RURAL	2,500– 49,999	50,000– 499,999	500,000– 999,999	1,000,000 AND OVER
Religious beliefs					
believe that religion is old-fashioned and out-of-date (1975)	12	18	20	19	35
have a great deal of confidence in the church or in organized religion (1975)	51	48	41	44	32
are very religious (1975)	30	29	24	27	20
Issues concerning personal morals and vices					
think abortion under any circumstances should be legal (1975)	9	19	23	29	31
would favor anti-abortion constitutional amendment (1975)	53	43	45	38	38
think use of marijuana should be made legal (1974)	21	21	27	33	35
believe it is wrong for people to have sex relations before marriage (1973)	61	50	44	41	34
would find topless nightclub waitresses objectionable (1973)	68	69	58	51	46
Minority-majority issues					
favor Equal Rights Amendment (1975)	53	59	55	65	67
would vote for woman for president (1976)	68	73	73	76	80
consider being married, with children, and no full-time job to be ideal lifestyle (women only, 1976)	53	39	45	38	38
Political issues					
favor registration of all firearms (1975)	50	64	71	77	81
would favor conservative over liberal political party (1975)	42	43	39	44	36
feel that war is outmoded as a way of settling differences between nations (1975)	37	45	48	51	48
are politically liberal (1974)	16	26	28	27	35
favor unconditional amnesty for draft evaders (1974)	29	26	38	39	40
favor reestablishing diplomatic relations with Cuba (1974)	58	62	60	70	71
have a great deal of confidence in labor unions (1973)	11	14	16	15	18

SOURCE: Various issues of the *Gallup Opinion Index*.
* Suburban residents are classified according to the size of their central cities.

instance, farmers tended to be more fundamentalist in religious beliefs, Puritanical, prejudiced, and conservative on political issues than persons in any other occupational category. In general, they resembled manual workers more than they resembled persons in higher-status occupations (although Glenn and Alston found farmers' attitudes on labor-management issues to resemble those of business and professional people).

Although a few of the farm-nonfarm differences in table 1 are fairly large, it should be kept in mind that we generally selected for reporting the largest differences we could find; therefore, the reported differences should not be considered representative of farm-nonfarm differences in general. Furthermore, the farm-nonfarm distinction accounted for only a small proportion of the total variation in responses even in the case of the items for which the differences were the largest. Since the rural-nonfarm population was no more than about 5 percent of any of the samples, even categorical differences between farmers and nonfarmers would not have produced substantial variation in the total samples.[9] Thus, in many respects the practical importance of even the largest farm-nonfarm differences is not very great. For instance, farmers do not constitute a "market" distinctive and large enough to be of much concern to most manufacturers and retailers, except those whose goods are specifically for the agricultural industry. On the other hand, farm-nonfarm differences do have some practical importance, the best example perhaps being in regard to politics. Farmers retain political influence disproportionate to their numbers (for instance, because "agricultural states," such as the Dakotas, with small populations but relatively large numbers of farmers, have two U.S. senators, the same as the populous industrial states), and any small portion of the electorate can be crucial to the outcome of a close election.

The theoretical importance of the farm-nonfarm attitudinal differences depends largely on whether they reflect largely socioeconomic, demographic, and religious-ethnic differences or whether they are in some way causally related to population concentration. Glenn and Alston conclude that most of the differences they found did not reflect differences in age, religious preference, region, income, or education; the differences existed among young non-southern Protestants as well as in the total population, and farmers often

9. Rural-farm people were about 5 percent of the total U.S. population in 1970 and are now only about 4 percent.

1. URBANIZATION

TABLE 3

SIZE OF COMMUNITY LIVED IN AT AGE 16, U.S. ADULT POPULATION, BY AGE, COMBINED
DATA FROM SURVEYS CONDUCTED IN 1972, 1973, 1974, AND 1975

	AGE							
	18–29	30–39	40–49	50–59	60–69	70–79	80 & Up	TOTAL
Open countryside	22.3	28.5	30.2	38.9	44.6	46.9	55.6	32.9
Dense settlements with less than 50,000 residents	30.4	30.2	34.1	27.3	29.8	31.4	22.2	30.3
Cities with 50,000 or more population and their suburbs	47.3	41.3	35.7	33.7	25.6	21.6	22.2	36.8
Total	100.0	100.0	100.0	100.0	100.0	100.0	100.0	100.0
N	1,565	1,119	1,027	989	781	462	117	6,060

SOURCE: The General Social Surveys conducted by the National Opinion Research Center
(James A. Davis, principal investigator).

differed from manual workers, whom they resembled in income and education. Although we have not subjected the data in table 1 to the controls used by Glenn and Alston, we are confident that the controls would not eliminate most of the differences, since the topics are similar to those studied by Glenn and Alston. Furthermore, socioeconomic differences can hardly account for most of the attitudinal differences, in view of the often substantial attitudinal differences between the farm and manual classes.

It is apparent from community-size breakdowns of responses to the items used for table 1 (not shown) and from responses to a number of questions asked on more recent national surveys (table 2) that the farm-nonfarm distinction is not the only rural-urban distinction useful for explaining attitudes and behavior. Again, it must be pointed out that we tended to select for reporting the items showing the greatest variation in responses by our independent variable, and thus the data do not indicate the typical degree of variation in expressed attitudes among communities of different sizes. However, the reported data are very nearly representative of all of the data we examined in one important respect:[10] when there is any appre-

ciable variation in responses by community size, the variation is usually monotonic rather than being a disjunctive difference between the smallest communities and all others. That is, the largest communities usually differ from the medium-sized communities about as much (and in the same direction) as the medium-sized communities differ from the smallest communities. This pattern of variation suggests that it is useful to conceive of a rural-urban continuum rather than a dichotomous rural-urban distinction. It also indicates that attitudinal and behavioral variation associated with degree of population concentration will not become unimportant simply because the most truly rural people become a very small proportion of the population. A rather substantial proportion of the population lives, and probably will long continue to live, in intermediate-sized communities;[11] and the differences between these people and the residents of the largest cities (and their suburbs) constitute rural-urban differences in one sense. Furthermore, there is no immediate prospect that rural-nonfarm people (residents of dense settlements of less than 2,500 population and non-farm residents of the open country-

THE IMPORTANCE OF RURAL BACKGROUND

Even if the only important differences associated with population concentration were between the "truly rural" people and others in the society, "ruralism" would not soon virtually disappear from American society, assuming that early socialization has enduring effects on individuals. Although few Americans are now "truly rural," a substantial proportion of the adults have rural backgrounds (see table 3), varying from around half of the elderly to about a fourth of the young adults.

Rural-urban differences in backgrounds undoubtedly contribute to the attitudinal and behavioral differentiation of the urban population, although apparently not in quite the way that some social scientists have speculated. For instance, Leo Schnore speculates that class differences in attitudes reflect to a large extent the fact that a larger percentage of the people in the lower than in the higher classes have rural backgrounds.[13] To test this hypothesis, we did a regression analysis of 19 attitudinal and behavioral variables from the 1974 General Social Survey (see table 4).[14] We first regressed each variable on prestige of occupation (males) or prestige of spouse's occupation (married females), and then we added size of place of residence at age 16 (rural-urban dichotomy) as a control variable. For most of the dependent variables, adding the control variable did reduce the strength of the association, but in no case was the reduction more than slight (see table 4). For males, the mean correlation coef-

---

10. We examined all of the data in recent (since the late 1960s) issues of the *Gallup Opinion Index*.

11. Thirty-one percent of the respondents to two national surveys conducted in 1974 and 1975 (the General Social Surveys conducted by the National Opinion Research Center) lived in cities with populations of from 2,500 to 249,999.

12. In 1970, rural-nonfarm people were 21.3 percent of the total U.S. population.

13. Leo F. Schnore, "The Rural-Urban Variable: An Urbanite's Perspective," *Rural Sociology*, vol. 31 (June 1966), pp. 131–43.

14. Since we were concerned with representativeness rather than with illustrating extreme cases, we selected the variables before we examined the data in order to avoid biasing the results via the selection process. For discussion of the "no peeking" rule, see Herbert H. Hyman, *Secondary Analysis of Sample Surveys* (New York: John Wiley, 1972).

TABLE 4

RELATIONSHIP OF OCCUPATIONAL PRESTIGE (MALES) OR SPOUSE'S OCCUPATIONAL
PRESTIGE (MARRIED FEMALES) TO SELECTED DEPENDENT VARIABLES,
WITH AND WITHOUT RURAL-URBAN BACKGROUND CONTROLLED,
WHITES, UNITED STATES, 1974

DEPENDENT VARIABLE	MALES		FEMALES	
	ZERO-ORDER CORRELATION	PARTIAL BETA	ZERO-ORDER CORRELATION	PARTIAL BETA
Frequency of church attendance	.116	.134	.021	.023
Republican party identification	.088	.112	.113	.118
Political conservatism	−.026	−.019	−.043	−.034
Belief that luck is more important than hard work in getting ahead	.017	.018	.038	.032
Frequency of socializing with relatives	−.167	−.155	−.112	−.121
Frequency of socializing with neighbors	−.005	.023	.046	.045
Frequency of socializing with friends who are not neighbors	.023	.006	.211	.191
Frequency of going to bar or tavern	.011	−.014	.067	.056
Expressed ideal family size	.023	.044	−.021	−.005
Permissiveness concerning premarital sex	.135	.095	.111	.089
Permissiveness concerning extramarital sex	.200	.178	.133	.125
Permissiveness concerning homosexual sex	.191	.171	.162	.151
Tolerance of communism	.148	.134	.142	.126
Belief in greater expenditures for education	.015	−.003	.084	.072
Belief in greater expenditures for welfare	−.058	−.042	.017	.007
Belief in greater expenditures for the military	−.249	−.230	−.155	−.142
Willingness to invite a black to dinner	.068	.055	.037	.021
Vocabulary test score	.473	.444	.317	.292
Number of children (persons age 45 and older)	−.181	−.169	−.138	−.127

SOURCE: The 1974 General Social Survey conducted by the National Opinion Research Center (James A. Davis, principal investigator).

NOTE: Data in this and subsequent tables are limited to whites in order to control race. Truncation is used for control since race interacts with some of the predictor variables. All dependent variables are scored to form ordinal or interval scales with at least three categories.

the case of several of the variables, size of community of residence at age 16 was a better predictor of the responses than size of present (at the time of the survey) community of residence (see table 5).[15] In the case of eight of the 19 variables for males and 14 of the 19 for females, the partial unstandardized regression coefficient is larger for size of community of residence at age 16 than for size of present community of residence. For males, the mean beta is .060 for size of community of residence at age 16 and .059 for size of present community of residence.[16] The corresponding means for females are .075 and .043.

Obviously, neither of the community size variables was an important predictor of most of the dependent variables we selected from the 1974 General Social Survey; most of the associations are neither statistically significant nor large enough to be important, even if they did not result from sampling error. This is true even for several variables which, according to the literature, should bear a rather strong relationship to community size. For instance, expressions of the ideal number of children for a family were virtually unrelated to size of present community of residence and only weakly related to size of community of origin. Some researchers require that a beta be at least .15 before it is considered worthy of interpretation; by that criterion, only the association among females of size of community of origin with the vocabulary test scores was large enough to be important. However, several other betas do not fall far short of .15 and, thus, probably reflect associations of some importance in the population. For males, these include the associations of size of present community of residence with permissive attitudes toward premarital and homosexual sex and with favorable attitudes toward formal education. For

ficient (which is equivalent to the zero-order beta) is .115 and the mean partial beta (standardized regression coefficient) is .107. For females, the values are .104 and .094, respectively. Therefore, at least in regard to the variables included in this analysis (which, of course, are not necessarily representative of all attitudinal and behavioral variables), the higher proportion of low-status than of high-status people who have rural origins does not seem to be an important source of so-called class differences.

However, it is important that, in

15. For this analysis, we used the same three-category community-size breakdown for community of origin and of current residence, namely, (1) open countryside, (2) dense settlements of less than 50,000 residents, and (3) cities of 50,000 or more population and their suburbs.

16. We disregarded the signs of the betas in computing these means.

1. URBANIZATION

TABLE 5
Relationship (Partial) of Size of Community Lived in at Age 16 and of Size of Community of Current Residence to Selected Dependent Variables, Whites, United States, 1974

	STANDARDIZED PARTIAL REGRESSION COEFFICIENT (BETA)			
	MALES		FEMALES	
DEPENDENT VARIABLE	COMMUNITY OF ORIGIN	COMMUNITY OF RESIDENCE	COMMUNITY OF ORIGIN	COMMUNITY OF RESIDENCE
Frequency of church attendance	−.007	−.051	.051	−.103
Republican party identification	−.067	−.038	−.020	−.017
Political conservatism	−.088	−.051	−.115	−.035
Belief that luck is more important than hard work in getting ahead	.062	−.004	.034	−.033
Frequency of socializing with relatives	.009	−.041	.065	−.033
Frequency of socializing with neighbors	−.066	−.022	.093	−.055
Frequency of socializing with friends who are not neighbors	.059	.082	.087	.019
Frequency of going to bar or tavern	.072	.083	.008	−.110
Expressed ideal family size	−.081	.034	−.081	−.001
Permissiveness concerning premarital sex	.073	.039	.050	.128
Permissiveness concerning extramarital sex	.095	.137	.077	−.011
Permissiveness concerning homosexual sex	.075	.146	.050	.027
Tolerance of communism	.084	.015	.055	.019
Belief in greater expenditures for education	−.032	.126	.091	.023
Belief in greater expenditures for welfare	−.028	.010	−.011	.073
Belief in greater expenditures for the military	−.074	−.074	−.074	.014
Willingness to invite a black to dinner	−.014	.096	.033	−.055
Vocabulary test score	.052	.051	.189	−.027
Number of children (persons age 45 and older)	−.096	−.016	−.119	−.043

SOURCE: The 1974 General Social Survey conducted by the National Opinion Research Center (James A. Davis, principal investigator).

NOTE: Only the two community-size variables are predictor variables in the regression equations.

females, these include the associations of size of present community of residence with permissive attitudes toward premarital sex and of size of community of residence at age 16 with number of children and with liberal political orientations.

A Multivariate Analysis

Of course, even the larger associations may not reflect direct effects of community size but rather may be spurious or reflect indirect effects through variables which intervene between community size and the dependent variables. If so, both the Wirth and the Fischer views of the effects of population concentration would tend to lose their credibility. To test for this possibility, we added nine background and current characteristics, all of which seemed likely to have some effect on some of the dependent variables, to the regression equation as predictors along with the two community-size variables.[17] We then selected each

17. We also recoded the community-size variables into the maximum number of categories consistent with retaining ordinal scales, which made the two variables incomparable with one another but allowed each to explain the maximum amount of variance in the dependent variables.

dependent variable with a zero-order correlation of at least .10 with one of the community-size variables and compared the correlation coefficient (zero-order beta) with the partial beta (see table 6).

Generally, the controls diminished the associations to an important degree, but only in a few cases were the associations reduced to virtually zero. We cannot be sure, of course, that we controlled all antecedent and intervening variables which could account for the remaining associations, as indicated by the betas, but it appears likely that population concentration, or some very close correlates, had rather direct effects on some of the dependent variables, such as vocabulary (females), fertility, attitudes toward family size, attitudes toward communism, and attitudes toward premarital sex. If so, we speculate that, with the probable exception of the effect on vocabulary, the effects were mainly a matter of the people in the smaller communities lagging behind those in the larger communities as attitudes and behavior have changed.

The multivariate analysis also allows tentative conclusions about the relative explanatory power of the community-size variables and the other predictor variables, most of which are often used in social scientific research. The means in table 7 indicate that the explanatory power of age and education exceeded those of both size of community of origin and size of community of current residence by a considerable margin. Even region of residence had slightly better predictive power, on the average, than either of the community-size variables. On the other hand, the community size variables did not fare badly in competition with some other variables often used as explanatory variables in social scientific research, such as occupational prestige and family income. Of course, the 19 dependent variables used for these comparisons are not necessarily representative, and the relative predictive power of the different independent variables varies

TABLE 6

Zero-Order and Partial Relationships of Community-Size Variables to Selected Dependent Variables, Whites, United States, 1974

Dependent Variable	Males				Females			
	Community of Origin		Community of Residence		Community of Origin		Community of Residence	
	Zero-Order Correlation	Partial Beta	Zero-Order Correlation	Partial Beta	Zero-Order Correlation	Partial Beta	Zero-Order Correlation	Partial Beta
Political conservatism	−.112	−.091	*	*	−.118	−.058	*	*
Frequency of socialization with friends who are not neighbors	.172	.079	.147	.084	.189	.090	*	*
Frequency of going to bar or tavern	.167	.108	.118	.065	.103	.023	*	*
Permissiveness concerning premarital sex	.171	.093	.118	.036	.212	.042	.211	.137
Permissiveness concerning extramarital sex	.162	.073	.204	.152	.101	.045	*	*
Permissiveness concerning homosexual sex	.173	.064	.204	.148	.132	.016	.109	.060
Belief in greater expenditures for education	.086	.028	.114	.090	.137	.085	*	*
Belief in greater expenditures for the military	−.158	−.087	−.110	.048	−.148	−.059	*	*
Vocabulary test score	.225	.077	.184	.053	.333	.215	.127	.005
Number of children (persons age 45 and older)	−.123	−.101	*	*	−.142	−.100	*	*

Source: The 1974 General Social Survey conducted by the National Opinion Research Center (James A. Davis, principal investigator).

Note: For the multiple regression analysis, the independent variables include all of the independent variables listed in table 7.

* Data not reported because zero-order correlation is less than .1.

a great deal among the 19 dependent variables.[18]

18. For a somewhat similar comparison, see George W. Lowe and Charles W. Peek, "Location and Lifestyle: The Comparative Explanatory Utility of Urbanism and Rurality," *Rural Sociology*, vol. 39 (Fall 1974), pp. 392–419. More recent research by Lowe and Peek, as yet unpublished, reveals that, for a large number of attitudinal variables from the General Social Surveys, a cluster of "status" variables has considerably greater predictive power than a cluster of rural-urban-community-size variables.

Conclusions

What, then, is the importance of the rural-urban distinction and of the community-size variable to those who would understand and deal with attitudinal and behavioral variation in the United States? The answer, clearly, is that the importance is more than negligible and that there is little reason to believe that the importance is diminishing

or will soon diminish very much. It would certainly be premature to suggest that students of rural-urban differences should find more fruitful topics to study.

On the other hand, the importance of rural-urban differences should not be exaggerated. The rural-urban variable, along with many other explanatory variables long favored by social scientists, is losing much of its apparent importance as re-

TABLE 7

MEAN PARTIAL RELATIONSHIP (BETA) OF TWO COMMUNITY-SIZE VARIABLES AND NINE
OTHER INDEPENDENT VARIABLES TO 19 SELECTED DEPENDENT VARIABLES,
WHITES, UNITED STATES, 1974

INDEPENDENT VARIABLE	MALES	MARRIED FEMALES
Size of community of origin	.067	.069
Size of community of residence	.059	.040
Region	.084	.076
Region of origin	.047	.071
Age	.159	.131
Family income	.049	.044
Subjective economic standing of family	.068	.071
Subjective economic standing of family at age 16	.041	.058
Occupational prestige (of spouse in case of females)	.055	.040
Father's occupational prestige	.041	.040
Years of school completed	.103	.102

SOURCE: The 1974 General Social Survey conducted by the National Opinion Research Center (James A. Davis, principal investigator).

NOTE: Means are computed without regard to signs of the betas. All 11 of the independent variables are in the regression equations. The 19 dependent variables are those listed in tables 4 and 5.

searchers increasingly use "proportional-reduction-in-error" measures of association and interpret their findings in terms of proportion of variance explained. For most attitudinal and behavioral variables, the predictive utility of the rural-urban variable is modest at best; "overinterpretation" of rather small differences between percentages has often obscured the fact that on most issues the rural and urban populations each has almost as much internal differentiation in attitudes as does the total population.

We, The Lonely People

We want and need a greater sense of community. Then why do we spend our lives resisting it?

Ralph Keyes

Ralph Keyes is a member of the Center for Studies of the Person in California. This article is an excerpt from his book entitled *We, the Lonely People* (Harper & Row, Publishers).

Kids have taken over the shopping centers.

Especially on weekends you see them, arrogant occupiers, an army marching up and down the mall, mugging at each other and stabbing their cigarettes at passersby.

While working for *Newsday*, I went to Long Island's Walt Whitman Shopping Center to expose this latest chapter in modern materialism.

The first day in, I hung around and asked kids why they spent so much time there. They seemed genuinely puzzled and usually could only mumble things like, "Well, you know, its warm . . . and I have friends here."

An Englishman I know who grew up in a small village in Yorkshire says the most striking quality of the town, and the thing he misses most, was the feeling of being *known* there. He said it wasn't even a spoken thing. Nobody would say anything out loud about your beating your wife. But they knew, you knew they knew, they knew you knew they knew—and in that there was comfort.

Today we talk about our "loss of community" in city and suburb. Often we discuss it intellectually while sipping scotch. Sometimes mystically, passing a joint. Or nostalgically over beer.

When we try to be more specific about just what "community" means, we usually think first of a place, the place where we live. I think this is what Car-

nation Milk has in mind when they implore me on their carton to "help keep our community litter free."

But when we consider where we find a "sense of community," it's rarely where we live. We use the word interchangeably, but it really means two different things.

A *sense* of community is what we find among the people who know us, with whom we feel safe. That rarely includes the neighbors.

It wasn't always so. For most of history man found his sense of community where he lived, with the people among whom he was born and with whom he died. For some that remains true today. But most of us in city and suburb live one place and find "community" in another. Or nowhere.

So many of us want back the more intimate sense of community, the one where the grocer knew our name and the butcher could comment on meat and life.

Business knows, and they're trying to sell that feeling back to us, some sense of community.

None of it works, and it won't work. The qualities that make a good mass marketer can't also produce a feeling of community. I find it a toss-up as to who loves me more, my local Shakey's Pizza Parlor or Howard Johnson's.

But business is hardly pernicious for trying. Their job is to be sensitive to markets, and there's obviously a market for intimacy. The market, however, is a package deal, part of a consumer's double message: give us all the advantages of a supermarket with all the familiarity of a corner store.

Sixty-nine percent of 200 Bostonians surveyed in 1970 agreed that "stores are so big these days that the customer gets lost in the shuffle." But 81 percent be-

lieved that "supermarkets are a great advance over the corner store."

We want both, and business tries to comply. It's an impossible task. If they're confused, it's because we're confused.

It's not that we don't want more community. We do. We crave community. We lust after it. "Community" is a national obsession. But we want other things more. I wanted to write this book more. Not getting involved with the neighbors is worth more to us than "community."

It's this confusion, this ambivalence, that confounds our quest for community. We yearn for a simpler, more communal life; we sincerely want more sense of community. But not at the sacrifice of any advantages that mass society has brought us, even ones we presumably scorn.

We didn't lose community. We bought it off. And rediscovering community isn't a matter of finding "the solution." We know how to do it. It's a question of how much we're willing to trade in.

I could find a Mom & Pop store if I really wanted one. But I don't. I prefer a supermarket's prices and selection. Also the anonymity, the fact that I'm *not* burdened by knowing the help.

Even as we hate being unknown to each other, we crave anonymity. And rather than take paths that might lead us back together, we pursue the very things that keep us cut off from each other. There are three things we cherish in particular—mobility, privacy and convenience—which are the very sources of our lack of community.

"It is astonishing," wrote Scottish journalist Alexander McKay in 1849, "how readily . . . an American makes up his mind to try his fortunes elsewhere." One historian says that "the M-factor"— movement, migration and mobility—is the shaping influence of our national character.

In nearly two decades of studying top corporation executives, industrial psychologist Eugene Jennings has found an increasingly close relationship between mobility and success, leading to what Jennings calls "mobicentricity." "To the mobility-centered person," he explains, "a new American phenomenon, movement is not so much a way to get someplace or a means to an end as it is an end in itself. The mobicentric man values motion and action not because they lead to change but because they are change, and change is his ultimate value."

Those studying communes have found a curious paradox. Experiments in communal living are top-heavy with the root-seeking children of nomadic corporation men. Yet these same utopian ventures are witness to a perpetual flow from one to the next, communards changing communes just as their fathers transferred between corporations. "Repeating the quintessentially American trait," writes an analyst of this movement, "when conditions of communal life become intolerable, the residents simply move elsewhere."

The worst part of mobicentricity may not be the moves themselves so much as the certainty that one will move again, and again and again. Why get involved with people, when you know you'll soon be leaving them? Why get close to anyone, when you know in advance that making friends, close friends, only means more pain at parting?

It all leads to a kind of "stewardess syndrome"—smiling warmly at strangers as you part after a few hours, or minutes, as if you had shared the intimacy of a lifetime.

I get this stewardess approach a lot in the counterculture. When I meet someone bearded and barefoot like myself, or a girl in work shirt and Levis, we're supposed to lock thumbs, whisper "brother" or "sister," and exchange the warmth of friendship for a few moments in passing. If there isn't time to get close, we may at least smoke some grass together, which is almost the same thing, or at least seems like it.

While we are on the move, appearances become all. Without time to come to know each other we must depend on outer signals. Eventually it becomes hard to remember that there's an inner person not so easily exhibited, a person more important than any badge

or secret handshake. The worst part of mobicentricity is being doomed to travel about seeking one's identity in the eyes of near strangers.

Mobility is a major enemy of the community of intimate friendship. But I'm not clear where it is cause and where effect: whether we're afraid to get close because we're always moving on, or whether we're always moving on because we're afraid to get close.

Mobility has also made a major contribution to the decline of neighborhood life, of our community of place. But in that it's had help, in particular from our love of privacy.

Privacy as an ideal, even as a concept, is relatively modern. Marshall McLuhan says it took the invention of print to tear man from his tribes and plant the dream of isolation in his brain. Historian Jacob Burckhardt says that before the Renaissance, Western man was barely aware of himself as an individual. Mostly he drew identity from membership in groups—family, tribe, church, guild.

But since the Renaissance, Western man has sought increasing amounts of isolation, of distance from his neighbors. In America, with more land in which to seek elbow room, and with more money to buy it, the ideal of the unfettered individual, rugged, free and secluded, has reached its zenith. Howard Hughes is only the logical conclusion, an inspiration to us all.

Increasing numbers of us suffer from an "autonomy-withdrawal syndrome," according to the architect-planner C.A. Alexander. Most people, explains Alexander, use their home as an insulation against the outside world, a means of self-protection. Eventually this withdrawal becomes habitual and people lose the ability to let others inside their secluded world. What begins as a normal concern for privacy soon resembles the pathological.

"The neighbors are perfect," reports University of Southern California football coach John McKay, "I don't know any of them."

A study of 75 white, middle-class, male Michigan suburbanites showed that most of their relationships with other men on the block took place standing up. This group of men defined a good neighbor as one who "is available for emergency aid; can be called on to trade mutual aid; lends and can be loaned to; respects privacy; friendly, but not friends." Only four of the men said

they had neighbors they also considered friends.

I'm constantly horrified/fascinated by the regular accounts of crime and carnage perpetrated by "respectable" but highly private men who turn out not to have been known at all by shocked friends and neighbors.

Recently an insurance executive apparently killed his wife, three children and mother-in-law, then left the bodies in their $90,000 New Jersey home. No neighbor noticed anything amiss until the newspapers started piling up on the porch and the lights burned out over a month's time. A news account explained that "the disappearance of the family caused little notice in the suburb, where executives move in and out frequently without making close friends."

We not only use our homes to avoid each other, but we also can do the same thing within the home, with just a little help from modern technology.

I once gave a speech on "The Generation Gap" to a women's club. In the discussion afterward, one fiftyish mother stood up and said: "I'm gonna tell you what brought on the whole thing—dishwashers. That's right, dishwashers. I got to know my kids better, they told me more, when we washed dishes together. One would wash, another rinse, and a third dry. We'd fight but we'd also talk. Now that we have a dishwasher, there's no regular time when we get to know each other."

She had fingered clearly something I was sensing only vaguely: that our household conveniences—our whole drive for a *convenient* life—have cut us off from each other. The cooperation and communication that used to accompany life's chores is being built out of our social systems.

Eating, according to contemporary nutritionists, has become less and less a family affair and more and more a matter of "slot-machine snacking." According to one estimate, 28 percent of our food intake is now in the form of snacks outside mealtime.

Consider, for example, the effect of individual pudding servings in a can. These not only make it unnecessary to work together in the kitchen preparing dessert, but also reduce the need to consider one's family as a unit, to compromise between chocolate and banana cream when it comes to fixing pudding. All members get their own flavor, right out of the can, whenever they want.

"The basic theme underlying food practices in contemporary American society is *individualism*," writes nutritionist Norge W. Jerome. "The structure, timing and ordering of meals (and snacks) as traditionally defined are yielding to individual patterns of food use."

This evolution of our eating patterns has been hard to document. "It may be easier to get people to talk with complete frankness about their sex life than about the eating patterns of the family," says motivational psychologist Paul A. Fine, who has conducted several surveys of meal habits for food manufacturers.

Fine says that today's average family eating pattern includes little or no breakfast, snacks during the morning, maybe lunch (but not for Mom unless little kids are home), big eating after school, a smaller and smaller supper and TV snacking that may be supplemented by after-bed refrigerator raids. The sit-down family dinner, he says, seldom takes place more than three nights a week in any family.

That seems a shame. Our family meals were warm, together times, times when the talk rivaled the food for attention. My best memories of home take place around the dining room table.

With our comings and goings inhibiting friendship, a love of seclusion eroding our neighborhoods and our passion for convenience atomizing the family, it's hardly any wonder we feel a "loss of community."

But the distinctions are artificial. Mobility, privacy and convenience are like a trio, first one playing, then the other, and all three finally coming together to play their song—at our request.

More than any single thing on the American scene, cars unite the triumvirate of values that are wrecking our sense of community. Automobiles are at once our main agent of mobility, the most private place to which we can retire and a primary source of convenience. When one asks what it is that we must trade in on community, the answer could very well be: our cars.

I once heard a woman describe in a most appealing way her two-and-a-half years on a commune. More than most, this commune seemed to have kept a stable core of people together over its brief/long life. She talked of their deep feeling of commitment to each other.

But she also pointed out that although most property was held in common, each communard kept a car—just in case he or she wanted to split. And if I

lived on that commune, I'd probably want to keep a car too—just in case I wanted to split. I prize my mobility, my right to get up and go, as much as anyone—and I love the car that permits it. It's freedom, and in San Diego as on Long Island, the car is an absolutely indispensable tool for survival. Without it you're crippled, a virtual prisoner.

The great, overlooked seduction of this earth module, the car, is privacy. Cars and bathrooms are the only places where most urban-suburbanites can be completely and blissfully—alone. And a car is better than the bathroom. No one can knock and tell you to hurry up.

I initially grew interested in the car as private space when friends of mine began screaming inside their automobiles.

The first person to tell me about this, a father of five in his late thirties, explained that within his van, driving to and from work, was the only time he felt free to rage—spit and holler—let it all out. He called it his Private Therapy Van. Just roll up the windows and howl, go crazy if you like. No one will ever know.

This intrigued me, and I began to talk with other friends, asking what they did alone in a car, mentioning that one guy I knew screamed. With striking frequency faces would light up and heads nod vigorously as they heard this: "Hey, me too," they'd say. "I scream in my car too sometimes, but I didn't know anyone else did."

Traffic patrolmen with whom I talked said singing is common within cars, especially among women, and many drivers seem just to be talking to themselves. They say you can tell the difference by whether the driver's head is keeping time with the movement of his lips.

The only problem with criticizing the way cars make us anonymous, unknown and nasty to each other is the assumption that we'd prefer it any other way. We do, of course, and yet . . .

It's that ambivalence. We say we'd like to be less cut off from and uncivilized with each other, but another voice within speaks differently. The private car is a place safe to be our other self.

The car itself has had a lot to do with cutting us off from each other by sealing us in cocoons on wheels and making it easy to drive away from each other. But its greater impact may be in the environments we erect to suit the car, environments built for mobility, privacy and convenience.

The process is self-feeding. The more we drive, the less pleasant it becomes to walk down streets that have become noisy, dangerous and smelly from cars. The less pleasant it becomes to walk, the more we drive. Eventually, custom becomes law.

In 1971 the city council of Dallas passed an antiloitering ordinance that made a crime of: "the walking about aimlessly without apparent purpose; lingering; hanging around; lagging behind; the idle spending of time; delaying; sauntering and moving slowly about, where such conduct is not due to physical defects or conditions."

Beverly Hills is the logical conclusion. There the police are notorious for questioning anyone caught walking at night. Long Island, also built to suit cars, is not much better. I spent a lot of my two years on Long Island feeling sorry for its residents—like myself. In all that time I can't remember ever meeting anyone by accident. Or having a place to hang out, a store within walking distance or anything within walking distance. Life in such environments can be ghastly.

The suburbs are simply not designed for congregation. One suburbanite says that in the subdivision where she lived the better part of a decade, seeing more than three people gathered on the street made her wonder whether a disaster had just occurred and perhaps she ought to inquire.

When we lived on Long Island, a small "7/11" was the only store close by—our neighborhood grocery. It was also a hangout for local kids in this purely residential area. When you went in to buy something, you'd have to plow through compacted youth, like police breaking up a demonstration.

Shortly after arriving in San Diego, my wife and I checked out the stores close by. The nearest one was 7/11. On their parking lot, kids were hanging around outside, with identical banana-seat bikes. Inside, the store was just as I remembered it: refrigerated goods in the rear, magazines up front, Slurpee machine by the cash register. All of this made me feel good, secure. There was a familiar place in this strange setting.

It seemed like a fresh insight—that I felt right at home at my local 7/11, almost as if we'd never left. Then I started reading up on franchisers and found that's exactly what they want me to feel.

Mobility has a built-in paradox. We move on in search of change. But the more we move, the more identical

23

things become in every region. And the process feeds itself. The more we move, the more alike things become. The more alike things become, the easier it is to move.

We fret about this growing sameness for a variety of cultural and aesthetic reasons but without considering the comfort uniformity provides for a people constantly on the move. As Lewis Mumford points out, the common grid pattern of our towns and cities has historically made strangers as much at home as veterans.

Since franchises grew up after World War II right along with the auto and freeway explosion, they have housed themselves in very visible buildings that have the advantage of being easily seen from a speeding car. When everything else is a blur through the windshield, Holiday Inn's green, red and yellow logo is a comforting point of stability. Their 1,500 buildings may seem distinct, but that's an optical delusion. There's really only one Holiday Inn, just as there's only one 7/11, one McDonald's and a single Colonel Harlan Sanders.

In Oakland the Institute of Human Abilities is franchising communes and human growth. They buy up dilapidated houses in the Bay Area, redub them "More Houses," then charge the young and lonely $200 a month to live there and fix up the places. For their money and effort, residents get more than just a place to live. They also get a hero, Victor Baranco, the "heavy" founder/philosopher-king of the Institute; a medallion with the More symbol; a variety of courses in human growth; *Aquarius* magazine; and 16 More Houses to be welcome at.

The More Houses people know what they're up to. "We are like Colonel Sanders," admits the institute's president and *Aquarius* editor, Ken Brown, 51. "We can reproduce our thing anywhere. The product is words. And the attraction is love."

The counterculture generally has built up a rather impressive network of familiarity within the national hometown—ranging from informal places to sleep, through friendly homes listed in guidebooks, communes and spiritual centers. The new nomads needn't feel much stress on the road.

Laundromats have become an excellent place to meet other citizens of the national hometown, straight and hip alike. Usually unguarded, often open all night, laundromats have become major American hangouts. There's something about laundromats that makes them a much safer, less threatening space than other public mixing points. It's just hard to seem dangerous with a box of Tide in your hands.

As a place to gather and share, laundromats differ only in form from the streams running by old hometowns where washers used to congregate. But laundromats have many more purposes to serve in the national hometown. After the Holiday Inn, they may be our leading community center.

Trust is what all these comfort points are about—the laundromats, the ashrams, the communes, the franchises. No matter how they clothe it or what they call it, the uniform gathering places—franchises in particular—are basically marketing trust. When we lived on a smaller scale, we would learn which merchants were trustworthy. Living now as we do throughout the country, we can only grope at symbols, and consistency is the best substitute for intimate knowledge.

Ironically, the last encounter group I attended spent its final day in the Holiday Inn room of one participant. In that room, on Sunday morning, one of the men in the group gave me an "Esalen massage." The experience made my body tremble and my mouth moan—as loudly as I would let it in the Holiday Inn. It felt great, great to let go, at least partway, and trust that group of people to see me shaking and exposed.

Afterward I exchanged hugs with all the participants and addresses with a few. We promised to visit, though it was months ago and we haven't yet. I still think we may.

A unique breed of "grouper" has grown up in southern California, and perhaps across the nation. With so many encounter groups going on, such people go from group to group getting stroked, enjoying their intimacy *seriatim*. To this group you reveal what a cad your wife is, to that group you cry about your vicious mother, and to the other about your brother. Then maybe trot out your wife again. If you handle the situation right, and it's not hard, each group of people will love and console you. A weekend's intimacy can sustain you till the next group.

I once asked a leader of a student-adult encounter group in a Long Island school district if they had a gossip problem, since participants lived near each other and could tell tales. "Oh, no," he replied. "We make sure that people in the groups are strangers to each other." Then he leaned forward affirmatively. "It's not the sort of thing you'd want to do with friends and neighbors."

Swinging is only the most obvious example of the growing acceptability of intimacy with strangers. Swingers have taken the trend a step further, removing even the need to feel good about the person with whom you're sharing intercourse or to seek actual closeness in the sex act. "It's fun," explains one New York swinger, "but I don't like most of the people involved in it."

It's as if we're trying to make our opportunities for intimate community, the times when we'll peek from behind the mask, as handy and convenient as a TV dinner. A time to cry, to reveal, to take off one's shoes and relax is a human necessity. To do so with friends, even with family (especially with family), is scary and risky. It might lead to rejection, even worse—to commitment.

The safest, most convenient alternative is to seek a few day's intimacy with strangers, love and let loose.

Psychologist Richard Farson says, "The people who will live successfully in tomorrow's world are those who can accept and enjoy temporary systems."

So what we're doing is developing temporary love systems, hit-and-run intimacy, self-destructing communities that are making closeness just as convenient and just as disposable as a two-week guided tour.

I'm fascinated, driving down the highway, by the number of campers that are complete with name-and-address plates just as if they were home. "The Newmans," a plate will say, "Bayside, Texas."

Sometimes a little message will be added, like, "Y'all come see us."

And the new campers find the community they seek. Their changing cast of neighbors will be gone in a few days, so there's little risk in getting close.

This is a lot of the appeal of hitchhiking. "It's a special feeling," wrote one guy hitching across the country. "Meeting other people and throwing in for a while together. There's a trust."

I once discussed this with Julie, my sister-in-law. She's a Berkeleyite who enjoys hitching around that town. Julie likes meeting people and talking with them. I commented that I really used to resent it when people would pick me up just for company, especially when I didn't feel like talking.

"Well, how far were you hitching?" she asked.

"Usually hundreds of miles," I replied.

Her face brightened. "Oh, I see the difference. I'm usually just hitching around town. Anything over ten blocks is a heavy commitment."

Airlines understand our hunger for intimacy-in-passing better than any sociologist alive. Disposable community has become their bread and butter.

United wants me to fly their "Friendly Skies," in "Friend Ships."

Southwest Airlines calls itself, "The Somebody Else Up There Who Loves You." Passengers boarding one of their flights are greeted by a stewardess saying, "Hi, I'm Suzanne, and we're so glad to have you on our flight. You-all buckle up your safety belts and don't dare get up. We don't want anything happening to you now, because we love you."

Airplanes are forced to *become* community and serve up intimacy because their customers' hunger is so great. The airlines knew that they had become the community they once served long before most of us had a notion. But we're beginning to catch up. That transformation—from *serving* community to *being* community—is revolutionizing our social institutions.

Now courts and juries have entered another incarnation and are floating free of any community except the one they have become themselves. Today's jury *is* the community, a family even.

And so the circle is completed. When we lived on a smaller scale, juries consisted of community members *known* to another member on trial. As we grew larger, we sought refuge in the objectivity of anonymity, of jurors *unknown* to the person being tried.

Now we're in the third stage. The courtroom is a community, the judge a father, each jury a family, and the defendants prodigal sons. Trials provide the opportunity to come to *know* each other once again, to become community. Justice has been communalized.

The evolution is from bureaucracy to brotherhood. Do you dislike waiting anonymously in line? Get to know the other people and make the queue family. Is the multiversity giving you "just-another-number" blahs? Shut it down and become a community.

Families Anonymous is just one of the self-help groups that are springing up in this country like dandelions after a rain. Many are anonymous, patterned after Alcoholics Anonymous. These range from Survivors Anonymous (for those left behind by suicides) to Pussy Anonymous (for men who are compulsive philanderers). Other groups, without being "anonymous," are bringing together Vietnam veterans to talk out their fears, POW wives to share frustrations or unemployed aerospace engineers to share despair.

Tocqueville anticipated this development a century and a half ago. He saw our drive to associate, even in the early 1830s, growing inevitably out of our rootlessness and the lack of relatedness he considered inherent in a democratic society. The only thing new in our drive to belong is the degree of disconnectedness Americans feel, and the added weight we put on our associations to be not only community but also family.

A biker says of his gang, "Our chapter is like a brotherhood. Strong. Strong. We're real tight. One of us cries, we all cry. One laughs, we all laugh. That's the thing about the Aliens. We're a family."

The Aliens. A family.

After completing the Dale Carnegie course, an insurance executive boasted, "Now there's a lot more cooperation in our department. . . . We enjoy working together so much we're really more like a family."

A family.

When Oregon's Governor Tom McCall decided against running for the Senate in 1972, he explained, "My prime commitment is to Oregon and the Oregon family. I feel I can do the most effective job for Oregon by finishing what the Oregon family reelected me to finish two years ago."

The Oregon family.

I don't know much about lexicography, but when a word becomes that popular and that diverse in the ways it's used, some of the original meaning has obviously been lost.

Dave Walden once belonged to the sports car community. He worked on cars and officiated at rallies. Dave had friends within the community, friends who really cared. When he had to go to the hospital, they visited.

But then Dave lost interest in sports cars and soon lost all contact with that community, as they with him. Their commitment was only to the sports car buff, not the person. The community was only in part.

We do seek community. There's no question about it. But also we're scared of it. So we seek a safe community, one in which we needn't be fully known. We want to preserve as much as we can of our privacy, our conveniences, as well as the freedom to pick up and move on.

The logical conclusion, the direction we're headed, is what Henry Burger calls "agapurgy," the industrialization of affection. An anthropologist at the University of Missouri, Burger says that although America has done badly at providing enough "tender loving care" to go around, we do have a demonstrated genius for mass production and sophisticated technology. Therefore, why not apply the strength to the weakness: build love machines; Friend-O-Mats; or, as he calls it, "the mass production of affect."

We're already in the primitive stages of agapurgy.

But it won't work. Agapurgy won't work any more than TV and magazine communities work—or dialed counseling, franchised friendship, bumper-sticker conversation, thumb-lock trust, encounter-group love, tribal clubs or self-help groups. None of them work as community because none is a place where we're known whole.

We want to be known, whole, and yet . . .

If any or all of our approaches worked, we wouldn't be suffering such an epidemic of loneliness.

A year before his death, W.H. Auden left New York and returned to England. The poet said he regretted leaving his adopted home of more than three decades but explained: "It's just that I'm getting rather old to live alone in the winter, and I'd rather live in community. Supposing I had a coronary. It might be days before I was found."

Auden fingered what, for me, is the minimum criterion of being in community, for being known: that my absence, as well as my presence, be noted.

The minimum question about whether a group of people is really a community for me is: "Would anyone notice if I didn't show up?"

It's a frightening question, perhaps the most scary one I could put to a group of people. I'd dread what the answer might be.

Better not to ask it at all—anywhere.

This fear, I think, fuels a lot of our frantic rushing around—the feeling that if we just keep moving we'll have an excuse never to raise such a question with any group of people.

Today we're free to choose and reject, be chosen or rejected. This right to choose is a liberation, and also a tyranny. It's much easier to be thrust into community from your mother's womb, with the alternative only to leave. The opposite choice—to ask to be included in community—is terrifying and excruciating, a choice rarely made.

Millions of us have gladly rejected the suffocation of total community, and even the partial oppression of churches or clubs, where we were once known and scrutinized. We feel well rid of that kind of oppression. At least I do. But we forget to provide anywhere for the fellowship that went hand in hand with suffocation. The sermons may have been a drag, but the potlucks weren't so bad.

Rather than moon about the old potlucks, though, we'd do better to build a new community now, at home. We keep remembering the small towns and stores because we want back some of their qualities—manageable size, familiar faces, a sense of being known. Few of us will ever again know the kind of total community that intermingled place and kin, work and friends—and fewer of us want to. Far more helpful is to find out where it is that we do feel community *today*, and to set about enhancing that feeling without getting hung up on obsolete notions of what a community should be.

Some see the building of community as a job for the government, the best path a political one. There is much that the government can do to create a climate more conducive to community. The government, for example, could evaluate all social and political programs according to a "community index," one that would judge programs purely in terms of their effect on human intercourse, whether they brought people together or drove them apart. A community index should not be the only one, but should weigh more heavily than it does now.

Urban renewal, for example, might get a zero for putting high rises and freeways above neighborhoods, people and community. Local laws that prevent unrelated groups of people from living together would rank at the bottom of a community index.

Some trends in America are encouraging, such as the growing "community-based" orientation in mental health, corrections and education. Most of what's going on in the ecology movement is an encouragement to community and ranks high on the community index. Anything that helps develop alternatives to cars has to be good.

Still, neither political reform nor revolution can bring about the kind of community I'm concerned about, the kind where people really know each other. The job of government is to mediate among millions of people. This gives it a set of priorities in which community building ranks low, and should. Feeding the hungry must come first, then redistributing income and keeping us from killing each other.

Take the issue of busing. From a political standpoint the crosstown busing of schoolchildren may be a necessary tool for integration and social justice. From the standpoint of community, busing is a disaster, another wrecker of our neighborhoods. In this case, as in so many, political priorities are at variance with those of community.

Building a sense of community will always be the work of those who want it. The government at times may be able to lend a hand, but only a hand.

An ideal community would be like a good family: the group from which one can't be expelled. Or like Robert Frost's definition of home—the place where, when you have to go there, they have to take you in. But that's ideal, and few of us will ever build such a community.

I've defined my attainable community as "the place where it's safe to be known." This has meaning for me, because trusting people to see me is so hard, and it feels so good when I do. It feels like community. And that kind of community can be built in a range of settings, from a commune to a bar or a church.

The elements that strike me as especially important for building a community include manageable size, a willingness to be exclusive, acceptance of oppression and at least some modicum of commitment.

Size is of the essence. Manageable numbers are basic to any group of people hoping to get close. Trust can be built only among familiar faces.

There's a simple experiment that can be done with a group to discover one's "comfort peak." Break down in pairs and chat with one other person. After a few minutes, join with another couple to become a foursome and chat some more. Then become eight and talk again, then sixteen, and thirty-two if you have enough time and people. The point at which you become uncomfortable, even stop talking, is probably your "comfort peak." For me, it's anything over 12.

I have a hunch that one reason juries get so intimate is their legal limit of 12 members.

The need to exclude is one of the harshest realities with which would-be community builders must cope. It grates against every humanistic instinct to openness, hospitality and tolerance.

But there's no alternative path to a truly intimate community.

If you have done the 2–4–8–16 experiment mentioned earlier, check yourself out. Did you resent the intrusion of newcomers once you had some rapport built with one or more members?

I usually do.

I'm not saying that it's necessary or even good to exclude *all* outsiders. A community with completely stable membership would get dull very quickly. But the crucial point for an intimate community is that it controls its own access, chooses new members and is not just like a hotel.

Recently I've been reading about an outfit called Leadership Dynamics Institute, which has developed a weird cross between encounter and the Inquisition. Participants in LDI's four-day groups are beaten, deprived of food and sleep and subjected to hours-long harangues from other members until they break down, confess their shortcomings and plead for the group's forgiveness. The late businessman William Penn Patrick, father of this method, says all but a few of the 2,000 participants in his $1,000 weekends have loved it—"a claim," says one news report, "that hotelmen who have sponsored the seminars somewhat incredulously support."

But it's not incredible at all. Individualism is a terrible burden, and when it is ripped away from us in exchange for submersion in a group, we're ecstatic, reborn, free at last from the tyranny of our selves.

There is an inescapable relationship between brotherhood and oppression. Any group setting out to build community must anticipate this relationship and deal with it. Being in community doesn't make you more free; it takes away some of your freedom in exchange for the warmth of membership. Ignoring or denying that trade-off just makes it harder to confront.

To deny the relation between community and conformity, to call them two different things, is to make community that much more difficult to achieve. To be in community requires the sacrifice of at least part of your individuality. To belong to a group you must accept the group's will at least sometimes, like it or not. That's as true at Esalen as it is in Levittown. For me and for anyone seeking community, it then becomes a question of how much autonomy to trade in. Is the community I want Synanon or a radio talk show?

A community simply cannot be built from people crouched and ready to take off, like foot racers awaiting the crack of a gun. Commitment is basic. There is just no way that a community can be forged from people trying to make up their minds about whether to belong—community-seekers who keep their bags packed and ready.

Fear of commitment may be the biggest barrier to the rediscovery of community, including marriage.

When I say "commitment," I don't mean a signature in blood, or even a long-term contract. What I do mean is a willingness to stay through friction, to work on problems when they occur, to be a little stuck with each other. That may not be "commitment" according to Webster, but it's more than many of today's "communities," even today's marriages, enjoy.

Without confusing temporary and committed community, some opt for the former. That's the approach of Richard Sennet, a young sociologist, who says that his kind of community is best found in the disorder of a city. "In the adult society I envision," writes Sennet, "there would be no expectation of human love, no community of affection, warm and comforting, laid down for the society as a whole. Human bonds would be fragmented and limited to specific, individual encounters."

That's an honest vision of a society in which I wouldn't want to live, one in which disposability would infect every relationship. But it's an alternative not masquerading as anything other than a community of transients. Confusion of that alternative, of disposable communities, with ones based on commitment is what creates problems.

As I wrap up three years of work on a book about community, I'm sitting here wondering—What is it that I have to say, in a nutshell? What's the essence, the kernel of what I've learned from studying community and seeking it?

I began with a fairly conventional perspective on how we became such a lonely people—that mass society dehumanized and cut us off from each other —but believed that with imagination and new approaches we might defeat these influences and restore our sense of community.

The more I studied the issue and tried to build a community for myself, the less I found that to be the case. The villain whose trail I kept stalking turned out really to be ourselves—myself; our—my —ambivalence about community; our wish—my wish—not to get too close, thwarting a real hunger to join together.

Something I've realized only slowly is that seeking "community" in the abstract dooms the search. Community is people. I find community only when I find other people. I'm open to a group only when I'm open to its members. When I start looking for some mystical "community" I usually miss the people.

The problem of community, which sociologist Robert Nisbet calls "the single most impressive fact in the twentieth century in Western society," is relatively modern. For most of man's history, group life was a given, and grew naturally out of the ways we were forced to be with each other—to live, work, wash clothes and die.

This is no longer true. We have less and less necessity to be together and fewer ways of knowing each other, while our need for community remains constant. So we're forced back on the only immutable reason for joining hands: the human need for company. Without place, cause, common work or religion, most of us must make that humiliating admission: I can't live alone.

Once someone—once I—can take the risk, break the ice and say how I really feel, it's amazing how many others turn out just to have been waiting their turn. Then the community begins.

In Praise of New York

A Semi-Secular Homily

Peter L. Berger

PETER L. BERGER *is professor of sociology at Rutgers and the author of, among other works,* Pyramids of Sacrifice. *The present essay is adapted from an address given by Mr. Berger to the 1976 meeting of the Metropolitan New York Synod, Lutheran Church of America.*

DIFFERENT cities acquire great symbolic significance at different moments in human history. Paris was significant in this way in the 18th and 19th centuries, as was London (though perhaps to a lesser degree), and Rome, over and beyond anything that was actually going on there, has retained its powerful symbolic character over many centuries. New York City undoubtedly has a comparable symbolic significance today. It is perceived as a symbol of modernity, of Western civilization, and (despite the often-repeated statement that "New York is not America") of the civilization of the United States. The curious thing is that it is very widely perceived as a negative symbol—that is, as a metaphor of everything that has gone wrong with our society.

Much of the rest of the country sees New York as one gigantic agglomeration of social ills: crime, poverty, racial hatred, mismanaged and corrupt government—not to mention dirt, pollution, and traffic congestion of virtually metaphysical dimensions. The same perceptions have been widely diffused abroad, and foreign tourists come here with the piquant ambivalence of apprehension and fascination that used to go with dangerous expeditions into the jungles of central Africa. Interestingly, New York City has negative symbolic value right across the political spectrum. As seen from the Right, New York

is the habitat of an anti-American intellectual and media establishment, bent on converting the entire nation into the decadent welfare state that the city, supposedly, has already become. Seen from the Left, New York is, above all, Wall Street—the heart of the beast, headquarters of capitalist imperialism, the cosmic cancer; Madison Avenue has a slightly lesser place in this particular demonological vision. Cutting across the political dividing lines there also exists today a widespread cultural mood of anti-urbanism. Vaguely linked with the ecology movement, this mood offers yet another incentive to deplore New York.

And yet, despite all this, New York City continues to be a magnet and even an object of love, sometimes fierce love. People, especially young people, continue to come in large numbers, irresistibly drawn to the city by expectations of success and excitement. And New Yorkers themselves, although they, too, frequently share the negative views of their own city, nevertheless continue to be inexplicably, perhaps dementedly, attached to the putative cesspool of perdition in which they reside. Such ambivalence suggests that the reality of New York is more complicated than its symbolic imagery. And so, of course, it is. For New York City—not New York in some romanticized past, not New York in some utopian future, but New York today—can, I would argue, best be understood as a signal of transcendence.

The currently fashionable anti-urbanism concentrates on the harsh empirical facts about the city. To speak of New York City as a signal of transcendence is neither to ignore nor to deny these facts. Rather, it is to try for a glimpse of

another reality, which is both hidden under and hinted at by the reality of this world. In other words, to speak of a signal of transcendence is to make an assertion about the presence of redemptive power in human life. Such assertions, needless to say, lie at the very center of the Judeo-Christian view of the world.

An exploration into the possibilities of New York as a signal of transcendence must begin with the root fact that it is not only a vast and vastly important city, but *the* city *par excellence*, the prototypical cosmopolis of our age. In other words, while New York may no longer be the largest city in the world, it is still the world's most potent symbol of urbanism and urbanity (two related but distinct matters). This is why visitors and new arrivals feel at home in New York so quickly. Every urban experience that they have had before has been, in a way, an anticipation of New York, and the encounter with the real thing thus has a strong note of familiarity, of *déjà vu* (quite apart from the fact that the major landmarks of New York are known everywhere and serve as instant orientations for the newcomers). Wherever skyscrapers reach up toward the clouds, wherever masses of cars stream back and forth over steel-girded bridges, wherever heterogeneous crowds pour through subways, underground concourses, or cavernous lobbies encased in glass—there is a bit of New York. Conversely, the New Yorker visiting other cities finds everywhere the sights and sounds, even the smells, that remind him of home. The mystique of New York City is, above all, the mystique of modern urban life, concentrated there more massively than anywhere else.

IT IS not accidental, I think, that the biblical imagery of redemptive fulfillment is so persistently urban. Jerusalem became the focus of religious devotion from an early period of the spiritual history of ancient Israel, and it has remained the holy city in both Jewish and Christian religious imagination ever since. And this same Jerusalem, of course, came to be transformed into an image of eschatological expectation—the Jerusalem that is to come, the heavenly city, "its radiance like a most rare jewel, like a jasper, clear as crystal." Biblical scholars disagree on the precise origins and status of the Zion tradition in the Old Testament, on the religious significance of Jerusalem at, say, the time of David and Solomon, and on the significance of the various images in the Apocalypse. Yet there seems to be far-reaching consensus on one rather simple point: the city as a sociopolitical formation marks a transition in human history from bonds based exclusively on kinship to more comprehensive human relationships. Perhaps this was not the case everywhere, but it was clearly so in the ancient Mediterranean world. Here cities—as markets, centers of political or military administration, and sanctuaries—served to weaken and eventually to liquidate the archaic bonds of blood, of clan, and of tribe.

Max Weber has argued that, in this, cities are incipiently "rationalizing"—that is, they constitute a social and political order based on reason, as against an older order based on magical taboos. This development reached a dramatic climax in the emergence of the Greek *polis*, but it is not fanciful to suggest that the biblical imagery of the city served as a religious legitimation of the same underlying liberation from the magic of the blood. Whatever else the city is, it is a place where *different* people come together and find a new unity with each other—and, in the context of the ancient world, that is a revolutionary event. What all this suggests is that the city is a signal of transcendence inasmuch as it embodies universalism and freedom.

If universalism is a root urban characteristic, then surely New York is the most universalistic of cities. And, of course, it is this quality of universalism that most impresses the newcomer and that is so often bragged about by the native. Here they are all pressed together, in this small space, all the races and all the nations of the earth. A short subway ride separates worlds of mind-boggling human diversity—black Harlem borders on the Upper West Side, the *barrio* on the territory of East Side swingers, the Village on Little Italy, Chinatown on the financial district. And that is only in Manhattan, beyond which lie the mysterious expanses of the boroughs—places like Greenpoint, Bay Ridge, or Boro Park, each one a world of meaning and belonging almost unpenetrated by outsiders. In this city you can enter a phone booth shaped like a pagoda, and make a reservation in a Czechoslovak restaurant (or, more precisely, in one of *several* Czechoslovak restaurants). You can spend weeks doing nothing else, if you have the leisure, than savoring the world's greatest concentration of museums, art galleries, musical and theatrical performances, and other cultural happenings of every conceivable kind from the sublime to the unspeakable. When I first lived in New York as a student, I had a job as a receptionist in a now-defunct dispensary on the Lower East Side. I still recall with pleasure my lunch hours: I would buy a bialy with lox in the old Essex Street Market, munch it while strolling through the teeming street life at the foot of the Williamsburg Bridge, and then have a quiet coffee with baklava in one of several Turkish cafés over on Allen Street, surrounded by old men smoking water-pipes and playing checkers (apparently their only occupation). What I recall most of all is the exhilarating sense that here I was, in New York City, where all these things were going on and where, in principle, everything was possible.

These mundane facts carry redemptive meaning. They point to the promise that all of humanity in its incredible variety is God's concern, and that the divine culmination of history will mean not the end but the glorious transfiguration of every truly human expression. The city of messianic fulfillment too will contain every human type and condition—and in this, necessarily, it will resemble New York. There is also the promise that the same culmination will be the reign of perfect freedom under God. Until then, all liberations are incomplete, some are illusory. All the same, wherever human beings are liberated from oppression or narrowness to wider horizons of life, thought, and imagination, there is a foreshadowing of the final liberation that is to come. It is in this sense—in the exhilaration of its pluralism and its freedom—that New York City is a signal of transcendence.

TO SOME extent the characteristics of universalism and freedom are endemic to urban life nearly everywhere, in varying degrees. The distinctiveness of New York comes from the enormous magnitude of these features here. The same may be said of another characteristic which, I propose, may be taken as a signal of transcendence: the city is a place of hope.

If there is any New York legend that is generally known, it is that of the immigrant, and the legend, of course, has as its most famous physical representation the Statue of Liberty. This legend is, above all, a story of hope. I myself arrived in America a short time after World War II, very poor and very young, after a long ocean voyage that sticks in my memory as an endless bout with seasickness. The ship sailed into New York harbor in the early morning, in a dense fog, so that very little could be seen at first. Then dramatically, the fog was pierced, and we saw first the Statue, which seemed perilously close to the ship, and then the skyline of Lower Manhattan. All the passengers (a motley crowd indeed) were assembled on the deck, and there was an awed silence. But, curiously, what impressed me most at the time was not these majestic sights; I had, after all, expected to see them. There was something else. As the ship sailed up the Hudson toward its pier, I was fascinated by the traffic on what I later learned was the West Side Highway. All these cars seemed enormous to me. But more than their size, it was their colors that astonished me. This was before New York taxis all came to be painted yellow; then, they came in every color of the rainbow, though yellow was predominant. Only, I didn't know that these garish cars were taxis. The exuberance of color, I thought, was characteristic of ordinary American automobiles. This, then, was my first unexpected sight in New York, and it pleased me greatly. I don't think I quite put it this way to myself, but implicit in my visual pleasure was the notion that someday I too might be driving past the skyscrapers in a bright yellow car of surrealistic proportions, engaged (no doubt) in some business of great importance, and enjoying the company of the most beautiful woman imaginable.

As immigrant stories go, mine has been lucky. Indeed, I could say that New York has kept all its promises to me. I know full well that this has not been so for all newcomers to the city. If New York has been a place of hope, it has also been a place of disappointed hope, of shattered expectations, of bitterness and despair. It has been fashionable of late to stress this negative aspect of the American dream —mistakenly so, I believe, because America has fulfilled many more expectations than it has frustrated. I would even go farther than that. The currently fashionable intellectuals, who decry the hopefulness of America, are far more in a state of "false consciousness" than the millions of immigrants who came and who continue to come to America full of hope.

Nevertheless, just as it would be false to speak of the universalism and the freedom of this city without also speaking of the sordid underside of these facts, so it would be dishonest to pretend that the hopeful message emblazoned on the Statue of Liberty is an accurate description of empirical reality. Of course it is not. And yet the proclamation of hope to all those who

came here across the ocean is a signal of transcendent portent. For all of us, men and women of this aeon, are on a long journey, across vast and dangerous seas, toward a city of hope.

THERE is more: New York is a place of useless labor. Just compare New York with an honest-to-goodness industrial city, like Detroit or Pittsburgh, or even Chicago. In these cities most people are engaged in labor that has at least an indirect relation to economic utility. Certainly there are such people in New York. The peculiarity of New York, however, is the large portion of its labor force employed in activities which only the most ingenious economic theory can interpret as a contribution to the gross national product. Leave aside the enormous number of people working in municipal government and other public services (and leave aside the very timely question of how long the city will be able to afford them): one is still left with legions of people making their livelihood, or at least trying to do so, through activities which, economically speaking, are bizarre. Promoters of Renaissance music, producers of non-verbal theater, translators of Swahili literature, purveyors of esoteric erotica, agents of nonexistent governments, revolutionaries in exile, Egyptologists, numismatic experts, scream therapists, guidance counselors for geriatric recreation, Indonesian chefs, belly-dancers and teachers of belly-dancing (and, for all I know, belly-dancing therapists)—not to mention individuals who are on university payrolls to provide instruction in phenomenological sociology.

A Chicagoan will know what to say to all this: these people can't be serious. Precisely! The opposite of being serious is being playful; the invincible playfulness of New York City is, I believe, in itself a signal of transcendence. *Homo ludens* is closer to redemption than *homo faber*; the clown is more of a sacramental figure than the engineer. And we have very good reason to expect that paradise will be a very playful affair—and in *that*, at the very least, it will resemble New

York more than Chicago.

New Yorkers, like the inhabitants of other large cities are supposed to be sophisticated. The word, of course, is related to sophistry—the ability to be clever with words, to be quick, to be surprised at nothing. This notion of sophistication is closely related to that of urbanity, and it is as much a source of pride for the urbanite as it is a provocation to others. Somebody once defined a true metropolis as a place where an individual can march down the street wearing a purple robe and a hat with bells on, beating a drum and leading an elephant by the leash—and only get casual glances from passers-by. If so, then surely New York is the truest metropolis there is. To some extent, of course, this is but another expression of the aforementioned universalism. But, in addition, the city is a place of magic. And in that too it offers us a signal of transcendence.

I don't mean occultism, though there is enough of that around as well. I mean magic in a more ample sense, what Rudolf Otto called the *mysterium fascinans*— namely, the quality of the surreal, the intuition that reality is manipulable, unpredictable, subject to the strangest metamorphoses at any moment. The British author Jonathan Raban, in his curious book *Soft City*, argues that modern urban life is characterized by magic, and *not* (as it is more customarily thought to be) by rationality. I think that there is much to be said for this view; Raban also maintains that New York has this magic in a particularly potent form. The magic of the city can be summed up in a sentence that points to a recurring experience: anything can happen here—and it could happen right now.

Magic always has its dark side, and it is hardly necessary to spell out the sinister possibilities of the insight that anything can happen. But it would be a mistake to limit the experience to its negative aspect. The city is a place of strangers and of strangeness, and this very fact implies a fascination of a special kind. Ordinary-looking houses contain unimaginable mysteries within. Casual encounters are transformed into revelations of shocking impact. Passions explode on the most unexpected occasions. All this helps to account for the excitement of the city, but it also makes for a general vision of the world. Reality is not what it seems; there are realities behind the reality of everyday life; the routine fabric of our ordinary lives is not self-contained, it has holes in it, and there is no telling what wondrous things may at any moment rush in through these holes.

This vision of the world is perhaps not itself religious, but it is in close proximity to the root insights of the religious attitude. The magic of the city should not be identified with religious experience, but it

may be said to be an antechamber of the latter. When people say that New York City is a surrealistic place, they are saying more than they intend. They are making a religious statement about the reality of human life: behind the empirical city lurks *another city*, a city of dreams and wonders. They are also making a statement about redemption: for redemption always comes into the world as a big surprise, even as a cosmic joke. Anything at all can come through the holes in the fabric of ordinary reality: a man leading an elephant by the leash—or Elijah returning in his fiery chariot to herald the dawn of our salvation.

BETWEEN Rutgers University, where I teach, and Brooklyn, where I

live, I regularly travel by crossing from Staten Island over the Verrazzano Bridge. It has often occurred to me, especially in the evening when the light is soft and the contours of visual reality seem to lack firmness, that the entrance to heaven may well look something like this wonderful bridge, with its majestic arcs and its breathtaking vistas on both sides. The transcendent hope of both Jewish and Christian piety is, quite simply, this: that in the evening of our lives we shall be part of this traffic and that we will know that, in the city on the other side of the bridge, what awaits us is home. I for one would not be overly surprised if the gatekeeper were to address me in a Brooklyn accent.

The Limits to Growth of Third World Cities

Lester R. Brown

Lester R. Brown is President and a Senior Researcher with Worldwatch Institute, 1776 Massachusetts Avenue, N.W., Washington, D.C. 20036, U.S.A. His numerous publications include *World Without Borders*, Random House, 1972, and *By Bread Alone*, Praeger, 1974, available through the World Future Society Book Service.

Projections by the United Nations show urbanization trends continuing unabated over the final quarter of this century. A world which was 29% urban in 1950 and 39% in 1975 is projected to be half urban by the year 2000. Can this rate of urbanization continue? Our research at the Worldwatch Institute on food and energy prospects and the future employment situation raises doubts as to whether projected urbanization rates will materialize. We do not expect the trends of the quarter century now beginning to be a simple extrapolation of the one just ended.

The basic premise that urbanization trends will continue unaltered, leading to a world of huge agglomerations by the end of this century, is underpinned by three implied assumptions: food surpluses produced in the surrounding countryside or imported from abroad will be sufficient to feed the burgeoning urban populations, cheap energy will be available to underwrite the additional energy costs of urban living, and sufficient productive employment will become available in the cities. Neither these underlying assumptions nor, therefore, the basic premise are likely to hold.

From Food Surplus to Food Deficiency

In order for people to move from the countryside to the cities, there must be a surplus of food produced in the rural areas that can be used to feed the dependent urban populations. These surpluses may come from domestic supplies or from foreign sources. From the first urban settlements several

Region	1934-38	1948-52	1960	1970	1976 Preliminary Estimates
		(Million Metric Tons)			
North America	+ 5	+23	+39	+56	+94
Latin America	+ 9	+ 1	0	+ 4	- 3
Western Europe	-24	-22	-25	-30	-17
E. Europe & USSR	+ 5	—	0	0	-27
Africa	+ 1	0	- 2	- 5	-10
Asia	+ 2	- 6	-17	-37	-47
Australia & New Zealand	+ 3	+ 3	+ 6	+12	+ 8

Source: Derived from FAO and USDA data and author's estimates.

Chart shows the changing pattern of world grain trade from the 1930s to the present. Over a mere 40-year span, most nations changed from net exporters to net importers. Plus signs indicate net exports; minus signs, net imports.

thousand years ago until the middle of this century, cities were sustained largely, if not entirely, by the food produced in the surrounding countryside. Since then more and more cities have come to depend on food imports from distant parts of the world. Accelerating urbanization since mid-century has been closely paralleled by the vast growth in food shipments from North America.

Forty years ago North American grain exports averaged five million tons yer pear. As of 1950 they had increased to 23 million tons, and by 1970 to 56 million tons. During the current year, North America will export an estimated 94 million tons of grain. In consumption terms, the farmers of North America are exporting enough grain to feed, at their respective consumption levels, 560 million Indians or 115 million Russians.

The world food trade pattern has been altered profoundly in recent decades. A generation ago, Western Europe, which was the most urbanized region, was also the only importing region. Each of the other continents was exporting grain in at least some quantity. By 1976, that situation has been changed beyond recognition.

Virtually the entire world has come to depend on North American food exports. Asia, Africa, Latin America, Western Europe, and Eastern Europe, including the Soviet Union, are net grain importers. A great amount of the food imported into these regions is used to feed the cities.

Analysis on a country by country basis shows that the world today consists almost entirely of food deficit countries. Those remaining as important exporters at the global level can be numbered on the fingers of one hand. While scores of new food importers have emerged over the past two decades, not a single new exporter has emerged! Growing deficits in some countries are due to the inability to expand food production apace with rapidly multiplying populations. In other countries, these deficits are a matter of mismanagement and of agricultural neglect, treating agriculture as a stepchild while giving the cities priority for new investments. All too often, deficits are the product of both factors.

Not only are nearly all countries today food importers, but a growing number now import over half of their

Reprinted from: *The Futurist* A Journal of Forecasts, Trends and Ideas About the Future. Published by: World Future Society An Association for the Study of Alternative Futures, 4916 St. Elmo Avenue, Washington, D.C. 20014.

grain supplies. Among these are Japan, Belgium, Senegal, Libya, Saudi Arabia, Venezuela, Lebanon, Switzerland, and Algeria. Others rapidly approaching a similar degree of dependence on imported foodstuffs include Portugal, Costa Rica, Sri Lanka, South Korea, and Egypt.

As rising import needs throughout the world have begun to exceed the exportable surpluses produced in the North American countryside, both the U.S. and Canadian governments have found it necessary to restrict access for some countries at least temporarily in order to avoid politically unacceptable rises in domestic food prices. Most recently Russian and Polish grain buyers were excluded from U.S. grain markets during the fall of 1975. The Canadian Wheat Board banned any new wheat sales from mid-July of last year until the harvest was completed in the fall.

Anticipating future difficulty in gaining access to U.S. food supplies, some industrial countries have negotiated long-term agreements which are intended to insure access to North American grain supplies. Among these are Japan, the Soviet Union, and Poland. After a quarter century of burdensome food surpluses and keen competition among exporters for markets abroad, the emerging competition among importers for assured access to supplies represents an ominous reversal.

If the trends of the past several years continue, the collective import needs of the 100-plus importing countries eventually will greatly exceed the exportable supplies from North America, particularly when the harvest is poor. This is creating a politics of food, a type of food diplomacy. The hostages in this game are the cities of the world that are sustained with imported food. They are living quite literally "from ship to mouth." The trend of cities becoming more and more dependent on imported food is everywhere evident, from Leningrad to Lagos, Cairo to Santiago, Tokyo to Bombay.

It is not likely that this rapid growth in dependence on imported foodstuffs from North America can continue for much longer. Yet the trend toward urbanization undoubtedly will lead toward ever-greater dependence on North American food. Inevitably, harsh decisions will have to be made by the U.S. and Canadian governments on who gets food and who does not.

Forward-looking Canadians foresee the day when the domestic demands of a growing, increasingly affluent population may reduce the exportable surpluses of food, much as they already have for energy. Overwhelming dependence by the world's cities on imported food supplies from a single geographic region in a world of food scarcity brings with it a vulnerability to external political forces and climatic trends that is risky indeed. This being the case, countries would do well to re-examine urbanization policies and consider whether continued rapid urbanization and the associated growing dependence on distant food supplies is in their national interest.

Energy Shortages May Limit Urban Life-Support Services

Urbanization and the availability of energy are closely related. The emergence of the first cities appears to have been closely associated with agricultural breakthroughs such as the harnessing of draft animals, the domestication of new agricultural plants, and the development of irrigation systems. In effect, these enabled humans to harness more energy for their own purposes—to capture more solar energy in plants or, in the case of draft animals, to convert otherwise unusable roughage into a form of energy that could be used to increase the food supply. Important though these new energy sources were, the agricultural surpluses they made possible were never enough to support more than a small proportion of the population living away from the land. Indeed, as recently as 1800 only 2.2% of the population of Europe resided in cities of 100,000 or more.

The energy breakthrough which permitted much larger populations, even majorities, to be sustained in cities was the discovery of fossil fuels, initially coal and later oil. The harnessing of fossil fuels, to generate steam for industrial power, gave birth to the industrial revolution, permitted the concentration of economic activity, and ushered in a new era of urbanization.

The large-scale migration of people from countryside to city requires an abundance of energy. In an urban environment, additional energy is required to satisfy food, fuel, housing, and transport needs. Assuming no change in consumption levels, each person who moves from the countryside to the city raises world energy requirements.

With food, urbanization raises energy requirements on two fronts. As the urban population increases relative to the rural food-producing population, additional energy is required in agriculture to generate this requisite food surplus. At the same time, more energy is needed to process the food and transport it to urban areas.

As more and more people move into the cities, each person remaining in agriculture must produce an ever-larger surplus. This, in turn, requires the broad substitution of mechanical energy for labor in food production. In a world where energy is becoming scarce and unemployment is rising, it makes little sense to continue this wholesale shift to mechanization in countries with large, unemployed rural populations.

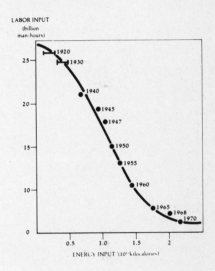

LABOR INPUT (billion man-hours)

ENERGY INPUT (10^{15} kilocalories)

Graph shows the substitution of energy for labor on U.S. farms since 1920. Man-hours of human labor have fallen by a factor of 16 while energy consumed has risen by a factor of 10.

It is customary to point with pride to the small percentage of the population living on the land in industrial nations such as the United States, where 5% of the society living on the land provides food for the remainder. This level of labor productivity in agriculture requires vast amounts of energy. David Pimentel, agricultural scientist at Cornell University, illustrates the magnitude of the energy requirements for modern agriculture by stating, "If the current four billion people in the world were to be fed at U.S. consumption levels, using U.S. energy-intensive agricultural techniques, and if *petroleum* were the only source of energy, and if we used the

1. URBANIZATION

world's petroleum reserve *solely* to feed the world population, the presently-known 415 billion barrel reserve would last a mere 29 years."

Although the amounts required for production are large, they are dwarfed by comparison with the amount of energy used to transport, process, and distribute food in a highly urbanized society. Within the United States, one-fourth of the energy used in the food system is used to produce food. Three-fourths of the total is used to transport, process, and distribute that same food after it leaves the farm.

The difficulties in meeting the food needs of city dwellers are in many ways paralleled by the difficulties in meeting their fuel needs. In both cases, supplies must come either from the countryside (in the form of charcoal, firewood, etc.) or be imported (as kerosene, fuel oil, etc.). Except for those few nations that have adequate domestic sources of hydroelectric or petroleum power, the grim alternatives are an ever-widening barren area around the cities, as they outgrow indigenous forest reserves, or growing dependence on unreliable and expensive fuel imports.

Urbanization also increases energy requirements for waste disposal. At the village level, waste disposal is not a major problem. Organic wastes are returned to the soil to enrich it, an important and integral part of nature's nutrient cycles of phosphorous, sulfur, and nitrogen. In this way they contribute to the food supply. But once large numbers of people congregate in cities, waste may no longer be an asset. Indeed, efforts to safely dispose of it often represent an additional drain on scarce energy resources.

The rapid urbanization characterizing so much of the world during the third quarter of this century occurred during an era of cheap energy, an era which may be historically unique. Oil production has already peaked in some major producing countries, including the United States and quite possibly Romania. Production declines in other countries will follow. With the end of the petroleum age now clearly in sight, the world must turn to other forms of energy, forms which may by their very nature affect the pattern of human settlement.

Until recently, it was assumed that the world would move from the fossil fuel era into the nuclear age. After a quarter century of experience with nuclear power, the world is beginning to have second thoughts about continuing down the nuclear path.

Failure to devise any satisfactory techniques of waste disposal, the inevitable spread of nuclear weapons along with nuclear power, and the prospect of terrorist groups acquiring nuclear materials and weapons are all beginning to raise doubts in even the most sanguine of minds.

Beyond the seemingly insoluble waste disposal and security problems, the economics associated with nuclear power are becoming questionable. In 1975 there were 25 times as many nuclear reactors cancelled or deferred in the United States as there were new orders placed. A principal executive within a company producing nuclear reactors described the industry as sick. It is undoubtedly sick; the real question is whether or not it may be terminally ill.

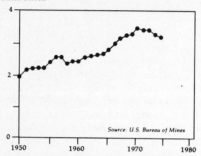

Billion Barrels

Source: U.S. Bureau of Mines

Graph shows U.S. petroleum production 1950-74. Downturn since 1970 is due to exhaustion of wells. Unless major new oil fields are discovered, production in the U.S. exclusive of Alaska is expected to continue to decline.

Given this very real possibility, urban planners need to consider the possibility of a world which will move not from the fossil fuel era to the nuclear era but toward growing reliance on solar energy. If the world moves toward a solar age, it means, among other things, that the population will need to be broadly distributed, for the simple reason that solar energy itself is broadly dispersed.

The mechanisms for capturing solar energy vary widely. They include solar collectors which are used both for heating and cooling; they include photovoltaics, which convert solar energy into electrical energy (the form that powers COMSAT's international communications satellites), and indirect forms of solar energy such as wind, water, and firewood. All forms of bioconversion including firewood are, of course, solar-based. The great attraction of solar energy is that the source is safe, secure, virtually endless, and rather widely available.

If the world goes solar, the optimum size of human settlements is likely to be far smaller than it would otherwise be. Planners should be considering the prospect of numerous relatively small communities, widely distributed for energy efficiency, rather than the continuing massing of people in large megalopolises.

Unemployment Problems Will Increase

A third assumption implied by the projections of urbanization trends is that jobs will be available in the cities. But this assumption is at least as questionable as those on food and energy. One of the most intractable problems facing governments in the years ahead is that of providing employment for the rapidly swelling numbers of young people coming into the job market. Projections by the International Labor Organization indicate that the industrial countries will need to create 161 million additional jobs during the 1970-2000 period, or an increase of 33%. The developing countries meanwhile must attempt to create 922 million new jobs, nearly double the number of jobs that exist today.

The labor force of India alone is expected to increase by 63 million during the current decade. Already plagued with widespread unemployment and underemployment, India is now beleaguered by 100,000 new entrants into the labor force each week. Mexico, with its comparatively small economic base, will shortly have nearly as many young people entering the job market each year as the United States.

The creation of jobs requires capital. Even the industrial countries with a relative abundance of capital have had difficulty in recent years in expanding employment rapidly; hence they have had the highest levels of unemployment since the Depression of the Thirties. What has been a problem for the industrial societies is becoming a crisis for the developing countries.

This explosion in the number of job seekers is coming at a time when it is becoming more difficult to raise capital for investment purposes. A growing body of economic literature is documenting the difficulty in maintaining satisfactory levels of capital formation. The United States, traditionally a source of capital for the rest of the world, is having difficulty meeting its own requirements. Japan's foreign investment rate has been cut severely. The centrally-planned economies of Eastern Europe and the Soviet Union are now borrowing heavily from Western capital markets.

With capital projected to be in short supply, as many jobs as possible must be created with that which is available. Creating jobs in the urban industrial sector requires far more capital than the creation of jobs in the rural agricultural sector. Thus, employment considerations also argue against rapid urbanization.

Food, Energy, Job Shortages Will Limit Cities

There are three reasons why urbanization trends cannot continue as projected until the end of the century: the inability of the countryside to produce sufficiently large food surpluses, the disappearance of the cheap energy needed to underwrite the urbanization process, and the impossibility of creating enough jobs in urban settings.

If the flow from the countryside to the city should continue unabated, some harsh correctives will likely begin to operate in the not-too-distant future. Among these will be food shortages in the cities, energy shortages that will hamstring the economy, and rising levels of unemployment. The secondary signs of stress will be uncontrollable inflation, increasing nutritional stress, growing depen-

Projected Growth in World Labor Force, 1970-2000				
	1970	2000	Additional Jobs Required	Change 1970-2000 (percent)
	millions			
More Developed Nations	488	649	161	+33
Less Developed Nations	1,011	1,933	922	+91

Source: International Labour Office.

dence on external food and energy imports, and an associated rise in external indebtedness. Finally, rising urban unemployment will possibly lead to social unrest and political instability.

Given this possible scenario, would it not be wise for governments to devise policies to slow urban growth before the constraints of natural and social systems limit their options? Before attempting to answer this, it would be well to examine the forces leading to the wholesale movement of people into cities. The forces at work fall into two broad categories, those originating in the countryside—the push forces—and those serving as attractants in the cities—the pull forces. The delineation is not always clear,

with forces often being simply opposite sides of the same coin.

The principal official policies which influence urbanization, both directly and indirectly, almost always reflect a bias toward the city, thus creating a natural magnet to draw people from the countryside. Michael Lipton, in his book *Why Poor People Stay Poor: Urban Bias and World Development* (Temple-Smith, London, 1976), graphically describes the nature of this rural-urban conflict:

> "The most important class conflict in the poor countries of the world today is not between labor and capital, nor is it between foreign and national interests. It is between the rural classes and the urban classes. The rural sector contains most of the poverty and most of the low-cost sources of potential advance, but the urban sector contains most of the articulateness, organization, and power. So the urban classes have been able to 'win' most of the rounds of the struggle with the countryside; but in so doing they have made the development process needlessly slow and unfair."

Food price policies designed to provide unrealistically cheap food for city dwellers through ceiling prices discourage domestic food production. More broadly, urban-oriented food policies discourage private investment in food production, and hence employment in the countryside. This distortion in the development process helps explain the increasing dependence on food imported from abroad, a situation which now exists in so many countries.

Street scene in Seoul, Korea, exemplifies the exciting life that many farm youths of the Third World aspire to attain by migrating to the cities. But most rural youths have no salable skills for employment in the limited number of jobs available in cities.

Photo: Carl Purcell, U.S. Agency for International Development

Apart from the distortions caused by shortsighted food price policies, public investment in most developing countries is heavily biased toward urban communities. It is not at all uncommon for a country with 70% of its

1. URBANIZATION

population in rural areas to allocate only 20% of its public sector investment to those same areas. In such a situation, investment per person can easily be several times as high for the urban dweller as for those living in the countryside.

The strong urban bias in public investment in social services, particularly education and health, further enhances the attractiveness of the cities. For example, an accident of birth can strongly influence access to a university education. Lipton points out that a child from an Indian town or city is 8.5 times more likely to go to a university than a village child. In addition to being a gross inequity, such a system is inefficient. University places are used to train less able urban children rather than more capable rural children.

A similar case exists with medical care. With investment in medical facilities concentrated in urban hospitals rather than rural clinics, the less urgent medical needs of the city take priority over the more urgent medical needs of the village. This policy leads to a wasteful allocation of scarce resources, which must inevitably take its toll in the form of reduced economic growth.

The social cost of this urban bias in the policies and priorities of governments is high. It seems certain to rise, particularly as the food, energy, and employment constraints on urbanization begin to operate. This unfolding situation calls for a pronounced shift in rural-urban priorities. The convergence of larger food deficits, rising unemployment, and a widespread physical deterioration of agricultural systems in all too many developing countries, suggest the outlines of a broad new public initiative, a way of meeting several needs simultaneously.

Solution Lies in Return to the Land

Apart from the great financial cost of providing jobs in an urban-industrial setting, there is a pressing need to sharply expand the effort to arrest and reverse the ecological deterioration of the countryside now underway in many heavily populated developing countries. This deterioration takes the form of deforestation, overgrazing, desert expansion, soil erosion, and the silting of streams, hydroelectric and irrigation reservoirs and canals.

During the past several years the global environmental crisis has been defined almost exclusively in in-dustrial or rich country terms, in terms of pollution. The two have become virtually synonymous, but there is another, perhaps even more serious facet of the environmental crisis. Erik Eckholm, in his book *Losing Ground: Environmental Stress and World Food Prospects* (Norton, 1976), describes it vividly:

"In the world war to save the habitable environment, even the battles to purify the noxious clouds over Tokyo and Sao Paulo, and to restore life to Lake Erie, are but skirmishes compared to the uncontested routs being suffered in the hills of Nepal and Java, and on the rangelands of Chad and northwest India. A far deadlier annual toll, and perhaps an even greater threat to future human welfare than that of the pollution of our air and water, is that exacted by the undermining of the productivity of the land itself through accelerated soil erosion, creeping deserts, increased flooding, and declining soil fertility. Humans are—out of desperation, ignorance, shortsightedness, or greed—destroying the basis of their own livelihood as they violate the limits of natural systems."

Perhaps the single most helpful effort in arresting this deterioration and restoring the countryside would be the mobilization of the population for massive reforestation projects. Reforestation serves several important ends. It reduces runoff, reduces soil erosion, lessens the frequency and severity of flooding, slows the siltation of irrigation reservoirs and canals and, over the longer term, it provides an important source of fuel and building materials. There is so much to be gained from a large-scale reforestation project in virtually every developing country that it is difficult to understand why more governments have not initiated programs for this purpose.

In a number of countries, particularly in Africa and to a lesser degree in Asia and Latin America, desert expansion poses a serious threat to agriculture. If the complex social and political problems can be overcome, this too is an area where the intensive investment of human labor in restoring destroyed vegetation, seeding grass, fencing, and planting tree belts can be very effective and can contribute to the capital stock and productive capacity of the country.

With water rather than land likely to be the principal constraint on

U.S. ship unloads mountain of sorghum grain at Dakar, West Africa, to be bagged and hauled by truck to the Sahel. Increasing numbers of people in Third World countries now depend upon imported grain for survival and would starve if the grain shipments ceased.

Photo: Carl Purcell
U.S. Agency for International Development

efforts to expand food production during the final quarter of this century, local water conservancy projects in the form of small catchments and earthen dams made from local materials can make an important contribution to rural water supplies. What is lacking in most countries is the political leadership and the means of mobilizing and organizing unemployed people.

Throughout history, societies often have mobilized for very specific objectives. From time to time the achievements have been singularly impressive: the construction of the pyramids in ancient Egypt, the rather massive restoration of the countryside in China (particularly reforestation, water conservation works, and terracing) over the past twenty-five years, and the landing of astronauts on the moon by the United States. The objectives, social structure and geographic location of these societies have varied widely, but each represents in its own way a rather spectacular accomplishment. The techniques of social organization differ markedly in these three particular situations, suggesting that each society needs to evolve its own techniques of social organization to achieve its goals.

There is an opportunity for the mobilization of literally hundreds of millions of chronically or seasonally unemployed people to improve the food production capacity of many countries, particularly developing ones. The need exists, it is a real one, and it is expanding day by day.

Government Support Needed for New Ruralism

Many of the problems confronting urban planners are a result of continuing, often uncontrolled, population growth and a strong urban bias in the allocation of resources. Part of the growth in urban populations is due to natural increase in the cities and part to migration from rural areas. In the most rapidly growing cities, the migration is the dominant component. The forces responsible for the human flood of several hundred million people from countryside to city between 1950 and 1975 are a combination of urban pull and rural push.

As we wrestle with the problems of human settlements, of the human habitat, it becomes increasingly clear that we are grappling in some measure with the problems of population, both current numbers and, in many countries, continued rapid natural increase. There are now four billion of us in the world, a figure we reached, according to the Population Reference Bureau, on March 28, 1976. This landmark occasion was not the cause for celebration, rather it was a matter which troubled people everywhere. The stresses and strains associated with continuing population growth in a world already inhabited by four billion people confront the urban planner on every front. (See "The Population Problem in 22 Dimensions," THE FUTURIST, October 1976.)

In our day-to-day wrestling with problems and events we tend to forget the fateful arithmetic of population growth. Occasionally we need to re-

Horticulturists confer in vinyl greenhouse at Pusan, Korea. Vegetables can be grown year-round in such facilities, offering new horizons in food production and labor-intensive agriculture for countries that have many unemployed people and not enough food.

Photo: Carl Purcell
U.S. Agency for International Development

mind ourselves that a 3% annual rate of population growth *leads to a nineteenfold increase in a century.* Algeria, with a 3.4% rate of population growth and with 15 million people today, would find itself with 285 million people, more than the total population of North America, just four generations hence. Similarly, if recent trends continue, Mexico, with 60 million people today, will have more than 1.1 billion people in a century. This would exceed the current population of Russia, India, and Bangladesh combined. I cite these numbers not because they are expected to materialize, but merely to emphasize the urgency of reducing birth rates where they remain high.

I put population policies at the forefront of efforts to cope with urbanization because if we do not succeed in putting the brakes on population growth, then our efforts on other fronts will be for naught. Along with this attention to population must come a major shift in government priorities away from the urban bias which has contributed to so many of the problems we face.

Many planners and analysts believe that the tide from the countryside to

the city cannot be slowed or stemmed, that it is inevitable. I am not among those. What is needed is farsighted national policies which give the countryside its due. It is at the national level where most important policies are formulated and programs are designed to shape the process of urbanization. And most of them have an overwhelming bias toward the urban centers at the expense of rural areas.

Correcting this imbalance is not an impossibility. Some countries have made a concerted effort to improve both productive capacity and living conditions in the countryside, and have derived broad social benefits from it. Among these nations—China, Taiwan, the United States, Tanzania, Cuba, and New Zealand—there is no common bond of geography, political system, or culture. The only common element is a desire to improve the lives of those living in the countryside as well as in the city.

In suggesting that the time has come for governments to abandon their urban bias, I am in no way suggesting that the city be abandoned. The evolution of cities represents an important facet of the social evolution of our species. As Barbara Ward has pointed out so effectively in *The Home of Man* (Norton, 1976), cities are an integral part of contemporary civilization, both repositories and custodians of culture. No one argues against cities nor does anyone argue for a world which is entirely urbanized. There should be a balance between the rural-urban distribution of people and economic activity. The question is what that balance should be in each country, and how it will be affected by the emerging food and energy situation and by changing economic and environmental conditions.

The massive movement from the countryside to the cities has been based over the past quarter century on conditions which do not appear to be sustainable. It is incumbent on political leaders to recognize this and to eliminate the overwhelming urban bias in resource allocation, adopting a much more balanced approach, one consistent with the new food, energy, and employment realities. The most effective efforts to ameliorate the problems facing cities may well be those to improve living conditions and productivity in the countryside.

The Pop Sociology of Suburbs and New Towns

Silvia Fava

Brooklyn College—CUNY

The mid-twentieth century is a sociologizing age, as the early twentieth was a psychologizing period, and still earlier periods were dominated by biological and mechanical frames of reference. We hear sociologizing at cocktail parties and kaffeeklatsches, in corporate boardrooms and in laundry rooms—and sometimes even in sociology classrooms. The household words and themes of pop sociology include *anomie,* alienation, the Protestant Ethnic, intergroup relations, the "empty nest stage" of family life, mass society, the generation gap, participatory democracy, the "other directed type," conflict, the role of women, the "power elite" and the "establishment" and, of course, the urban crisis.

In many ways the world is now viewed in sociological images—groups, affiliations, social class and social mobility, deviance and control, the processes of change, the structure of institutions, demographic and ecological balance. We have now reached the point where few college freshmen have to be taught that socialization has another meaning than the nationalization of steel and coal production. Sociological thinking has become part of what John Kenneth Galbraith called "the conventional wisdom—the structure of ideas that is based on acceptability."[1]

Much of the sociology we find around us is pop sociology. The overriding characteristic of pop sociology is that it involves no suspension of judgment or assessment of evidence and is therefore stereotyped and unscientific. Pop sociology's second major feature—the ideological, moral or evaluative tenor of its statements—is linked to its stereotyped approach and, in fact, often explains why such an approach was applied. These two defining traits of pop sociology lead to a host of subsidiary characteristics. Pop sociology is "instant"—it never fails of an answer because judgment is seldom suspended. It is simple and clear. Indeed it is oversimplified, for it has few definitions or delineations of statements; pop sociology is relatively untested. It is also all-encompassing; it applies sociological approaches broadly to all areas and topics. Pop sociology is often geared to a wide audience in response to a social "crisis." In sum, pop sociology may be provocative but it is also superficial, often to the point of inaccuracy or confusion. Pop sociology is not new; it is deep-seated and probably as old as sociology. What is new is the widespread currency of pop sociology.

As indicated above, the most important characteristic of pop sociology is its lack of rigor or systematic thought. Pop sociology is seldom empirical or "factual" but that is not its crucial lack; whether empirical or speculative it fails in giving a reasoned base and thorough search. These very failings give pop sociology its virtues. Precisely because it is free-flowing and unfettered by a broad conceptual apparatus, pop sociology may provide useful insights. One of the uses of pop sociology lies in providing hypotheses for new research. Unfortunately this is not typically the course of pop sociology; rather it is offered, without *caveats,* to a wide public as "answers" and conclusions.

Although usually presented in simple language, pop sociology must be distinguished from the attempts to "translate" technical sociological concepts, language and findings into layman's terms. Such "translation"

From *American Studies*, Urban issue, Vol. 14. No. 1, Spring 1973. Copyright © 1973 by American Studies Association. Reprinted by permission of American Studies and the author.

is the aim of the project, Sociological Resources for the Social Studies, sponsored by the American Sociological Association and supported by the National Science Foundation. The volume on urban sociology is a notably successful attempt at clearing out the underbrush and presenting the major contributions in a responsible, interesting and lucid way.[2]

Several illustrations may clarify the nature of pop sociology. The youth rebellion, particularly on campuses, is the focus of pop sociology that we are probably most familiar with at the present time. The explanations include affluence and poverty, each of which is used to "explain" disregard of property and propriety; permissive parents who don't keep their offspring in line and restrictive parents who have to be rebelled against; rebellious youth is characterized as still struggling to find itself via identity crises and is also characterized as exceptionally mature and clearthinking.[3] A year or so ago the major focus of pop sociology was the "culture of poverty" in which the concepts of culture and subculture were bandied about so loosely as to be almost shapeless, particularly when they were applied to discussion of the lower-class black family.

Pop sociology is widespread in the mass media and practiced by the "man in the street." But it is also often found among professional social scientists themselves, particularly when they are pressed into making quick analyses of profound issues for a waiting public. Thus, an issue of the *New York Times Magazine*[4] featured a symposium, "Is America by Nature a Violent Society?" in which the following analyses were made:

> However repulsive and shocking H. Rap Brown's quip may seem—"Violence is as American as cherry pie"—his motive for saying it must not obscure the fact that he was telling it like it is.
>
> The American white-collar set have so little direct experience with violence that it is difficult for them to conceive of it as an ever-present reality—or possibility—in a person's daily life, although they know that the Indians were herded onto the reservations by force, that violence was used both to keep Negroes in slavery and to free them, and that assault and battery, rape and murder occur every now and then. The older people in the labor movement know something of the historic confrontations between trade unionists and the forces of law and order, though young workers know almost nothing of the great labor struggles of the past. Negroes understand the reality of violence better than most Americans, for most of them have witnessed it in varied forms, even if they have not experienced it. But all Americans need to face the fact that American society—as compared with some others in the world—is a very violent society. Self-delusion is self-defeating. We can never lower the level of violence unless we admit that it is omnipresent and understand the forces that generate it. (St. Clair Drake)

The next participant in the symposium says:

> In a period which has seen the German massacre of the Jews, the communal horrors of Indian partition, the convulsive destructiveness of the last days of L'Algerie Francaise, the mass executions accompanying the Indonesian change of regime, the terrible civil wars in Nigeria and the Congo, and the wild riots in Sharpesville, it is difficult for the hardiest celebrant of the American Way of Life to claim for his country any special gift for violence. We are, it turns out, a people like any other. There is nothing particularly distinctive about the ways we destroy one another.
>
> The notion that "violence is as American as cherry pie" is one more cliche which we invoke to prevent our seeing our situation for what it is.... (Clifford Geertz)

Why should we take pop sociology seriously? Perhaps for somewhat the same reasons that caused pop sociology to become prominent now: the predominantly *social* nature of many of the problems around us today: civil rights, family interaction, the aged, population growth and redistribution; the emergence of large-scale organization and bureaucracy in virtually every phase of life including the school, religion, and leisure; and the very rapid social change on a scale without precedent in human history. The pervading nature of these pressures leads to a sense of urgency in understanding and in finding solutions.

The urgency of our concern often produces elements of pop in the many attempts to apply social science, especially sociology, to policies and programs on specific current issues. Since so many of these current issues are urban-located or urban-related, approaches to urban phenomena are often infected with pop. The pressure on sociology and other social sciences for "answers" to the urban enigma are widespread. The pop approach and reform may often be related, as sociologically unsound or half-baked programs are put into effect based on *convictions* rather than evidence. Thus, a *belief* in participatory democracy—or in the stultifying impact of suburban life—may lead to projects or to individual and group actions which are not well-supported by data or logic. All action programs tend to be "arts" rather than "sciences," as administrators know. Yet even a brief look at the community action field—whether the war on poverty, community control of schools, decentralization of government, advocacy planning, or other instances that might be cited—suggests that action programs often have in addition some pop qualities, pseudo-expertise and ideological bias, compounded by urgency, concern and widespread interest.

How is suburbia a manifestation of pop sociology? Suburbia has a legitimate claim as the first of the major social changes that attracted broad public attention and was widely disseminated through the mass media.[5] The "teenager" syndrome and the early Kinsey reports on sexual behavior are, I believe, the other two major examples of pop sociology in the immediate post-war period.

Suburbia entered the public awareness about the time World War II ended, when the building-boom in outlying areas became a visible signal of something new on the horizon. Sociologists had been studying and writing about metropolitan development, of which suburban development is a part, for several decades before then; United States suburbs themselves date at least into the latter part of the nineteenth century and had become widespread by 1920. It is neither the time lag between professional and public awareness nor the popularity of the topic which makes suburbia "pop," however, although these do enhance the process. It is the spurious accuracy and partisanship which make pop sociology of many public, and some professional, presentations of suburbia. The result is a debased public currency of suburbia.

The pop image of suburbia revolves around the related themes of a contrast between the central city and the suburb, and stultifying, homogeneous conformity. Thus, the suburbs are presented as bedroom communities, residential outposts of the white, educated, affluent middle class for which Scarsdale has become the national byword. The central cities are the home of the blacks, the poor, and the locales of the problems besetting American society. This stereotypical central city-suburban contrast has long since been shown false in the professional literature.

There is no one kind of suburb (neither is there one kind of city), hence there is no one central city-suburb contrast. It follows there are no uniquely urban or suburban problems. The sociologist Leo Schnore, has been working for at least a decade on detailing the various types of central city/suburban contrast and seeking the dynamics explaining the formation of types of metropolitan area.[6] Using education as an index of socio-economic status, he delineated six different patterns of variation between central city and suburb. Only one of these exemplified the pattern reflected in the pop conception of suburbs, in which the lowest classes are overrepresented in the central city and the higher the educational status the more suburbanized the population.[7] The New York metropolis exhibits this classic pattern, while Los Angeles exemplifies another and Tucson and Albuquerque still other patterns. The classic pattern appears to be associated with the larger metropolitan areas and those which are "older," that is, which reached large size relatively early. In the "newer" and smaller metropolitan areas suburbanization may not be so far advanced toward the classic pattern, or population may actually be redistributing in accord with newer, different industrial and transport processes.

On the basis of the professional literature, then, a simple contrast between high status suburbs and low status cities is at best only partly true. Similarly, if we turn to the pop picture of the stultifying and conformist nature of suburban life we find that professional sociology has shattered this image. At least as long ago as Bennett Berger's 1960 study,[8] there have been data available to show that suburbanites are not miraculously reborn in the suburban setting. Politics and voting behavior, religion, family life, personality formation, educational goals and practices, leisure pursuits, interactive patterns in the neighborhood and participation in voluntary organizations have all been put under the microscope in literally dozens of studies. They show there is no single way of suburban life nor any uniform effect of the suburban experience on those who live in suburbs.

The reality of the suburban impact on individuals' lives and thought is far more complex than pop sociology would lead us to believe. One study dealt with the question of whether there are distinctive suburban psychological characteristics, particularly the assertion that suburban residence fosters anti-intellectual attitudes.[9] The data included questionnaire responses from over 33,000 college seniors graduating in 1961 from 135 colleges in the United States. Initial comparisons showed no significant differences in intellectual attitudes between college seniors who had been raised in cities and those who had been raised in suburbs.

However, further analysis showed that there *is* a relationship between suburban residence and anti-intellectualism, but that it is more complex than commonly supposed. When the items measuring anti-intellectualism were cross-tabulated with the kind of communities students said they *wished* to live in rather than by the communities the students had grown up in, then the suburb-oriented students differed significantly from the urban-oriented students in anti-intellectualism. That is, those who indicated a *desire* to live in the suburbs were less likely to be concerned with access to cultural activities and less likely to think of themselves as intellectuals. The final analysis suggests that anti-intellectualism in suburbia is partly a result of family-cycle (more married students prefer suburbs and they are likely to have less time for intellectual activities), partly a result of selectivity (the students expressing a preference for suburban living are more anti-intellectual) and partly a result of the influence of community of origin (regardless of their marital status and intellectual attitudes, students who were brought up in suburbs more often expressed a desire to live in suburbs than those who had been raised in the city).

The vision of a homogeneous and conformist suburbia has been negated by sociological research, yet the pop version remains and continues to be spread by the mass media. Why? The answer, I think, lies in the ideological aspect of popness. The pop sociology of the suburbs is not only inaccurate, it is inaccurate for a reason. (In saying this, I do not mean that there exists a conscious plot to make it inaccurate.)

The ideological aspect of pop suburbia has two main components. The first relates to the persistence of the myth of homogeneity. According to one sociologist, the belief that suburbs are homogeneous operates to sustain a belief in the "American dream" of equals cooperating in a democratic society. The American dream is undermined by the realities of long-standing economic and ethnic differentiation and by our fundamental ambivalence toward melting-pot as opposed to pluralist development. In view of the flaws in the American dream it becomes important to reaffirm it in the major new setting of American life, the suburbs. Thus, the myth of the homogeneous, classless suburbia persists.[10]

Although the foregoing observations were based on impressionistic data they are lent some substance by Herbert Gans' study of Levittown, New Jersey, in which he concludes, after several years of participant-observation and close study that one of the shortcomings that Levittown shares with other American communities is an

inability to deal with pluralism. People have not recognized the diversity of American society, and they are not able to accept other life styles. Indeed, they cannot handle conflict because they cannot accept pluralism. Adults are unwilling to tolerate adolescent culture, and vice versa. Lower middle class people oppose the ways of the working class and upper middle class, and each of these groups is hostile to the other two. Perhaps the inability to cope with pluralism is greater in Levittown than elsewhere because it is a community of young families who are raising children. Children are essentially asocial and unacculturated beings, easily influenced by new ideas. As a result, their parents feel an intense need to defend familial values; to make sure that their children grow up according to parental norms and not by those of their playmates from another class. The need to shield the children from what are considered harmful influences begins on the block, but it is translated into the conflict over the school, the definitional struggles within voluntary associations whose programs affect the socialization of children, and, ultimately into political conflicts. Each group wants to put its stamp on the organizations and institutions that are the community, for otherwise the family and its culture are not safe.[11]

The second ideological component of pop suburbs relates to the allegedly conformist, anti-intellectual features of suburban life. Most likely this evaluation is a function of the fact that most writers on suburbs are upper middle class intellectuals who are projecting onto the suburbs their dissatisfaction with the "bourgeois" and to them debased standards in lower middle class suburbs. Most recently this tendency has been revealed in the characterization of Spiro T. Agnew. One newspaper columnist, under the title, "The Sterile Paradise of Suburban Man," says:

Agnew's biography sounds like Warren Harding's might if Harding had been a character in a novel by Sinclair Lewis and Lewis had been writing in the 1960s. He [Agnew] is so typical of the new suburban man that he almost seems to parody his class. . . . The people to whom he speaks are at least as afraid of losing what they already possess as they are eager to acquire more. For every daydream of personal success they have two nightmares of armed, marauding Negroes who will burn down their communities. They do not want to nationalize the giant corporations . . . they only want the great businessmen they've been raised to respect . . . to protect them and stop encouraging their enemies, the black and the student dissenters. . . . And his audiences seem eager to live in the sterile paradise his speeches promise. As far as many of America's new suburbanites are concerned, Agnew, son of a poor Greek immigrant, the luckiest Horatio Alger in this country's history, is describing the enchanted, protected land their parents and grandparents came all this way to find.[12]

Another author says: ". . . Agnew the Vice President is no more than the commonplace made exceptional, the conventional made controversial, instinct promoted into intellect and suburbia made sublime."[13] This kind of bias would account for the lingering tendency of even professional sociologists to write condescendingly of suburbs. To the upper middle class professional the "city" is the place where civilization resides.[14]

In the broadest sense it appears that the suburban myth of harmony, greenery and cultural kitsch is the contemporary staging ground for the long-standing American preference for rural life. In the modern age, when, through the sheer lack of farm experience on the part of the vast majority of the population, agrarianism has lost its force as a normative standard, the familiar dialogue between ruralism and urbanism may peter out. In place of the nineteenth-century discussions of whether the city or the country is more "civilized," we may have discussions of whether urban or suburban life is more "cultured." In place of the city versus the country debate we may have the city versus the suburb. This does not necessarily mean that suburbs are replacing the country in the sense of being rural; it does mean that the suburbs, like all community forms, have the power to arouse emotion and partisanship. As new community forms arise, they become invested with symbolic meaning and enter the arena of public opinion.

After studying the political structure of suburbs, Robert Wood, a political scientist, concluded that it represented a renaissance of the small-town and village ideal.[15] Suburban governments, according to Wood, are typically small, ineffective and expensive, unsuitable for coping with metropolitan area problems. Yet suburbanites stubbornly resist efforts at a consolidation into larger governmental jurisdictions, and small-scale suburban governments are, in fact, proliferating. Wood points out that the attachment to suburban government is ideological, stemming from a belief that the small community produces the best life, and the best government.

> Suburbia, defined as an ideology, a faith in communities of limited size and a belief in the conditions of intimacy, is quite real. The dominance of the old values explains more about the people and politics of the suburbs than any other interpretation. Fundamentally, it explains the nature of the American metropolis. . . . If these values were not dominant it would be quite possible to conceive of a single gigantic metropolitan region under one government and socially conscious of itself as one community. The new social ethic, the rise of the large organization, would lead us to expect this development as a natural one. The automobile, the subway, the telephone, the power line certainly make it technically possible; they even push us in this direction.
>
> But the American metropolis is not constructed in such a way; it sets its face directly against modernity. Those who wish to rebuild the American city, who protest the shapeless urban sprawl, who find some value in the organizational skills of modern society, must recognize the potency of the ideology. Until these beliefs have been accommodated reform will not come in the metropolitan areas nor will men buckle down to the task of directing, in a manner consonant with freedom, the great political and social organizations on which the nation's strength depends.[16]

It has become increasingly difficult to maintain the simple pop sociology view of suburbs as evidence mounts, from the 1970 census and other sources, of the diversity of suburbs and the increasing resemblance of older suburbs to cities, in terms of structure and problems. Crime and delinquency rates have been rising rapidly in many suburbs, as has the drug problem; welfare, pollution, traffic congestion and unbalanced budgets have emerged as major issues; office decentralization has accelerated in many large metropolitan areas and some shopping centers have become miniature downtowns in the range and variety of goods and services offered—and as locales for vandalism and burglary, as congregating places for "undesirables." "Black suburbs" have become increasingly important, although this trend does not appear to be accompanied by racial or economic integration, despite the mounting attack on suburban exclusionary zoning. Both the professional literature and the mass media have begun to reflect this new view of suburbia.[17]

Suburbs are now being succeeded by a new community focus of pop sociology, New Towns, the large planned communities of which Reston, Virginia, and Columbia, Maryland, are often cited as examples.[18] Suburbs were the focus of community pop sociology in the period of public awareness of metropolitan emergence; New Towns are the expression of community pop sociology in the era of the mature metropolis.

New Towns represent a new policy for the same set of needs expressed earlier in the image of suburbia. There is the same anti-urbanism, the fear and distrust of the city, expressed now in the desire to control and manage urban growth and density by carefully pre-cast new communities. As with suburbs there is also the same concern with diversity, the containment of conflict and the maintenance of outward harmony and equality. There are, however, two important ways in which New Towns contrast markedly with suburbs. First, New Towns, usually called New Communities in this context, have become a legislatively-enacted goal of the federal government. Although it has been argued that home mortgage legislation, subsidies for highway construction and other governmental policies indirectly fostered suburban expansion,[19] there was never specific suburban legislation.

The official support of the federal government for New Towns dates to the passage of the Demonstration Cities and Metropolitan Development Act of 1966. This Act expanded FHA mortgage coverage, through the Department of Housing and Urban Development, to include privately financed New Communities. However, these provisions were hedged with so many restrictions that the New Communities provisions were not put to effective use. Many of these restrictions were removed by the Housing and Urban Development Act of 1968, legislation which has been called the urban equivalent of the Homestead Act of 1862. Title IV of the 1968 Act, entitled "New Communities," expanded the financial backing of New Communities and this prompted a large number of applications to HUD by private developers.[20] By 1971 five New Communities had received federal financial guarantees. The Housing and Urban Development Act of 1970, under Title VII, "Urban Growth and New Community Development," carries federal support of New Towns several important steps further,[21] and has attracted widespread interest from private and public developers.[22] By Spring 1973 fifteen New Communities had received federal guarantees of the specified financial obligations.

The second major way in which New Towns in the United States contrast with suburbs is in the explicit concern in the New Towns with social issues. Thus, Title IV of the 1968 Act includes as one of the conditions of eligibility that the New Community include the "proper balance" of housing units for families of low and moderate income. The 1970 Act lists among the ten reasons for developing new communities that "continuation of established patterns of urban development . . . will result in . . . (1) unduly limited options for many of our people as to where they may live, and the types of housing and environment in which they live; . . . (2) further lessening of employment and business opportunities for the residents of central cities and of the ability of such cities to retain a tax base adequate to support vital services for all their citizens, particularly the poor and disadvantaged; (3) further separation of people within metropolitan areas by income and by race."[23] Each New Community proposal presented by HUD must contain a special social plan indicating how it proposes to implement the stated goals.

In understanding the social concerns of the New Communities legislation one must recognize that the New Towns movement in the United States gathered momentum in the 1960's in the wake of the "urban crisis." Important milestones in the mounting urban concerns of that period include the first message on cities to Congress by any President, President Johnson's March 1965 message on "Problems and Future of the Central City and Its Suburbs," and his February 1968 message, "The Crisis of Our Cities"; a series of comprehensive reports[24] documenting in staggering detail a group of urban problems: poverty, unparalleled growth, gross housing inadequacy, racial segregation, crime and violence; and the piecemeal recognition of the changing nature of the American city as metropolitan development entered a new phase heralded by suburban dominance.[25]

New Towns are clearly a matter of public policy. How does our public and professional view of them partake of pop sociology? Essentially because New Towns are seen as a solution to many urban and indeed national ills for which critical evidence on specific social questions involved is lacking or ambiguous. Ideology has taken the place of evidence; matters of belief have become accepted as matters of fact.

Such socially-relevant terms as "participation," "balance," "diversity" and "optimum size" have seldom even been defined in the context of New Towns discussion. New Towns involve assumptions regarding the nature and desirability of neighborhood interaction; high-rise and multi-family vs. low-rise and single-family homes; the impact of density and community size on the human psyche; the importance of propinquity as a catalyst for meaningful contact; the merits of community self-sufficiency; the benefits of diversity and balance; the manner in which housing choices are made; the virtues of local participation and decentralization.

An overview of the published work on New Towns indicates the pop nature of public and much professional thinking on the social goals of New Towns. There is a Niagara of material: for example, at least seven bibliographies on New Towns in the United States.[26] Allowing for duplication there are several thousand separate published books, articles and reports. They come from a broad spectrum of national circulation magazines (*Harper's, U.S. News and World Report, Saturday Review*) and from the professionals journals, house organs and publications of sociologists, planners, architects, builders, large corporations, housers and public officials. The literature is overwhelmingly pro-New Town, indicating a broad dissemination and acceptance of the New Town idea, which is underscored by the passage of the 1970 Housing and Urban Development Act and by the testimony in its favor from witnesses representing a wide variety of groups.

Only a relatively small proportion of the published work deals with the social aspects of New Towns in the United States; most treats architecture, design, finance, management and legislation. This emphasis seems significant in view of the importance of social goals both in the federal legislation and in many of the privately financed New Towns.

For the purpose of pop sociology, there are two significant characteristics of the existing socially-relevant material. First, the empirical material is typically fragmentary, low-level description with little possibility of generalizability. In this, the literature on the New Towns resembles the pop sociology of suburbia. The two are also alike in that definitional problems compound the difficulty of generalizing. One man's New Town is another's satellite city and still another's "large development." Second, much of the material has no empirical base at all, but is hortatory—it merely advises and states the desirability of New Towns to achieve social goals and policies. Given these two characteristics it follows that the "how" of achieving the social goals of New Towns is not often specified.

Behind the pop treatment of suburbia lay a backlog of professional research which needed popularization; for the New Towns, there was no such backlog. The central issue of racial and economic integration in New Towns is a case in point.[27] While this situation offers opportunity for well-focused research on major public policy implications of New Towns, it also warns against unexamined acceptance of the pop sociology view of New Towns as the brake halting the movement toward "two societies." There are only two investigations of any depth related to this matter; neither is conclusive. In one study a multiple-choice questionnaire which had been developed from long depth interviews, was administered to almost 800 residents of New Towns in two different metropolitan areas of California.[28] The results indicated that a major reason for buying in New Towns was the belief that "planning" protected the community against the intrusion of economic and racial diversity.

The other study examined a matched sample of ten new communities differing in location, age and degree of planning. It concluded that degree of residential satisfaction with the community as a whole was positively associated with degree of planning.[29] The analysis of reasons for satisfaction with the immediate neighborhood was less clear, although dwelling unit density, the condition of the neighborhood (whether it is "well kept up") and compatibility of neighborhood residents were important features. The authors stress the difficulties in measuring compatibility, which they found related to attitudes rather than to the expected socio-economic and demographic homogeneity. "For people in our sample it appears that shared attitudes and evaluations concerning the neighborhood and community were most salient in defining neighbors as both 'friendly' and 'similar.' . . . In other words, when consensus (homogeneity) exists among neighbors about qualities of the residential environment, the neighbors themselves tend to be more positively evaluated."[30]

The matter of operationalizing the concept of "homogeneity" (and, of course, "heterogeneity" and "balance") remains, although both New Towns studies above indicate the importance of some kind of local homogeneity, as do studies in such diverse New Town settings as Britain[31] and Israel.[32] The burden of these studies is not to discourage policy planners from aiming at racial and economic integration and "balance" in New Towns. On the contrary, it should point up the necessity of going beyond the labeling of pop sociology which simply defines "balance" as a goal.

The pop sociology of New Towns offers a current opportunity to utilize the immediacy and provocativeness of the pop approach in generating wide interest, while avoiding the instant "solutions" of pop. If sociology is to be useful in dealing with vital issues such as the form of future urban growth then action must be taken. However, the public and the government must recognize more fully the need for experimental approaches which permit tests of the validity of unproved assumptions. As we have indicated, the pop sociology of suburbs and New Towns provides many such assumptions. What has been lacking is the spelling out of assumptions and the attendant hidden hypotheses with which pop sociology abounds and the systematic testing out of these hypotheses in a variety of simulated or actual suburbs or New Town contexts. The result would give us knowledge about the social processes at work and the limits of such knowledge. We would have laid the basis for improved decision-making in selecting the goals for further community development. More broadly we would have substituted sociology—warts and all—for the silicone curves of pop sociology.

footnotes

1. *The Affluent Society* (Boston, 1958), 18.

2. Helen MacGill Hughes, compiler and editor, *Cities and City Life* (Boston, 1970). It is most instructive for an understanding of pop sociology to compare the Hughes book with even a superior, relatively well-balanced treatment of urban phenomena in the pop genre: Vance Packard's *A Nation of Strangers* (New York, 1972).

3. In contrast to the pop treatment of youth, see Philip C. Altbach and Robert S. Laufer, eds., *The New Pilgrims: Youth Protest in Transition* (New York, 1972). This reader includes historical and cross-cultural materials and relates youth protest to the strucure of society as an aspect of generational conflict, social class and radical movements; an appended bibliography by Kenneth Keniston contains several hundred items reviewing research and further indicates how youth movements are imbedded in the overall social system.

4. April 28, 1968.

5. For example in such works as: Frederick Allen, "The Big Change in Suburbia," *Harper's*, CCVIII, 1249 (June, 1954); Hal Burton, "Trouble in the Suburbs," *Saturday Evening Post*, CCVIII, 12-14 (September 17, 24; October 1, 1955); R. Gordon, K. Gordon, and M. Gunther, *The Split Level Trap* (New York, 1961); Sidonie Gruenberg, "The Homogenized Children of the New Suburbia," *New York Times Magazine* (September 19, 1954); Harry Henderson, "The Mass Produced Suburbs," *Harper's*, CCVII, 1242-1243 (November-December, 1953); T. James, "Crackups in the Suburbs," *Cosmopolitan*, CLI, 4 (October, 1961): John Keats, *The Crack in the Picture Window* (Boston, 1956); Alice Miel, *The Shortchanged Children of Suburbia* (New York, 1968); A. C. Spectorsky, *The Exurbanites* (Philadelphia, 1955); William H. Whyte, *The Organization Man* (New York, 1956); Peter Wyden, *Suburbia's Coddled Kids* (Garden City, 1960).

6. See for example, the articles collected in Parts II and IV of Leo F. Schnore, *The Urban Scene* (New York, 1965); also his "Measuring City-Suburban Status Differences," *Urban Affairs Quarterly*, III, 1 (September, 1967) and Schnore and Pinkerton, "Residential Redistribution of Socioeconomic Strata in Metropolitan Areas," *Demography*, III, 2 (1966). For a different approach which also supports the diversity of the central city-suburban contrast see, Advisory Commission on Intergovernmental Relations, *Metropolitan Social and Economic Disparities* (Washington, D.C., 1965) and Advisory Commission on Intergovernmental Relations, *Metropolitan Fiscal Disparities*, vol. 2 of *Fiscal Balance in the American Federal System* (Washington, D.C., 1967).

7. "Urban Structure and Suburban Selectivity," in Schnore, *The Urban Scene*.

8. *Working-Class Suburb* (Berkeley, 1960).

9. Joseph Zelan, "Does Suburbia Make a Difference," in S. F. Fava, ed., *Urbanism in World Perspective* (New York, 1968).

10. Bennett Berger, "Suburbia and the American Dream," in Fava, *Urbanism in World Perspective*.

11. Herbert J. Gans, *The Levittowners* (New York, 1967), 414.

12. Paul Cowan in *The Village Voice* (New York) October 10, 1968.

13. Peter Jenkins, "Agnew is the Common Man Made Exceptional," *New York Times Magazine* (October 29, 1972), 94.

14. The reviews of Gans' *The Levittowners* have already noted that it is the first major sociological work on suburbs which does not condescend to the new middle classes. Gans "does not find them comic or menacing, barbarians to be subdued or living corpses to be exhumed," says Marvin Bressler in his review of Gans' book in *The Public Interest* (1968), 102.

15. Robert C. Wood, *Suburbia, Its People and Their Politics* (Boston, 1958), chapter 1.

16. *Ibid.*, 18-19.

17. John B. Orr and F. Patrick Michelson, *The Radical Suburb* (Philadelphia, 1970); Scott Donaldson, *The Suburban Myth* (New York, 1969); "The Suburbs: Frontier of the '70's," special issue of *City*, V (January-February, 1971); "Suburbia: A Myth Challenged," cover story in *Time*, XCVII, 11 (March 15, 1971); "The Outer City: U.S. in Suburban Turmoil," series of five articles in the *New York Times* (May 30-June 3, 1971).

18. A useful definition of New Towns in the United States is that they are ". . . *large-scale developments* [1,000 acres or more] *constructed under single or unified management, following a fairly precise, inclusive plan and including different types of housing, commercial and cultural facilities, and amenities sufficient to serve the residents of the community. They may provide land for industry, offer other types of employment opportunities, and may eventually achieve a considerable measure of self-sufficiency. With few exceptions, new communities under development today are within commuting distance of existing employment centers."* Advisory Commission on Intergovernmental Relations, *Urban and Rural America: Policies for Future Growth* (Washington, D.C., 1968), 64. HUD has estimated that in 1947-1969 there were 63 new communities built or under construction in the U.S. which met such a definition. Virtually all were built under private financing since they predated the federal supports for New Towns. "HUD Survey and Analysis of Large Developments and New Communities," *Urban Land.* XXIX (January, 1970), 11-12.

19. See for example, B. Weissbourd, "Segregation, Subsidies, and Megalopolis," in Fava, ed., *Urbanism in World Perspective.*

20. The 1966 Act had required developers to obtain funds from private lenders and was restricted to mortgages on land; the 1968 Act authorized HUD to guarantee the bonds and other obligations issued by developers of New Communities to finance land acquisition and its development for building.

21. Major new provisions: (1) the federal government will assume responsibility for formulating a national urban growth policy which includes the encouragement of a variety of planned new communities; (2) the Domestic Council in the Office of the President will send to Congress every two years, beginning in 1972, a Report on Urban Growth covering the preceding ten years; (3) the creation within HUD of a Community Development Corporation working with public bodies and private developers to spur new community development through a system of loans, guarantees, and technical assistance to provide for planning, land acquisition, development, public facilities and services; (4) loans for new communities totaling $240 million are authorized ($20 million limit per community) as are $500 million in guarantees of obligations of private *and* public developers ($50 million limit per community).

22. For example, see Eleanore Carruth, "The Big Move to New Towns," Fortune, LXXXIV, 3 (September, 1971).

23. Housing and Urban Development Act of 1970, Part B, Sec. 710 (b).

24. An incomplete list would include: National Commission on Urban Problems (the "Douglas Commission"); President's Commission on Urban Housing (the "Kaiser Commission"); National Advisory Commission on Civil Disorder (the "Kerner Commission"); Advisory Commission on Intergovernmental Relations, *Urban and Rural America: Policies for Future Growth.*

25. The 1970 census showed, for example, that in only 7 of the 25 metropolitan areas with over a million in population, did the central city population outnumber that of the suburban areas surrounding it; in 1960 central city population outnumbered suburban in 15 of the same 25 metropolitan areas.

26. Joy Akin, *The Feasibility and Actuality of Modern New Towns for the Poor in the United States* (Monticello, Ill., 1970); James A. Clapp, *The New Town Concept: Private Trends and Public Response* (Monticello, Ill., 1970); HUD, *New Communities: A Bibliography* (Washington, D.C., 1969); T. C. Peng and N. S. Verna, *New Towns Planning, Design and Development: Comprehensive Reference Materials* (Lincoln, Neb., 1971); Melvin C. Branch, "New Towns," in his *Comprehensive Urban Planning* (Beverly Hills, Calif., 1970); Housing and Home Finance Agency, *New Communities: A Selected Annotated Reading List* (Washington, D.C., 1965); *Minnesota Experimental City Progress Reports,* 2nd edition, Appendix A, "A Compendium of Publications relating to Socio-Cultural Aspects," and Appendix D, "Bibliography" (Minneapolis, 1969).

27. The question has been examined in detail elsewhere. See Sylvia F. Fava, "The Sociology of New Towns in the U.S.: 'Balance' of Racial and Economic Groups" (paper delivered at the American Institute of Planners Conference, Minneapolis-St. Paul, October 1970).

28. Carl Werthman, Jerry S. Mandel and Ted Dienstfrey, *Planning and the Purchase Decision. Why People Buy in Planned Communities* (Berkeley, 1965).

29. John B. Lansing, Robert W. Marans and Robert B. Zehner, *Planned Residential Environments* (Ann Arbor, 1971).

30. *Ibid.,* 125.

31. B. J. Heraud, "Social Class and the New Towns," *Urban Studies,* V (February, 1968); and Heraud, "New Towns: The End of a Planner's Dream," *New Society,* XII, 302 (July 11, 1968).

32. Judith Shuval, "Relations between Ethnic Groups," Appendix A to "The Integral Habitational Unit at Kiryat-Gat," *Ministry of Housing Quarterly* (Israel), III (December, 1967), 92-98.

2. Varieties of Urban Experiences

Many different urban contexts exist in our society. There are small neighborhoods resembling little communities with tidy homes and gardens; ethnic enclaves populated by a particular religious or cultural group; slums, usually referring to an area of the city that has been neglected, run down and characterized by poverty and crime; and very wealthy areas protected by high fences, doormen, or other devices to enforce privacy. Suburban areas are equally diverse. At one time suburban communities were characterized as "bedrooms" for the central cities; residents slept in suburbia and traveled downtown to work. Today, however, more people in the United States live and work in suburbia than commute to the central city. There are poor suburban communities, wealthy ones, occupational suburbs, ethnic suburbs, and even bohemian suburban areas.

Urban areas are continuously changing. Suburban areas are annexed by central cities thus becoming residential neighborhoods, residential areas become industrial cities and a Polish neighborhood is transformed into a Mexican neighborhood. Change is often dramatic and swift but it can also come about gradually through the processes of assimilation and drift.

There are different responses to urbanization among individuals. Some enjoy the excitement and dynamics of the crowded city; others are crushed under the weight of concrete jungles. The urban area may represent hope for employment and good fortune to some; but it can be the scene of tragedy and misery for others. Some ethnic groups have found urbanization a congenial practice, whereas others have adjusted very slowly to the demands of such a life.

Describing, comparing, and understanding the similarities and differences between urban contexts is an important task of social scientists. Another task is to analyze the everyday experiences of living in an urban area. From such analyses we can begin to understand the dynamics of social interaction which lie at the root of urban existence.

A number of questions might be considered after reading the material contained in this section. Does living in an urban area by itself change behavior? Is metropolitan life distinctively different from rural life? How do suburban communities differ from central cities? Why do some neighborhoods survive despite changing surroundings? In what situations does a sense of community flourish or decline? How can we sufficiently control the experiences of urban life in order to maximize pleasure and diminish discomfort?

The End of the Exurban Dream

John Tarrant

The 4:59 pulls out of Grand Central. The train carries 850 commuters. Many of them will get off at Westport, 44 miles and an hour and ten minutes away.

The 4:59 emerges from the tunnel into the daylight at 96th Street. It runs on elevated tracks along upper Park Avenue. Old tenements flank the tracks. Their windows are broken; the interiors appear burned out. Other buildings look to be in no better shape, but they are occupied. It's a pleasant evening. A girl sits on a fire escape. A man leans out a window. An old fat woman waters a small plant on a sill. All these people are black. They look blankly at the passing train. The commuters inside the train do not look back. They talk; they read; they poise briefcases on their knees, open them, and riffle through papers. Some pull down the shades.

The train stops at 125th Street. A few people get on. They do not look like the rest of the passengers. The train is crowded; there is no place for them to sit. The 4:59 gets under way again. The last landmark it passes before crossing the river is a large blocklike structure bearing the words CITY OF NEW YORK DEPARTMENT OF WELFARE.

Just past the marshaling yards in Mott Haven, the Bronx, the train stops. The commuters scarcely notice. Then there is a sudden shattering of glass. A commuter ducks away from his starred window. Two small black boys stand on the opposite embankment. One makes an obscene gesture. They run away.

The train groans into motion and lumbers on, to arrive in Westport twenty minutes late. Some of the commuters are still muttering that something has to be done about these kids who throw stones at the train.

These are Exurbanites, en route from where they work to where they sleep and play.

The term *Exurbanite* was coined by the late A. C. Spectorsky to describe the individual who can't abide the city and who thinks of the suburbs as meaning dull conformity, and who thus moves farther out into the country.

Exurbia is the epitome of conspicuous consumption. As Thorstein Veblen saw it, a beautiful lawn was the means by which a householder could display his wealth to the world. It was the equivalent of the potlatch, the feast at which the Indian of the American Northwest destroys and gives away his possessions to show that he is a man of stature. The lawn, used for neither food-growing nor forage, proclaims to all that the owner is a man so well off that he need not raise animals or cultivate the land.

But Exurbia is more than that. Exurbia is a system of affluent enclaves across the country, from Westport to Pasadena. The inhabitants of this wealthy archipelago—in Winnetka, in University Park, in Webster Groves, in Petaluma—constitute an elite within the American society. The Exurban elite is powerful. Its members operate the levers that control how we are entertained, what we buy, and how we live.

An elite provides leadership, sets standards, embodies a way of life to be emulated and goals to be striven for. The economic role of the titled classes in Great Britain dwindled in the early years of the nineteenth century, but the function of this group as setter and maintainer of social norms continued for more than a hundred years.

The concept of Exurbia has been built on four cornerstones:

Exclusion: zoning that mandates large, single-family homes on spacious grounds.
Education: public-school systems of recognized superiority that propel the children of Exurbia on to college.
Women: wives who have been willing to take on the bulk of the parental role and, in addition, do volunteer work on which much of the community's functioning depends.
"Distancing": isolation and insulation from problems, cities, neighborhoods, and indeed, the other members of one's family.

All four cornerstones are crumbling.

Exurbia—the Good Life—has meant a lot to Americans. Between 1950 and 1970 the population of suburbia grew considerably in relation to the cities. In *The Real America*, Ben Wattenberg likens the migration to the suburbs to the American Dream of the 1930s and 1940s: "What is it? 'The little white house with a picket fence around it,' of course. That's where June Allyson always wanted to move."

This American Dream comprises certain elements. One is the *house*—not a room, not an apartment, not a semi-detached, but a house of one's own. Another is *land*. That picket fence surrounds some grass, flowers, a few trees. Once, the possession of a piece of land was a necessity of human existence. It's no longer a matter of life or death, but we still have the urge to own ground.

There are other things that go with the house in the suburbs. Nationwide, the median family income of suburbia is about $3.000 more than elsewhere. The schools are better. People have better jobs, live more bountiful lives.

But these blessings do not come with suburbia. They are more effect than cause. People who are better educated and have better jobs move to the suburbs. Those who have the best jobs move to the super-suburban purlieus of Exurbia. What they get when they arrive there is the opportunity to do what Wattenberg says that human beings want deeply: "to associate with their 'own kind.'"

No doubt about it, there are voices raised in opposition to the whole idea of suburbia. Books of fact and fiction denigrate the suburbs as characterless boxes containing conformist neurotics. It would appear, though, that most Americans have paid little attention to these attacks. All they know is that they want to live there. Suburbia—and its acme, Exurbia—stands for Journey's End: the reward for all those who engage in the "pursuit of happiness" that Jefferson bequeathed to us in the Declaration of Independence. Typically, in a survey of national attitudes commissioned by the New York *Times* and carried out by the Gallup Organization in 1975, people again and again said that one of their chief aspirations was a nice home in the suburbs.

Those who are trying to reach Exurbia—and those who have already gotten there—describe the reasons for the quest in similar terms. They want good schools, a better chance for the kids, a nice place to live, fresh air, nice neighbors, and more fun out of life.

However, the Exurban elite is now an endangered species. Exurbia is threatened. Its members are beset with problems. And, unlike the cases of such other endangered species as the whooping crane and the sperm whale, nobody gives a damn about the Exurbanite except the Exurbanite.

Recently two Connecticut suburbs passed up federal grants totaling more than a million dollars. Other suburbs are doing the same.

One way to look at this phenomenon would be to call it a triumph of principle over greed. Another way would be to call it a victory of hysteria over common sense. Exurban towns are beginning to back away from the Washington trough because they are afraid that acceptance of the money will open the gates to let *them* in. In Exurbia, *them* means poor people, blue-collar people, blacks—anybody who can't afford a big house on a large piece of ground. The development is one more thrash in the mounting death throes of Exurbia.

The Exurban Good Life is finished. The pressure outside the barricades is growing. Within the walls, resistance to change is feverish, but spirit and vigor are waning. Exurbia is dying because its life sources are drying up and its organic defenses are eroding. The restrictive zoning codes are under powerful and effective assault in federal and state courts and legislatures. The expensive educational systems seem to have produced as many illiterates as

less highly touted plants which have at least the virtue of being cheaper. The Exurban family, always in difficulty, is coming apart. The female volunteer, once the mainstay of a broad range of community services, wants to get paid for what she does.

And Exurbia is getting old. We don't have the zip we once possessed. The Good Life is now hard work, and anyway, who can afford it?

My hometown is Westport, the archetype and queen of the Exurbs. Years ago I got used to the smiles and knowing looks stimulated by my telling people where I was from. Once there were sly references to the wild parties, the wife-swapping. You don't hear that sort of thing much anymore, since in Exurbia we have subsided into well-groomed middle age.

There was grudging envy behind the reactions. I had arrived in Westport; I had *made it*. It came to me that Westport, and the other Westports forming the Exurban Archipelago, were in many ways an illusion. Illusion has its uses. A house in Westport was, for a lot of us, a focus for driving effort while we were struggling to get there and a culmination of the dream when we moved in. Now illusion seems to be all that's left.

Word got around to some people in town that I was working on a book about the end of Exurbia. On the railroad platform one morning a commuter friend asked me about it. This was one of our razor-sharp achievers, a successful corporate climber, a mover and shaker. I told him that my proposition was that our present way of life would soon be finished. I began to tell him that I thought this was by no means a bad thing.

"That's where you're wrong," he assured me. "Thank God we still have a system that rewards accomplishment, and that we can live in places where we want to live, without having apartments and the scum of the city pushed in on us."

Around that same time I was talking with a woman, an earnest, dedicated person, deeply into the preservation of the environment. "I can't believe you're right," she said. "We simply cannot let all this beauty, all this good air and open space, go down the drain into an ugly megalopolis."

The "system" my commuter friend was referring to is, of course, the free-enterprise system. He is a pillar of it. He is a robust defender of restrictive zoning laws. My friend would listen with bridled impatience to the argu-

ment that there is scarcely any constitutional backing for such a practice, but he would dismiss it as craziness.

My earnest ecological friend laments the incursion of megalopolis on the Exurban preserve. She doesn't ask herself what it costs the surrounding regions and the world at large to maintain us in our isolated splendor. For Exurbia is very wasteful of scarce resources. We live far apart from each other. It is enormously expensive to mount services in areas so sparsely populated, and the effort eats up finite resources. Naturally we drive everyplace; somewhere the air is being polluted so that we can run our cars, heat and cool our houses, and enjoy our appliances. Meanwhile a nearby city is festering; there is no place to which its inhabitants can move. Environmental concern in Exurbia is usually of quite limited focus.

The illusions of the elite. Illusions and elites are valuable. They help us to visualize the goals toward which we aspire. But not when the elite becomes irrelevant, begins to constitute a drag on the society rather than a spur—when its energies focus too much on its own preservation. The Exurban elite, and its habitat, are no longer functional. The dream is just not working out.

Consider zoning. About 60 years ago the concept was introduced as a device for city planning. It has turned into a means of keeping "undesirable" people out. For a long time we in Exurbia took zoning for granted. Now zoning is taking its lumps. The New Jersey Supreme Court decrees that Mount Laurel, a suburb of Philadelphia, can no longer keep out all but single-family houses. Towns like this, says the court, must make available "an appropriate variety of housing." This is because suburbs must assume their "fair share of the regional need."

Never mind that lawyers will found fortunes debating the meaning of "fair share" as it is applied to case after case. The key word here is *regional*. Confirmed Exurbanites talk about "regional approach" in the same way that Civil War Georgians talked about Sherman's armies. "Regional" means that the suburb can no longer say to the neighboring city, "That's your problem." It means that problems of housing, land use, education, and transportation have to be handled on a regional basis, which sometimes overrides the sacred boundaries of the town lines. There goes the neighborhood!

The forces dedicated to breaking local zoning are moving ahead on several fronts. They have soft-pedaled through the federal courts the approach which attacks restrictive regulations on the basis that they are violations of the U.S. Constitution. The U.S. Supreme Court is notably leery of undertaking a full-scale review of zoning, perhaps because, as many lawyers feel, the justices fear that there is insufficient constitutional support for the concept. Federal courts have shown a recent tendency to say that it is not enough to show that the *effects* of zoning laws are discriminatory; the complainants have to prove that the *intent* of the laws is discriminatory. Since it is a lot tougher to demonstrate intent than effect, antizoners are not enthusiastic about this ploy. Nevertheless, there are cases on the high-court docket that carry the potential for a sweeping ruling on zoning.

The opponents of Exurban exclusion have higher hopes for what is called the "Hartford approach." The essence of this strategy is that restrictive zoning is contrary to the wishes of Congress as expressed in specific pieces of legislation. Antizoners sue to keep the suburbs from receiving money from Washington, money which would be forthcoming under various laws in the Housing and Urban Development area. The city of Hartford started it by suing to cut off such funds to its surrounding suburbs. The suits have stood up well in higher courts. Some Exurban community leaders have concluded gloomily that they will have to forgo the federal money in order to maintain the "character of the community"; thus a small suburb decides to discontinue its application to obtain a mouth-watering million dollars.

Cities throughout the country are watching the Hartford experience closely. Some—Buffalo, for example—may be moving into the arena. Here in Westport we are becoming uncomfortably aware that the cities flanking us—Norwalk and Bridgeport—are stirring in the direction of cutting off our small but welcome federal grants.

And then the state legislatures are getting into the act. For years in Connecticut the same thing would happen at every legislative session. Some fire-eating city representative would put in a bill to break suburban zoning. Nobody worried; the bills always died in committee. Last session it was a little different. A bill was introduced that might have enabled a city to buy land in a suburban town, and then put up low-cost apartments there for the city's residents, overriding local zoning. This measure did not die as quickly as its predecessors. It got out of committee.

It passed both houses of the legislature. Finally, after some deliberation, the bill was vetoed by Governor Grasso. There will be other sessions and other bills.

So we are not to be left alone in our peaceful enclaves. We look forward dolefully to a series of confrontations with the cities. If we lose just one of them, *they* will be upon us.

That's what's happening outside the stockade. Meanwhile, within the fortifications, how is the morale of the defenders? Not so good. We are becoming morose, irritable, and panicky. We are losing our cool. We are of course not monolithic in our feelings about zoning. Some want a limited number of apartments. A few want a lot of apartments. Most cling to the status quo. Exchanges between proponents of different views are getting mean.

In one Fairfield County town a pro-apartment member of the zoning body had found himself on the short end of every vote. At a recent meeting the same old problem came up. A large tract was about to come onto the market. How could the town prevent the building of (hushed voices) apartments?

The proapartment member addressed his colleagues: "Look. What's the worst that can happen? They will put up a six-story building and 200 blacks will move in. Maybe we'll get lucky. Maybe one of them will be a brain surgeon." Whereupon the member withdrew in disgust from the commission, leaving his shocked associates to vote down yet another multi-family-housing application.

But our frustrations are by no means confined to our differences over zoning. We look at our educational system and we wonder what happened. Once high-rolling executives moving into our area were advised, "Buy a place in Westport [or whatever the currently recommended town happened to be] .They have a fabulous school system." Since this usually dovetailed with the prevalent claim of Exurbanites that they were doing it all for the kids, education became a mainstay of the rationale. And why shouldn't the education system in Exurbia be fabulous? Under the long-standing custom by which schools are paid for out of local property taxes, the affluent town can—and does—spend more than twice as much per pupil as less fortunate locations.

Several things have happened to this precinct of the Dream. For one thing, as the hard-nosed management types say, the system has not proven to be cost-effective. Too many of the products are deficient. The kids get out without being able to read, write, or

add very well, and besides, they have no discipline.

There was a time when the sky was the limit for education in Westport. All this changed in June, 1974. A large education budget had been proposed. The seismograph showed tremors. Opponents of the expenditure got enough petition signatures to force a referendum. Proeducationists assumed that this threat would be staved off, as had all the others in the past.

This time it was different. The budget was drubbed resoundingly. The "no" voters comprised a large number of elder Westporters who no longer had a personal stake in the system. They carried along with them a bloc of people who were disgusted with the local school and who were determined to send a message to the education establishment. The era of unlimited spending on schools had ended in Westport. It is ending, with similar convulsions, throughout the Exurban Archipelago.

As if this were not enough to put an end to the old approach to school spending, the *coup de grace* is being applied by courts and legislatures. Late in 1974 a Connecticut Superior Court judge ruled that primary reliance on local property taxes for schools violates the state constitution. Courts in other states have been saying the same thing for some time. Whether or not a community can buy better education because it is rich enough to afford the expenditure—and this is an increasingly dubious proposition—it is unfair and legally taboo for Westport to spend $1,731 per pupil while, say, Griswold can spend only $779. The whole thing has been dumped in the laps of the legislators, who will come up with some kind of formula which equalizes educational spending. Regionalization rears its head again.

The American family is in trouble, but the Exurban family is in trouble in some special ways. The traditional Exurban family conformed to an identifiable pattern. The husband: a hard-driving, successful executive or professional who has reached the upper financial brackets. The wife: an educated and capable person, content with the role of well-off suburban matron and devoted to the raising of the kids and the doing of volunteer good works. The children: two or three attractive achievers who will flourish in the local schools, go on to good colleges, and eventually take their places in the established elite, reflecting credit on their parents and on Exurbia.

The Exurbanite is older and less resilient than he once was. He is beginning to feel anxious about his capability on the job. And when he is in trouble on the job, he is in trouble everyplace, because that's where most of his real life takes place.

A lot of affluent suburbanites are out of work. Others are trying to get along on reduced incomes. And a great many fear that this is about to happen to them. This almost always means difficulty for the family. The job is traditionally a kind of San Andreas Fault of the suburban marriage. While the Exurbanite is involved in his job there are groans and shifts, stresses and strains. He devotes too much energy and time to work, not enough to the family. When he loses the job, that can be an earthquake.

The children of Exurbia are in trouble too: not all of them, but a significant number. The drug problem has been with us for a long time. It seems to rise and fall in intensity; mostly we seem to become more resigned to it.

Now there is booze. Drinking in high school is commonplace. Junior-high teachers no longer react with utter astonishment to the sight of a student coming to class drunk. Tippling has been reported in the elementary grades.

Once Exurbia experienced practically no crime except for mild vandalism. Now Exurban police are trying to cope with a rash of burglaries. For a while many clung to the comfortable assumption that the housebreakings were the work, by and large, of hoodlums who came into town from the cities. The authorities know better. An Exurban police chief says, "These are our own kids who are doing this. And they are very hard to catch."

One of the things that make the burglars hard to catch is the fact that they do not dispose of the loot through established fences. I was told that a band of young burglars from Westport would get on the New Haven train with their portable booty—in a grotesque parody of the commuting routine—ride to New York, and get off at 125th Street to barter the goods on the street for drugs.

And the traditional Exurban matron has undergone what may be the most significant change of all. She simply will not settle for the role any longer. Once at parties you would hear women talking about their volunteer activities. No more. If a woman happens to do volunteer work, she is apt to keep it to herself. It's not socially acceptable anymore. The thing to do is to have a job for which you get paid. More than half the women over sixteen in Westport are in the labor market.

There are a number of consequences. What was always, in effect, a one-parent family has become a no-parent family. The Exurban family structure has never conformed to the ideal of "togetherness." Togetherness was what you had to endure if you couldn't afford any better. When we move to the affluent suburbs, what we cherish is *apartness*. We are removed from the houses of our neighbors. The place is big enough so that we never have to see our children; we can install separate telephones for them to ensure even greater distancing. And spouses do not have to see much of each other either.

So, as the besiegers mill around outside the walls, the strains grow within the enclave. Our will to resist is sapped. It is no longer a question of *if* the barricades will be breached. The question is *when*, and how bad it will be.

In ten years or so Westport will be a satellite city of about 80,000, one of the sat-cits growing in the interstices between megalopolises where Exurbia once bloomed. For a while some of the old mystique will remain: but for a new generation Westport will no longer be the apex of the American Dream, but just a stop on the New Haven line between Norwalk and Bridgeport.

The place will present a denser and more variegated aspect. There will be apartments, some of the garden variety, some multistoried. They will rent for various prices; some will be occupied by low-income families. New houses will be smaller, grouped in developments, standing on smaller lots, not large tracts of acreage. There will be neighborhoods; residents will talk with and get to know those who live close to them. Human legs will make a comeback as a means of transportation.

The die-hard Exurbanite will have certain options. He may choose to sit tight on his two acres, but he will have trouble ignoring what is going on around him. Those apartments down the road will block his view of Long Island Sound. When he drives downtown on Saturday morning he will find the place full, not just with more people but with *different* kinds of people. And he will learn that stubborn adherence to yesterday's ideal of the Good Life is a very expensive proposition. His tax will reflect the reality that the big house on the big spread is no longer a commonplace of the community but a distinct and idiosyncratic luxury.

Or, he can move into some future WestportWorld, a combination of Disneyland and posh condominium, which will be one answer for those who have really made it and who wish to enjoy the old Exurbanite amenities. Here one will be able to live in isolated splendor. Here *they* will not encroach. However, *they* will no longer be zoned out. The Exurbanite who dwells in the pleasant confines of WestportWorld will have the Good Life because he is paying a great deal for it. Elegant seclusion will be a function of private property rather than restrictive ordinance.

To me, the prospect of WestportWorld is a sad spectacle. The dying of a dream is always a melancholy thing. The present Exurbanite may feel that he has been cheated of the fruits of success. Younger people, on the threshold of a move to Exurbia, may conclude that such an act is as quixotic as Rhett Butler's enlistment in the Confederate Army after the fall of Atlanta.

However, on the bottom line of life, the balance of all this may be distinctly in the black. In one sense we are not seeing the death of a dream, but rather its displacement toward something more fruitful and relevant to reality.

Consider the children. Within the regionalized approach to education which is an inevitable corollary of the growth of the sat-cits, educational spending and opportunity will come into a form of balance unknown in the past. It is not just a matter of allocation of dollars. Westport may be getting ready to shut down a "new" elementary school, built less than twenty years ago, because there is a diminishing number of children to attend it. In the neighboring cities, older school buildings bulge at the seams. As less affluent families move into the once forbidden confines, such schools will come to life again.

Exurbia's children will no longer grow in a hothouse atmosphere, never meeting adults and other children who are much different. Moreover, when the children of Exurbia are grown, they will not become automatic exiles from the places in which they grew. As it stands now, young adults who were raised in Westport cannot afford to live here. When the change comes they will be able to come back to where their roots are, and to contribute their vigor to the community.

In general, the opening of Exurbia will lead to the rejoining of the isolated elite with the mainstream. As the barriers come down, we will see a forced equalization of concern. We Exurbanites will no longer be able to avert our eyes from the problems of the people of the cities. From here on in, *they* will be *we.* And we have talent and a measure of residual energy that can be brought to bear on these problems. The meshing of effort will not be easy. There will be discomfort and suspicion as Exurbia comes together with Urbia. But the growing unity of interest between those who are used to power and those who have been excluded from it will begin to ameliorate—if not solve—the problems of the metropolitan area.

For some confirmed Exurbanites it will be a rejuvenating experience. Nowadays your card-carrying commuter gets on the 4:59 out of Grand Central and sits with rigid sphincter, reading dismal memoranda about downside risks and the need for belt-tightening. His train lumbers past cities about which he does not give a damn to deposit him in the enclave whose once bright promise has grown into a somewhat oppressive reality. He suspects it's coming to an end, and he is despairing about what will happen next.

The reality is: What happens next may well engage moral and intellectual energies which the Exurbanite has not used for years. The management philosopher Peter Drucker says that the middle-aged executive needs a second vocation—not just a hobby—to keep himself from atrophying. Well, here is that vocation: the building and betterment of a wider community.

Yes, it's the End of Exurbia. If we work it right it's the start of something better.

We want your advice.

Any anthology can be improved. This one will be—annually. But we need your help.

Annual Editions revisions depend on two major opinion sources: one is the academic advisers who work with us in scanning the thousands of articles published in the public press each year; the other is you—the person actually using the book.

Please help us and the users of the next edition by completing the prepaid reader response form on the last page of this book and returning it to us. Thank you.

Bologna, Italy: Urban Socialism in Western Europe

Thomas R. Angotti and Bruce S. Dale

THOMAS R. ANGOTTI is a research and planning consultant in Rome and has recently been working on projects in Libya, Yugoslavia, and Italy. BRUCE S. DALE, an architect, has collaborated on public housing and planning projects in Italy and is now associated with Urban Deadline Architects in New York.

The net effect of publicly financed urban renewal programs in the United States has been to break up old residential neighborhoods and displace their low-income residents. As a result of urban renewal programs, low-rent, working-class housing in the central core is replaced by luxury housing, commercial or administrative buildings. The displaced residents are forced to accept more expensive housing, often in worse neighborhoods, with a minimum of assistance in relocation. Various aspects of this removal process have been clearly described and documented by other commentators such as H. Gans, J. Jacobs, and C. Hartman.[1]

Working-class housing, when centrally located, is considered fair game for speculative redevelopment. And it is traditional in America and in Europe for working-class families to live in the central core—originally to be near their workplaces, then for economy and convenience. In the process of metropolitan growth these communities are often taken over by speculators and subjected to renovation (or demolition and reconstruction) by private and public interests alike. A period of housing decay may

precede renewal but is tolerated, even encouraged, as an intermediate stage which will facilitate future profits by reducing acquisition costs and inviting large-scale redevelopment.[2] Whether or not rehabilitation is directly assisted by public programs, the net effect is always the same: destruction of working-class communities in the central core. Basically very little has changed since Engels observed this process in *The Housing Question* (1872).

The expansion of the big modern cities gives the land in certain sections of them, particularly in those which are centrally situated, an artificial and often enormously increasing value; the buildings erected in these areas depress this value, instead of increasing it, because they no longer correspond to the changed circumstances. They are pulled down and replaced by others. This takes place above all with centrally located workers' houses, whose rents, even with the greatest overcrowding, can never, or only very slowly, increase above a certain maximum. They are pulled down and in their stead shops, warehouses and public buildings are erected. Through its Haussmann in Paris, Bonapartism exploited this tendency tremendously for swindling and private enrichment. But the spirit of Haussmann has also been abroad in London, Manchester and Liverpool, and seems to feel itself just as much at home in Berlin and Vienna. The result is that the workers are forced out of the center of the towns towards the outskirts; that workers' dwellings and small dwellings in general become rare and expensive and often altogether unobtainable, for under these circumstances the building industry,

which is offered a much better field for speculation by more expensive dwelling houses, builds workers' dwellings only by way of exception.

In recent years there has been increased interest in historic preservation as a means of redevelopment. Although not very widespread, it has generally aided the process of increasing land and housing values by generating middle- and upper-income neighborhoods. Preservation programs have resulted in rent increases due to higher land values in renewed central locations.[3] Based on a nostalgia for past social values and their symbolic representation in physical form, in addition to pecuniary interests, historic preservation has rarely improved housing and environmental conditions for the people with the greatest need. Rather, restoration is oriented toward the improvement of individual structures, to the exclusion of low-income tenants. Public intervention has generally taken the form of protective legislation for preserving individual structures of unusual historic value from either occupancy by low-income people or speculative redevelopment (e.g., Beacon Hill, Boston; Vieux Carré, New Orleans; Georgetown). There are also examples of the use of renewal subsidies, as in Providence and Mobile, but the results have been the same: exclusive and sterile communities. Society Hill in Philadelphia and Old Town in Alexandria, Virginia, set the standards for this undesirable goal.

THE EXAMPLE OF BOLOGNA
Bologna, Italy, is the first industrial city in the Western world to have a central city renewal program that

2. URBAN EXPERIENCES

aims to preserve the historical and social character of the urban environment by not displacing low-income people from their homes. This renewal program is probably the only one of its kind in a capitalist country. Its success is due to a basic political commitment by a communist administration to reinforce the social foundations of the central core by improving the physical environment, increasing the level of services available to residents, and promoting democratic participation in decision making.

The main theoretical basis of the Bologna program is a concept of the city, including its services and buildings, as a public good (*bene pubblico*). Simply stated, it means that the needs of the people—all of the people—come before profit. Within the limits of the Italian economic and legal structure the program attempts to eliminate land speculation in both the center and the periphery of the city. Following P.L. Cervellati and R. Scannavini, the main features of the plan which stem from these general principles are:

1. The use of public housing subsidies for conservation and renovation rather than new construction.
2. Democratic participation in the planning process at the neighborhood as well as city-wide level.
3. Adoption of a comprehensive planning approach which takes into account the role of the historic center in overall metropolitan and regional growth.
4. Conversion of historic buildings to collective use.
5. Development of a rigorous scientific system of classification of building types and strict regulation of rehabilitation.[4]

In its original form the 1969 master plan for Bologna declared that the city had no economic or social justification for continued growth if the human quality of urban life were to be preserved. Hence a moritorium on all new construction was declared. The citizens, however, did have the right and need for improved housing, which was the reason for a new focus on the historic center. Improved hous-

ing had to come from the existing housing stock. It was in the historic center that public investment could fulfill the dual intention of conserving an inestimable historic heritage and providing better housing for the lower-income population. Expansion and new construction had tended to produce largely luxury apartments of which Bologna already had an adequate supply. Publicly financed renovation was therefore seen as a mechanism capable of providing adequate low-income housing.

The Bologna plan was introduced by a municipal government which has been dominated by the Italian Communist party since the end of World War II. It is the largest Communist party in the West and has recently obtained either majority control or participation in most of Italy's major city governments (Milan, Turin, Venice, Genoa, Florence, Naples) and many smaller municipalities. The only two major cities still controlled by the Christian Democrats, who have dominated Italian politics since the end of the war, are Rome and Palermo. In the local elections of June 15, 1975, national totals showed the Communist party within two percentage points of the lead held by the Christian Democrats. The Communist party's proposal of an "historic compromise" uniting democratic forces from a wide political spectrum to solve the country's problems is therefore in the process of being tested in numerous local situations. [The contemporary Italian political context was the subject of "Crisis in Italy: The Strategy of Coalitions" by Roy Bennett, *Social Policy* 6, no.3 (November/December 1975)—*Ed.*]

Bologna (population: 500,000) is a light manufacturing center in northern Italy and principal crossroads for rail and motor traffic. The historic center, located within the Renaissance walls, had a population of 85,000 in 1971. This represents a loss of many thousands of residents, mostly young and male, since 1945. This decline in the center corresponds to the growth of industry and housing in the city's periphery in the last few decades.

Bologna was an important agricultural center from Roman times through the Middle Ages: the central core still displays the grid layout typi-

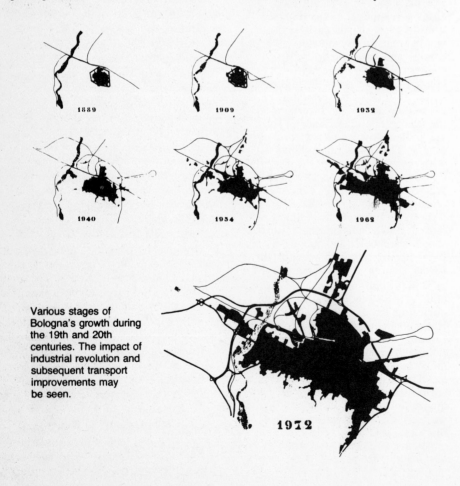

Various stages of Bologna's growth during the 19th and 20th centuries. The impact of industrial revolution and subsequent transport improvements may be seen.

cal of Roman settlements. The University of Bologna was founded in the twelfth century when the city was acquiring importance as a commercial and artisan center, and it continues to occupy a large amount of land in the center. Fortified stone walls were built in 1380 and taken down in 1902; the present ring road around the center follows the path of the old walls.

After the unification of Italy in 1861, Bologna assumed national importance as a strategic node in the new rail network and as an industrial center. The unprotected agricultural land around the city was taken over by speculators in a process of unplanned residential and industrial development. Unlike American cities, Bologna (and many other European settlements) never developed large industries in the central core as it was already densely developed prior to the industrial revolution.

The city's first master plan in 1889 gave official sanction to the clearing of housing in the central core for road expansion. Throughout our century, medium and small industries have continued to expand in the periphery while agriculture in the region has declined. The growth of tertiary activities in the core has left many working-class neighborhoods fragmented, with large stocks of deteriorating housing being renovated for speculative gain. Portions of the central city were cleared by the Fascists for strategic and "aesthetic" purposes in the 1930s. In addition, American bombing during the last war destroyed considerable amounts of the housing stock in the historic center. Postwar speculation in the periphery has led to large municipal expenditure to support the newer high-rent housing.[5]

The Bologna program seeks to halt these detrimental trends by:

1. Stopping speculation in the periphery and limiting growth, generally through implementation of the city's new master plan.
2. Improving services and recreational space in the center.
3. Financing housing rehabilitation.
4. Restricting growth of tertiary activities in the center and decentralizing commercial and administrative functions.

5. Improving transport links between the center and other parts of the region.
6. Facilitating pedestrian movement in the center.
7. Maintaining a stable socially mixed population.[6]

The earliest proposals for a revaluation of the historic center were presented in preliminary studies carried out by Leonardo Benevolo in the 1960s. These studies led to the 1969 master plan supplement for the historic center, completed by the city planning office. The methodology employed in the preparation of this supplement relied heavily on an historical analysis and an extensive inventory of the historical buildings conducted by the city's technicians. They identified 13 zones within the center characterized by low-income population, substandard housing, and poorly utilized public facilities, with a notable absence of accessible public open space. The population of the 13 zones represented about 15 percent of the center's total population, with about 80 percent of the families living in rented units, 60 percent of which lacked bath or shower, while 68 percent lacked heating. The majority of the buildings were clearly overcrowded.[7] This survey also enumerated the remarkable historic legacy of Bologna, particularly a heritage of seventeenth-century artisan housing interwoven with religious and aristocratic buildings.

In 1972 a housing plan for the historic center identified five zones for priority treatment, involving 6,600 residents. The plan conformed to a program for planning and management of municipal services which meshed with the city's desire to maintain the historical integrity of its monuments by using them to house the community's services. The center was further divided into 10 historical and morphologically distinct zones which were characterized by existing prevalent building typologies. Recommended restoration plans designated Renaissance and Baroque churches to serve as community centers, providing space for schools, day care, meeting halls, and a variety of cultural activities—museums, art galleries, theaters, etc.[8]

The issue of citizen participation in Bologna led in 1964 to the formation

of neighborhood councils (4 in the center, 18 in the city) as a means of decentralizing administrative functions and facilitating direct public involvement. Representation on the councils is based proportionally on the votes received during municipal elections by each party within the council's district. In each neighborhood numerous advisory committees function as well, and all plans and proposals are reviewed at the neighborhood level. These councils have been consulted repeatedly throughout the development of the plan and have been given official status and responsibilities within the plan's administration.

Although the plan did not receive full official approval until July 1975, many of its proposals have already been initiated. Since March 1973, 400 million lire ($600,000) of national governmental funds have been spent for real estate acquisition and restoration, plus another 200 million lire ($300,000) in city funds. Three public facilities have been finished: two multiple-service centers, including two schools and a museum. Dwelling units for 360 persons have been completed, and contracts for a theater, multipurpose hall, and housing for an additional 144 persons are presently being bid.[9]

The first completed housing was built on a vacant city-owned lot and is being used for relocating people temporarily while their apartments are being renovated. In July 1975, the city received final approval for a proposed long-term contract which will allow it to expand renewal operations to privately owned dwelling units (see discussion below). Large or corporate real estate holders in the renewal area shall have their properties expropriated; others will be encouraged to sell to the city. Small property owners (owners of one, two, or three apartments) who do not wish to sell are obliged to sign a long-term agreement with the city which guarantees the status of tenants, limits rents, and provides for low-interest loans to cover renovation expenses.

A basic premise of the Bologna plan is that peripheral urban development involves high capital and social costs and feeds speculation. Studies undertaken by the city show that cost of renovation of central city housing is lower than the cost of new construction in the periphery. In the center costs average 200,000 lire ($300) per square meter or 5–6 million lire ($8–10,000) per capita for all construction and services. In the periphery costs average 218,000 lire ($325) per square meter or 7–8.5 million lire ($11–13,000) per capita. The higher cost in the periphery is due primarily to the cost of new infrastructure. Renovation also offers a savings on social costs which are difficult to quantify: the cost of displacing households, increasing travel time between residence and work, isolating people, destroying community structure, etc.[10]

Private housing construction in Bologna has slowed to the lowest level since the war. Zoning has preserved the best development land for public and cooperative housing which now account for more than half of all new building. The city has also begun to rehabilitate early public housing and improve services in portions of the periphery which have been neglected in the past. Thus the city's objective is to eliminate imbalances throughout the entire urban region.

PHYSICAL RENEWAL

Bologna is a physically attractive city. The dominant periods of development, the Renaissance and the Baroque, have left ubiquitous arcaded sidewalks, which insure separation of motor and pedestrian traffic, and a grid pattern overlaid by radial axes and two circumferential routes which facilitate traffic flow. These features are accompanied by a large stock of original period buildings partially defined by a variety of zoning policies which reflect the original concerns of their Renaissance and Baroque planners, who often produced odd-shape building lots, but were generous in the design of urban open spaces. We should note that the philosophy which underlies Bologna's restoration is based on the distinction between the historic monument as art, where aesthetic value dominates, and the monument as urban design, where the whole object including its function and relationship to its urban environment is valued. Changes are not to be based on aesthetic taste alone.

The basic principles underlying physical renewal are: a rigorous scientific analysis and classification of physical structure and function; ap-

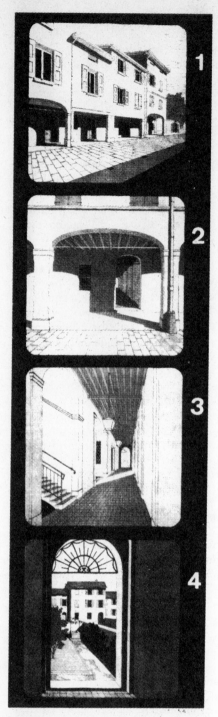

Four major architectural elements dominant in the housing of Category C.

plication of a set of codes, incentives, and restrictions to the various physical classifications that guarantees the integrity of historical values and permits adaptability to present needs; and evaluation of individual physical structures within the overall context of the future role of the central core and urban region rather than as static isolated objects.

The individual buildings are to be treated by either a *scientific* or a *conservative* restoration. A scientific restoration requires historical research to determine the original elements of the structure and their original use; the intention is to return the building to its original state, accommodating equivalent modern functions without making structural changes. A conservative restoration requires a similar process of research but does not necessarily require the removal of all later modifications. Alterations to facilitate the utilization of the building are permitted. In the case of artisan housing, discussed below, we have an example of a conservative restoration producing satisfactory modern housing while preserving intact a seventeenth-century building.

The first step in formulating the plan for the historic center was an extensive inventory of buildings and internal spaces, including an analysis of their structural characteristics and original functions. This analysis resulted in four main categories by building type: large containers,[11] small containers, small residential units, and other, less historically consistent, small residential units.[12] *Large containers* are typically churches and convents considered suitable for public use and easily adapted for purposes different from, but compatible with, their original ones. Such buildings are ideal for cultural and educational centers, museums, libraries, community theaters, neighborhood service centers, clinics, nurseries, and day-care centers. *Small containers* are fairly large buildings organized around a central courtyard and have served as university buildings or noble palaces. Alteration of use is difficult due to the size of interior spaces and their vaulted ceilings, particularly on the first floors. *Small residential units* are typically located on narrow building lots and were occupied by artisans and the working class of the sixteenth through eighteenth centuries. The single unit is generally repeated in series for entire blocks. *Other small residential units* are typically private residential structures which do not fall within any other category, are of minor historical interest, and may be composed of a variety of typological components. Units in this classification will remain private residences or accommodate other functions compatible with their structure.

In addition to this general classification of building types, the city produced a detailed set of restrictions on building alteration comprised of three major codes: restoration, rehabilitation, and demolition. Every building within the historic zone has been evaluated, classified, and coded for eventual restoration.

Preparation for restoration in residential areas began with a thorough iconographic research of the city archives and a volumetric reconstruction. After identification of the principal elements, which define the typology, further studies identified the principal variations and determined the state of conservation and the various alternatives for restoration. Taking artisan housing as an example of a residential unit, we find it to be typically single family units, two or three story buildings with two blind walls running the full depth, one or two windows in front and back, with occasional skylights and a variety of interior spaces. In some cases the entire lot is covered with open courtyards providing light and air. The buildings have frequently been modified to allow for more than one family occupancy, but ground floors generally remain intact with artisan workshops, neighborhood stores, and storage rooms for tenants and shopkeepers. These buildings were identified as potentially adequate housing for students, single persons, elderly, young couples, or working-class families. The restoration program, using modern space standards, is able to modify this type of structure designed for an extended family to satisfy the housing needs of today's social composition. Each restored building will have a certain variation of apartment types to allow for a social mix. The ground floor of each will also have a shop or professional office and an entrance way connecting directly to the central stair block, the rear yard, and common spaces. These common areas will accommodate the following services: day-care centers and nurseries, meeting rooms, washrooms and laundries, playgrounds, centralized heating (rare in Italy), kitchen/restaurants for students and elderly, and other civic center functions.

In most cases renovation of large containers involves a change in use from private institutional functions, mainly religious, to local neighborhood services. In some cases, functions remain the same; for example, religious libraries are simply expanded and remodeled for public use. If market forces were allowed to take hold when institutions abandon use of the containers, many of these structures would eventually revert to commercial or high-rent residential use or be demolished to permit new construction. On the other hand, a purely conservative approach to restoration would limit them to underutilization without any purposeful social function.

The process of restoring large containers involves three major steps: (1) analysis of the building's exterior including changes by historical period; (2) analysis of needs for the use of the building by neighborhood and city planners; (3) analysis of interior flexibility and distribution of space. One of the first examples of renovation of a large container is "The Barracano," formerly an orphanage and now a multipurpose community center. The Renaissance structure has been converted for use as a nursery school, student center with library, and community center with meeting rooms and offices. The complex also includes an art museum and public theater. The inner courtyard now provides a pleasant green retreat for the public as well as a play area for nursery school children. The total cost of conversion was the relatively small amount of 120 million lire ($180,000).

At the neighborhood level there are programmed modifications of the sewer system; improvement of gas, water, and electric utilities; installation of heating plants and piping; temporary relocation within 500–800 yards of the original housing; and a reorganization of storage facilities. A decentralized school system with parent participation and supervision is also projected. The plan also proposes to increase the availability of green spaces at the neighborhood level and to help meet citywide and regional demands as well as local ones. Creation of pedestrian zones and the expansion of playground spaces and indoor recreation areas are also envisioned. Neighborhoods in the center will be linked by public transit to the large open spaces on the hill overlooking the city (strictly preserved by the master plan) and to the periphery.

HOUSING AND SOCIAL CHANGE

A major cornerstone of Bologna's original housing program, before its revision in 1972, was the principle of collective ownership and management of property. Private property within renewal parcels was to be taken by eminent domain and returned after renovation to locally organized cooperatives. This was based on the assumption that private property was the major obstacle to rational renewal. A very meticulous and innovative interpretation of the Italian 1971 housing law was the basis for the unprecedented taking of land for the renovation of old housing, rather than just for construction of new housing. The cost of expropriation was linked to a formula which basically led to payments far below market price.

The initial reaction to the housing plan was quite favorable among practically all segments of the public. Small property owners, however, became sharply aligned against the tenants who stood to benefit from the scheme. They argued that the expropriations were discriminatory and that they were being deprived of their small holdings while owners outside the historic center were not touched.

The right wing and center parties exploited the small owners' discontent and denounced the program, launching a national campaign to stop it, claiming that it was a threat to all private property.[13] There was also a marked absence of support from the central committee of the Communist party. The historic compromise had been designed to expand the party's political base to include the middle class, and this would be hindered, the party believed, by the small nonspeculative property owner's fear of the original plan. The prospect of delaying the program with legal proceedings and widening internal divisions within the left led the city council eventually to reverse itself and withdraw the expropriation clause, substituting a contract between city and owner which would guarantee the status of tenants, limit rents, and provide for low-interest loans and grants.

The failure of planners and the political leadership to obtain the use of eminent domain was due to two major errors. The first, an error of objective analysis, considered small property owners in the same class as medium and large owners and speculators. Many small owners are

2. URBAN EXPERIENCES

in fact working-class families that use housing as a form of savings and as old age insurance. It is idealistic and unrealistic to treat all property holdings as if they were the fruits of mercenary speculation. Although private property is a major obstacle to rational planning, it is the large corporate land owners and the speculators who are the greatest violators. The elimination of private property with general acceptance requires a national revolutionary change. It cannot be fully achieved at the local level independently.

The second error was failure to discuss expropriation at all levels of the political structure. By not encouraging public debate and developing awareness of the necessity of this tool to realize equitable housing, the city officials found themselves with insufficient support. At the very least it was a case of unclear political strategy.[14]

The renewal program must be seen as only part of a larger political struggle. Small and medium property owners may become allies of the left or may otherwise strengthen the forces of reaction. Insistence on the use of expropriation could only have served to separate the working class from its natural allies and stall the realization of an important reform.

Substituting the contract for expropriation in the program does not essentially compromise the basic principles. The use of this contract will alter significantly the relationship between landlord and tenant. The contracts are to be negotiated by the neighborhood councils with city supervision. The basic model of the contract also contains guarantees that protect tenants from high rents and eviction. Let us examine some aspects of the contract model recently approved by the Bologna City Council.

The contract provides for three principal means of financing renovation: outright grants from the city, loans with subsidized interest payments, or a combination of the two. Most of the contracts will probably provide for loans rather than grants, since the latter are to be used only in cases where the owner is a resident and lacks adequate income to satisfy the loan conditions. Grants are 20-year contracts and the loans will be for 15, 20, or 25 years. Grants may cover the full costs of renovation and loans will normally cover up to 80 percent of the costs.

Rents are fixed at established public housing rent levels. The average family will pay 12 percent of its income for rent. New tenants must meet public housing qualifications. The city reserves the right to sublease an apartment for a tenant who does not have sufficient income to meet established rents (thus subsidizing rents) or if the tenant's income becomes too high, to increase rent. The city may also lease an apartment if it is left vacant for more than four months. Under the grant agreement, the owner of the dwelling has the right to occupy an apartment for the duration of his/her lifetime. The legal heirs may occupy the unit if they reimburse the city for the cost of renovation plus inflationary increases. As most of the people in this category are of low-income families, it is expected that most of the units will revert to the city for eventual conversion to cooperative housing.

The contracts providing for interest subsidies are the most critical to the success of the program. Theoretically, property owners could take advantage of the loan subsidy and subsequent increase in the market value of their housing and, after the contract period is over, gouge on rents and make removal of low-income tenants a reality. This eventuality, however, is unlikely for these reasons:

1. Italian rent control laws do limit rent increases.
2. Since profit is not included in the rent formula, owners may be encouraged to sell to the city which has the option to buy.
3. Corporate speculators are excluded from contracts and will have their holdings expropriated.
4. The city reserves the right to utilize its powers of eminent domain should the owner fail to carry out any part of the agreement.
5. The city can use every incentive and regulatory device at its disposal to promote conversion of housing units from private to cooperative ownership.

It is clear that owners will be able to continue using housing as equity, but their incomes will be severely limited. It is quite likely that some will sell to the city during the contract period and many of the units will be turned over to cooperatives without much opposition. It is also very likely that important political changes in Italy will create conditions for deeper and more lasting reforms within the next decade or two.

The Bologna municipal government has become a model of progressive administration, not only in the field of urban planning and renewal but in others as well. For example, the level of social services has been raised, a programmed budgeting system has been initiated, and an efficient public transportation system—free during peak hours and for students and the elderly—is in operation.[15] In addition, the methodology of the Bologna renewal program has been applied to a number of other Italian cities: Ferrara, Bergamo, and Ancona.

At the technical level there is much in common between the Bologna program and successful renewal programs in socialist countries (e.g., Czechoslovakia, Poland, USSR). Bologna is, however, unique in Western Europe. On the 50 other pilot projects selected as part of the European Architectural Heritage Year sponsored by the Council of Europe, Bologna is the only one which guarantees low-income residents continued tenancy and applies public housing funds to historic renovation projects. It is one of the few taking a comprehensive approach to renovation, preserving and improving whole urban living environments rather than single isolated monuments.[16]

In the long run the contradictions between private property and public purpose will have to be confronted. Renewal without removal is only possible within a capitalist system if there is a progressive political base. Progressive municipal policy in Bologna has used public housing subsidies, which are necessary in a social system based on private ownership and profit. It has used strict enforcement of planning regulations in both center and periphery, and has restrained, though not ended, speculation.[17] It has begun to develop a decision-making structure which by Italian standards is democratic. Finally, the renewal program has clearly demonstrated that central city housing can be rehabilitated without removing people and destroying working-class neighborhoods, that the historical integrity of the environment can be maintained and used for social purposes, and that the housing question must be confronted first at a political level.

NOTES

1 Herbert J. Gans, "The Failure of Urban Renewal," *Commentary* (April 1965), pp. 29–37. Jane Jacobs, *The Death and Life of Great American Cities* (New York: Random House, 1961). Chester W. Hartman, "The Housing of Relocated Families," *Journal of American Institute of Planners* 30 (November 1964), pp. 266 ff.; *Yerba Buena: Land Grab and Community Resistance in San Francisco* (San Francisco, California: Glide, 1974).

2 Roger Starr, chief administrator of the New York City Housing and Development Administration, has proposed a deliberate policy of encouraging total abandonment of deteriorating areas such as the South Bronx in New York. *New York Times,* February 3, 1976.

3 R.L. Montague, III and T.P. Wrenn, *Planning for Preservation* (Chicago: ASPO, 1964).

4 P.L. Cervellati, and R. Scannavini, eds., *Bologna: politica e metodologia del restauro nei centri storici* (Bologna: Societa editrice Il Mulino, 1973).

5 This has created apparent contradictions between housing and urban environment in the core and periphery. For instance, while there is general overcrowding in the center, significant vacancies exist in the periphery. The situation is even more critical in Italian cities which have had larger in-migration (Milan and Rome) where services have barely kept up with urban expansion. See A. Belli, ed., *Citta e teritorio: pianificazione e conflitto* (Naples: Coop. editrice di Econonis e Commercio, 1974), and Nella Ginatempo, *La casa in Italia* (Milan: Mazzotta, 1975).

6 Cervellati and Scannavini, *Bologna.*

7 City of Bologna, *Piano regolatore generale,* 1973; Claudio Claroni, ed., *Piano per il centro storico: stato delle abitazioni e struttura della popolazione* (City of Bologna, 1971).

8 City of Bologna, *PEEP/ Centro storico,* 1973.

9 Ibid., *La convenzione per il risanamento dei 5 comparti PEEP/ Centro storico,* 1975.

10 Cervellati and Scannavini, *Bologna.*

11 The term "containers" (*contenitori* in Italian) refers to the building's large interior spaces capable of holding public functions.

12 Cervellati and Scannavini, *Bologna.*

13 One conservative newspaper commented, "If this plan, after all is said and done, is actually carried out, will it not create a precedent which is capable of bringing about a national economic crisis, a crisis of the very idea of private property itself? *Giornale d'Italia,* December 4, 1972.

14 Paolo Ceccarelli and Francesco Indoviana, eds., *Risanamento e speculazione nei centri storici* (Milan: F. Angeli, 1974).

15 While Rome, New York, and many other cities have continuously increased their bus fares, Bologna offers free bus transport to everyone from 5 to 9 a.m., and from 5 to 9 p.m. Pensioners can travel free at any time, and students do so with a monthly pass at a nominal charge.

16 Council of Europe, *European Programme of Pilot Projects* (Strasbourg: Committee on Monuments and Sites, 1973).

17 This might be compared to the situation in Rome where a third of all housing in the periphery was built illegally and where there are 60,000 vacant units.

Parochial, Diffuse or Stepping-Stone?
SIX KINDS OF NEIGHBORHOODS

It's not income, ethnic group, or social level that determines whether a neighborhood is friendly or cold, active or indolent. The failure of urban renewal and Model Cities programs may ultimately rest on bureaucratic ignorance of neighborhood structure.

Donald I. Warren and Rachelle B. Warren

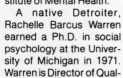

Donald I. Warren received his Ph.D. in sociology at the University of Michigan. He taught at Wayne State University from 1965 to 1968, and then returned to the University of Michigan, where he is presently Director of the Program in Community Effectiveness at the Institute of Labor and Industrial Relations. Warren is author of *Black Neighborhoods: An Assessment of Community Power* (University of Michigan Press, 1975). Research reported in this article was done under a grant from the National Institute of Mental Health.

A native Detroiter, Rachelle Barcus Warren earned a Ph.D. in social psychology at the University of Michigan in 1971. Warren is Director of Qualitative Field Studies for the Program in Community Effectiveness (a division of the Institute of Labor and Industrial Relations at the University of Michigan) and teaches in the department of sociology. Her current research interest is the psychological and social effects of unemployment—particularly as it affects blue-collar women.

An expanded version of this paper can be found in handbook form in *The Neighborhood Organizer's Guidebook*, The University of Notre Dame Press.

THE STREETS WERE ALMOST EMPTY as we looked for Betty's home, which was in a suburban, working-class neighborhood at the fringe of Detroit. The only evidence of occupation was mute; cyclone-fence boundaries and "beware-of-dog" signs partitioned the area into Monopoly-board squares. As a new resident in the neighborhood, Betty Wagner was finding the partitions quite real, and quite distressing.

In the old neighborhood, "Everyone shared and it was easy to get people involved; everyone was so close-knit there." After a year in the new area, "I've come to hate it," she said. "We can't get a PTA going, or managers for the kids' baseball teams; the old people are on their own . . . and I can't even have Tupperware parties."

Without realizing it, Mrs. Wagner had moved from her kind of neighborhood to one where she was a fish out of water. In her old neighborhood, "We take care of our own" was a common expression, and activists like Mrs. Wagner found it relatively easy to gain the support of their neighbors for all kinds of group projects. In the new neighborhood this task was much more difficult and would have required a set of techniques quite different from those Mrs. Wagner was accustomed to using. Unfortunately, she became so frustrated with her "crazy neighborhood" that she gave up her activist role altogether.

It is not surprising that Mrs. Wagner failed to understand the dynamics of her new neighborhood. Even social scientists who have made it their business to understand how neighborhoods function and how to organize them for action have clung for years to inadequate, one-dimensional views of neighborhoods as "strong" or "weak," "cohesive" or "non-cohesive," "organized" or "disorganized." Such dichotomies fail to take into account the extreme variability in neighborhood structures that we have discovered in more than eight years of research at the University of Michigan.

Class, Income, Ethnicity. To better understand and describe the variety of highly specialized roles that neighborhoods can play in the lives of their residents, we developed a typology based on three important principles of organization: interaction, identity and connections. Our research shows that these three factors are critical for understanding the different situations people like Mrs. Wagner find themselves in when they want to take action at the neighborhood level. Taken together, these elements constitute a neighborhood's structural characteristics, the differences in neighborhood organization that cut across social-class, income and ethnic lines.

In terms of specific questions to ask about a neighborhood, these dimensions can be put this way:

A *Interaction:* During the year do people in the neighborhood get together quite often?

B *Identity:* Do people in the neighborhood feel that they have a great deal in common?

C *Connections:* Do many people in the neighborhood keep active in political parties and other forces outside the neighborhood?

Depending on how each question is answered, a specific neighborhood will fall

Different Strokes for Different Neighborhoods
A COMMUNITY LEADER'S HANDBOOK

Have you thought about mobilizing your neighborhood to accomplish something, but don't know exactly where to begin? This brief guide can help you diagnose your neighborhood and select the best prescription for effective action.

Our research has identified eight neighborhood characteristics that are pivotal for organizational action and change. We have listed these characteristics in terms of eight questions to ask yourself about your own neighborhood.

We also have identified seven strategies that are frequently used by successful activists. These strategies are listed on the chart and marked according to their probable effectiveness.

To devise your own strategies, first answer each question. Then, for each "yes" answer, look across the list of strategies to find which action would be your best first step (+), which ones would be your best follow-up actions (★), and which ones would be so costly in time or money that it wouldn't make sense to use them (NO).

Now let's examine the choices:

1 INTERACTION. If your neighbors are in frequent contact with one another, the most efficient first step is to try to mobilize a few key neighbors. They will quickly spread your message. Door-to-door contact and media advertisements might work, but they are costly or time-consuming. Developing a new local group and setting up a pipeline to city hall are useful follow-up actions.

2 HETEROGENEITY. If your neighbors'

(continued on following page)

NEIGHBORHOOD ACTIVISTS' GUIDE

Diagnosing the Neighborhood — Characteristics	Taking Action						
	Publish News-letter	Conduct Door-to-Door Campaign	Advertise In Mass Media	Contact Key Neighbors	Use Organization Lists	Form Grass-Roots Group	Set Up Pipeline to City Hall
1 **Interaction.** During the year do people in the neighborhood get together quite often? YES	★	NO	NO	+	★	★	★
2 **Heterogeneity.** Are there many people of different backgrounds, lifestyles, or social levels who live in the neighborhood? YES	★	+	NO	★	★	NO	NO
3 **Identity.** Do people in the neighborhood feel they have a great deal in common? YES	+	★	★	NO	★	★	★
4 **Mutual Aid.** When someone has something on his mind that is bothering him, are neighbors willing to help? YES	★	★	★	NO	NO	NO	+
5 **Privatism.** Do people in the neighborhood place more value on their family privacy than on being in touch with neighbors? YES	NO	NO	+	★	★	NO	NO
6 **Insulation.** If a bill collector came around asking about a neighbor, would people in your neighborhood refuse to give out any information? YES	★	+	NO	★	NO	★	NO
7 **Connections.** Do many people in the neighborhood keep active in groups outside the neighborhood? YES	★	NO	★	★	+	★	★
8 **Turnover.** Are there many people who move in and out of your neighborhood? YES	+	★	★	NO	NO	★	★

lifestyles are many and various, it is hard to find a suitable "language" for a newsletter or advertisement. Your neighbors may misperceive your message. Door-to-door, personal canvassing seems to be the only effective first step, even though it is time-consuming.

3 IDENTITY. Suppose your neighborhood has little going for it except that people like it and feel a certain sense of identity. Publishing a newsletter can be an effective starter. It can inform even the newest resident about what is going on. And once your neighbors find out, they may readily help you with the follow-up steps.

4 MUTUAL AID. If neighbors are willing to help each other but there is little formal leadership, the best first step is to get help from city hall. Your neighborhood needs expertise. Neighbors may develop leadership skills eventually, but in the meantime having a pipeline to city hall can be a good holding pattern.

5 PRIVATISM. If your neighbors put a premium on privacy, it is difficult to develop a base for collective action. Media advertising is an effective first step, followed by efforts to mobilize neighborhood people through the community groups they belong to.

6 INSULATION. A neighborhood that has strong boundaries because of language, ethnicity or other insulating factors often has greater strength in resisting change than in anticipating neighborhood problems. A good first strategy is the personal approach, door-to-door canvassing. Without some initial icebreaking, you may find that your actions will meet with stiff resistance, particularly if you are not a long-time resident.

7 CONNECTIONS. If your neighbors have many ties to outside groups, your first task is to reach them through these groups. This approach is often more effective than publishing a newsletter or advertising in the media. Setting up a pipeline to city hall could be redundant, since your neighbors probably have connections there already.

8 TURNOVER. In a neighborhood where residents move in and out frequently, the would-be activist has overwhelming problems. A good initial tactic is to publish a newsletter to let newcomers have some idea of what is going on and to remind long-time residents that the neighborhood does have some community. Setting up a grassroots group comprised of newcomers and oldtimers is a good follow-up tactic.

—Donald I. Warren and
Rachelle B. Warren

---

into one of six types. In all cases, we have respected the privacy of the neighborhoods we have studied and have therefore assigned them pseudonyms.

INTEGRAL • An ad in a suburban newspaper brought us to Rolling Acres's annual two-day street sale. Like the sale, the relationships we saw on display were temporary. Normally, neither fences, dogs, nor people are visible, yet an unseen organization works to keep each bush and shrub well-groomed.

The mayor, city council members, and leaders of many civic groups live in Rolling Acres, providing a firm link to the city. Yet the neighborhood stands alone, proud of its uniqueness, its own newspaper, and its "Home-Improvement Association," which keeps the bushes in line. This is a neighborhood we rate as responding "yes" to the questions of identity, interaction, and linkage to the outside.

PAROCHIAL • Oakdale elementary-school district was dense with activity the day we strolled through its streets. This long-established suburban city is white, working class, and isolated.

On the warm afternoon of our visit, men just released from their day shifts in the auto factories stood in knots of five or six, drinking beer and watching neighborhood kids play ball in the streets. Nearby, neighbors worked together to complete a house addition while sidewalk superintendents offered unsolicited advice. Many people greeted us with "nice day" or "how 'ya doing" as we passed by.

Although people in a parochial neighborhood interact frequently, and feel very much a part of the area, they are isolated from the outside community; "we take care of our own" is the prevailing sentiment.

DIFFUSE • Four youths pummel a tetherball temporarily lashed to a street sign, while down the block a group of teenagers offer advice to two young men working on a dragster. Rosegarden Homes sits on the periphery of Detroit, in a working-class neighborhood distinguished by its sameness of homes, children and attitudes.

People we meet talk freely about national and statewide issues, and Walter Cronkite is closer to them than their next-door neighbor. People are friendly, acknowledging us with a "Hi," but place a premium on privacy. Neighbors have a good deal in common, but they share very little; most say they would go to their family, rather than their neighbors, for aid. Like most diffuse neighborhoods, people clearly identify with the community, but they have little interaction with each other, and feel little connection with the outside community.

STEPPING-STONE • Moving vans are a permanent part of the landscape in the Pembleton-elementary-school district, where the dominant housing style is modified house trailer, temporary living quarters for the white-collar workers at nearby auto companies.

The neighborhood is open and friendly; old residents greet newcomers with a veritable Welcome Wagon of goodies, written materials, and smiles.

A young man distributing campaign literature thought it was a wonderful place: "Man, this is a great neighborhood for getting things done. There may be a new crop (of residents) every four years, but they sure jump right in." Stepping-stone communities are usually that way, as a result of the close interaction between people and their ties to the larger community. The transient nature of the neighborhood, however, means that people often don't feel a strong connection to that particular area.

TRANSITORY • We saw the same unique pattern repeated at house after house: two chairs—never three or four—strategically placed on small front porches so that it was impossible for passersby to pause on the stoop for conversation. Centered amidst the ubiquitous cyclone fences that separate property lines are license-plate-sized "beware-of-dog" and "no-trespassing" signs. Here and there an abandoned, overturned tricycle gives evidence of the children who were permitted to play outside in the bleak, cold setting.

There is neither interaction nor community identification in this type of neighborhood. As we walked down the barren streets on a sunny afternoon, neighbors peered from their windows, and disappeared if our eyes met. We were never invited into homes, and our occasional backyard interviews revealed widespread distrust within the neighborhood. "No one cares," the Welcome-Wagon lady told us.

ANOMIC • These neighborhoods are al-

WHEN PEOPLE NEED HELP, WHERE DO THEY GO? To neighbors or to outside agencies? The answer varies with the type of neighborhood they live in, according to a study carried out in 43 Detroit-area neighborhoods.

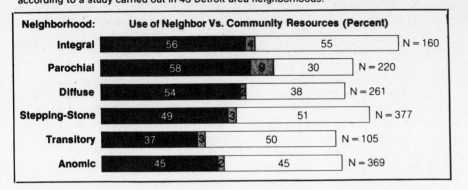

Neighborhood:	Use of Neighbor Vs. Community Resources (Percent)		
Integral	56	4	55	N = 160
Parochial	58	9	30	N = 220
Diffuse	54	2	38	N = 261
Stepping-Stone	49	3	51	N = 377
Transitory	37	3	50	N = 105
Anomic	45	2	45	N = 369

Black portion at left of each bar graph represents percent of persons in each type of neighborhood who used neighbors for at least five of seven kinds of aid, ranging from keeping an eye on children playing to organizing protest against some city action. Mutual aid is highest in the parochial neighborhood, lowest in transitory.

White portion at right shows use of outside agencies for such services as health care, family counseling, police, recreation, employment. Use is highest in integral neighborhood, lowest in diffuse.

Shaded portion in middle represents a third pattern—where neighbor goes to neighbor for referral to outside source. This happens most in parochial neighborhood, least in diffuse.

Total length of each bar shows how much in total resources each neighborhood draws upon. Integral neighborhood is highest, diffuse and transitory lowest.

most ephemeral, consisting of a lack of everything. There is little interaction between the residents, most of whom don't feel a part of the community, and few of whom engage in any activities outside the neighborhood. These communities are extreme. Some, like Skyview, consist of luxury condominiums where our inquiries met with suspicion and silence. A few people explained the community's attitude as "We don't like people nosing into our business."

A short drive carried us to a neighborhood in Detroit's inner city, where the burned and boarded remains of four-flat residences provided a stark contrast to the previous buildings. Yet here, too, people were isolated and uninterested. We stopped a postman and asked the meaning of a small orange and black sign in some of the nearby house windows. "I don't know," he said, "that's not my block, anyway."

Odds Against Success. Our memories of the neighborhoods are clear, and the first impressions significant. But there is an important lesson for the novice interested in neighborhood observation or citizen action; these vignettes represent initial impressions and points of entry. One must go beyond the windshield survey and casual walking tour in the final analysis.

Mrs. Wagner had the misfortune to move from a parochial to an anomic neighborhood. In the anomic neighborhood, the odds are weighted heavily against the success of any kind of neighborhood action—although, as we shall see later, the anomic neighborhood is by no means unreceptive to certain types of influence.

Although our typology cuts across social-class, income and ethnic lines, the residents' social characteristics do influence the organizational pattern. For example, the integral neighborhood is more prevalent among the more affluent residents of urban communities. These

people have the jobs, the group contacts, and the access routes to power that are often lacking in middle- and lower-income groups. At the same time, our studies show that not all of the higher-income families live in integral neighborhoods. Many of them live in anomic or parochial neighborhoods.

Another important factor is the rate at which families move into and out of a neighborhood. The stepping-stone and transitory neighborhoods in particular have a high turnover. So does the integral neighborhood. But this factor by itself need not shape the organizational structure. Some neighborhoods can and often do find ways to get people involved quickly in local activities. Others put up barriers to new arrivals if they are considered deviant in some way or simply not "old-timers."

While structural factors are important in understanding how neighborhoods function, it is also necessary to examine the process of influence that goes on. Every neighborhood is in reality an information-processing center, either keeping information out, absorbing it uncritically, or filtering its content by providing various interpreters to control the way individual residents evaluate the meaning of the information. It is no accident that *community* and *communication* share the same Latin root, *communitas*.

Three Brands of Activist. Several of our colleagues at the University of Michigan recently studied the communication patterns in two medium-sized Midwestern communities. We included questions in their study that allowed us to take a systematic look at how neighborhoods affect the flow of information. We first grouped people on the basis of our six-fold typology, then looked at how much time they spent watching television and reading newspapers, how many people in local government or business or key commu-

nity people they knew, how often they talked with friends and neighbors about the things they read or watched on TV, and to what extent they relied on a neighbor to interpret events in the world around them.

Before examining how this process works in the six neighborhood types, it is necessary to point out that our research distinguished three breeds of neighborhood activist. All three types figure importantly in the neighborhood information process. There are officers in various kinds of voluntary organizations, such as block clubs and PTAs. There are less visible people who belong to no formal organizations but who have a reputation for getting things done. And there are "opinion leaders," people who are approached frequently by their neighbors for advice about a particular problem or for information about where to get help.

Now let us look again at our six neighborhood types, this time with a view to understanding how each one functions or fails to function.

INTEGRAL • This neighborhood is like a vast radar network. It picks up resources and information from many outside points. Residents have influential jobs and links with many kinds of community groups. At the same time they are active within their neighborhood. Thus they are able to bring new information and techniques into the neighborhood and to let outside institutions, such as city government or professional groups, know what people in their neighborhood are thinking. In this way they can heighten the sensitivities of outsiders to the concerns of their neighbors. These "linking persons" have a real power base. They can get outside organizations to act consistently with their own goals without actually taking over those organizations and without the necessity of setting up similar groups in their own neighborhood. The leader's main job in the integral neighborhood is to carry messages from local residents to outside organizations and back again.

PAROCHIAL • In many ways the structure is identical to that of the integral neighborhood. People interact often and have a network of neighborhood groups. But unlike the integral neighborhood, it faces inward. Information seldom passes directly into the neighborhood; it is filtered and modified by key opinion leaders. These leaders have strong commitments to their neighborhood but are less likely than integral leaders to transmit to their neighborhood the concerns of the larger community. The main job of the activist in the parochial neighborhood is to protect the neighborhood against outside influences that are not consistent with the neighborhood's norms while, at the same time, interpreting to residents what the outside world is doing.

DIFFUSE • Residents identify with this neighborhood because they find it a pleasant place to live; but they seldom get together and do not depend on the neighborhood as a basis for shaping or protecting their lifestyle. Information flows slowly, and the neighborhood is often relatively slow in taking action even though there is a great deal of organizational potential.

Only under conditions of crisis does this neighborhood become organizationally active. Once galvanized, neighbors often find a new sense of solidarity but it may not last long. Although there is no rigid boundary between the neighborhood and the outside world, neither is there any institution to facilitate the flow of information. Outsiders who try to set up programs in this neighborhood may be surprised at the low level of acceptance; it feels cold. Basically, this is an underdeveloped neighborhood, in the sense that neighbors do not rely on each other for aid and support but go directly to outside sources. The activist in this neighborhood usually works primarily with outside groups and only secondarily acts as a carrier of messages to the neighborhood.

STEPPING-STONE • This neighborhood is somewhat like the integral neighborhood in that it has a high degree of internal organization as well as a large number of residents with outside connections. But the residents have no strong commitment to the neighborhood. Often they are mobicentric young executives who move in to be close to the job but who move out again for the next job. The neighborhood

usually has formal mechanisms to integrate new residents quickly. As soon as their bags are unpacked, a welcoming committee greets them and tells them about neighborhood groups they may join. But residents usually continue to be more active in outside than in local groups. The activist uses neighborhood groups mainly as a training ground for community leadership.

TRANSITORY • The population turnover is so great and the institutional fabric so restricted that there is little action in this neighborhood. It often breaks down into cliques of long-time residents who belong to the same groups and never allow newcomers in. Neighbors feel they have little in common and usually avoid local entanglements. There may be pockets of intense activity but there is no cohesion. Individual activists have their own constituencies and seldom know each other. Local groups often are dominated by people who are members of outside groups and have literally taken over a local leadership function. These leaders usually become inactive when their constituents move on.

ANOMIC • This neighborhood has virtually no leadership structure. A few residents may have connections to outside groups but remain inactive on their home turf. Individuals and families are on their own, confronting outside institutions without any kind of support from their neighbors. If they are affluent, they may be isolated in their condominiums and enjoy their anonymity. If they are poor, they will find little help in solving their problems. Usually they are distrustful of outside groups but almost never can they get help or guidance from anyone in their neighborhood. There simply aren't any local opinion leaders or recognized activists. The residents are large consumers of the mass media, and the messages come through unfiltered. Any leadership role is strictly an individual action.

Larger Lessons. Our examination of neighborhood structure and process provides a useful, systematic description of neighborhood life in America's urban areas. We have used it over the years to study rioting patterns, alienation, energy conservation, response to mass-media influence, and mental health in many communities. We are certain that other social scientists will find it to be a much more useful tool than the stereotyped, one-dimensional views of neighborhoods that

have guided them in the past. Important Federal programs, such as Urban Renewal, Model Cities, and the now-fashionable community-development efforts, are all based on inadequate definitions of neighborhood—a fact that may help explain their failures.

Our research also can be put to practical use, providing guidelines for anyone who wants to organize a neighborhood for action [see "Different Strokes for Different Neighborhoods," *AE page 63*].

But it also provides some larger lessons, for the survival of democracy depends in large measure on the quality of political and social life in one's own neighborhood. These microworlds very often are the training ground of future political leaders as well as the crucible in which most people confront the often prodigious problems of our urban culture.

Totalitarian systems of the 20th century have achieved success not through the ideological appeals they have put forth but through their control over the neighborhood life of individuals. The Nazis, for example, systematically destroyed voluntary organizations and neighborhood forces outside the Party. The dangers of "mass society," where individuals are manipulated by the mass media and become ready adherents to totalitarian causes, have always seemed to present a distorted picture of modern society. And it is true that most of the neighborhood types we have examined seem strong enough to resist such manipulations.

And yet in the anomic neighborhood we have the prototypical setting for such processes to achieve a frightening reality. Our research shows that people in anomic neighborhoods are the highest consumers of mass media, watching more hours of television per day than the other neighborhoods and relying to a far greater degree on the mass media than on friends and neighbors for advice and information. The anomic neighborhood has little protection from media manipulation; it lacks opinion filters to "check out" rumors or mass-media appeals.

Franklin D. Roosevelt, who led the nation's fight against fascism in the Second World War, once said that "If there are remoter nations that wish us not good but ill, they know that we are strong; they know that we can and will defend our neighborhoods." Doubtlessly the statement still holds true. But, as we have seen, some of our urban neighborhoods are ill-fitted to defend themselves.

Anonymity and Neighboring in an Urban, High-Rise Complex

Jacqueline M. Zito

Jacqueline M. Zito is on the faculty of the Columbia University school of medicine and research associate on a study of a community center for health assistance. Her major interests are in the areas of the sociology of medicine and psychiatry.

A GOOD DEAL HAS BEEN WRITTEN about such distinctive urban areas as the racial ghetto and the ethnic enclave but little attention has been paid to an equally distinctive urban living space—the high-rise, multi-building complex of "middle-class" apartment-dwellers. Non-residents tend to deplore the alleged anonymity and isolation of life in these places that supposedly combine minimum living space with maximum social distance. Big-city apartment dwellers are said not only not to know their neighbors, but not to care to know them.

This study attempts to ascertain the extent and nature of interaction among tenants in one such apartment complex. It finds that, in keeping with the prevailing cliches, social relations in this particular apartment complex were characterized by a high degree of anonymity and social isolation. There was also a pervasive ignorance about neighbors as well as little inclination to establish friendly relations with fellow residents.

In order to ascertain the nature of social relationships in such an apartment complex, one must seek answers to the following questions: How do people actually define "neighbor" and what is the ecology of a social "neighborhood" in a high-rise complex? Are neighborly and friendly relations sought and found among people within the project or found elsewhere? If they are sought among fellow residents, are these friendly relationships easily established? Furthermore, what is the nature of these neighborly relations and "neighboring patterns" in a high-rise complex? Does architecture help or hinder sociability, and to what extent does physical propinquity encourage or discourage social relations? Stated alternatively, the major areas of inquiry are: (1) the extent of anonymity and isolation within an urban high-rise complex; (2) the degree and nature of social contacts among residents, particularly within and outside the complex; (3) the nature of sociability among neighbors; (4) the ecology of social relations (that is, the definition of a social "neighborhood" in a high-rise complex); and (5) the influence of architecture on sociability and the effect of physical propinquity on social relations.

_____
AUTHOR'S NOTE: I am grateful to Professor Herbert Gans for suggestions on conceptualization and for his interest in the study.

"Anonymity and Neighboring in an Urban, High-Rise Complex," by Jacqueline M. Zito is reprinted from *Urban Life and Culture* Vol. 3, No. 3 (October 1974) pp. 243-263 by permission of the Publisher, Sage Publications, Inc.

67

SETTING

The complex, here called Manhattan Towers, occupies four full city blocks. Its eight, 29-story buildings contain 4,000 apartments housing 12,000 residents. The buildings, identical in appearance, are not only tall, but also wide and narrow. On each floor, sixteen apartments open off a hall corridor running the width of each building.

Entering through the revolving doors centered in front of each building, one finds oneself in a large, sparsely furnished lobby containing a scattering of potted plants. A carpeted area with a low table and several chairs is set against a wall decorated with a mosaic or, in some buildings, a mirror. The carpeted seating area often serves as a meeting place for residents, especially for elderly and retired tenants. Several doctors' offices are on each main floor. In one building, there is also a beauty salon; in another, a boutique; in a third, an art gallery.

Manhattan Towers was completed eleven years ago, requiring two years of construction. It was one of the first such multi-building complexes constructed on the West Side of Manhattan. Confronted by financial problems even during construction, the owners not only offered lower rents than for comparable apartments on the more fashionable East Side, but, as further inducement, offered one month rent-free. Currently, the rents remain somewhat lower than equivalent-sized apartments on the East Side. However, apartments are now in demand, as indicated by a lengthy waiting list.

The apartments range in size from "studios" (combination living room and sleeping area) to three-bedroom. Balconies are part of some studio and one-bedroom units and most of the two- and three-bedroom apartments.

Manhattan Towers offers a tailor and cleaning service for each building, plus outdoor and indoor parking (garage), cable T.V., the usual laundry-room facilities and housekeeping services. Maintenance services—heating, air-conditioning, plumbing, and so forth—are rather efficiently and swiftly provided by management. A pre-school day center designed for children of working parents has recently been added and there is 24-hour doorman service for each building, as well as two security guards on duty around the clock. The neatly kept grounds around the complex include a mall, consisting of some trees and benches, as well as several playground areas.

Manhattan Towers' rental agents call it a "middle-class, high-rise residential community." The majority of tenants are middle-aged (between 40 and 65), married, and Jewish, their incomes ranging from $15,000 to $30,000. Approximately twenty-five percent earn over $30,000. Almost a third of those sampled were college professors, physicians, lawyers or corporate executives. About 80% of the tenants are married; another 15% are retired or widowed; the remaining 5% are single. Most of the married couples are either childless or their children are grown and no longer live with them. About one-fourth have children and about 50% of this group have small, pre-school age children. Most children go to private schools.

The dearth of teenagers in the building reflects the mobility pattern of tenants. Newly married, childless couples move in, live here while their children are young, then move away as their children get older (usually during their elementary-school years if they have not already done 'so before they begin school). The few such couples that do not depart are usually those whose profession and personal tastes require living in a large, cosmopolitan city.

Older married couples very often move in after their children are grown and remain here, thinking of Manhattan Towers as a permanent home. This is also true of older retired people. On the other hand, younger, single tenants are the most transient residents, usually moving after a few years.

During the day, maids are a common sight in elevators, mailrooms, laundry rooms and play areas. A fair number of the tenants are known to the general public, being writers, news commentators, and entertainers (musicians, actors, actresses, dancers, etc.). In addition, there are a large number of foreign residents: it is not uncommon to hear Chinese, French, German or Hebrew spoken in elevators and public areas.

METHODOLOGY

This study employs three techniques of data collection: open-ended personal interviews, mail questionnaires, and participant observation. Originally, a personal interview was planned with a random sample of 50 residents but in pretesting, many obstacles were encountered. It was often difficult to elicit innocuous information, even when talking through a door; gaining entrance to apartments in order to interview tenants was almost impossible. Moreover, intervening circumstances made matters worse: a week after I began my study, a young woman was raped in her apartment. Several days later, a couple returning home late one evening suprised burglars; the wife was beaten and the husband murdered.

These events made tenants wary of strangers and unwilling to cooperate with personal interviewing. Having completed only 19 interviews, the personal interview schedule was then revised into a mail questionnaire. Using "apartment" as the sampling unit, 20% of the apartments in one building (that is, 90 apartments) were randomly sent questionnaires. The return rate was 73.3%. Income and educational levels appear to have had no effect on returns.

The third source of data was participant observation throughout the building complex and the immediate neighborhood, including elevators, laundry rooms, local stores, and so forth.

SATISFACTION AND SOCIAL COMPOSITION

Reasons for Choosing to Live at Manhattan Towers

"Security" and "convenience" (that is, doormen, maintenance service, available housekeeping services) are cited by over 95% of the respondents as major reasons for choosing to live in a high rise complex. When asked why they specifically chose Manhattan Towers rather than another high-rise project, the majority (52%) mention "reasonable rent" and "value in terms of apartment size" as the prime determinants. Tenants generally feel they have the "best buy for the rent you pay." Locale is the second most often mentioned reason (37%) for choosing this particular complex; Manhattan Towers is near major lines of mass transit as well as a large cultural center. Table 1 describes in more detail reasons for choosing to live at Manhattan Towers.

Perceived Satisfaction with Living in Manhattan Towers

Tenants specify more advantages than disadvantages about living in the complex, with advantages outnumbering disadvantages by 5 to 1. The most often cited disadvantage is "lack of security" (33%). There are also a few complaints about elevator service, and a few younger couples believe the complex "is just too massive for any real communications between people." These complaints, however, are few in comparison to the positive comments reported. For example, while only 2% mention the "view" as a reason for moving in, over half report this as the major unanticipated advantage. The "view" includes a panoramic exposure to the Hudson River and the flow of river traffic—ocean liners, barges, tugboats, sailing vessels, and so forth.

The convenient location (for access to mass transit, work, cultural centers, shopping) and the spacious layout of the apartments are the next most often cited advantages. In addition, one-third of the respondents mention security and good service as positively perceived reasons for maintaining residence.

Using the number of perceived advantages and disadvantages mentioned by tenants as a measure of satisfaction and dissatisfaction with Manhattan Towers' living conditions, we may conclude that residents generally are quite satisfied.

Homogeneity Among Residents

Residents view themselves as being similar to other tenants in terms of religion, cultural background, education and income level. However, they do not perceive similarity in terms of interests or leisure activities. (Another study of an urban high-rise also found that residents perceived homogeneity in

TABLE 1
REASONS FOR CHOOSING TO LIVE AT MANHATTAN TOWERS

	% Response (n=85)
Apartment-Related Reasons:	
1. Value-"best buy for the rent"	52
2. Amount of space in apartments	3
3. Attractiveness of apartment and building	2
4. View from apartment	2
Subtotal	59
Location Reasons:	
5. Easy access to transportation	21
6. Proximity to job	9
7. Advantages of living close to a large cultural complex	5
8. Schools and facilities for children	0
9. Neighborhood	2
Subtotal	37
Other Reasons:	4
Total %	100

terms of economic level, but not in terms of interests [Michelson 1973b: 18].) More than 60% of respondents name more ways in which they feel similar to other residents on their floor than ways in which they feel dissimilar. While other floor residents are perceived as "personally different sort of people than we are," when asked to describe similarities or differences in terms of interests, age, religious preference, cultural background, educaticnal level, income level, and leisure activities, the results are as shown in Table 2.

Only 20% report similarity in terms of interests and only 37% in terms of age. No respondent under 40 feels he shares similar interests with his neighbors or that they are of a similar age. In fact, the under-40 group unanimously perceives other tenants as older. In contrast, tenants over 40 and under 65 years old uniformly feel they and their fellow residents are of similar ages and have similar interests.

The residents feel similar in religious preference (58%), cultural background (56%), education (58%), and income level (61%). Fifty-eight percent of the respondents perceive similar religious preferences. Every respondent who said he feels similar to other tenants in terms of religious preference is Jewish. Every non-Jewish respondent feels he has religious preferences different from other tenants. This may lead us to conclude that there is a perceived "Jewishness" to Manhattan Towers. In fact, most of the names on mailboxes are of Jewish origin, and almost three-fifths (58%) of the sample are apparently of Jewish origin.

Perception of educational homogeneity varies in terms of the education of the respondent (and/or spouse). In every case, those who perceive their educational level as similar to that of other tenants are college graduates (often, college-plus). On the other hand, those reporting dissimilar educational level do not have college degrees. The perceived norm for educational level in Manhattan Towers would appear to be college graduate or plus. In fact, 80% of those surveyed have received at least a college education.

Economic homogeneity is also perceived by residents. The majority (68%) of respondents believe their neighbors have an annual income between $15,000 and $30,000. In every case where the total family income was not within this $15,000 and $30,000 range, dissimilar income as compared with other tenants is reported. Conversely, respondents who have family incomes between $15,000 and $30,000 consistently perceive a similar income level with that of other residents.

In sum, there appears to be a shared perception by the majority of tenants as to what the average resident of Manhattan Towers is like: more than 40 years old, Jewish, a college graduate, with an annual income of between $15,000 and $30,000, and possessing professional status.

TABLE 2
PERCEIVED HOMOGENEITY AMONG RESIDENTS

Traits	% Respondents (n=85)			
	Similar	Dissimilar	Don't Know	Total %
Interests	20	62	18	100
Age	37	57	6	100
Religious preference	58	36	6	100
Cultural background	56	30	14	100
Education	58	34	8	100
Income	61	24	15	100
Leisure activities	16	64	20	100

ANONYMITY AND ISOLATION

Life in a high-rise complex is often thought to be characterized by a high degree of anonymity and isolation. My findings suggest that this is true, at least for the middle-income, urban high-rise project studied.

One young, single psychologist reports not speaking to any other resident in the two years he lived in Manhattan Towers, but he may be an exception. Most people at least say "hello" or nod to some residents on their floor. However, only 8% of those surveyed "could recognize" everyone on their floor, and even fewer (2%) know the family names of every tenant on their floor. Furthermore, while more than half (56%) of the respondents can recognize at least half the people on their floor and say "hello" or nod when passing in the halls, or in elevators, the mailroom, lobby and sometimes in local stores, there appears to be a pervasive lack of specific knowledge about other tenants—not merely those in ones' own building, but also those on the same floor. That is, even tenants who have a "chatting relationship" are unlikely to know one another's occupations or life styles, except impressionistically. Although a high degree of anonymity and lack of specific knowledge about neighbors may appear to contradict the rather accurate perceptions of self-other similarities and differences reported above, this is only an apparent contradiction. Judging from their own rent, tenants have some idea of the income level necessary to live in Manhattan Towers. This income level also connotes educational level and life-style. Furthermore, residents see, overhear, and talk with other tenants in elevators, lobbies, and so forth: conversation, dress, deportment, and age all provide identity clues. Thus it is possible for tenants to have quite accurate self-other perceptions without actually knowing their neighbors.

Many residents are not interested in knowing their neighbors, nor do they especially care to establish even neighborly relationships with tenants on their floor, let alone within the building or the complex. This is especially true of working couples, childless couples, and unmarried men and women. Sixty-eight percent of the respondents report that they prefer to make friends outside the project. Except for non-working wives with young children and older people, most residents appear to do their socializing elsewhere.

People do not move to Manhattan Towers to establish friendships within the complex or to meet new and interesting neighbors. Only 2% of the tenants surveyed say they moved to the complex because they had friends living there. No one claims to have moved in order to make new friends among other tenants. This does not mean residents are uninterested in establishing new friendships; they simply look for them elsewhere—in organizations, political clubs, the local synagogue or churches, or professional associations.

While some tenants (61%) report having one or a few (meaning two or three) friends living in the complex, an overwhelming majority—86%—of these friendships were established before moving to Manhattan Towers through contacts made outside the complex (in work or school, or organizations, clubs, church or synagogue) or through mutual acquaintances. Friendships were not usually established with neighbors or with other tenants in the complex. Neighbors do not usually become friends. While most respondents (62%) may say "hello" or even chat with neighbors, they do not consider them to be their "friends" and most prefer such social distance. When I inquired as to the reasons for this preference, the most frequent reply was the desire for a certain amount of anonymity, and the privacy and freedom it brings. As one tenant states "Cordial relations with my neighbors are all right, but friendships as such are strictly out."

Evidently, establishing friendship relations with one's neighbors brings obligations most residents neither desire nor have the time for. This is especially true for working couples, childless couples, and job-holding "singles." One professional couple suggested that their life-style and daily routines were simply not conducive to cultivating local friendships or even neighborly relations. "We work most of the day, often go out in the evening, have no children and go away often on weekends.

When do we have time to *see* our neighbors, even if we did want to?"

Even if they desired to do so, there are few opportunities for residents to become acquainted. Although half of the respondents say they know someone from another building, these acquaintanceships arise in organizational settings (very often a political club), sometimes the P.T.A. or through a mutual acquaintance; or, if one has small children, from encounters at the play areas. However, if one is neither a joiner, extroverted nor possessed of children, it is quite difficult to become acquainted with tenants in other buildings. One potential "linkage" organization is the Tenant's Association; but it is ineffectual—only about 200 tenants belong to it.

New tenants have little opportunity to meet neighbors or other residents. Informal, get-acquainted gatherings are almost non-existent. Only one couple reported even attempting such an affair. A young physicist and his wife, several weeks after moving in, tried to become acquainted by inviting some neighbors over for Sunday brunch. Their "southern hospitality" was chilled when only two showed up.

Not only are informal gatherings almost non-existent, but knocking on a new neighbor's door to introduce oneself is also rare. It is not the norm for the new tenant, or the tenant already in residence to do this. Almost 90% of the respondents and almost everyone I have talked to say they met their neighbors in the halls or elevators or when coming into or leaving their apartments. However, new tenants may meet neighbors when a problem occurs, such as a complaint about a barking dog or an emergency.

The norm appears to be "benign neglect." Unless a tenant has indicated willingness to be friendly, even a self-introduction is considered a violation of privacy. Nevertheless, some residents are interested in establishing neighborly or friendly relations. Who they are, and how they go about establishing and maintaining such relationships, will be examined now.

LOCALIZED RESIDENTS

A minority of tenants are concerned to establish neighborly relations and make friends. These are the "localized residents," that is, tenants who are at home much of the day: non-working mothers, older people, and some non-working wives without children. "Non-localized residents"—defined as those who are away most of the day, such as single working men and women, professionals and, working couples—comprise the majority of respondents (68%). The localized residents, especially the non-working mothers with preschool aged children, and older people, appear to have more need to find local friendships since they are the least mobile, socially and physically. Small children and old age are confining However, even among this group, the desire for neighborly and/or friendly relations is limited and restricted to those in a similar situation (mothers with young children want to meet women in similar circumstances, old people want to meet other old people). Furthermore, while many such tenants desire more social contact, this should be interpreted in terms of desiring low-keyed companionship, not necessarily close friendship.

Non-working Mothers with Pre-school Age Children

For the non-working mother, especially with young children not yet attending school, meeting other tenants is not terribly difficult. About two-thirds of such mothers surveyed say they met most of their neighbors through their children. The playground areas are the meeting places for mothers. In the afternoon, weather permitting, one can usually find about a dozen or so in any one of three play areas.

Often, mothers meet through mutual acquaintances—who are also mothers. During warmer weather, they usually congregate several (2-4) times a week, meeting at the same playground area or in each other's apartment for coffee-klatsches, while the children play. In colder weather, they meet almost as frequently, but more often indoors, visiting in each other's apartment during the early afternoons. These coffee-klatsches usually consist of two or three mothers, rarely more.

It is difficult, however, to say how much of this type of interaction is perceived as "friendship" by the tenants. While these mothers do see a good deal of each other, the cementing factor in their relationship appears to be children. They rarely go places together (shopping, for example) or take children places together (for example, a museum). They rarely visit as couples and their husbands never get together by themselves. After their children begin school or they go back to work, such visiting and "coffee-klatsching" decreases.

When the children reach school age, they tend to seek out friends more on their own. Friends from school visit and they make friends with other children in the building. Certainly their parents guide their choices, and parents of school-age children may introduce their children to each other soon upon moving in. However, the quality and frequency of interaction among their mothers is slightly different from mothers with pre-school children. While the children may play together almost daily, usually outdoors in the playground, or in the lobbies, and frequently visit each other's apartment, their mothers see less of each other. This is evidently because being older, the need for supervising their play is reduced. While these children are rarely accompanied by an adult, mothers occasionally do take their children to another apartment to play but rarely stay to visit They are seeking playmates for their children, not friendships with other parents (although this sometimes may occur).

Thus, the age and presence of children in a family is an important variable in determining the nature and frequency of neighboring among women. If their interests are similar, more enduring friendships will probably develop. Children, especially small children, may provide more of a need for social contacts among mothers and influence their frequency of interaction, but compatibility appears to determine whether more intense social relationships will develop (Gans, 1967: 155-6).

Older Residents

The older tenants want, and find, friendly relations, usually with other older people. They seem to prefer the companionship of those sharing their social position and condition— retired, living on limited incomes, usually having children and grandchildren who serve as topics of discussion. Apparently, a good many know other residents like themselves, perhaps having a relative living in the complex or in the surrounding area. Once in residence, they meet other older people, usually through a mutual acquaintance.

They seem not only to know many other older people in the building (they always seem to know each other when getting into the elevator) but they also know almost as much about what is happening in the building as the doorman. They tend to chat with anyone who will stop, but most often find mutual friendships among themselves.

Their main areas for meeting and socializing are outdoor benches, certain areas in the playground or in the rear of the buildings (usually the sunny areas), weather permitting. Weather not permitting, the lobbies and mail room substitute. Encounters usually occur several times a week and are devoted to chats and gossip about each other, the building, grandchildren and so forth. The women may do needlework; the men may play chess or checkers. Casual apartment visiting is rare, except among those who have been long-time friends.

Housewives without Children

Non-working housewives without children who remain at home also qualify as "localized residents." These women would like to have cordial relations with neighbors and have established some friendships with other tenants. Their need is not as great as that of residents with children who must find playmates for their offspring, or that of older people who are less mobile than they. They have more difficulty than either group in establishing friendly relations because of lack of opportunity to meet neighbors and the relatively small numbers of persons like themselves. Most childless wives work, even if only part-time, or involve themselves in clubs, organizations, or volunteer work.

In some such cases, husbands are brought together. If the foursome proves compatible, it may meet once every month or two. Such housewives usually get together with two or three women like themselves who are also home all day. This may happen on a weekly or biweekly basis. They visit in each other's apartments, go out for lunch, shop, or attend a movie or theater matinee.

A HIGH-RISE SOCIAL "NEIGHBORHOOD"

If you live in a four-block, eight-building, 4000-apartment complex, whom do you consider your "neighbor"? The residents of Manhattan Towers define "neighbor" as much in terms of "friendliness" (that is, cordial relations) as in terms of physical propinquity. "Neighbor" is not, of course, defined uniformly by the residents. To some it means proximity—18% of the respondents say a "neighbor" is everyone on their floor; 15% say everyone on "their" side of the elevator (which includes half of the corridor). Most importantly, the majority (65%) of tenants surveyed define "neighbor" as someone living on their floor or within their building with whom they are friendly. "Friendliness" is defined as casual chatting in halls, elevator, laundry room, mailroom, lobby, in local stores, and public areas; but, not necessarily, visiting in each other's apartments.

Propinquity is important since residents are more exposed to residents living on their floor. Propinquity alone does not, however, determine if tenants occupying a particular location along the corridor will be considered "neighbors." Were location the prime determinant of friendly relations or the definition of "neighbor," those occupying apartments closest to the respondent should have been mentioned as neighbors or friends more than other tenants.

Although other studies have shown that social relationships are influenced, and even determined, by the site plan, (Gans, 1967: 181; Merton, 1947; Caplow and Forman, 1950; Festinger et al., 1950) this does not appear to be true in Manhattan Towers. Respendents do not mention tenants in closer apartments or on the same floor more often than they mention tenants at the other end of the hall or on another floor; 54% of those surveyed deem as their neighbors tenants living on another floor within the building. Although about half the tenants deemed neighbors by fellow tenants live on the same floor, the proximity of their apartments varies. Hence, while proximity may facilitate social contacts, it does not appear to determine friendly relations or definition of others as "neighbor" (Gans, 1967: 154-9).

On the other hand, observation gives some support to the previous findings of propinquity studies (Merton, 1947; Caplow and Forman, 1950) which have stressed the impact of the "front door," in this case the apartment door. While tenants choose as neighbors residents who live nearby (across the hall, next door, and so forth) as often as they choose residents at the other end of the hall, or on another floor, they define as "neighbors" people living directly across the hall more often than those living in adjacent apartments. There appears to be more interaction with the occupants of apartments across the corridor. Almost three-fourths of the respondents report having "nothing to do with" (29%) or "minimal contact with" (43%), adjacent apartment dwellers. The "minimal contact" was restricted to "friendly greetings" if you encounter each other. But, about half the respondents report they are "friendly" and have more interaction with tenants living directly across the corridor.

The most frequent explanations for lack of contact between adjacent neighbors are dissimilar interests, age gap, or lack of interest in establishing neighborly contact. Only 8% of the respondents admit they are friendly with adjacent neighbors, and even this friendliness was mainly limited to "watering their plants, taking in their newspaper when they're away on vacations, or just chatting for a few minutes when we meet in the hall."

Such explanations do little to account for why residents are more neighborly with tenants in facing apartments. Tenants who *do* have neighborly relations with adjacent tenants and/or with tenants living across from them, were asked why this is so. The most often stated reasons are "similar interests" and "compatibility." However, this is the prime determinant given for all their friendly and neighborly relations. They find the people living across the hall to be compatible twice as often as those living next door. Perhaps, the face-to-face aspect of the two doors being directly across from each other provides more opportunities for visual contact, making it more difficult to ignore the other. Such encounters may serve to impose more opportunities to become acquainted and more opportunities to discover mutual compatibility and shared interests.

NEIGHBORING PATTERNS

The frequency and intensity of social interaction among neighbors (that is, neighboring patterns) in Manhattan Towers vary depending on whether a tenant is a "localized resident" who is home most of the day or a "non-localized resident" away most of the day. Other important determinants of the nature of these social relationships are the presence of children in a family, and the age of the children.

Overall, there is relatively little neighboring in Manhattan Towers. Sixty-two percent of the tenants surveyed report they visit no neighbor regularly, even on a weekly or monthly basis. ("Visit" is defined as visiting inside other apartments.) For many, visiting means encountering a neighbor and being invited inside the apartment to chat, perhaps every two months or so. Of those who say they do visit neighbors regularly, more than half (58%) name only one neighbor (or family); 23% name two neighbors and 19% name three. None reports visiting more than three neighbors or families on a regular basis.

Localized Residents

"Localized Residents" are definitely in the minority of tenants surveyed, comprising 32% of the respondents. They visit with more neighbors, more often, than the non-localized tenants. Among them, mothers with pre-school age children regularly visit more neighbors, more often, than any other group of localized residents, usually about three neighbors, several (2-4) times a week. Non-working mothers with children in school, non-working childless mothers, and older people visit fewer tenants and less frequently. They usually visit two neighbors once or twice a week. The absence of children from the home during the day definitely decreases neighborly relations and sociability among tenants.

Non-Localized Residents

"Non-localized Residents" visit far fewer neighbors and far less often than the "localized residents." Forty-two percent of these tenants say they visit with no neighbor as frequently as weekly or monthly. Visiting is usually haphazard, meeting a neighbor and being invited inside the apartment to chat, perhaps several times a year. (Unless couple visiting is involved; in which case, it is more planned.) Of those who do visit neighbors regularly, over half (64%) name only one neighbor or family with whom they do so; 20% name two neighbors; and 16% name three. No non-localized resident reports visiting more than three neighbors (or families) on a regular basis. For the majority (78%) these regular visits are limited to once a month; for the remainder, visiting occurs every two months.

Visiting is rarest for the single working man and the working couple. They report visiting no one regularly. Most visiting among non-localized residents is among women, almost always among those who are married. Non-localized men, whether married or single, do not usually mingle, unless retired. Couple visiting (except for parties) is rare, especially if both spouses work. They visit neighbors on a much less regular basis. Furthermore, couple visiting involves more than neighboring: compatibility is required of four rather than two and more of a commitment toward friendship is needed. Couple visiting thus usually takes place when husbands work together or know each other, or when wives who are friendly introduce their husbands, who find themselves compatible.

SUMMARY AND CONCLUSIONS

A high degree of anonymity is found to exist within Manhattan Towers, a high-rise complex although tenants are not actually unfriendly to each other. Most report chatting with and saying "hello" often to fellow tenants. But the desire for sociability and friendship among neighbors appears minimal.

Exceptions are the "localized residents," who have more need and opportunity for neighborly and friendly relations with other tenants. "Being home during the day" is apparently a significant determinant of sociability and neighborly relations. This conclusion is supportive of that of Gates et al. (1973) who find that "opportunity to meet neighbors," which is a result of "being home during the day" and "length of residency," is a more important determinant of "neighborly relations" than the "need for neighbors" or the existence of a sufficiently large pool of neighbors.

Neighborly relations, while not totally determined by proximity, are defined more in terms of cordiality and compatibility than in terms of "functional" friendship—defined as depending on people for mutual aid, sociability, companionship, solace, and so forth. Tenants look more toward friends living outside the complex rather than toward neighbors for such relationships. Most neighbors call on each other only in emergencies.

The fact that friendships and socializing are concentrated away from the complex is a result not only of the desire for anonymity (and the privacy it brings) but also a result of life-styles in high-rise complexes. Many of the wives work; their friendship pattern is typical of working men—concentrated away from home, since they are not at home during the day.

Michelson found similar friendship patterns in his study of high-rise apartments in Toronto. Perhaps, as he suggests, this accounts for the "anti-social image of high-rise apartments." Daily routines are conducive to non-local friendship formation (Michelson, 1973b: 19). Residents of a middle-class, high-rise, complex such as Manhattan Towers are generally highly educated; both husband and wife are more likely to be professionals. Hence, friendship patterns appear to be a function of the wife's employment and the general absence of children which combine to create a distinctive pattern of sociability and friendship formation.

Further, it is desirable to consider a latent function of anonymity in a high-rise complex. It permits privacy among the propinquitous. With 12,000 individuals residing in eight, 29-story buildings in a four-block square, privacy and psychological distance between people is difficult, if not impossible to obtain, without a high level of mutual anonymity. If lack of privacy and pressure for neighborliness prevails in such close and crowded quarters, the milieu might well be psychologically intolerable. In a chokingly close, urban environment, a high level of pervasive sociability could be psychically suffocating. Anonymity not only provides psychological distance, it also allows more freedom to come and go without interruption, thus permitting time-pressed residents to maintain their life routines and meet their preferred social obligations.

Finally, while the high degree of anonymity and isolation of life in this high-rise project has been documented, nothing has been said, on the other hand, about the quality of life, as perceived by the people living here. A high degree of satisfaction with their living conditions is reported by the tenants. Advantages outnumber disadvantages by five to one. Furthermore, loneliness appears to be quite uncommon. When asked,

"About how often do you get lonely living here?", all but two families (who had recently come from small towns) said "hardly ever" or "quite rarely." With the same two exceptions, no one feels lonelier in Manhattan Towers than where they had lived previously. About half of the sample do admit loneliness at times; however these respondents are more likely to have fewer ties outside of Manhattan Towers. With the exception of elderly widowers, marital status and age have far less relationship to loneliness than the number of social relationships a resident maintains outside the complex.

The narrative comments on the mail questionnaires and interviews give a general impression of satisfaction and pleasure. These are people, anonymity and local isolation notwithstanding, who are not especially lonely. Nor are they displeased with their manner of life in this urban, high-rise complex. Most lead busy lives. More important, they appear to be reasonably satisfied with their life-style.

REFERENCES

CAPLOW, T. and R. FORMAN (1950) "Neighborhood interaction in a homogeneous community." Amer. Soc. Rev. 16 (June): 357-366.

FESTINGER, L. (1950) "Architecture and group membership." J. of Social Issues 7, 1 and 2: 152-163.

——— S. SCHACTER, and K. BACK (1950) Social Pressures in Informal Groups. New York: Harper.

GANS, H. (1967) The Levittowners. New York: Pantheon.

GATES, A., H. STEVENS, and B. WELLMAN (1973) "What makes a good neighbor?" Presented at the meetings of the American Sociological Association, New York City.

MERTON, R. K. (1947) "The social psychology of housing," in W. Dennis (ed.) Current Trends in Social Psychology. Pittsburgh: Univ. of Pittsburgh Press.

MICHELSON, W. (1973a) "The reconciliation of 'subjective' and 'objective' data on physical environment in the community: the case of social contact in high-rise apartments." Presented at the meetings of the American Sociological Association, New York City.

MICHELSON, W. (1973b) "Environmental change." University of Toronto Center for Urban and Community Studies. (mimeo)

The City Family's Budget

August Gribbin

Urban families must spend significantly more in some places than in others to maintain an "average" standard of living, but wherever they lived, they had to pay more last year than the year before just to stay even, the Bureau of Labor Statistics reported last week.

The agency released data comparing family spending in various cities for 11 standard items bought last year and in 1975. Costs for low-budget families generally rose in the year by 5 per cent, and for intermediate and high-budget families by 6 per cent. Nationwide, the low budget family must pay out $10,041 a year to maintain its standard of living, intermediate-budget families $16,236, and high-budget families, $23,759.

The results are based on the spending required by a hypothetical family consisting of a fully employed husband aged 38, his nonworking wife, a son aged 13, and a daughter aged 8. Outlays go for routine replacement of worn goods, personal taxes, transportation, food, medical care, and the like.

The bureau assumes that wealthier families tend to buy items of generally higher quality and in greater quantity than poorer families. Low-budget families would tend to use public transportation more often than the other groups and to own a six-year-old car. The intermediate family would possess a two-year-old car, and the high-budget family a two-year-old or newer model.

Low-budget families would purchase suits every four years; intermediate and high-budget families would buy better quality suits every three years. The wife in the low-budget family would get a shampoo and hair set 0.7 times a year, the intermediate family wife would obtain the same service 4.6 times, and her high-budget counterpart would buy this service 16.3 times a year.

The low- and the intermediate-budget families would buy 18 quarts of milk weekly, and the high-budget families would buy 20½ quarts. Low-budget families would buy 11¾ pounds of meat, poultry, and fish a week, while intermediate families would purchase 17½ pounds, and high-budget families 20¾ pounds.

The table shows yearly outlays required of families to maintain their standard of living in 40 cities and 4 nonmetropolitan urban areas.

Living Costs for Average Families of Various Economic Groups in Selected Locations, 1975-1976

Place	Low Budget	Intermediate Budget	High Budget
URBAN UNITED STATES	$10,041	$16,236	$23,759
Metropolitan Areas	10,189	16,596	24,492
Nonmetropolitan Areas	9,382	14,625	20,486
NORTHEAST			
Boston	11,104	19,384	29,187
Buffalo, N.Y.	10,198	17,175	25,017
Hartford, Conn.	10,601	17,238	24,207
Lancaster, Pa.	9,799	15,685	22,194
New York-Northeastern New Jersey	10,835	18,866	29,677
Philadelphia-New Jersey	10,343	16,836	24,482
Pittsburgh	9,697	15,515	22,418
Portland, Maine	10,412	16,633	23,280
Nonmetropolitan Areas	9,876	16,040	22,105
NORTH CENTRAL			
Cedar Rapids, Iowa	9,702	15,976	23,198
Champaign-Urbana, Ill.	10,564	16,578	24,104
Chicago-Northwestern Indiana	10,380	16,561	23,804
Cincinnati, Ohio-Kentucky-Indiana	9,448	15,708	21,974
Cleveland, Ohio	10,023	16,412	23,486
Dayton, Ohio	9,466	15,101	22,022
Detroit	9,865	16,514	24,226
Green Bay, Wis.	9,626	16,008	23,881
Indianapolis	9,876	15,911	22,586
Kansas City, Mo.-Kan.	9,677	15,628	22,968
Milwaukee, Wis.	10,306	17,307	25,221
Minneapolis-St. Paul	10,085	16,810	24,556
St. Louis-Illinois	9,612	15,623	22,437
Wichita, Kan.	9,816	15,102	21,628
Nonmetropolitan Areas	9,673	14,926	21,068
SOUTH			
Atlanta	9,222	14,830	21,410
Austin, Tex.	8,887	14,209	20,628
Baltimore	10,280	16,195	23,715
Baton Rouge, La.	8,914	14,472	21,334
Dallas	9,114	14,699	21,393
Durham, N.C.	9,600	15,525	22,205
Houston	9,532	14,978	21,482
Nashville, Tenn.	9,102	14,821	21,307
Orlando, Fla.	9,271	14,378	20,878
Washington, D.C.-Maryland-Virginia	10,650	16,950	24,769
Nonmetropolitan Areas	8,828	13,855	19,442
WEST			
Bakersfield, Calif.	9,599	15,004	21,214
Denver	9,765	15,906	23,078
Los Angeles-Long Beach	10,523	16,016	23,977
San Diego, Calif.	10,007	15,989	23,687
San Francisco-Oakland	10,920	17,200	25,315
Seattle-Everett	10,770	16,204	22,935
Honolulu	12,711	19,633	30,086
Nonmetropolitan Areas	9,996	14,627	20,606
Anchorage	16,492	23,071	33,273

THE NEW GANGS OF CHINATOWN

Berkeley Rice

Once the quietest
of ethnic neighborhoods,
Chinatown is now
exploding with violence.
What happened?

THE CHINATOWNS of America's large cities used to be islands of law and order, filled with industrious, dignified adults, and children raised to respect parental and other authority. Not any more. A 10-year flood of young immigrants from Hong Kong has brought a wave of crime and fear. In New York's Chinatown, teen-age gangs roam the streets at night, threatening, robbing, and shooting their own countrymen. In Los Angeles and San Francisco, the situation is less alarming, but still a major problem for the police.

Most of the clichéd explanations for gang violence used in discussions of urban ghettos apply equally well to the gangs of Chinatown. But experts on Chinese culture and those who have worked with Chinese youths say Chinatowns are different from other ghettos, different in ways that present greater obstacles for these kids, and that make their gangs more prone to violence.

Last September, in New York, a shootout on Bayard Street between two rival youth gangs left five members of the White Eagles wounded. In October, a group of eight Black Eagles, wielding guns and meat cleavers, burst into the Wong Kee Restaurant on Mott Street and attacked two 19-year-old Ghost Shadows who had just begun their dinner. The shots went astray, but both victims were hacked up—one critically—by the cleavers. A few days later, Peter Lee, 15, was shot and killed in front of his apartment house on Elizabeth Street by three members of the White Eagles. That evening, two members of the Ghost Shadows entered the men's room of the Sung Sin Chinese Theater and shot and killed Bing Quinn Lee, 19. One

week later, a group of Flying Dragons walked into the crowded lobby of the Pagoda Theater and opened fire on two Ghost Shadows, killing David Wong and wounding Peter Chin.

Those few weeks were a bit worse than usual, but the usual has become increasingly alarming to residents of New York's Chinatown. At least 30 people were shot in gang-related incidents last year, and many others were victims of robberies, burglaries, and muggings by gang members. Elderly Chinese are particularly afraid to go out after dark. As one of them told a reporter, "So much fighting. The young people go bang, bang, bang." Some stores and restaurants have begun closing early. Some restaurants will admit only non-Chinese or recognized customers at night. Streets that used to be crowded and festive until midnight are now pretty quiet by nightfall.

None of these troubles seems to affect the hordes of New Yorkers and tourists who pour into Chinatown every day, nor should it, for the gangs have not intentionally assaulted any lo fon or non-Orientals. So the busloads of tourists continue to parade through Chinatown's 200 restaurants, its gift shops, and groceries.

Chinatown is a teeming section of lower Manhattan whose crowded tenements have housed successive waves of Irish, Jewish, and Italian immigrants. Because of various exclusionary acts and immigration quotas, the Chinese population in New York City remained around 10,000 until 1965, when the quotas were lifted. Since then, immigrants coming mainly from Hong Kong have raised the city's Chinese population to more than 150,000, with 30,000 to 50,000 of them crammed into Chinatown. The estimates vary, depending on whom you ask, and whether you include illegal immigrants. About 20,000 more Chinese enter the U.S. every year, nearly half of them ending up in the New York area. The rest are bursting the seams of Chinatowns in San

Francisco, Los Angeles, and Boston. In New York, they have crossed the border of Canal Street into what used to be exclusively part of Little Italy.

A large percentage of the new immigrants are teen-agers from Hong Kong, where youth gangs have thrived for years. Once here, many of them end up joining the gangs in Chinatown. According to the police, there were no youth gangs in Chinatown before the big wave of immigrants began in 1967. In fact there were hardly any young Chinese, since immigration was restricted to older, single men. The few who grew up here worked dutifully in their parents' restaurants and laundries, and caused no trouble.

Police officials estimate a total of 200 to 250 youth-gang members in Chinatown today, with a few dozen in each gang. All males, they range in age from new recruits of 13 to leaders in their late 20s. Most speak the Cantonese dialect to each other, although they also understand English. None is interested in being interviewed. As one said, walking away from an inquiring reporter, "It's just the Chinese way, man. Don't want to get involved, especially with outsiders." As a Chinatown youth worker explained, "The gangs down here don't go for media exposure like the guys up in the Bronx. These kids are out for money, not publicity."

A visit to the 5th Precinct House on Elizabeth Street produces striking statistical evidence of the recent surge in teen-age crime. Until 1966, the police made fewer than 10 arrests a year of Chinese youths under 21. Since then, the number of arrests has climbed to nearly 200 a year, and most of them gang members. Even that is a conservative estimate, because much of the crime in Chinatown goes unreported.

The gangs have divided Chinatown into their own territories, which change as one gang gains supremacy over another. At the moment, the Ghost Shadows control the most lucrative area, along Mott Street; the Flying Dragons have Pell, Division, and Bowery streets; the Black and White Eagles (recently merged) patrol Elizabeth Street; and the Wah Ching (recently arrived from San Francisco, and called Ching Lee here) rule Catherine Street.

The gangs' principal support comes from Chinatown's flourishing gambling dens. Gambling is a traditionally popular activity among Chinese everywhere, and particularly so in a foreign culture that still offers Orientals limited opportunities for financial success. Chinatown's emporiums, housed mostly in basement rooms along the principal streets, offer patrons a choice of fan-tan, pi-gow, which is a Chinese version of blackjack, and Chinese or 13-card poker.

Though illegal, the gambling dens are tolerated by most Chinese community leaders because they provide a victimless form of recreational vice for the hard-working residents, who have few other outlets. Since the community doesn't seem to mind, the police tend to look the other way, staging infrequent but highly publicized raids. (Some claim the gambling dens buy protection from the police as well as the gangs.) The more prosperous parlors on Mott Street gross more than $500,000 weekly, and estimates of the total weekly take for the dozen or so dens in Chinatown run about $3 million.

With that kind of money at stake, the gambling dens naturally worry about security, particularly the gang problem. To keep uninvited intruders out, and to guarantee that winners make it home unmolested, they hire their own gangs, a relationship that lasts only as long as the gang offers such protection. For example, the Ghost Shadows took control of Mott Street away from the Eagles when the Eagles developed the perverse habit of mugging the very gamblers they were assigned to protect.

In addition to collecting regular payments from the gambling houses, the gangs also run a prosperous protection racket, demanding payoffs from restaurant owners and other merchants for insurance against "gang violence"— meaning themselves. Most pay up. Those who refuse may find themselves robbed, burglarized, or shot. They must also endure groups of gang members who simply sign "Dragons" or "Eagles" on their dinner checks and walk out without paying. Customers of uncooperative restaurant owners may find pieces of bullet-ridden plate glass in

their Egg Foo Young, which can give a place a bad name.

"Extortion is a unique kind of crime," says 5th Precinct Detective Neil Mauriello. "It's not hit and run. It's a permanent relationship. They're going to come back regularly. In the old days they'd say, 'Give us some money or we'll kill you.' Now they ask for donations for their welfare fund, or for bail for some friends in jail. They'll even go out to Chinese restaurants and merchants in other parts of the city, and stick them up if they don't pay off."

Mauriello, 34, and his partner, Detective Phil Agosta, have watched the growth of Chinatown's youth gangs since the new wave of immigrants began arriving from Hong Kong. "Prior to 1967," he recalls, "there was very little crime here, and no gangs. It was a community of mostly old men. There were very few Chinese kids in the schools." Flipping through his thick file books on gang members, he explained, "The new ones are coming mostly from Hong Kong, which is loaded with gangs. But we're beginning to get some native-born members.

"These aren't really youth gangs, like up in the Bronx. Up there the kids are in it for the ego. They care about their jackets, and their turf. The gangs here are real gangs, not youth gangs. They're organized crime. They're not into wearing jackets. They're into getting money. They now have more shootings and murders than any other gangs in the city."

Across the East River in the Italian section of Brooklyn, where Mauriello grew up, neighborhood gangs were also common, but different. "Sure, we got into trouble all the time too," he recalls, "but not for money. We just got into fights with other kids. These Chinese gangs used to just rough each other up back in the '60s. But now they've got guns, real good ones, like Lugers and Walther automatics worth $300 to $400."

The gangs do seem to spend much of their income on guns. When police recently arrested the 27-year-old leader of the Flying Dragons for the October killing at the Pagoda Theater, they found a shotgun, a carbine, two revolvers, an automatic pistol, and a dozen boxes of ammunition at his house and at his gang's clubhouse. "None of this shooting is close up," says Mauriello. "And none of these guys knows any of that Kung Fu or karate stuff. You'll get a couple of Ghost

Shadows and they'll take some guns and go out for a ride, looking for some Flying Dragons. They'll just pull up in a car, jump out, and start shooting."

When they start shooting, most residents know enough to get out of the way, for few gang members have had the luxury of small-arms training, and they are not noted for accuracy. Besides, the shooting is often performed by inexperienced younger members trying to establish reputations for daring rather than precision. This explains why innocent non-Oriental bystanders have occasionally been shot by mistake, because they didn't have sense enough to hit the floor when a group of Chinese youths stormed into a restaurant with their guns.

Mauriello took me for a walk around Chinatown one afternoon to show me what outsiders don't see. As we headed down Mott Street, he said, "You used to be able to recognize the gang kids. They'd have long hair. But now you can't tell them apart from the others." He pointed out several gang members I couldn't distinguish from other teenagers on the streets.

On Pell Street, we bumped into a young man whose brother, an illegal alien, had recently been convicted of a gang murder. On Division Street, we ran into a bunch of Flying Dragons sitting in a green van. They looked nervous when Mauriello walked up and greeted them. He reminded one of them to appear in court the next day as a witness to a shooting in the Go Luck Restaurant that left seven people injured and an innocent woman killed.

For the police at the 5th Precinct, getting local Chinese residents to testify as witnesses or even to talk about the gangs has been a frustrating obstacle to successful prosecution. The Chinese are traditionally close-knit and close-mouthed, traits particularly pronounced among those living in the alien culture of America. The Chinese keep their dirty linen within the family. They consider it a serious loss of face when the parents cannot keep their offspring in line. Because of their concern for face, the language barrier, their fear of retaliation by the gangs, and their distrust of non-Oriental authorities (the 5th Precinct has only one Chinese police officer), Chinatown residents, even those victimized by the gangs, rarely cooperate with the police. The morning after the big shootout on Bayard Street, for example, during which at least 20 shots were fired, residents of the block questioned by the police suddenly spoke no English, or claimed they had no idea a shooting had occurred.

Despite the gangs' repeated extortion of local Chinese merchants, the victims deny any knowledge of such troubles. Joseph Mei, Vice President of the Chinese Consolidated Benevolent Association, the most influential businessmen's organization, told a reporter: "We have no problem at all about youth gangs in Chinatown." What he may mean is that as long as you keep your mouth shut you don't have any problems. If you go around telling the cops you have trouble with the gangs, you're likely to have some serious problems, like getting killed.

Those who try to explain the emergence of youth gangs in Chinatown often come up with the standard problems faced by most ghetto-bound teenagers—no jobs, poor education, poor housing—and these reasons certainly exist in Chinatown. Most gang members there are high-school dropouts, and few can find jobs. They also have language problems, and run up against anti-Oriental job discrimination. Thousands of Chinese teen-agers from Hong Kong are forced to attend schools here with children because they don't speak English. Even if they finish school, they face a future seemingly limited to the narrow confines of Chinatown, with job opportunities mostly in restaurants or laundries. As one gang member asked, "Get an education? What for? I finish high school, I work in a restaurant. So what?"

Compared to unemployment or low-paying jobs as waiters, gang membership looks pretty good. The take from the gambling houses and the extortion of merchants can bring in $1,000 or more each week for gang leaders, and even the younger street soldiers can make $100 to $200. For them, it beats working. They buy flashy cars and clothes, and eat in the expensive restaurants their nongang peers must work in.

To find out more about why some Chinese youths join the gangs and others don't, I paid a call on Sam Cipolla, who runs Chinatown Life, a neighborhood youth center located on the second floor of a run-down building on Chatham Square. A youth worker in Chinatown for 11 years, Cipolla blames much of the teen-age violence on the city's failure to provide adequate facilities for other forms of recreation. "What has the city ever done for Chinatown?" he asks. "Nothing!" There's no park, and no public gym in the whole area. The only public basketball court, on Mulberry Street, is in terrible shape. It has the same cracks it had when I grew up here in Little Italy 30 years ago."

Chinatown Life sponsors highly successful basketball teams, tries to find jobs, and provides a clubhouse with pool tables for those who stay out of the gangs. "We try and stay on top of the kids here," says Cipolla. "We try and get them before they go into a gang. Once they join, you can't touch 'em."

"Why not?" I asked.

"If a kid is pulling down $300 to $350 a week in the gang, what can you offer him? A job in a laundry?"

"The gangs do their recruiting around the schools," Cipolla told me. "They scare kids into joining by threatening them if they don't. Some of the kids have family problems. Most of them have trouble in school because of their language problem, and drop out without finishing. Without a high-school diploma you're not going to get a job. And even with one there are no jobs these days. So with no school, no job, no gyms, no parks, there's nothing else for them to do. The gangs are the next best thing. In fact they're the only thing."

A young Chinese social worker who counsels teen-agers tells how some of them come to join the gangs: "When a young man grows up in Chinatown, he is very conscious of the gangs. If you're not a jock, you're in a gang. If you're not in a gang, you'd better be protected. You better have your friends to back you up if the gangs pick on you. You may not have a friend in the gang, but your friend's friend may be in a gang. And if he's attacked, you should stand by him."

This social worker, who prefers anonymity, feels that the excitement and danger offered by life in the gangs is more important than the lack of jobs or poverty. "Many of these kids could go back to school, or live with their parents, and be comfortably well-off. But they would rather go out on their own. They all have families in this area. It's just that once they get active in the gangs they tend to separate from their families. They will turn to their parents if they need money for bail, or if they need a place to stay, but only as a last-ditch situation, after running out of everything else, their connections, and their friends."

"When they war, they're not fighting against society. They're just fighting the other gangs for power and money. They are very much into American values, with the big cars and the big money. The macho image has a lot to do with it. The martial arts and the street image are very important to their 'face.' It's very much of a peer-pressure thing. Like, 'Wow, you just walked into the restaurant and you shot him.' Their presence has to be known. A gang is not effective if people don't see them on the streets. When they pace up and down the streets, they feel very powerful. They know people fear them, so they just naturally see themselves as the new warrior class of Chinatown."

While the police in Chinatown have occasionally been accused of brutality, many people wonder why they don't just round up all these young warriors and lock them up. The problem with this solution is they usually have no evidence. And often, even when they do, not much happens, and the gang members know it. If a young kid of 14 or 15 gets picked up for shooting somebody, and the police are lucky enough to convict him, he merely gets processed as a juvenile in Family Court, and may not even go to jail. Even the older gang members know they'll only get a slap on the wrist for the first offense. As one local observer puts it, "The street gangs here regard the American criminal-justice system as a revolving door."

Many experts attribute the rise of the gangs to the breakdown of the traditional authority of the Chinese family. Betty Lee Sung, a professor of Asian Studies at City College of N.Y., explains this idea in her book, The Story of the Chinese in America: "Where Chinatowns were once static societies, perpetuating a rural way of life known in the villages of southern China, the new immigrants are mainly from Hong Kong, where they have lived a pseudo-Western, urban way of life.... Many of the new arrivals come with little kinship or geographical ties to the more homogeneous groups from southern China. And they have little language or education to help them fit into American society.... They straddle the fences between two cultures. ... Parental authority, once absolute, has been undermined by comparison with more permissive attitudes in American families."

2. URBAN EXPERIENCES

Sung also feels that the shock of economic reality leaves the immigrants unsettled, and troubled. "The biggest shock to the newcomers," she writes, "is the lowering of their status. In their home villages in China, the overseas Chinese were highly regarded. Steady remittances enabled their families to live in comfort, and above the station of ordinary farm families....Few of the immigrants' families in China ever wondered about the hard work behind the remittance checks. Can you imagine the immigrant's dream of coming to the 'Gum Shan,' the Mountain of Gold, only to find himself doing other people's dirty clothes?"

Another scholar, an anthropologist, has asked, "What makes you think that Chinese youth, with poor housing, social, educational, and economic discrimination, and conflict with a new culture, might escape what the Irish and Italian children went through, or what black and Puerto Rican children go through?"

Whatever the scholarly explanations, the Chinese who have worked hard here for years resent the troubles brought by these newcomers. "Those Hong Kong teen-agers have come over here and spoiled our good name," complained one American-born old-timer. "They think they are better than we are, and refuse to accept jobs in the restaurants, laundries, and groceries. They are not used to work because their families just cashed the remittance checks sent to Hong Kong by the fathers....They don't do well here in school because they have difficulty with the language, and they can't get decent jobs for the same reason....They just hang around Chinatown and idle their time away."

Until someone figures out a way to get these kids off the streets, and into schools, jobs, or some productive activity, they will continue to terrorize the merchants of Chinatown, and shoot up the streets in their attacks on rival gangs. Unfortunately for them, the days of the warrior class are gone, at least in this country, and particularly in Chinatown. Someone must discover another role for them to play.

Bystander "Apathy"

Bibb Latane and John M. Darley

*Bibb Latané is Professor of Psychology at Ohio
State University in Columbus, Ohio.
John M. Darley is Professor of Psychology in the Department
of Psychology at Princeton University.*

*Do the work that's nearest
Though it's dull at whiles
Helping, when you meet them,
Lame dogs over stiles.*

In the century since it was written, this minor bit of exhortatory doggerel has become sheer camp. We have become too sophisticated to appreciate the style—many believe that we have become too cynical to appreciate the moral. Working at dull tasks is now taken as a sign of dullness, and helping lame dogs is no longer much in vogue. At least, that is the impression we get from the newspapers.

On a March night in 1964, Kitty Genovese was set upon by a maniac as she came home from work at 3 A.M. Thirty-eight of her Kew Gardens neighbors came to their windows when she cried out in terror—none came to her assistance. Even though her assailant took over half an hour to murder her, no one even so much as called the police.

This story became the journalistic sensation of the decade. "Apathy," cried the newspapers. "Indifference," said the columnists and commentators. "Moral callousness," "dehumanization," "loss of concern for our fellow man," added preachers, professors, and other sermonizers. Movies, television specials, plays, and books explored this incident and many more like it. Americans became concerned about their lack of concern.

But can these epithets be correct? We think not. Although it is unquestionably true that witnesses in such emergencies have often done nothing to save the victims, "apathy," "indifference," and "unconcern" are not entirely accurate descriptions of their reactions. The thirty-eight witnesses to Kitty Genovese's murder did not merely look at the scene once and then ignore it. Instead they continued to stare out their windows at what was going on. Caught, fascinated, distressed, unwilling to act, but unable to turn away, their behavior was neither helpful nor heroic; but it was not indifferent or apathetic either.

Crowd Behavior

Actually, it was like crowd behavior in many other emergency situations; car accidents, drownings, fires, and attempted suicides all attract substantial numbers of people who watch the drama in helpless fascination without getting directly involved in the action. Are these people alienated and indifferent? Are the rest of us? Obviously not. It seems only yesterday we were being called overconforming. But why, then, don't we act?

There are certainly strong forces leading us to act. Empathy or sympathy, innate or learned, may cause us to share, at least in part, a victim's distress. If intervention were easy, most of us would be willing to relieve our own discomfort by alleviating another's suffering. As Charles Darwin put it some years ago, "As man is a social animal it is almost certain that . . . he would, from an inherited tendency, be willing to defend, in concert with others, his fellow men; and be ready to aid them in any way, which did not interfere too greatly with his own welfare or his own strong desires."

Even if empathy or sympathy were not strong enough to lead us to help in emergencies, there are a variety of social norms which suggest that each of us has a responsibility to each other, and that help is the proper thing to do. "Do unto others as you would have them do unto you," we hear from our earliest years. Although norms such as these may not have much influence on our behavior in specific situations, they may imbue us with a general predisposition to try to help others.

Indeed, in many non-emergency situations, people seem surprisingly willing to share their time and money with others. According to the Internal Revenue Service, Americans contribute staggering sums to a great variety of charitable organizations each year. Even when tax deductions don't fan the urge to help, people still help others. When Columbia students asked 2,500 people on the streets of New York for 10¢ or 20¢, over half of these people gave it.

If people are so willing to help in non-emergency situations, they should be even more willing to help in emergencies when the need is so much greater. Or should they? Emergencies differ in many ways from other types of situations in which people need help, and these differences may be important. The very nature of an emergency implies certain psychological consequences.

Characteristics of Emergencies

Perhaps the most distinctive characteristic of an emergency is that it involves threat or harm. Life, well-being, or property is in danger. Even if an emergency is successfully dealt with, nobody is better off afterwards than before. Except in rare circumstances, the best that can be hoped for if an emergency occurs is a return to the status quo. Consequently, there are few positive rewards for successful action in an emergency. At worst, an emergency can claim the lives not only of those people who were initially involved in it, but also of anybody who intervenes in the situation. This fact puts pressures on individuals to ignore a potential emergency, to distort their perceptions of it, or to underestimate their responsibility for coping with it.

The second important feature of an emergency is that it is an unusual and rare event. Fortunately, although he may read about them in newspapers, or watch fictionalized accounts on television, the average person probably will encounter fewer than half a dozen serious emergencies in his lifetime. Unfortunately when he does encounter one, he will have had little direct personal experience in handling such a situation. Unlike the stereotyped patterns of his everyday behavior, an individual facing an emergency is untrained and unrehearsed.

In addition to being rare, emergencies differ widely, one from another. There are few common requirements for action between a drowning, a fire, or an automobile accident. Each emergency presents a different problem, and each requires a different type of action. Consequently, unlike other rare events, our culture provides us with little secondhand wisdom about how to deal with emergencies. An individual may cope with the rare event of a formal dinner party by using manners gleaned from late night Fred Astaire movies, but the stereotypes that the late movies provide for dealing with emergencies are much less accurate. "Charge!" "Women and children first!" "Quick, get lots of hot water and towels." This is about the extent of the advice offered for dealing with emergencies and it is singularly inappropriate in most specific real emergency situations.

The fourth basic characteristic of emergencies is that they are unforseen. They "emerge," suddenly and without warning. Being unexpected, emergencies must be handled without the benefit of forethought and planning and an individual does not have the opportunity to think through in advance what course of action he should take when faced with an emergency. He must do his thinking in the immediacy of the situation, and has no opportunity to consult others as to the best course of action or to alert others who are especially equipped to deal with emergencies. The individual confronted with an emergency is thrown on his own resources. We have already seen that he does not have much in the way of practiced responses or cultural stereotypes to fall back upon.

A final characteristic of an emergency is that it requires instant action. It represents a pressing necessity. If the emergency is not dealt with immediately, the situation will deteriorate. The threat will transform itself into damage; the harm will continue or spread. There are urgent pressures to deal with the situation at once. The requirement for immediate action prevents the individual confronted with an emergency from leisurely considering the possible courses of action open to him. It forces him to come to a decision before he has had time to consider his alternatives. It places him in a condition of stress.

The picture we have drawn is a rather grim one. Faced with a situation in which there is no benefit to be gained for himself, unable to rely on past experience, on the experience of others, or on forethought and planning, denied the opportunity to consider carefully his course of action, the bystander to an emergency is in an unenviable position. It is perhaps surprising that anyone should intervene at all.

A Model of the Intervention Process

If an individual is to intervene in an emergency, he must make, not just one, but a *series* of decisions. Only one particular set of choices will lead him to take action in the situation. Let us now consider the behavioral and cognitive processes that go on in an individual who is in the vicinity of an emergency. What must he do and decide before he actually intervenes? These may have important implications for predicting whether an individual will act.

Let us suppose that an emergency is actually taking place. A middle-aged man, walking down the street, has a heart attack. He stops short, clutches his chest, and staggers to the nearest building wall, where he slowly slumps to the sidewalk in a sitting position. What is the likelihood with which a passerby will come to his assistance? First, the bystander has to *notice* that something is happening. The external event has to break into his thinking and intrude itself on his conscious mind. He must tear himself away from his private thoughts or from the legs of the pretty girl walking the street ahead of him and pay attention to this unusual event.

Once the person is aware of the event as something to be explained, it is necessary that he *interpret* the event. Specifically, he must decide that there is something wrong, that this ambiguous event is an emergency. It may be that the man slumped on the sidewalk is only a drunk, beyond any assistance that the passerby can give him. If the bystander decided that something is indeed wrong, he must next decide that he has a *responsibility* to act. Perhaps help is on the way or perhaps someone else might be better qualified to help. Even in an emergency, it is not clear that everybody should immediately intrude himself into the situation.

If the person does decide that he should help, he must decide what *form of assistance* he can give. Should he rush in directly and try to help the victim or should he detour by calling a doctor or the police? Finally, of course, he must decide how to *implement* his choice and form of intervention. Where is the nearest telephone? Is there a hospital nearby? At this point, the person may finally begin to act in the situation. The socially responsible act is the end point of a series of decisions that the person makes.

Obviously, this model is too rational. It seems unlikely that a bystander will run through the series of choice points in a strictly logical and sequential order. Instead, he may consider two or three of them simultaneously and "try on" various decisions and their consequences before he finally arrives at his overall assessment of the situation. Since he has no commitment to any intermediary decision until he has taken final action, he may cycle back and forth through the decision series until he comes up with a set which serves both his needs and the needs of "reality."

Second, the bystander in an emergency is not a detached and objective observer. His decisions have consequences for himself just as much as for the victim. Unfortunately, however, the rewards and penalties for action and inaction are biased in favor of inaction. All the bystander has to gain from intervention is a feeling of pride and the chance to be a hero. On the other hand, he can be made to appear a fool, sued, or even attacked and wounded. By leaving the situation, he has little to lose but his self-respect. There are strong pressures against deciding that an event is an emergency.

Social Determinants of Bystander Intervention

Most emergencies are, or at least begin as, ambiguous events. A quarrel in the street may erupt into violence, but it may be simply a family argument. A man staggering about may be suffering a coronary or an onset of diabetes; he may simply be drunk. Smoke pouring from a building may signal a fire; on the other hand, it may be simply steam or airconditioner vapor. Before a bystander is likely to take action in such ambiguous situations, he must first define the event as an emergency and decide that intervention is the proper course of action.

In the course of making these decisions, it is likely that an individual bystander will be considerably influenced by the decisions he perceives other bystanders to be taking. If everyone else in a group of onlookers seems to regard an event as nonserious and the proper course of action as non-intervention, this consensus may strongly affect the perceptions of any single individual and inhibit his potential intervention.

The definitions that other people hold may be discovered by discussing the situation with them, but they may also be inferred from their facial expressions or their behavior. A whistling man with his hands in his pockets obviously does not believe he is in the midst of a crisis. A bystander who does not respond to smoke obviously does not attribute it to fire. An individual, seeing the inaction of others, will judge the situations as less serious than he would if alone.

But why should the others be inactive? Unless there were some force inhibiting responses on the part of others, the kind of social influence process described would, by itself, only lead to a convergence of attitudes within a group. If each individual expressed his true feelings, then, even if each member of the group were entirely guided by the reactions of the others, the group should still respond with a likelihood equal to the average of the individuals.

An additional factor is involved, however. Each member of a group may watch the others, but he is also aware that others are watching him. They are an audience to his own reactions. Among American males, it is considered desirable to appear poised and collected in times of stress. Being exposed to the public view may constrain the actions and expressions of emotion of any individual as he tries to avoid possible ridicule and embarrassment. Even though he may be truly concerned and upset about the plight of a victim, until he decides what to do, he may maintain a calm demeanor.

The constraints involved with being in public might in themselves tend to inhibit action by individuals in a group, but in conjunction with the social influence process described above, they may be expected to have even more powerful effects. If each member of a group is, at the same time, trying to appear calm and also looking around at the other members to guage their reactions, all members may be led (or misled) by each other to define the situation as less critical than they would if alone. Until someone acts, each person sees only other nonresponding bystanders, and is likely to be influenced not to act himself. A state of "pluralistic ignorance" may develop.

It has often been recognized that a crowd can cause contagion of panic, leading each person in the crowd to over-react to an emergency to the detriment of everyone's welfare. What we suggest here is that a crowd can also force inaction on its members. It can suggest, implicitly but strongly, by its passive behavior that an event is not to be reacted to as an emergency, and it can make any individual uncomfortably aware of what a fool he will look for behaving as if it is.

This line of thought suggests that individuals may be less likely to intervene in an emergency if they witness it in the presence of other people than if they see it alone. It suggests that the presence of other people may lead each person to interpret the situation as less serious, and less demanding of action than he would if alone. The presence of other people may alter each bystander's perceptions and interpretations of the situation. We suspect that the presence of other people may also affect each individual's assessment of the rewards and costs involved in taking action, and indeed we will discuss this possibility in some detail later. First, however, let us look at evidence relevant to this initial process. The experiments reported below were designed to test the line of thought presented above.

2. URBAN EXPERIENCES

Where There's Smoke, There's (Sometimes) Fire

In this experiment we presented an emergency to individuals either alone, in the presence of two passive others (confederates of the experimenter who were instructed to notice the emergency but remain indifferent to it), or in groups of three. It was our expectation that individuals faced with the passive reactions of the confederates would be influenced by them and thus less likely to take action than single subjects. We also predicted that the constraints on behavior in public combined with social influence processes would lessen the likelihood that members of three-person groups would act to cope with the emergency.

Male Columbia students living in campus residences were invited to an interview to discuss "some of the problems involved in life at an urban university." As they sat in a small room waiting to be called for the interview and filling out a preliminary questionnaire, they faced an ambiguous but potentially dangerous situation as a stream of smoke began to puff into the room through a wall vent. Some subjects filled out the questionnaire and were exposed to this potentially critical situation while alone. Others were part of three-person groups consisting of one subject and two confederates acting the part of naive subjects. The confederates attempted to avoid conversation as much as possible. Once the smoke had been introduced, they stared at it briefly, made no comment, but simply shrugged their shoulders, returned to the questionnaires and continued to fill them out, occasionally waving away the smoke to do so. If addressed, they attempted to be as uncommunicative as possible and to show apparent indifference to the smoke. "I dunno," they said, and no subject persisted in talking. In a final condition, three naive subjects were tested together. In general, these subjects did not know each other, although in two groups, subjects reported a nodding acquaintance with another subject. Since subjects arrived at slightly different times and since they each had individual questionnaires to work on, they did not introduce themselves to each other, or attempt anything but the most rudimentary conversation.

As soon as the subjects had completed two pages of their questionnaires, the experimenter began to introduce the smoke through a small vent in the wall. The "smoke" was finely divided titanium dioxide produced in a stoppered bottle and delivered under slight air pressure through the vent. It formed a moderately fine-textured but clearly visible stream of whitish smoke. For the entire experimental period, the smoke continued to jet into the room in irregular puffs. By the end of the experimental period, vision was obscured in the room by the amount of smoke present.

All behavior and conversation was observed and coded from behind a one-way window (largely disguised on the subject's side by a large sign giving preliminary instructions). When and if the subject left the experimental room and reported the smoke, he was told that the situation "would be taken care of." If the subject had not reported the smoke within six minutes of the time he first noticed it, the experiment was terminated.

The typical subject, when tested alone, behaved very reasonably. Usually, shortly after the smoke appeared, he would glance up from his questionnaire, notice the smoke, show a slight but distinct startle reaction, and then undergo a brief period of indecision, and perhaps return briefly to his questionnaire before again staring at the smoke. Soon, most subjects would get up from their chairs, walk over to the vent, and investigate it closely, sniffing the smoke, waving their hands in it, feeling its temperature, etc. The usual Alone subject would hesitate, again, but finally walk out of the room, look around outside, and, finding somebody there, calmly report the presence of the smoke. No subject showed any sign of panic; most simply said, "There's something strange going on in there, there seems to be some sort of smoke coming through the wall. . . ." The median subject in the Alone condition had reported the smoke within two minutes of first noticing it. Three-quarters of the twenty-four people run in this condition reported the smoke before the experimental period was terminated.

The behavior of subjects run with two passive confederates was dramatically different; of ten people run in the condition, only one reported the smoke. The other nine stayed in the waiting room as it filled up with smoke, doggedly working on their questionnaires and waving the fumes away from their faces. They coughed, rubbed their eyes and opened the window—but they did not report the smoke.

Subjects in the Three Naive Bystander condition were markedly inhibited from reporting the smoke. Since 75 percent of the Alone subjects reported the smoke, we would expect over 98 percent of the three-person groups to include at least one reporter if the groups had no influence on their members. In fact, the groups had a large influence with only 38 percent of the eight groups in this condition with even one person reporting. Of the twenty-four people run in these eight groups, only one person reported the smoke within the first four minutes before the room got noticeably unpleasant. Only three people reported the smoke within the entire experimental period.

Subjects who had reported the smoke were relatively consistent in later describing their reactions to it. They thought the smoke looked somewhat "strange," they were not sure exactly what it was or whether it was dangerous, but they felt it was unusual enough to justify some examination. "I wasn't sure whether it was a fire, but it looked like something was wrong." "I thought it might be steam, but it seemed like a good idea to check it out."

Subjects who had not reported the smoke also were unsure about exactly what it was, but they uniformly said that they had rejected the idea that it was a fire. Instead, they hit upon an astonishing variety of alternative explanations, all sharing the common characteristic of interpreting the smoke as a nondangerous event. Many thought the smoke was either steam or airconditioning vapors, several thought it was smog, purposely introduced to simulate an urban environment, and two (from different groups) actually suggested that the smoke was a "truth gas" filtered into the room to induce them to answer the questionnaire accurately (surprisingly, they were not disturbed by this conviction). Predictably, some decided that "it must be some sort of experiment" and stoically endured the discomfort of the room rather than overreact.

Despite the obvious and powerful report-inhibiting effect of other bystanders, subjects almost invariably claimed that they had paid little or no attention to the reactions of the other people in the room. Although the presence of other people actually had a strong and pervasive effect on the subjects' reactions, they were either unaware of this or unwilling to admit it.

The results of this study clearly support the predictions. Individuals exposed to a room filling with smoke in the presence of passive others themselves remained passive, and groups of three naive subjects were less likely to report the smoke than solitary bystanders. Our predictions were confirmed—but this does not necessarily mean that our explanation for these results is the correct one. As a matter of fact several alternatives are available.

Two alternative explanations stem from the fact that the smoke represented a possible danger to the subject himself as well as to others in the building. Subjects' behavior might have reflected their fear of fire, with subjects in groups feeling less threatened by the fire than single subjects and thus less concerned to act. It has been demonstrated in studies with human beings and with rats that togetherness reduces fear, even in situations where it does not reduce danger. In addition, subjects may have felt that the presence of others increased their ability to cope with fire. For both these reasons, subjects in groups may have been less afraid of fire and thus less likely to report the smoke than solitary subjects.

A similar explanation might emphasize, not fearfulness, but the desire to hide fear. To the extent that bravery or stoicism in the face of danger or discomfort is a socially desirable trait (as it appears to be for American male undergraduates), we might expect individuals to attempt to appear more brave or more stoic when others are watching than when they are alone. It is possible that subjects in the Group condition saw themselves as engaged in a game of "Chicken," and thus did not react.

Although both of these explanations are plausible, we do not think that they provide an accurate account of subjects' thinking. In the post-experimental interviews, subjects claimed, *not* that they were unworried by the fire or that they were unwilling to endure the danger; but rather that they had decided that there was no fire at all and the smoke was caused by something else. They failed to act because they thought there was no reason to act. Their "apathetic" behavior was reasonable—given their interpretation of the circumstances.

A Lady in Distress

Although it seems unlikely that the group inhibition of bystander intervention observed in Experiment 1 can be attributed entirely to the fact that smoke represents a danger to the individual bystander, it is certainly possible that this is so. Experiment 2 was designed to see whether similar group inhibition effects could be observed in situations where there is no danger to the individual himself for not acting. In addition, a new variable was included: whether the bystanders knew each other.

Male Columbia undergraduates waited either alone, with a friend, or with a stranger to participate in a market research study. As they waited, they heard someone fall and apparently injure herself in the room next door. Whether they tried to help, and how long they took to do so, were the main dependent variables of the study. Subjects were telephoned and offered $2 to participate in a survey of game and puzzle preferences conducted at Columbia by the Consumer Testing Bureau (CTB), a market research organization. Each person contacted was asked to find a friend who would also be interested in participating. Only those students who recommended friends, and the friends they suggested, were used as subjects.

Subjects were met at the door by the market research representative, an attractive young woman, and taken to the testing room. On the way, they passed the CTB office and through its open door they were able to see a desk and bookcases piled high with papers and filing cabinets. They entered the adjacent testing room which contained a table and chairs and a variety of games, and they were given a preliminary background information and game preference questionnaire to fill out. The representative told subjects that she would be working next door in her office for about ten minutes while they completed the questionnaires, and left by opening the collapsible curtain which divided the two rooms. She made sure that subjects were aware that the curtain was unlocked and easily opened and that it provided a means of entry to her office. The representative stayed in her office, shuffling papers, opening drawers, and making enough noise to remind the subjects of her presence. Four minutes after leaving the testing area, she turned on a high fidelity stereophonic tape recorder.

The emergency: If the subject listened carefully, he heard the representative climb up on a chair to reach for a stack of papers on the bookcase. Even if he were not listening carefully, he heard a loud crash and a scream as the chair collapsed and she fell to the floor. "Oh, my God, my foot . . . I . . . can't move . . . it. Oh . . . my ankle," the representative moaned. "I . . . can't get this . . . thing . . . off me." She cried and moaned for about a minute longer, but the cries gradually got more subdued and controlled. Finally, she muttered something about getting outside, knocked over the chair as she pulled herself up, and thumped to the door, closing it behind her as she left. The entire incident took 130 seconds.

The main dependent variable of the study, of course, was whether the subjects took action to help the victim and how long it took him to do so. There were actually several modes of intervention possible: a subject could open the screen dividing the two rooms, leave the testing room and enter the CTB office by the door, find someone else, or most simply, call out to see if the representative needed help. Four experimental conditions were run. In one condition (Alone, $n = 26$) each subject was by himself in the testing room while he filled out the questionnaire and heard the fall. In a second condition (Stooge, $n = 14$), a stranger, actually a confederate of the experimenter, was also present. The confederate had instructions to be as passive as possible and to answer questions put to him by the subjects with a brief gesture or remark. During the emergency, he looked up, shrugged his shoulders, and continued working on his questionnaire. Subjects in the third condition (Strangers, $n = 20$ pairs) were placed in the testing room in pairs. Each subject in the pair was unacquainted with the other before entering the room and they were not introduced. Only one subject in this condition spontaneously introduced himself to the other. In a final condition (Friends, $n = 20$ pairs), pairs of friends overheard the incident together.

Results: Across all experimental groups, the majority of subjects who intervened did so by pulling back the room divider and coming into the CTB office (61 percent). Few subjects came the round-about way through the door to offer their assistance (14 percent), and a surprisingly small number (24 percent) chose the easy solution of calling out to offer help. No one tried to find someone else to whom to report the accident. Since experimental conditions did not differ in the proportions choosing various modes of intervention, the comparisons below will deal only with the total proportions of subjects offering help.

Seventy percent of all subjects who heard the accident while alone in the waiting room offered to help the victim before she left the room. By contrast the presence of a nonresponsive bystander markedly inhibited helping. Only 7 percent of subjects in the Stooge condition intervened. These subjects seemed upset and confused during the emergency and frequently glanced at the passive confederate who continued working on his questionnaire. The effective individual probability of helping among pairs of strangers was 23 percent and among friends 45 percent—but still significantly below the Alone rate.

Pairs of friends often talked about the questionnaire before the accident, and sometimes discussed a course of action after the fall. Even so, in only 70 percent of the pairs did even one person intervene. While, superficially, this appears as high as the Alone condition, there must again be a correction for the fact that twice as many people are free to act.

Although pairs of friends were inhibited from helping when compared to the Alone condition, they were significantly faster to intervene than were pairs of strangers. The median latency of the first response from pairs of friends was 36 seconds; the median pair of strangers did not respond at all within the arbitrary 130-second duration of the emergency.

Subjects who intervened usually claimed that they did so either because the fall sounded very serious or because they were uncertain what had occurred and felt they should investigate. Many talked about intervention as the "right thing to do" and asserted they would help again in any situation.

Many of the non-interveners also claimed that they were unsure what had happened (59 percent), but had decided that it was not too serious (46 percent). A number of subjects reported that they thought other people would or could help (25 percent), and three said they refrained out of concern for the victim—they did not want to embarrass her. Whether to accept these explanations as reasons or rationalizations is moot—they certainly do not explain the differences among conditions. The important thing to note is that non-interveners did not seem to feel that they had behaved callously or immorally. Their behavior was generally consistent with their interpretation of the situation. Subjects almost uniformly claimed that, in a "real" emergency, they would be among the first to help the victim.

Interestingly, when subjects were asked whether they had been influenced by the presence or action of their coworkers, they were either unwilling or unable to report that they had. Subjects in the passive confederate condition reported, on the average, that they were "very little" influenced by the stooge. Subjects in the Two Strangers condition claimed to have been only "a little bit" influenced by each other, and friends admitted to "moderate" influence. Put another way, only 14 percent, 30 percent, and 70 percent of the subjects in these three conditions admitted to at least a "moderate" degree of influence. These claims, of course, run directly counter to the experimental results, in which friends were the least inhibited and subjects in the Stooge condition most inhibited by the other's actions.

These results strongly replicate the findings of the Smoke study. In both experiments, subjects were less likely to take action if they were in the presence of passive confederates than if they were alone, and in both studies, this effect showed up even when groups of naive subjects were tested together. This congruence of findings from different experimental settings supports the validity and generality of the phenomenon: it also helps rule out a variety of alternative explanations suitable to either situation alone. For example, the possibility that smoke may have represented a threat to the subject's personal safety and that subjects in groups may have had a greater concern to appear "brave" than single subjects does not apply to the present experiment. In the present experiment, nonintervention cannot signify bravery! Comparison of the two experiments also suggests that the absolute number of non-responsive bystanders may not be a critical factor in producing social inhibition of intervention. One passive confederate in the present experiment was as effective as two in the smoke study; pairs of strangers in the present study inhibited each other as much as did trios in the former study.

How can we account for the differential social inhibition caused by friends and strangers? It may be that people are less likely to fear possible embarrassment in front of friends than before strangers, and that friends are less likely to misinterpret each other's inaction than are strangers. If so, social influence should be less likely to lead friends to decide there is no emergency than strangers. When strangers overheard the accident, they seemed noticeably concerned but confused. Attempting to interpret what they had heard and to decide upon a course of action, they often glanced furtively at one another, apparently anxious to discover the other's reaction yet unwilling to meet eyes and betray their own concern. Friends, on the other hand, seemed better able to convey their concern nonverbally, and often discussed the incident and arrived at a mutual plan of action. Although these observations are admittedly impressionistic, they are consistent with other data. During the emergency, a record was kept of whether the bystanders engaged in conversation. Unfortunately, no attempt was made to code the amount or content of what was said, but it is possible to determine if there was any talking at all. Only 29 percent of subjects attempted any conversation with the stooge; while 60 percent of the pairs of strangers engaged in some conversation, it was mostly desultory and often unrelated to the accident. Although the latter rate seems higher than the former, it really is not, since there are two people free to initiate a conversation rather than just one. Friends, on the other hand, were somewhat more likely to talk than strangers—85 percent of the pairs did so. Friends, then, may show less mutual inhibition than strangers because they are less likely to develop a state of "pluralistic ignorance."

These first experiments show that in two, widely different types of emergency settings, the presence of other people inhibits intervention. Subjects were less likely to report a possible fire when together than alone, and they were less likely to go to the aid of the victim of an accident when others were present. Is this a general effect? Will it apply to all types of emergency? Are there situations in which the presence of other people might actually facilitate bystander intervention? One possible set of circumstances in which we might expect social facilitation of intervention is when an emergency is caused by a villain. People who fail to intervene in real emergencies sometimes claim they were afraid of the consequences of intervention—afraid of direct attack, afraid of later retribution, afraid of having to go to court. In situations involving a villain, even if one person is afraid to take action, the presence of other people as potential risk-sharing allies might embolden him to intervene. Under these circumstances, there might actually be a group facilitation of intervention. To test this possibility, two Columbia undergraduates, Paul Bonnarigo and Malcolm Ross, turned to a life of crime.

The Case of the Stolen Beer

The Nu-Way Beverage Center in Suffern, New York, is a discount beer store. It sells beer and soda by the case, often to New Jerseyans who cross the state line to find both lowered prices and a lowered legal drinking age. During the spring of 1968 it was the scene of a minor crime wave—within one two-week period, it was robbed ninety-six times. The robbers followed much the same *modus operandi* on each occasion. Singly or in a pair, they would enter the store and ask the cashier at the checkout counter, "What is the most expensive imported beer that you carry?" The cashier, in cahoots with the robbers, would reply "Lowenbrau. I'll go back and check how much we have." Leaving the robbers in the front of the store, the cashier would disappear into the rear to look for the Lowenbrau. After waiting for a minute, the robbers would pick up a case of beer near the front of the store, remark to nobody in particular, "They'll never miss this," walk out of the front door, put the beer in their car, and drive off. On forty-six occasions, one robber carried off the theft; on forty-six occasions, two robbers were present.

When the cashier returned from the rear of the store, he went to the checkout counter and resumed waiting on the customers there. After a minute, if nobody had spontaneously mentioned the theft, he casually inquired, "Hey, what happened to that man (those men) who was (were) in here? Did you see him (them) leave?" At this point the customer could either report the theft, say merely that he had seen the man or men leave, or disclaim any knowledge of the event whatsoever. Overall, 20 percent of the subjects reported the theft spontaneously, and 51 percent of the remainder reported it upon prompting. Since the results from each criterion followed an identical pattern, we shall indicate only the total proportion of subjects in each condition who reported the theft, whether spontaneously or not.

Results: Whether there were one or two robbers present made little difference. Customers were somewhat but not significantly more likely to report the theft if there were two robbers (69 percent) than if there was only one (52 percent). Sex also made no difference; females were as likely to report as males. The number of customers, on the other hand, made a big difference. Thirty-one of the forty-eight customers, or 65 percent mentioned the theft. From this, we would expect that 87 percent of the two-person groups would include at least one reporter. In fact, in only 56 percent of the two-person groups did even one person report the theft. Social inhibition of reporting was so strong that the theft was actually somewhat (though not significantly) less likely to be reported when two people saw it than when only one did.

In three widely differing situations the same effect has been observed. People are less likely to take a socially responsible action if other people are present than if they are alone. This effect has occurred in a situation involving general danger, in a situation where someone has been the victim of an accident, and in a situation involving one or more villains. The effect holds in real life as well as in the laboratory, and for members of the general population as well as college students. The results of each of these three experiments clearly support the line of theoretical argument advanced earlier. When bystanders to an emergency can see the reactions of other people, and when other people can see their own reactions, each individual may, through a process of social influence, be led to interpret the situation as less serious than he would if he were alone, and consequently be less likely to take action.

Taking Action

So far we have devoted our attention exclusively to one stage of our hypothesized model of the intervention process: noticing the situation and interpreting it. Once an individual has noticed an emergency and interpreted it as being serious, he still has to decide what, if anything, he will do about it. He must decide that he has a responsibility to help, and that there is some form of assistance that he is in a position to give. He is faced with the choice of whether he himself will intervene. His decision will presumably be made in terms of the rewards and costs of the various alternative courses of action open to him.

In addition to affecting the interpretations that he places on a situation, the presence of other people can also alter the rewards and costs facing an individual bystander. Perhaps most importantly, the presence of other people can alter the cost of not acting. If only one bystander is present at an emergency, he carries all of the responsibility for dealing with it; he will feel all of the guilt for not acting; he will bear all of any blame others may level for non-intervention. If others are present, the onus of responsibility is diffused, and the individual may be more likely to resolve his conflict between intervening and not intervening in favor of the latter alternative.

When only one bystander is present at an emergency, if help is to come it must be from him. Although he may choose to ignore them (out of concern for his personal safety, or desire "not to get involved"), any pressures to intervene focus uniquely on him. When there are several observers present, however, the pressures to intervene do not focus on any one of the observers; instead the responsibility for intervention is shared among all the onlookers and is not unique to any one. As a result, each may be less likely to help.

Potential blame may also be diffused. However much we wish to think that an individual's moral behavior is divorced from considerations of personal punishment or reward, there is both theory and evidence to the contrary. It is perfectly reasonable to assume that, under circumstances of group responsibility for a punishable act, the punishment or blame that accrues to any one individual is often slight or nonexistent.

Finally, if others are known to be present, but their behavior cannot be closely observed, any one bystander may assume that one of the other observers is already taking action to end the emergency. If so, his own intervention would only be redundant—perhaps harmfully or confusingly so. Thus, given the presence of other onlookers whose behavior cannot be observed, any given bystander can rationalize his own inaction by convincing himself that "somebody else must be doing something."

These considerations suggest that, even when bystanders to an emergency cannot see or be influenced by each other, the more bystanders who are present, the less likely any one bystander would be to intervene and provide aid. To test this suggestion, it would be necessary to create an emergency situation in which each subject is blocked from communicating with others to prevent his getting information about their behavior during the emergency. Experiment 4 attempted to fulfill this requirement.

A Fit to be Tried

Thirteen male and 104 female students in introductory psychology courses at New York University were recruited to take part in an unspecified experiment as part of their class requirement. When a subject arrived in the laboratory, he was ushered into an individual room from which a communication system would enable him to talk to the other participants (who were actually figments of the tape recorder). Over the intercom, the subject was told that the experimenter was concerned with the kinds of personal problems faced by normal college students in a high-pressure, urban environment, and that he would be asked to participate in a discussion about these problems. To avoid possible embarrassment about discussing personal problems with strangers, the experimenter said, several precautions would be taken. First, subjects would remain anonymous, which was why they had been placed in individual rooms rather than face-to-face. Second, the experimenter would not listen to the initial discussion himself, but would only get the subjects' reactions later by questionnaire.

The plan for the discussion was that each person would talk in turn for two minutes, presenting his problems to the group. Next, each person in turn would comment on what others had said, and finally there would be a free discussion. A mechanical switching device regulated the discussion, switching on only one microphone at a time.

The emergency. The discussion started with the future victim speaking first. He said he found it difficult to get adjusted to New York and his studies. Very hesitantly and with obvious embarrassment, he mentioned that he was prone to seizures, particularly when studying hard or taking exams. The other people, including the one real subject, took their turns and discussed similar problems (minus the proneness to seizures). The naive subject talked last in the series, after the last prerecorded voice.

When it was again the victim's turn to talk, he made a few relatively calm comments, and then, growing increasingly loud and incoherent, he continued:

> I er um I think I I need er if if could er er somebody er er er er er er er give me a little er give me a little help here because er I er I'm er er h-h-having a a a a real problem er right now and I er if somebody could help me out it would it would er er s-s-sure be sure be good . . . because er there er er a cause I er I uh I've got a a one of the er sei—er er things coming on and and and I could really er use some help so if somebody would er give me a little h-help uh er-er-er-er-er c-could somebody er er help er uh uh (choking sounds) . . . I'm gonna die er er I'm . . . gonna die er er I'm . . . gonna die er help er er seizure er (chokes, then quiet).

The major independent variable of the study was the number of people the subject believed also heard the fit. The subject was led to believe that the discussion group was one of three sizes: a two-person group consisting of himself and the victim; a three-person group consisting of himself, the victim and one other person; or a six-person group consisting of himself, the victim, and four other persons.

Varying the kind of bystanders present at an emergency as well as the number of bystanders should also vary the amount of responsibility felt by any single bystander. To test this, several variations of the three-person group were run. In one three-person condition, the other bystander was a female; in another, a male; and in a third, a male who said that he was a premedical student who occasionally worked in the emergency wards at Bellevue Hospital.

Subjects in the above conditions were female college students. To test whether there are sex differences in the likelihood of helping, males drawn from the same subject pool were tested in the three-person, female bystander condition.

Two final experimental variations concerned acquaintanceship relationships between the subject and other bystanders and between the subject and the victim. In one of these conditions, female subjects were tested in the three-person condition, but were tested with a friend that they had been asked to bring with them to the laboratory. In another, subjects were given prior contact with the victim before being run in the six-person group. Subjects underwent a very brief "accidental" encounter with an experimental confederate posing as the future victim. The two met for about a minute in the hall before the experiment began. During this time, they chatted about topics having nothing to do with the experiment.

The major dependent variable of the experiment was the time elapsed from the start of the victim's seizure until the subject left her experimental cubicle. When the subject left her room, she saw the experiment's assistant seated at the end of the hall, and invariably went to the assistant to report the seizure. If six minutes elapsed without the subject's having emerged from her room, the experiment was terminated.

Ninety-five percent of all the subjects who ever responded did so within the first half of the time available to them. No subject who had not reported within three minutes after the fit ever did so. This suggests that even had the experiment been allowed to run for a considerably longer period of time, few additional subjects would have responded.

Eighty-five percent of the subjects who thought they alone knew of the victim's plight reported the seizure before the victim was cut off; only 31 percent of those who thought four other bystanders were present did so. Every one of the subjects in the two-person condition, but only 62 percent of the subjects in the six-person condition ever reported the emergency. Variations in the sex and medical competence of the other bystander had no important or detectable effect on speed of response. Subjects responded equally frequently and fast whether the other bystander was female, male or medically experienced.

Coping with emergencies is often thought to be the duty of males, especially when there are females present, but there was no evidence that this is the case in this study. Male subjects responded to the emergency with almost exactly the same speed as did females.

Friends responded considerably differently from strangers in the three-person condition. When two friends were each aware of the victim's distress, even though they could not see or be seen by each other, they responded significantly faster than subjects in the other three-person groups. In fact, the average speed of response by subjects who thought their friend was also present was not noticeably different from the average speed of response in the two-person condition, where subjects believed that they alone were aware of the emergency. This suggests that responsibility does not diffuse across friends.

The effects of prior acquaintance with the victim were also strong. Subjects who had met the victim, even though only for less than a minute, were significantly faster to report his distress than other subjects in the six-person condition. Subjects in this condition later discussed their reactions to the situation. Unlike subjects in any other group, some of those who had accidentally met the victim-to-be later reported that they had actually *pictured* him in the grip of the seizure. Apparently, the ability to *visualize* a specific, concrete, distressed individual increases the likelihood of helping that person.

Subjects, whether or not they intervened, believed the fit to be genuine and serious. "My God, he's having a fit," many subjects said to themselves (and we overheard via their microphones). Others gasped or simply said, "Oh." Several of the male subjects swore. One subject said to herself, "It's just my kind of luck, something has to happen to me!" Several subjects spoke aloud of their confusion about what course of action to take: "Oh, God, what should I do?"

When those subjects who intervened stepped out of their rooms, they found the experiment's assistant down the hall. With some uncertainty but without panic, they reported the situation. "Hey, I think Number 1 is very sick. He's having a fit or something." After ostensibly checking on the situation, the experimenter returned to report that "everything is under control." The subjects accepted these assurances with obvious relief.

Subjects who failed to report the emergency showed few signs of the apathy and indifference thought to characterize "unresponsive bystanders." When the experimenter entered her room to terminate the situation, the subject often asked if the victim were all right. "Is he being taken care of?" "He's all right, isn't he?" Many of these subjects showed physical signs of nervousness; they often had trembling hands and sweating palms. If anything, they seemed more emotionally aroused than did the subjects who reported the emergency.

Why, then, didn't they respond? It is not our impression that they had decided *not* to respond. Rather, they were still in a state of indecision and conflict concerning whether to respond or not. The emotional behavior of these non-responding subjects was a sign of their continuing conflict; a conflict that other subjects resolved by responding.

On the one hand, subjects worried about the guilt and shame they would feel if they did not help the person in distress. On the other hand, they were concerned not to make fools of themselves by overreacting, not to ruin the ongoing experiment by leaving their intercoms and not to destroy the anonymous nature of the situation, which the experimenter had earlier stressed as important. For subjects in the two-person condition, the obvious distress of the victim and his need for help were so important that their conflict was easily resolved. For the subjects who knew that there were other bystanders present, the cost of not helping was reduced and the conflict they were in was more acute. Caught between the two negative alternatives of letting the victim continue to suffer, or the costs of rushing in to help, the non-responding bystanders vacillated between them rather than choosing not to respond. This distinction may be academic for the victim, since he got no help in either case, but it is an extremely important one for understanding the causes of bystanders' failures to help.

We asked all subjects whether the presence or absence of other bystanders had entered their minds during the time that they were hearing the seizure. We asked the question every way we knew how: subtly, directly, tactfully, bluntly, and the answer was always the same. Subjects had been aware of the presence of other bystanders in the appropriate conditions, but they did not feel that they had been influenced in any way by their presence. As in our previous experiments, this denial occurred in the face of results showing that the presence of others did affect helping.

Social Inhibitions

We have suggested two distinct processes which might lead people to be less likely to intervene in an emergency if there are other people present than if they are alone. On the one hand, we have suggested that the presence of other people may affect the interpretations each bystander puts on an ambiguous emergency situation. If other people are present at an emergency, each bystander will be guided by their apparent reactions in formulating his own impressions. Unfortunately, their apparent reactions may not be a good indication of their true feelings. It is possible for a state of "pluralistic ignorance" to develop, in which each bystander is led by the *apparent* lack of concern of the others to interpret the situation as being less serious than he would if alone. To the extent that he does not feel the situation is an emergency, of course, he will be unlikely to take any helpful action.

Even if an individual does decide that an emergency is actually in process and that something ought to be done, he still is faced with the choice of whether he himself will intervene. Here again, the presence of other people may influence him—by reducing the costs associated with non-intervention. If a number of people witness the same event, the responsibility for action is diffused, and each may feel less necessity to help.

Although both processes probably operate, they may not do so at the same time. To the extent that social influence leads an individual to define the situation as non-serious and not requiring action, his responsibility is eliminated, making diffusion unnecessary. Only if social influence is unavailable or unsuccessful in leading subjects to misinterpret a situation, should diffusion play a role. Indirect evidence supporting this analysis comes from observation of non-intervening subjects in the various emergency settings. In settings involving face-to-face contact, as in Experiments 1 and 2, non-interveners typically redefined the situation and did not see it as a serious emergency. Consequently, they avoided the moral choice of whether or not to take action. During the post-experimental interviews, subjects in these experiments seemed relaxed and assured. They felt they had behaved reasonably and properly. In Experiment 4, on the other hand, face-to-face contact was prevented, social influence could not help subjects define the situation as non-serious, and they were faced with the moral dilemma of whether to intervene. Although the imagined presence of other people led many subjects to delay intervention, their conflict was exhibited in the post-experimental interviews. If anything, subjects who did not intervene seemed more emotionally aroused than did subjects who reported the emergency.

The results of these experiments suggest that social inhibition effects may be rather general over a wide variety of emergency situations. In four different experiments, bystanders have been less likely to intervene if other bystanders are present. The nature of the other bystander seems to be important: a non-reactive confederate provides the most inhibition, a stranger provides a moderate amount, and a friend, the least. Overall, the results are consistent with a multi-process model of intervention; the effect of other people seems to be mediated both through the interpretations that bystanders place on the situation, and through the decisions they make once they have come up with an interpretation.

"Safety in Numbers?"

"There's safety in numbers," according to an old adage, and modern city dwellers seem to believe it. They shun deserted streets, empty subway cars, and lonely walks in dark parks, preferring instead to go where others are or to stay at home. When faced with stress, most individuals seem less afraid when they are in the presence of others than when they are alone. Dogs are less likely to yelp when they face a strange situation with other dogs; even rats are less likely to defecate and freeze when they are placed in a frightening open field with other rats.

A feeling so widely shared should have some basis in reality. Is there safety in numbers? If so, why? Two reasons are often suggested: Individuals are less likely to find themselves in trouble if there are others about, and even if they do find themselves in trouble, others are likely to help them deal with it. While it is certainly true that a victim is unlikely to receive help if nobody knows of his plight, the experiments above cast doubt on the suggestion that he will be more likely to receive help if more people are present. In fact, the opposite seems to be true. A victim may be more likely to get help, or an emergency be reported, the fewer people who are available to take action.

Although the results of these studies may shake our faith in "safety in numbers," they also may help us begin to understand a number of frightening incidents where crowds have listened to, but not answered, a call for help. Newspapers have tagged these incidents with the label "apathy." We have become indifferent, they say, callous to the fate of suffering others. Our society has become "dehumanized" as it has become urbanized. These glib phrases may contain some truth, since startling cases such as the Genovese murder often seem to occur in our large cities, but such terms may also be misleading. Our studies suggest a different conclusion. They suggest that situational factors, specifically factors involving the immediate social environment, may be of greater importance in determining an individual's reaction to an emergency than such vague cultural or personality concepts as "apathy" or "alienation due to urbanization." They suggest that the failure to intervene may be better understood by knowing the relationship among bystanders rather than that between a bystander and the victim.

Our results may explain why the failure to intervene seems to be more characteristic of large cities than rural areas. Bystanders to urban emergencies are more likely to be, or at least to think they are, in the presence of other bystanders than witnesses of non-urban emergencies. Bystanders to urban emergencies are less likely to know each other or to know the victim than are witnesses of non-urban emergencies. When an emergency occurs in a large city, a crowd is likely to gather; the crowd members are likely to be strangers; and it is likely that no one will be acquainted with the victim. These are exactly the conditions that made the helping response least likely in our experiments.

In a less sophisticated era, Rudyard Kipling prayed "That we, with Thee, may walk uncowed by fear or favor of the crowd; that, under Thee, we may possess man's strength to comfort man's distress." It appears that the latter hope may depend to a surprising extent upon the former.

3. Contemporary Urban Problems

The urban crisis has become an all too familiar phrase. The difficulties of providing services for residents in a metropolis can be serious, especially since many cities have attracted the poor, the elderly, and those citizens who require special consideration. An important characteristic of urban life, however, is not disorganization but the presence of organization everywhere. It is incredible that thousands of people manage to live closely together only because a vast and complex system provides food, shelter, and work for a variety of different people. It would be unrealistic to believe that such a system could remain unaffected by rapidly changing conditions throughout the world. The strains between the demands for urban services and the adaptability of urban systems has always been a central feature of urban life, but today the strains are particularly severe.

One important feature of American urban society has been the change that has reduced the eonomic strength of central cities. Factories located in the central cities are old. Land costs, better highway and rail transportation, as well as more efficient, versatile communication systems have made it possible to disperse modern industry. Retail stores are located in large shopping centers away from downtown areas. Those in central cities are often faced with demands for help from needy residents. In some nations a strong central government can allocate resources between rural and urban areas. For example, the government of developing nations encourages rural migration to cities for the purpose of industrialization. But in the United States, local governments operate more independently, resulting in intense competition between the cities and suburbs, and between urban areas throughout the nation. These rivalries are aggravated by problems of poverty, discrimination, and economic change.

Cities have become the dynamic centers of education, culture, and civilization. Urban dwellers often regard themselves as very fortunate individuals because they are able to enjoy a wide variety of experiences and enrichments. This view is maintained by many who wish to find ways to preserve the sophisticated qualities of the metropolis as well as resolve the key issues of human needs.

It is important to consider some questions while reading the articles in this section. How can the economies of urban areas be revitalized? In what way does urban growth determine social problems? What are some of the problems that can result from crime, poor housing, and poverty? How can resources be more equitably distributed throughout the nation? Are urban problems today too severe to be handled by each area independently?

The Undisciplined City
In a Resource Short World

Lowell W. Culver

Author Lowell W. Culver, an urbanologist, was a founder of the Tacoma, Washington, Area Urban Coalition in 1968. He currently is University Professor of Public Service at Governors State University in Park Forest South, Illinois.

The U.S. city is suffering from a serious breakdown of discipline, says an urbanologist. Population and economic trends offer grounds for hope, but greater discipline will be needed to cope with the world's rising population and dwindling resources. The standard of living will likely go down, but, in human terms, the quality of life may improve as people move toward greater cooperation and self-sacrifice.

U.S. metropolitan areas, with few exceptions, are characterized by crazy quilts of competing governmental units, undisciplined by public bodies of area-wide jurisdiction or by a regional public consciousness. Many of the separate local units are either too small to provide adequate services or are financially incapable of doing so. Others, due to lack of will or imagination, legal

or structural barriers or incompetence, have failed to discipline their human and physical resources for the general benefit of their citizenry.

Of the some 1250 separate units of government making up the six-county Chicago metropolitan complex, 268 are municipalities, ranging in size from under 200 to over 3,000,000 inhabitants. Half have populations of less

than 5,000; 75 have less than 2,000. Other than the newly formed Regional Transportation Authority (RTA), hobbled initially by political controversy, no entity exists which can act authoritatively for the entire area.

The metropolitan city is further debilitated by the undisciplined actions of some of its inhabitants who, out of greed, mental derangement, hatred,

Reprinted from: *The Futurist* A Journal of Forecasts, Trends and Ideas About the Future. Published by: World Future Society An Association for the Study of Alternative Futures, 4916 St. Elmo Avenue, Washington, D.C. 20014.

personal frustration, or estrangement from life, spread fear throughout the metropolis, threatening normal relationships between people and endangering efforts at developing satisfactory accommodations between blacks and whites. Nowhere is the breakdown of personal discipline, primarily among youth, more marked than in the inner city, where the principal sufferers are the aged, minorities, and the poor.

Crime is a major deterrent to the revitalization of the inner city, not only by jeopardizing the viability of minority and non-minority businesses, but by causing the more capable and therefore more mobile inhabitants to flee to safer areas.

The undisciplined city is an "unheavenly city," a city without direction, where growth is uncoordinated, decision-making is fragmented, and common responsibility for the problems of the inner city has been abandoned. Archaic governmental forms and funding sources continue to exist, leadership is lacking, and personal discipline to a large extent has broken down.

Discipline vs. Democracy: The Urban Dilemma

While man may prove incapable of creating an urban paradise, given the limits on resources and the perennial gap between present conditions and expectations, he will find it essential to create a more disciplined urban environment. The question is whether free men can discipline themselves through democratic processes. Fear, hatred, and civil unrest may so immobilize man's capacity for constructive resolution of society's conflicts that he resorts to the defensive city (in which people are separated from one another by distance, physical obstacles, or armies of police) or succumbs to an authoritarian state with its subsequent loss of freedom for the nation's cities. The period we are now entering may therefore be one of the most critical in U.S. history for the survival of democratic institutions.

Complicating improvement of the urban environment are possible future shortages of energy, food, and raw materials, and a questioning of the country's ability to sustain economic growth and make available to a larger portion of the population the affluence to which many have become accustomed. Greater affluence for the masses may ultimately be possible only at the expense of those who are already affluent.

Some of our most serious problems—increased crime and delinquen-cy, overcrowded schools, generational and racial conflict, minority unemployment, and deteriorating neighborhoods—are a direct outgrowth of the post-World War II baby boom and shifts in population; the dispersed and docile rural poor have moved to urban areas and become concentrated and potentially explosive masses, and it is doubtful that massive infusion of public funds will have a major impact on them. Little of the federal revenue-sharing money is presently being used for social programs. In fact, revenue-sharing may be having the detrimental effect of shoring up non-viable units of local government and thereby delaying the establishment of sorely needed regional coordinating mechanisms which have the capacity to plan and make decisions on such important regional questions as transit, water supply, solid and liquid waste disposal and the location of commercial and industrial facilities. Only in a relatively few instances, notably in metropolitan Portland (Oregon) and Seattle, have regional multi-purpose bodies been established to deal with such concerns. This, in part, reflects the changing interests of reformers who, in recent years, have turned away from metropolitan solutions to those of a neighborhood nature. Revenue-sharing may, however, have the beneficial outcome of stimulating greater citizen involvement in local government affairs.

City Governments Must Modernize

While it is unrealistic to expect a purely governmental solution to all of society's ills, government can still play an important role in preventing a worsening of conditions in the cities. For example, new initiatives are needed in the employment, health, housing, nutrition, and welfare fields. Government must come to grips with the economic inequalities perpetuated by continuing inflation, the present tax structure and the marked power imbalances between different segments of labor and between labor and management. The operation of government, particularly on the local level, must be modernized. As a member of the Washington State Urban Affairs Council, I found that local government in that state was often hobbled by excessive fragmentation without compensating coordinating mechanisms, by ineffective planning tools, by cumbersome provisions for implementing structural change, and by unreasonable restrictions on the ability to raise and spend revenue. Numerous special districts were found to operate virtually under a cloak of secrecy, as "invisible governments." Similar examples can be cited from other states. No wonder the voter has become confused and disillusioned with the political process.

Although it has become increasingly clear that there is no magic formula, no combination of federal programs, no sum of money that will "solve" the

The American Birth Rate

Census Bureau Population Projections for the Year 2000

Series	Assumed Fertility Rate	New Projection	Old Projection
A	3.35	(discontinued)	(discontinued)
B	3.1	(discontinued)	322,277,000
C	2.8	300,406,000	305,111,000
D	2.5	285,969,000	288,293,000
E	2.1	264,430,000	271,082,000
F	1.8	250,686,000	

A fertility rate of 2.11 per family is considered replacement level; it is the level of fertility at which a population will replace itself under projected mortality rates and in the absence of migration in or out of the country. The fertility rate fell below the replacement level in both 1972 with 2.02 children per family and 1973 with 1.9 per family. Census Bureau preliminary figures for 1974 indicate a rate of 1.86 per family.

The decline of the U.S. birth rate has caused the Census Bureau to revise its population projections. In the year 2000, there may be 50 million fewer people in the U.S. than previously estimated. As population growth subsides, Culver believes, cities will be able to deal more effectively with pollution and racial conflicts and give more attention to housing needs, education, and public services.

3. URBAN PROBLEMS

problems of the cities, this does not mean that the future is without hope. Already, significant demographic and economic changes are occurring, which, over the long run, will considerably relieve the pressures on our urban centers and assist in bringing about a more disciplined state of affairs.

Low Birth Rate Offers Hope for Cities

First and foremost has been the remarkable decline in the nation's birth rate. In 1973 it dropped to the lowest level in American history and substantially below the population replacement point, and preliminary figures indicate that the trend continued in 1974. More importantly, the drop does not appear to be a temporary aberration, as it is occurring even though the number of women of childbearing age is one-third larger today than in 1957 when post-World War II births peaked, and during a period of relative prosperity, in contrast to the economic conditions which drove down birth rates during the 1930s. The emancipated women of today have for the first time a real choice in determining family size and are opting for greater material status and personal careers over large families.

The low birth rate is a development of far-reaching importance. It means that, in the future, youth will make up a smaller portion of the population; by 1989 there will be over seven million fewer people in the crime-prone 15-24 age category, which should result in a lessening of youth crime. It also portends a lessening of population pressures on our major metropolitan areas. With a possible 50 million fewer people in the year 2000 than projections indicated in the 1960s, there will be more moderate claims on municipal budgets and on the nation's natural resources, less demand for new housing and capital investment, greater resources for education and public services, less pollution, less prejudice and racial conflict, and greater opportunity to plan for orderly growth than if the nation's urban centers had been called upon to absorb the additional millions.

The consequences for our metropolitan areas are striking. Art Myren, field representative for the Northeastern Illinois Planning Commission, the official comprehensive planning agency for northeastern Illinois, notes that the six-county Chicago area is entering a whole new period of history as a result of declining growth patterns. Instead of the 3.4 million additional inhabitants originally foreseen for the year 2000, revised forecasts now indicate an increase of 2 million, enabling the area to

Ragged Indian school children symbolize widespread world poverty that is closely related to American affluence. If Asia and Africa consumed resources at a rate equal to the U.S., the increased competition for and depletion of natural resources would force Americans to settle for a lower standard of living. Dwindling petroleum supplies already are depressing living standards for many people.
Photo: U.S. Department of Agriculture

buy valuable time in which to establish new parameters, perimeters, and perspectives. Residents of urban regions, he observed, are becoming increasingly concerned with the environmental impact of unrestricted growth, and "quality of life" has gradually replaced an emphasis on quantity and the notion that "more is better."

Recently released Department of Commerce projections indicate that as a result of declining births the labor force, currently growing by about 1.7% a year, will grow by 1.8% until 1980 and then slow to 1.1%. With fewer individuals entering the labor force in the 1980s, the public and private sectors may be forced to hire and train those considered unprofitable in today's labor market. Moreover, the potential for a larger dependent population in the future will create a need for increased participation of women, youth, and the elderly in the nation's labor force.

Family Size Will Affect Quality of Life

Smaller families mean high percapita income, even for the poor. An improved quality of life for many families will be possible only through a restriction in family size. With the threat of future shortages of food, fuel, and raw materials, family size may not

be a matter of choice, even for the affluent. Certainly, with a stabilization of the population, the U.S. will improve its capacity to cope with the period of shortages which lies before it. Hopefully, with the wave of humanity reduced to a ripple, the importance of each and every individual will increase and the nation will become more concerned with quality instead of quantity.

Another factor of change has been the economic growth of the South, which has created opportunities for rural blacks and whites in southern urban centers and considerably slowed their out-migration. The 1970 census indicated that for the first time since 1880 the South had a net gain by in-migration. While well over a million blacks left the South during the 1960s, their out-migration was less than in the previous two decades. Conditions in the northern cities have also made migration a less attractive alternative to rural and small town America.

Resource Shortages Threaten American Lifestyle

No recent development, however, poses at once such a threat for disruption of the American lifestyle and a potential for demanding a greater discipline of the nation's citizenry than future shortages of energy, food, and natural resources and their increasing costs.

The affluence which Americans have come to take for granted has, in part, been possible because of widespread poverty in the world and the ability of the U.S., along with a comparatively few other countries, to command the world's resources at relatively cheap prices. If the states of Africa and Asia had consumed the materials of well-being at a rate equal to the U.S., competing with Americans in world markets and adding to the depletion of available supplies, Americans would long ago have had to settle for a more modest lifestyle. The fact that other nations have not been as wasteful as the U.S. has bought us some time to deal with the problem of diminishing resources before it is too late. Nevertheless, the shifting of enormous sums of money to energy and mineral-rich countries and possible further transfers to developing areas, coupled with predictions for a doubling of the world's population from an estimated 3.8 billion today to over 7 billion in the next thirty years, promises greater competition and escalating prices for most commodities, and the U.S. can no longer expect to be able to obtain resources from abroad in any quantity.

Economic Nationalism Will Be Reborn

Higher consumption levels in the developing countries will eventually threaten the affluence of the industrial nations and stimulate a rebirth of economic nationalism, as governments attempt to insure future supplies of natural resources and foodstuffs for their own people. Canada's decision to phase out exports of oil to the United States is a case in point. Concern for the future will also be reflected in stricter immigration policies on the part of the affluent countries. In the long run, only a highly disciplined society which wastes little, makes maximum use of its existing human and natural resources, and limits its population will have any chance of maintaining a degree of affluence in the future.

Scarcity will make the politics of planning easier, as placement and compatibility of both public and private development will be determined increasingly by energy and resource costs. Products which have little social utility will not be produced. Comprehensive systems of recycling will be developed to recover all reusable materials. Eating habits will undergo a radical change, both in terms of the quantity and kinds of food consumed.

More economical means of transporting people will be perfected. Less dependence on the automobile will tend to increase face-to-face contacts. Near-

"Energy shortages may force the economy to become more labor-intensive, requiring larger work forces and expanding personal contacts which machines have progressively diminished."

ness to amenities will be an increasingly important factor in determining the placement of housing. Energy shortages may force the economy to become more labor intensive, requiring larger work forces and expanding the personal contacts which

"It may prove impossible to bring everyone up to the level of affluence enjoyed by today's average American. Indeed, people everywhere may have to settle for a somewhat reduced level of living."

The American birth rate has dropped steadily in the last decade and in 1973 went below the population replacement level. The low birth rate, if it continues, should lessen the population pressures on the cities and improve their capacity to cope with shortages of natural resources.

Births and Birth Rate per 1,000 of the Mid-Year Population 1955-1974

Year	Births	Birth rate	Year	Births	Birth rate
1955	4,128,000	24.9	1965	3,801,000	19.6
1956	4,244,000	25.1	1966	3,642,000	18.5
1957	4,332,000	25.2	1967	3,555,000	17.9
1958	4,279,000	24.5	1968	3,535,000	17.6
1959	4,313,000	24.3	1969	3,605,000	17.8
1960	4,307,000	23.8	1970	3,750,000	18.3
1961	4,317,000	23.5	1971	3,588,000	17.3
1962	4,213,000	22.6	1972	3,258,000	15.6
1963	4,142,000	21.9	1973	3,141,000	14.9
1964	4,070,000	21.2	1974	3,166,000	15.0
Ten year total	42,345,000		Ten year total	35,041,000	

*Based on preliminary Census Bureau figures. The slight increase over 1973 is attributed to a 2% increase in the number of women of child-bearing age rather than to an increase in the rate of births.

The lowest birth rate prior to 1967 was 18.4 per thousand recorded in 1933 and 1936.

Source: U.S. Bureau of the Census, *Current Population Reports*, Series P-25, No. 465, unpublished data and Census Bureau preliminary figures.

Motor vehicles crowd into New York City, pouring exhaust fumes into the atmosphere and clouding the skyline. Energy and resource shortages may force cities to develop more economical forms of transportation. The decline of the automobile will cause an increase in face-to-face human interactions, Culver predicts.

Deteriorating urban neighborhoods, such as the one in Washington, D.C., shown here, are populated largely by rural poor people who poured into the cities seeking a better life. As their expectations are dashed by the cold realities of inflation, high energy prices, and possible future shortages of food and raw materials, Culver warns, a potentially explosive situation will develop.
Photos: The Urban Land Institute, Washington, D.C.

machines have progressively diminished.

As changing material conditions alter our attitudes and values, we will begin to question much of the waste and personal extravagance which characterizes our present society. Because everyone's fate will be bound up in the actions of everyone else, there will be greater restraint on individual actions, but also greater incentive for cooperative effort.

Ceilings May Be Placed on Incomes

The period of transition will not be an easy one and will place democratic government under continuing strain, as economic groups vie with one another for the trappings of affluence, much as governments on the international scene will compete for the world's resources. There will be an increasingly hostile attitude towards strikes and their use to enhance the economic position of a small economic segment to the detriment of the larger society. Present concern for minimum floors on income will turn to placing upper limits on income. Consumption of non-essentials will be contained by high prices and taxes, and essentials will be kept within the reach of most income levels through a complicated system of subsidies and rebates based on publicly determined allotments per individual or family.

Against the desires for an improved condition for the city's less affluent masses are the growing realities of future material shortages and limits to economic growth. What the U.S. can make of its cities is closely linked with what happens in the rest of the world, the resources that must be shared, and the population levels that these resources must bear. It may prove impossible to bring everyone up to the level of affluence enjoyed by today's average American. Indeed, Americans may have to settle for a somewhat reduced level of living. But if self-discipline, self-sacrifice, and greater human cooperation are the pre-conditions for survival, as they were for many, both rich and poor, during World War II, we may find ourselves better off in human terms than in the recent past, which recognized no limits to economic growth and set us apart as human beings.

Urban Growth and Decline

Thomas Muller

THOMAS MULLER is Director of Evaluation Studies at The Urban Institute Land Use Center, and is the author of *Fiscal Impacts of Land Development* (The Urban Institute, 1975).

Major migrations from center cities to suburbs, and from old industrial regions to new ones, are deepening the urban crisis.

The current fiscal plight of many cities and some states has brought forth an avalanche of "how do we compare to New York City" reports in the media. Fiscal issues, previously considered too dull to gain public attention, have moved from the back to the front pages of local newspapers.

To understand the fiscal situation of our large central cities and populous northern states, two concurrent phenomena of the 1970s need to be examined: the accelerating migration of people and jobs from the central cities to the suburbs and ex-urban areas, and the movement of households and employment from most of the northeast and north central states to the South and West. Both movements, if Bureau of the Census estimates are reliable, have been unprecedented in magnitude since 1970. It appears that the South and West combined will surpass the balance of the nation in population by 1978.

Regional relocation

Since the beginning of this decade, the net movement of 2.5 million persons into the South and West from other regions, twice the rate of the previous five years, has resulted in above-average per capita gains in income and wealth in the recipient states. Since 1973, only two states in the northeast and the

north central region have had net in-migration: sparsely populated New Hampshire (which is benefiting from high taxes in contiguous Massachusetts); and Maine. This is a drastic shift from the 1960s, when Connecticut, New Jersey, and Massachusetts attracted large numbers of new residents. At the same time, all states in the South and West, with three exceptions—the industrial "border" states of Delaware, Maryland, and Louisiana—have been attracting in-migrants.

You owe me ten shillings,
Say the bells of St. Helen's.
When will you pay me?
Say the bells of Old Bailey.
When I grow rich,
Say the bells of Fleetditch.
Pray, when will that be?
Say the bells of Stepney.
I am sure I don't know,
Says the great bell at Bow.

Employment changes in the private sector have been even more dramatic than the movement of people. While between 1969 and 1974 New York had negative job growth, Illinois zero growth, and other northern industrial states only minor increases,

"Urban Growth and Decline," by Thomas Muller, *Challenge*, May/June 1976. Copyright © 1976 by International Arts and Sciences Press, Inc. Reprinted by permission of International Arts and Sciences Press, Inc.

private jobs expanded by 35 to 44 percent in Arizona, Colorado, and Florida.

Among factors contributing to the regional migration of industry, one needs to include technological improvements which have reduced the benefits of centralized facilities, energy cost differentials, and lower wages for industrial workers in the South and parts of the West. Beyond job opportunities, families find the warmer, sunnier climate and lower living costs attractive, offsetting lower wages. Air conditioning has made work in regions of high summer heat and humidity more tolerable. Many of the elderly, particularly the more affluent, retire to the "sun belt," shifting pensions, social security, and other transfer payments, as well as their savings, to these areas.

Many areas attracting people and industry pay a high price for their economic expansion: a pleasant environment, which induces much of the growth in the first place, may deteriorate under the weight of rapid development. Los Angeles was a mecca attracting thousands of young households until the late 1960s. Since then, an increasing number of families have left as pollution and congestion have taken their toll. The congested southeast Florida "gold coast" has also lost some of its glitter, causing many people to move to less crowded parts of the state. Large growing cities not only rival the older declining cities in population; their crime rates are comparable, too. Other, mostly suburban, areas under growth pressure are formulating various measures to preserve the status quo; in other words, some communities are actively attempting to keep out what others are anxious to attract. Thus, while today's growing areas may have bright current and short-term economic prospects, they should be prepared to face the same aging process as our older cities are experiencing today.

Migration from cities

Net migration from central cities reached a total of 7 million persons between 1970 and 1975, representing a fourfold annual increase over the 1960s. The sharpest out-migration was felt in the largest central cities. Since those who migrate are typically younger and better educated, and have higher incomes than those remaining behind, the central cities are left with a disproportionate number of households requiring social assistance of some kind. The outer suburbs and ex-urban areas, on the other hand, can list among their attractions the availability of low-density residential housing (more than two out of every three

suburban units built continue to fit this pattern), broadening job opportunities, and a perceived, if frequently illusory, better "quality of life"—presumably with decent schools and relative freedom from crime, congestion, and pollution in all its forms.

Sharply rising energy and housing costs, according to some predictions, were supposed to stem or reverse this tide of out-migration from the urban cores. This does not appear to have occurred so far. While numerous young households—mainly childless and relatively affluent—are returning to the city, they are numerically overwhelmed by middle-income families, both white and black, who are leaving the core. The rate of out-migration from Denver, Los Angeles, San Francisco, or Atlanta does not differ substantially from that found in New York, Philadelphia, or Detroit. But there is a difference: in the South and West, the movement represents primarily an intra-metropolitan relocation to suburbs of the former city of residence, whereas many moves in areas of declining population are across regional boundaries.

Equally important, most cities in the growing regions of the country are annexing contiguous areas, thus "capturing" those seeking an escape from higher city taxes and other problems. The total population increase in these cities is almost totally attributable to annexation rather than to growth within their pre-1960s boundaries. Annexations by large central cities of the northeast and north central states, however, are almost nonexistent. Thus, of the thirty-four cities with 200,000 or more residents and a growing population between 1960 and 1973, all but three—Honolulu, Miami, and Yonkers—annexed substantial territory, while among the twenty-nine with a decline, only one, Birmingham, added extensively to its land area. Personal income in these growing cities is generally close to the suburban average, while the city-suburban income gap is widening among those incurring a population loss.

Fiscal factors

To the extent that these intraregional and interregional movements are part of a dynamic economy and reflect the preferences of households, public intervention to halt the trends is likely to be ineffective and would probably cause further dislocations in the economy. The issue to explore is to what extent current population movements are attributable to fiscal policies at the local and state levels, as well as to activities of the federal government.

If one looks at a set of common municipal services, one discovers that the aging, high-density central cities of the northeast and north central regions, almost all of which are losing population, frequently have twice as many municipal workers per capita performing these services as do their own suburbs, cities of similar size in other regions, or smaller jurisdictions in their own states. In addition, the wages of these workers are frequently 20 percent or more above the level of their counterparts in the suburbs. Resulting high payrolls, combined with increasing debt levels and the compelling need for social services, place the urban core at a tax disadvantage relative to its suburbs as well as to nonmetropolitan areas competing for industry. There are reasons for higher per capita municipal payrolls in the older cities—stronger unions, greater inefficiencies, diseconomies associated with congestion, and entrenched bureaucracies. But whatever the causes, the effect—to "push" middle-income families out of central cities—is easily recognized as a major factor in the fiscal crises of New York and other cities. In the past, these jurisdictions could count on their business firms and, to a lesser degree, commuters to contribute their tax dollars, thus keeping a lid on tax burdens. Now, however, more and more businesses and commuters not only threaten to leave, but do in fact leave, eliminating sources of additional revenue. The unwillingness or inability of local officials to keep the cost of locally funded services in line with revenue without tax rate increases no doubt contributes to the apparently continuing exodus of middle-income families.

At the next level, those states with fiscal problems spend much more for public assistance and aid to local school districts (with resultant heavier tax burdens) than do states in growing regions. Massachusetts and New York, two notable examples, have 11 percent of the nation's population, but they account for 14 percent of AFDC cases and 25 percent of total public assistance payments. The average payment to a family on welfare in New York or Massachusetts is over three times the level in Florida or Texas. While higher payments no doubt reflect a greater concern for the needy (typical welfare payments in the South, even taking into account lower costs of living, are insufficient to provide minimal necessities) the long-run fiscal effects, given current intergovernmental aid formulas, can prove to be detrimental to all.

Higher contributions to school districts are more difficult to justify on grounds of social equity. There is no prima facie evidence that students in the cities of New York receive a better education than those attending public schools in southern urban school districts. None of the education specialists contends

that outlays of $2,000 per pupil in the Empire State, compared to about $1,000 in North Carolina and Virginia, or $900 in Texas, represent a twofold improvement in educational quality.

Probably the most damaging outcome of high public outlays in declining areas is their effect on the cost of living. If we compare the two urban areas with the highest living costs—New York and Boston—we find that income and property taxes alone explain a substantial share of the almost 30 percent difference in outlays for a typical family as between these two metropolitan areas and the urban regions of Texas and Florida, states without income taxes. A Boston family earning $10,000 pays $2,000 in state and local taxes; a comparable Jacksonville family pays $360.

Federal activities, including the interstate highway system and FHA housing, as well as deductibility of property tax and interest payments by homeowners, are frequently cited as factors contributing to relocation from central cities to suburbs. But programs initiated in the 1960s, such as urban renewal and increased aid for urban mass transit, have offset, at least in part, the federal "pro-suburban" bias. Nevertheless, the household decision to leave the urban core for an alternative location which does not require a change in employment has been motivated primarily by private preferences. In contrast, direct federal civilian and military employment, defense contracts, and other programs clearly redistribute tax dollars from the industrial states of the North and Midwest to the southern and western regions. For example, the four large industrial states of New York, Pennsylvania, Michigan and Illinois contribute 28 percent of all federal individual income taxes, but receive only about 10 percent of all federally generated payrolls. By contrast, the growing states of Arizona, North Carolina, and Texas have larger federally generated payrolls than the four industrial states, but pay less than 8 percent of federal income taxes.

Federal expenditures related to the three major wars in the Pacific in as many decades, the availability of large tracts of land, and various political decisions have resulted in federally generated payrolls accounting for about 10 percent of all personal income in many growing areas, compared to about 4 percent in populous northern states. Thus, over 75 percent of defense-related employment in 1975 was concentrated in the South and West. The importance of federal wages can be illustrated by Florida, where the average earnings of federal employees exceed those of workers in the private sector by over 60 percent. Similarly, wages in defense industries are above the private sector average.

This form of income redistribution made sense in the 1940s and 1950s, if one considers the large gap in income and industrialization between the North and South during that period. However, the differential has narrowed substantially in subsequent decades. In terms of buying power among middle-income families, a complete reversal may indeed have taken place.

Future prospects

There is little evidence that intrametropolitan or regional shifts are basically attributable to fiscal or other economic policies at any of the three levels of government. What does emerge from the mass of statistical evidence, however, is that excessive taxes, particularly at the local level, probably accelerated somewhat a rate of movement which it would now be difficult, if not unwise, to break.

An accumulation of generally uncoordinated federal actions promoted part of the regional job shift, and is presently aiding in maintaining the momentum. What one thus observes is a set of many individual private decisions operating in the same direction as public actions.

If this premise is correct, what about the future? No sudden reversal of recent trends is likely. The traditional economic role of many, but not all, central cities has been altered by changes in technology and personal preferences, while the aging process itself has taken its toll. It is simply too expensive to provide mass transit in older central cities by tunneling under layers of previous development as the population declines. The energy crisis was supposed to rejuvenate the city; instead, builders are still providing smaller units in the suburbs and, until gasoline prices stabilized, manufacturers were building more small cars. The political strength of cities has also been diluted by population shifts. It is perhaps not commonly realized that only one American out of seven lives in a large city. In the 1930s, one out of every twelve inhabitants lived in New York or Chicago; in the mid-1970s, fewer than one out of twenty lives there. This is more than a statistical curiosity: it is an index of political reality in the big central cities, revealing their lack of strength and their dependence on "outsiders" to take up their cause.

What urban policies should our nation adopt? At one extreme, some advocate a "benign neglect" stance: let the old cities deteriorate further. Others argue for crash federal programs, stating that in their absence economic upheaval will be followed by social unrest. Unfortunately, the advocates of both positions are handicapped by a lack of understanding as to why some cities with classical characteristics of decline have managed to avoid severe problems, while others in similar circumstances have acute fiscal crises. Simply funneling money via various uncoordinated programs is not the answer, as previous experience has shown. However, a number of cities will require direct additional financial aid as an interim measure. Such help will have no lasting effect unless politically painful internal reforms are initiated, including controls on accelerating municipal payrolls and underfunded pension programs.

Federal payrolls and contracts could also be more equitably distributed among regions. This would primarily strengthen the economies of states in the manufacturing belt. They would therefore be in a better fiscal position to aid their aging cities. Such policies, however, if they were to avoid serious inefficiencies, could take a decade or more to implement, and would thus have little immediate impact.

Recent analysis seems to be bringing us closer to an understanding of the issue of urban decline. We now have a better base than we had previously to launch a debate on the most effective response we can make to help cure our ailing cities and regions.

America's Long Urban Turmoil

Charles H. Trout

Charles Trout is chairman of the Department of History at Mt. Holyoke College. He is the author of Boston During the Great Depression.

How does the dreary litany go? Fall River, Sandusky, Kokomo? Ailing cities. Shrinking cities. The industrial base shrivels; unemployment soars; services deteriorate; crime increases.

Meanwhile, residents of most of our large metropolitan centers experience an even more chilling decline in the quality of their environment. Asthmatics fare poorly in the smog of Los Angeles; Washingtonians dodge muggers in the streets; New Yorkers watch their city sink into a fiscal abyss, while San Franciscans know that one day they may plummet into the San Andreas fault. Over the years, Americans have witnessed the creation of doughnut cities: there may be a hot time in the old suburbs tonight, but downtown, where proud central business districts used to be, there are silent, gaping holes.

People leave the cities whose deaths are lingering, the result of anything but benign neglect. No one quite has the decency to put them out of their misery, and Agnew's law—"If you've seen one slum, you've seen 'em all"—prevails. Urban dwellers, made cynical by a decline of amenities, accept for the most part quietly the truth that in the Buycentennial Year, no one is going to buy them much of anything.

A decade ago, city populations bargained through purposeful violence, or waited expectantly for the payoffs promised by the Great Society. Today the careworn residents, dulled by disappointments, slip into what social psychologists call "anomie." The capacity for outrage diminishes, and political alienation can be measured by the declining participation in municipal elections. The demise of protest politics, in turn, raises an obvious question. Can contemporary urbanites be expected to endure increasing discomforts indefinitely? Big city types have a reputation for being tough, nervy, resilient, full of bounce and pride. It may have been so once, but is it so still? Let us see.

In ancient times, city dwellers frequently did not have to ask about their future, for death tended to fall swiftly on errant metropolises. No glacial erosion of urban services in those days! Because of carnal wickedness, Sodom and Gomorrah were leveled by fire and brimstone "rained. . . from the Lord out of heaven." An earthquake, legend has it, pushed Atlantis under the sea. Vesuvius erupted, stopping Pompeii and Herculaneum in their tracks. Cato the Elder, not fond of destructive urban rivalry, pushed for the obliteration of Carthage. Into North Africa rolled the Roman legions. Carthaginians turned their temples into workshops; women gave their hair for bowstrings. After a bitter siege, Carthage fell. Not a building, in good repair or substandard, was left upright; the land was cursed. To symbolize the reduction of Carthage to open fields, the Roman plow was driven over the ruins. Like the residents of the lost and buried city of Persepolis, the denizens of Carthage, as well as those of other ancient citadels, were in no position to restore their cities, even had they wanted to bring about physical and spiritual renewal.

However, in somewhat more recent episodes of overnight urban catastrophe, city dwellers—ones not suddenly buried under lava—have risen Phoenix-like from the ashes. Indeed, Atlantans after General Sherman marched their way, Chicagoans after Mrs. Leary's incendiary cow, and San Franciscans after the 1906 earthquake all supply lessons from which today's city dwellers might derive inspiration. In those disaster-stricken places, an aroused citizenry mobilized as if for war. Residents hauled rubble, collected garbage, fought fires, formed *ad hoc* police squadrons—and assumed many of these tasks without charge. Black and white, immigrant and early settler, men and women momentarily forgot their differences, performed the labors of Hercules, and basked in civic pride as their cities were reshaped. Chicagoans, for example, who after the great conflagration of 1871 surveyed "mountains of brick and mortar, and forests of springing chimneys," soon were boasting that "the flames swept away forever the greater number of monstrous libels on artistic house building." During most of 1872, an amazed visitor noted, "There was built and completed in the burnt district of Chicago a brick, stone or iron warehouse every hour of every working day." "It is difficult to realize the fact," a Britisher observed a bit later, "that the busy thoroughfare through which we were passing, with its beautiful buildings constructed of immense blocks of marble, exquisitely chiseled, was but three years before a heap of charred ruins."

The smoldering ruin of urban decline does not, it seems, strike similar sparks of determination from its victims. Even so, it is unlikely that a disconsolate mayor today is going to take a torch to his city in the forlorn hope that his constituents will, like those feverishly energetic Chicagoans of the 1870s, rouse themselves from torpor. Even with the examples of Civil War Atlanta and post-earthquake San Francisco before him, no municipal executive will pray heaven to destroy his city in the wistful expectation that the lightning might pry loose funds from penurious state and federal governments, that citizens confronted by catastrophe might patch up their quarrels and put their shoulders to the civic wheel. The examples of Watts, Calif. and Chelsea, Mass., both of which suffered fiery fates within the last decade of so, ought to be sufficient to stay the hands of mayors intent upon arson. Of neither place could it be said, as was observed of post-fire Chicago: "Everything is rapid, everything is keen.

From *The Nation*, May 8, 1976. Reprinted by permission.

3. URBAN PROBLEMS

There are hardly any idlers on the streets. Everyone has an object in immediate view—and is walking fast to reach it."

If mayors would be ill-advised to push the "destruct" button, could it be that ordinary citizens, when faced with overabundant unhappiness, might themselves perpetrate deeds sufficient to animate lethargic governments? History surely affords instances when city dwellers, made wretched by intolerable conditions, bestirred themselves without the stimuli of invading armies, earth-shattering quakes or fiery holocausts. The most spectacular cases where angry urbanites have accomplished awesome short-term results, it is true, have been European. Moreover, the most dramatic urban disturbances had something to do with injustices not exclusively confined to cities. Still, Abraham Beame and his counterparts might think about the aggrieved residents of Paris, circa 1785-95.

Appalled by prices which were advancing three times . fast as wages, victims of government which spent 75 p(cent of its money on maintaining an army and discharging war debts, and unenthusiastic about starvation, Parisians of the 1780s turned to bread riots. When denied bread, they lashed out against speculators. When denied cake as well, they lopped off a few heads. Believing the old order to be corrupt and despotic, and miserable in the decaying tenements for which they paid exorbitant rents, Parisian *enragés* embraced Revolution with a capital "R." In 1792-93, insurgents distributed food, candles, soap and other commodities to those with proper credentials (food stamps, Paris style?). Estates were confiscated, and common citizens frolicked in parks which had been the exclusive preserves of the nobility. While the sons and daughters of the aristocracy were transported to the safety of faraway places, children of the working class paraded in the Jardin des Tuileries and watched the execution of Louis XVI at the Champs de Mars. Exclusive craft guilds were declared illegal, and all the trades were free for every citizen to enter.

Urban Americans, generally chary of extremism, may find this and other European models unappealing. Nevertheless, our own history has been punctuated by occasional acts of expressive violence growing out of a distinctly urban set of conditions. In 19th-century Philadelphia, Irish immigrants, fighting back against rampant nativism, resorted to direct attacks upon the Mayor and his citizen-posses. Railway workers in 1877, and again in 1894, acted out their discontents by burning car barns and uprooting track from Martinsburg to Pittsburgh to Chicago; the weapon of the general strike against intolerable hours and wages, usually occurring during periods of depression, has been applied in Chicago, Seattle, Minneapolis and elsewhere. Upset by soaring property levies, residents of Chicago in 1929 staged a taxpayers' strike which resulted in a cashless city. During the Great Depression, councils of the unemployed, marching under banners which read, "United We Eat, Divided We Starve," invaded the city halls of America. Eviction riots occurred in still other cities. In the 1960s, urban Negroes selectively looted the stores which they counted among their worst exploiters.

As Michael Wallace and Richard Hofstadter have pointed out, however, most episodes of American violence have been repressive, not expressive. Rather than directing wrath at government officials, discontented urbanites have turned upon convenient scapegoats. At an early stage, for example, certain urban areas became combat zones for socially accepted violence. White residents of Cincinnati in 1829 solved their racial problem when "some 200 or 300 of the lowest canaille" went on an anti-black rampage. When the violence had run its course, more than half the city's substantial population had fled. In the ensuing years, appalling episodes of anti-Negro violence were to break out north of Dixie: South Boston in 1976 is but the tip of a very large iceberg. Native Americans, concerned about competition for jobs, burned the Ursuline Convent in Boston and lugged cannons into Southwark, the Irish section of Philadelphia. Street-corner rumbles between immigrant groups eventually gave way to more serious ethnic struggles: in 1902, some 25,000 Jews passed through a New York Irish neighborhood behind the coffin of Chief Rabbi Jacob Joseph. When the funeral procession was attacked, the marchers retaliated, police moved in, and dozens were injured. Four years later the good people of Atlanta, ostensibly dismayed by the dives along Decatur and Peachtree Streets, acted in the name of moral reform by launching a reign of terror against blacks. During the zoot-suit riots of World War II, residents of Los Angeles found a convenient target in the city's Chicano neighborhoods. Informal vigilantism, often pitting have-nots against other have-nots, has habitually been substituted for action aimed at the sources of urban power.

Although more conventional political activism has also been resorted to in the past, in general the results have been disheartening. When New Yorkers discovered, among other things, that Boss Tweed had spent $175,000 on carpets, $7,500 on thermometers, and $400,000 on safes for a new county courthouse, they turned him out. A year later, voters restored Tammany to power. The nation's first tenement law was enacted in 1867; the growth of festering slums accelerated. As Melvin Holli has noted, progressive cosmeticians too often went to work on the structural aspects of municipal government; too few interested themselves in social reform. Municipal work forces, filled with dozing supernumeraries who owed their posts to the crassest forms of patronage, were trimmed to more efficient size during the 1930s, as a sop to beleaguered property owners. When the Great Depression ended, however, the jobs were restored—in spades. No concomitant improvement of services occurred; no greater responsiveness to citizens' desires was manifested. Much like Gogol's Akaki Akakievich, the humble Russian whose stolen overcoat led him on a futile goose chase through St. Petersburg's bureaucracy, the 20th-century urbanite has repeatedly encountered apathy, mediocrity, callousness.

If Americans have been reluctant extremists, and if it is pointed out that they have lacked models of successful citizen protest sustained over long periods of time, someone is bound to say that the nation's urban misery quotient has never been as high as that registered by, say, Parisians at the time of the French Revolution. Who knows? Misery, after all, is hard to calibrate. But while filthy streets and subways, polluted air, mini-Watergates, the friendly neighborhood junkie, the not-so-friendly neighborhood mugger, the run-down local P.S. 235, and the cop on the take do not produce widespread joy, neither do they send the misery quotient zooming off the charts. A full-scale revolt against the automobile in the city, against crushing taxes, against dog dung on the sidewalks is unlikely. Indeed, the American urbanite's capacity for discomfort is immense and has always been thus.

America's 17th-century city dwellers, with only murmurs of protest, accommodated themselves to robberies, prostitution, public displays of drunkenness, putrescent tanning pits which emitted noxious smells, and other "Grievous & Noisom" irritants. The inefficacy of citizen protest—indeed, the surprising infrequency of citizen uprisings—against misery-producing conditions during early American history was often to be repeated. To be sure, there were exceptions: in mid-19th-century Philadelphia, street gangs ran amok. In fact, the Philadelphia heavies, variously named "The Bouncers," "The Killers" and "The Rats," made the Sharks and Jets who pranced through *West Side Story* look like a feckless band of Fauntleroys. Respectable citizens clamored for a professional police force. Soon, they got one, and the "City of Brotherly Fear" became infinitely more peaceable. And in the Progressive era, self-anointed elites, distressed by immigrant politicians whose chicanery, according to Lincoln Steffens, represented "The Shame of the Cities," organized themselves into municipal reform associations. Private traction magnates, who owed their franchises to machine politicians, were replaced by public corporations. Municipal gas and electric departments were created; watchdog agencies in state legislatures were established; New Yorkers, tired of choking on the air emanating from Hoboken and other Garden State industrial cities, pushed for interstate controls; other cities pursued metropolitanization. But in the main, urban rebellions (almost never could they have been termed "revolts") have been rare. When they have occurred, they have been tempered by local habits, by historical legacies which have vitiated most of the bolder designs for urban change. The 1930s, when Franklin D. Roosevelt's New Deal entered the American city, is a case in point.

During the early years of the Great Depression, urban upkeep ground to a halt. Boston City Hall symbolized what was happening throughout the country: "Paint turned a grim brown; there was darkness, gloom and filth everywhere. The rich hangings in the Council Chambers were so dirty that you couldn't touch them without causing a dust storm." Men with self-inflicted wounds came to hospitals in search of three meals and a bed; women, covered with newspapers, slept on park benches. Residents of New Orleans peddled "Louisiana's golden oranges" supplied to the jobless at $2.70 a crate; in Boston, a city council member feared the day when there would be "on every corner men not selling apples but standing beside apples which they are trying to sell." Mass unemployment and plunging revenue collections forced cities to pare budgets and divert funds from public works to municipal welfare departments. Ill-housed, ill-fed, ill-clad and ill-served by government at every level, the army of unemployed turned to self-help cooperatives in places like Seattle and Dayton, to demonstrations in front of city halls, to May Day parades, to hunger marches. Apoplectic over the federal government's nonresponse, *The Nation* in August 1932 published one of the most scathing indictments of an American President ever to find its way onto the printed page, an article entitled "Is It to Be Murder, Mr. Hoover?" Voters answered "No!" and ushered Franklin D. Roosevelt to power.

Without question, the New Deal brought immense benefits to cities. For the first time, the national government entered the field of public housing. Work relief agencies furnished jobs to millions, and before the Works Progress Administration closed its doors, it had repaved thousands of miles of city streets, laid sewers, built hospitals, and repaired schools. Traffic moved more swiftly over bridges, through tunnels, and beneath underpasses largely financed by Washington. Subway extensions, airport expansion, and a network of municipal parks were all part of the New Deal contribution. Under federal auspices, artists painted murals in public buildings, musicians performed in civic orchestras, and "opera on the dole" debuted in city after city.

In the wake of New Deal reform, the blue-collar classes provided glimpses of authentic radicalism: from the docks of San Francisco to the gates of Republic Steel, workers took to the streets in a quest for social justice. Thousands of municipal workers were unionized; the NAACP increased its membership tenfold, and its branches turned their attention away from a federal anti-lynch law to struggles against local discrimination. In many cities, as Edwin O'Connor observed in *The Last Hurrah*, Roosevelt's "celebrated impersonation of the Great White Father" had "put the skids" under urban bosses. "No need to depend on the boss for everything," one of the novel's characters recalled, for "the Federal Government was getting into the act. Otherwise known as social revolution."

But despite the important changes in intergovernmental relationships forged by New Dealers, there had been no social revolution. As Mark Gelfand observes in *A Nation of Cities*, "Roosevelt's pursuit of the urban vote may have turned national politics upside down, but it left the physical contours of the urban environment much the same." Roosevelt, argues Gelfand, catered to "the numerous interest groups that comprised the urban population. His program was urban only in the sense that it assisted people who lived in cities. . . ." The New Deal, adds Gelfand, "never came to grips with the city as an economic and social entity." Roosevelt's commitment to public housing was modest indeed; federal assistance to the urban jobless was always deemed a temporary expedient; public works projects were piecemeal and almost never reflected a planned, comprehensive attack upon urban blight; segregation of urban blacks increased; income was not redistributed; ambitious plans for the construction of spanking new cities were whittled down to three modest greenbelt communities.

When federal programs were installed in cities, they did not enter a vacuum. Rather, they encountered entrenched elites with encrusted habits. New Deal agencies quickly absorbed the traits of the cities into which they had come, and this localization of federal programs, in turn, blunted the Roosevelt administration's urban thrust. In Boston, for example, Green Power prevailed in local politics, the Irish receiving a shocking portion of federal jobs. Virtually all of the first 6,000 public-housing units were placed in Irish neighborhoods. The jobless in Cleveland, Fargo and New Orleans were indirectly punished when Roosevelt, impelled to discipline anti-New Deal Governors, for a time cut off or drastically reduced benefits. Real estate interests in Louisville and countless other places impeded federal housing when they moved in the courts against eminent domain proceedings. In order to reduce municipal taxes, Mayors diverted funds intended for the jobless to regular city projects; city councils, knowing that their constituents would not tolerate budget deficits, frequently scotched Public Works Administration projects because local treasuries were required to put up matching funds. By capturing control of work relief, urban bosses were often created, not destroyed, by the New Deal: Pittsburgh would serve as a case in point. Like Potemkin villages, the physical accomplishments of the New Deal sparkled, but behind the façades in city after city, familiar ideas and practices were solidly in place. Even in one of the nation's most traumatic decades, apostles of change chanced upon few converts.

In *World Of Our Fathers*, Irving Howe recalls a moment when Jewish women of New York's East Side, enraged by the price of kosher beef, staged a mini-revolt. The fracas "started on Monroe Street between Pike and Market, where Mrs. Edelson and Mrs. Levy—unremembered heroines of protest—refused to pay the new prices. Clashes occurred in front of butcher shops, a 'Ladies Anti-Beef Trust Association' was formed, immigrant housewives poured kerosene over meat, and, as the *Forward* wrote, 'hundreds of women, screaming and cursing the swindlers of the poor,' roamed through the streets."

However, isolated mini-revolts, no matter how courageous, have not transformed cities. Neither, for the most part, has the democratic faith in small, incremental change. Failing the reincarnation of Mrs. O'Leary's cow, today's cities will very likely continue to suffer citizen apathy, segmented reform, the persistence of self-interested bureaucracies and an exodus to the suburban crab-grass frontiers.

The Clamor over Municipal Unions

Roger M. Williams

Today's public-employee unions face nationwide resentment over their escalating demands and public-be-damned attitudes

FOR five days last April, the only police car on the streets of Mansfield, Ohio, was driven by Mayor Richard A. Porter. With a badge in his pocket and an armed auxiliary patrolman at his side, Mayor Porter filled in for an entire police force that had stayed off the job with an alleged sickness whimsically known as the "blue flu." As it turned out, the mayor-cop's most dangerous assignment was cooling down the hot rodders on Mansfield's Park Avenue West. But among the city's 58,000 residents, apprehensions ran high. Anger ran equally high among its 85 policemen, who wanted a substantial wage increase. It was the type of face-off that has become exasperatingly familiar in American cities, where public employees are striving to better their lot while municipal governments are striving to solve expanding problems with declining revenues.

Within the last year, New York and San Francisco have received national publicity because of their struggles with—and eventual triumphs over—public-employee unions. Much less visible is the frequency with which similar struggles are taking place in cities the size of Mansfield and smaller, with strikes, slowdowns, and mass demonstrations; and with all kinds of public workers involved.

Over a period of a few months in 1976, California alone had this array of small-city labor disputes: Redondo Beach, a police slowdown; Hayward, a strike of non-uniformed workers; Tulare, a heated confrontation with police and firemen, who were represented by an outside consultant; Morro Bay (population 8,875), a long wrangle with police over unionization and their demand that the chief be fired; several Bay Area cities, teacher strikes—after passage of a state law providing for collective bargaining in an effort to avoid such strikes. And all that was in addition to problems in the state's major cities. San Francisco was suffering its third major public-employee strike in two years. Oakland was seeking an escape from a budget-busting $2 million to $3 million arbitration award to its firemen. San Diego was witnessing the spectacle of its mayor pushing through an anti-strike referendum while its firemen were buying billboard space in Los Angeles urging people not to come to San Diego.

Well within the memories of most of us, public employees were so docile a group that they scarcely seemed part of the American labor movement. Public work was regarded as a short step above the dole, the refuge of lazy, dimwitted people willing to exchange decent wages and the respect of their fellowmen for security and an undemanding job. Public-employee uprisings were few, and they met severe censure. The Boston police strike of 1919, which helped make then Massachusetts governor Calvin Coolidge President, was squelched so effectively that 55 years passed before policemen dared strike in another large American city—Baltimore.

The lowly status of public employment was cemented in the past by two notions: that municipalities, like the king, were sovereign, and that public workers deserved neither of the crucial rights won by workers in the private sector—the rights to strike and to bargain collectively. (At the expense of those rights, the public employee did gain early statutory protection on wages, hours, and working conditions.) The first broadly based public workers' union, the American Federation of State, County, and Municipal Employees (AFSCME), was not formed until the mid-1930s, and its original members were quasi-professional rather than blue-collar. By the early 1960s, however, AFSCME and similar organizations formed the fastest-growing— virtually the *only* growing—segment of the trade-union movement. They remain so today. Roughly half of America's 11 million public employees (including teachers) are now organized, compared with 20 to 25 percent of the work force in the private sector. And AFSCME, by far the largest and most powerful of the public unions, has 700,000 members, a threefold increase in a dozen years. It bargains for an additional half-million workers who do not have to join because their municipalities prohibit union shops and frown on agency shops, which compel employees to contribute to the union that serves them, whether or not they join that union.

All but 16 states permit collective bargaining by at least some levels of public employees. The holdouts are concentrated in the Rocky Mountains, the Great Plains, and the South. While no reliable and comprehensive statistics comparing public- and private-sector earnings are available, public workers without question have greatly narrowed the gap in the past couple of decades. Such highly publicized phenomena as transit workers retiring at pensions that exceed their salaries and street sweepers earning $17,000 a year have made public employment seem like the twentieth century's longest gravy train. Although there have been abuses of this type—all acceded to by supposedly responsible elected officials—they distort the true picture of incremental, generally reasonable gains made by workers who started far down the economic ladder.

For the past few years, however, the challenge for public-employee unions has been to cope with a backlash against their continued successes and their periodic displays of a public-be-damned attitude. Backlash combined with a chronic fiscal crisis has cost New York City's municipal unions 55,000 jobs, as well as scheduled pay increases and assorted perquisites. Yet even now the unions are periodically castigated by conservative politicians and elements of the press. In San Francisco, where municipal unions have exercised inordinate power, voters responded last November by overwhelmingly approving a group of anti-union referenda. One measure requires the firing of any city employee who strikes; a second sharply restricts the application of the pay formulas that have escalated city workers' wages; a third, which one local union official justifiably calls "ludicrous," provides that in stalemates over wages, voters will decide what the wage rates will be. In many other cities municipal unions have been settling for little or no increase in wages and benefits.

In some localities, an anti-union stance has measurably enhanced the popularity of politicians. After years of capriciously boosting city pay scales, the San Francisco board of supervisors "hung tough" in a crippling strike last spring and won the approval of a clear majority of the electorate. The supervisors added another laurel a few months later by removing from the airport commission the head of the plumber's union (plumbers and other crafts employees had attained the highest pay scales under the city's permissive policies). In San Diego, Republican major "Pete" Wilson has been testing the depth of anti-municipal-union sentiment as a possible base for a gubernatorial race in 1978.

The courts also have taken a hand in checking what critics contend are excesses committed by public-employee unions. A New York State court last fall punished the United Federation of Teachers (UFT) by stripping it of the right to have its members' dues automatically deducted from payrolls by the employer; that right, prized by unions, had been removed on only one other occasion in New York. The U.S. Supreme Court last June ruled 5 to 4 that the minimum-wage and maximum-hour provisions of the federal Fair Labor Standards Act cannot be extended to cover employees of state and local governments—a decision that has municipal managers rejoicing. Its effect will be to save municipalities countless millions of dollars and, in some cases, to save them from bankruptcy. Jerry Wurf, the gruff, outspoken president of AFSCME, complains that the decision "reasserts the doctrine of state sovereignty and goes back to the Articles of Confederation," but there is little prospect of overturning it until Jimmy Carter gets a crack at naming a Supreme Court Justice or two.

To many labor leaders, this severe slowdown in municipal-union gains reflects an effort to make public employees scapegoats for urban problems; to Albert Shanker, president of the UFT, it is no less than "war" against the employees; to the National League of Cities and other representatives of municipal management, on the other hand, it is a necessary redressing of the balance of power between cities and their unions. "Even some people in labor circles have a growing awareness that they've had it a little too easy," says Alan Beals, Vice-president of the league.

While few labor leaders would admit to that heretical view, there is some agreement in the two rival camps over the causes of the current backlash. The principal cause, they concur, is sheer economic necessity. By and large, America's cities are broke. Many have been broke for several years, but they have only recently been able to convince their unions of that. Fiscal subterfuges that enabled pay raises to be funded out of seemingly empty treasuries are no longer possible. New York City's sleights of hand are everybody's favorite example, but New York has had no monopoly on the practice.

In Mansfield, city officials regularly "raped"—as Mayor Porter puts it—the street-improvement fund in order to give employees annual raises and thereby purchase labor peace. Last year, when the street fund was depleted, Porter showed the police the empty piggy bank, and they responded with their blue-flu strike. (They finally settled, on condition that any funds left over in the budget go to salary increases.)

There is also agreement that the mechanics of municipal labor relations have not worked well, even where there has been collective bargaining. Legislatures have exercised undue influence over city labor matters, sometimes refusing to establish a rational and unencumbered bargaining procedure, other times permitting city unions to make an end run around city officials in order to obtain additional goodies from the state—a practice known in the trade as "double dipping" or "taking a second bite of the apple." A classic case of a successful end run saw the New York legislature, at the behest of then governor Nelson Rockefeller, grant New York City sanitation workers a hefty pension after 20 years of service. Although Rockefeller is a Republican, he courted the labor vote. He often got it, and in deals like the sanitation pension, he left New York City to pay the bill.

Further, both sides agree that the level of professionalism in municipal labor relations is painfully low. Jerry Wurf says, "There are a lot of guys making Edsels in the public sector"; and Victor Gotbaum, the head of New York City's AFSCME District 37, calls local government "one of the most mismanaged institutions in the U.S." Alan Beals of the National League of Cities admits that "too often cities fail to have their houses in order with the necessary expertise and good guidelines."

The unions, however, are not always superior in this respect. New York City's Patrolmen's Benevolent Association is notorious for its lack of leadership, which has led to squabbling within the association ranks and, last fall, to riotous protests over changes in police work schedules and the city's refusal to meet pay demands. In a spectacle that even hardened New Yorkers found hard to accept, New York's "finest" stood by while young punks attacked and robbed people at public gatherings; the cops then resisted arrest themselves and even attacked their fellow officers.

ON THE controversial question of pensions, Jerry Wurf insists that pensions for the vast majority of public employees remain either modest or downright inadequate. And AFSCME's William Hamilton points out that early pensions for police and firemen resulted not from union pressure but from a long-ago decision by city fathers not to have sixty-year-olds walking the beat or fighting a fire—for their good as well as the good of the citizenry. Thoughtful observers agree that, political temptations aside, neither union nor management has realistically projected the costs of huge pension agreements. That certainly seems to have been the case in Oakland, where actuaries last year calculated that the city would have to contribute 200 percent of its firemen's salaries in order to fund their pension plan.

More basically, Wurf blames the unwillingness of states to enact sharply progressive income taxes for the benefit of their cities. "Budget-cutting and firing workers without relation to social needs is not the answer," he says. "It's Billy-the-Kiddish. They ought to deal with the tax mechanisms, with who pays how much for what services."

They—governors and legislatures—resist doing that because it is bad politics, especially in this time of animosity toward the city and indifference to its problems. Unless Jimmy Carter proves even more sympathetic to them than big-city mayors expect, the cities of America are going to be left substantially to their own resources. Finger-pointing politicians call that "living within one's means," a pious phrase that ignores the disproportionate share of national burdens that the cities must bear. It is cruelly ironic that as these burdens mount, America's cities have ever fewer resources for withstanding them. Caught in this fiscal meat grinder are the cities' employees.

Aren't the employees and their unions partly to blame for their current plight? They are. Because they started late and low, and because they instinctively obeyed Samuel Gompers's labor dictum of "more," the public-employee unions plunged into municipal treasuries like a starved man whose only thought is to eat as much as he can swallow. When they met resistance on wages, they pushed up their "bennies"—benefits—in maneuvers costly to the public but too complicated for it to understand. Although strikes were forbidden by law, they struck whenever necessary. Again because it was bad politics, public officials rarely applied the law and put the union leaders in jail or imposed heavy fines.

The public-employee unions have had important advantages. City officials have seldom been willing to "take a strike" because of the disruptions and political fallout a strike by city workers can produce. Further, municipal government can operate at a deficit, and officials granting raises do not have to pay for them during their own terms of office; "settle now–pay later" has been the rule in some cities.

Perhaps most important, municipal labor relations have been inextricably tied to elective politics. If the workers at American Motors don't get a raise, they can't vote the company president out of office. Nor can they prevent him from moving up to being president of Ford by branding him "anti-labor." But public employees, joined with family and friends in a politically cohesive force, can and do exercise that kind of clout, in contributions as well as at the ballot box. The United Federation of Teachers is widely credited with having elected both New York City mayor Abraham Beame and Governor Hugh Carey of New York—and the UFT's present difficulties are a surprise to politicians who wonder why Beame and Carey aren't taking better care of the union. The fact that they aren't demonstrates the dangerous reverse side of playing municipal politics. Elected officials gauge the pressures from all sides and react accordingly; Beame and Carey have decided that the demands of the UFT must for the present give way to the demands of the general public.

POLITICS has always had too great an influence on the municipal labor process. In the old days, police and firemen's associations dealt with city officials as though they were all members of the same ward organization. San Francisco's recent labor troubles stem largely from the fact that, for decades, the board of supervisors set wage and benefit scales through informal conversations about what the city could afford rather than through businesslike bargaining; in San Francisco, a "union town," that seemed like smart politics. Until recently, southern city officials, even in progressive Atlanta, left the pay of sanitation workers scandalously low simply because the workers were politically powerless blacks.

In a different political setting, New York of the 1960s, Mayor John Lindsay oriented his labor relations to the blacks and Puerto Ricans who had helped elect him and who were then becoming a large part of the city's non-uniformed work force. And AFSCME's District 37, which won the right to bargain for the vast majority of those new employees, has been a formidable factor in New York City politics ever since then. "Everything Thirty-seven does is keyed to politics," says a New York labor leader. But the political dealings of AFSCME locals are obscured by the national union's strong statements on major public issues.

Although politics can never be erased from any municipal undertaking, there are ways to reduce political influence and establish a sensible procedure for labor relations. Municipal unions should realize that the "more" approach has reached its limit, as the sophisticated among them now realize that the crudest forms of disrupting public services do their cause more harm than good. The current anti-union backlash may at least drive home the fundamental truth that public employees need the goodwill of their community and must expect to prosper and wane along with that community.

ELECTED officials, for their part, can resist the temptation to play personal politics with every labor dispute that comes along. A mayor need not cave in to heavy pressures from a union nor "back end" a settlement so that his successors—rather than he—will have to pay for it. He can put his case to the public, thereby forcing the union to justify its demands and conditioning the public to accept a strike if one occurs. Observers on both sides of last year's San Francisco strike agree that the key to the city government's victory was public willingness to suffer a strike in order to curb what it felt to be an excess of union power. That definitely was the key in Seattle, where Mayor Wes Uhlman rode out a 104-day strike by utility linemen—and settled it in 1976 by giving the strikers less than they'd been offered at the outset.

3. URBAN PROBLEMS

The mechanics of municipal labor relations can also be placed on a more rational basis. Collective bargaining in one form or another is the only workable procedure. States that forbid bargaining and cities that dodge it will wind up with larger problems than the ones they're trying to avoid. Strikes should not be illegal except for public-safety and -health employees, and not even for them unless their private-sector counterparts—employees of private hospitals, for instance —are also forbidden to strike. The best procedure may be what Jerry Wurf calls "voluntary arbitration," under which unresolved issues, and only those, are submitted to an impartial third party. Whatever the procedure is, it probably should be conducted in full public view, as Kansas City recently began doing after 32 years of closed-door hearings.

"Increased productivity," a much touted solution, is too often a public-relations gimmick having no real impact on the problems. Unions should instead be encouraged to come up with ways to save the city money on manpower. In Santa Clara County, California, Local 715 of the Service Employees International Union has done just that, convincing county officials that hundreds of the employees whom the union represents can get the job done by working up to 20 percent fewer hours—for up to 20 percent less pay. Local 715 also has recommended against hiring—or retaining— employees it feels are not essential to the county government.

A. H. Raskin, veteran labor analyst of *The New York Times*, observes that even collective bargaining is valuable "only as long as both sides want it to work." Raskin adds that in New York and many other cities so-called bargaining now simply means unions trying to keep the status quo or give up as little as possible. That should be a temporary situation, lasting until the cities return to something like fiscal stability. When they do, it will be time for municipal unions and municipal officials to approach each other openly and professionally, bearing in mind the interests of the communities they are supposed to serve.

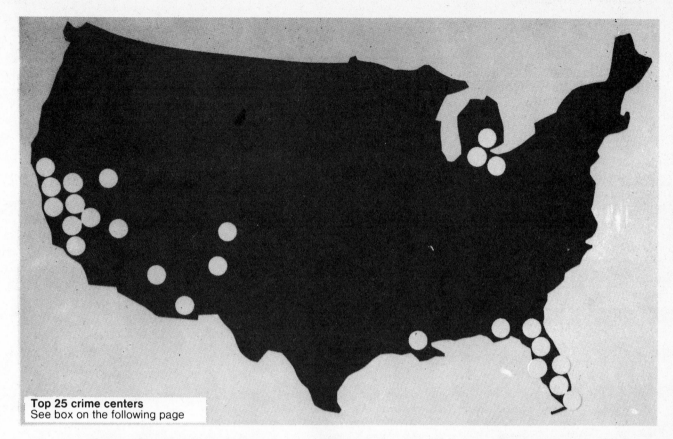

Top 25 crime centers
See box on the following page

Crime in the sunshine

Ernest Lendler

The popular belief is that crime is an urban problem and that America's crime centers are the bleak, crowded, cold cities of the East and Midwest. But, according to the most reliable statistics available, that just isn't the case. The fact is, there is more crime in the sunny and warm states of the West and South than in any other part of the country. And the crime capital of America, according to these statistics, is not New York or Chicago or Washington D.C.; it is Phoenix, Arizona.

The "Sunshine Crime Belt" is not new, nor has its existence been hidden away. But it has been easy to ignore. Early each year the FBI releases general statistics on crime (i.e., rape was up 9 percent nationally in 1974), in the nation's most populous cities, and that report generally makes a big splash in the press. But it is months before the Bureau issues a comprehensive area by area report on crime—its Crime Index—so those figures, though of greater significance, are rarely reported.

The information in the Crime Index is broken down into seven catagories (murder, rape, robbery [use of threat of force in theft], aggravated assault [including attempted murder and rape], burglary [unlawful entry], auto theft and larceny-theft [theft without violence]), and it provides the single definitive evaluation of criminal activity in specific parts of the country.

One of the major criticisms of the Index is that it is compiled by Standard Metropolitan Statistical Area, usually one city and its surrounding county (the same areas on which all major government statistics are based) rather than simply by city. But to report by individual city, according to the FBI, would be "unfair" to the smaller cities and towns, since many would find themselves with extraordinarily high rates. In a city by city accounting, San Clemente, California, for example, would have higher robbery, larceny-theft and rape rates than New York City. Other small California cities would fare even worse: Inglewood has a crime rate of 10,100 incidences per 100,000 population; Lynwood, over 12,100; South Lake Tahoe, over 13,100; and Compton, over 16,100. New York's rate—6,100—is tame by comparison.

Within the "Sunshine Crime Belt," most police and elected officials initially deny that their areas have high

From *New Times*, May 2, 1975. Reprinted by permission of the author.

crime rates and acknowledge the problem only after being confronted with the Crime Index. Even then, there are some who deny the validity of the statistics. Lt. Post of the West Palm Beach Police Department, for instance, insists that "there is no way we can compare to New York. Crime is worse in New York from what I read. There is no doubt in my mind about that."

However, once officials begin to list reasons for their high crime rates, three causative factors become apparent; the climate, social instability and an absence of fear of crime. Ray Marky, an assistant attorney general in Florida, has found that "weather has a lot to do with crime. In the heat of summer tempers flare, and I have read reports that crime increases with the temperature. I mean, who wants to go out to stalk a woman when it's zero degrees outside?" The Florida legislature has just finished a study of the state's crime

and has concluded that the situation might require drastic measures. "We are going to have to do something." as Marky puts it, "or it's going to become a zoo around here."

According to Mike Sophy, a special assistant to the Arizona attorney general, the desert air attracts undesirables. "Even the criminals are deciding where they want to live," he says. "It's just as profitable to rob houses in Phoenix in the sun instead of someplace in the snow." He adds that high quality drugs are cheaper in the Southwest than in the East. Phoenix Assistant Police Chief Richard Porter is quick to point out that "our rate of increase is decreasing" and that,above all, it is Phoenix's property crime rate that is exceptionally high. There appears to be a reason for that, however; "It's so easy to steal around here," says one Phoenix cop, "that no one really has to use force to get what you own."

Top 50 crime centers

(Statistics are for metropolitan areas. The figures in the right-hand column of all charts are the number of crimes per 100,000, as reported by the FBI.)

1. Phoenix, Arizona	8,165.2	18. Bakersfield, California	6,560.7	37. Jacksonville, Florida	5,861.8
2. Daytona Beach, Florida	7,861.4	19. Santa Cruz, California	6,489.1	38. Lawton, Oklahoma	5,840.3
3. Ann Arbor, Michigan	7,746.9	20. Santa Rosa, California	6,464.3	39. Lakeland—Winter Haven, Fla.	5,785.6
4. Las Vegas, Nevada	7,526.3	21. Modesto, California	6,441.9		
5. Fort Lauderdale—Hollywood, Fla.	7,519.8	22. Kalamazoo-Portage, Mich.	6,432.3	40. Melbourne—Titusville—Cocoa, Fla.	5,756.2
		23. Orlando, Florida	6,404.3		
6. San Francisco—Oakland, Calif.	7,277.8	24. Tucson, Arizona	6,391.5	41. Little Rock—North Little Rock, Ark.	5,733.8
7. Fresno, California	7,214.5	25. Baton Rouge, La.	6,362.7		
8. West Palm Beach—Boca Raton, Fla.	7,125.2	26. Riverside—San Bernardino—Ontario, Calif.	6,247.7	42. Spokane, Washington	5,714.5
9. Reno, Nevada	7,000.8	27. Eugene—Springfield, Ore.	6,232.2	43. Corpus Christi, Texas	5,705.1
10. Albuquerque, New Mexico	6,966.4	28. Portland, Oregon	6,174.7	44. St. Louis, Mo.—Ill.	5,675.1
11. Stockton, California	6,819.4	29. San Jose, California	6,147.6	45. Austin, Texas	5,618.9
12. Miami, Florida	6,726.8	30. Sacramento, California	6,146.2	46. Pensacola, Florida	5,613.1
13. Los Angeles—Long Beach, Calif.	6,628.5	31. Detroit, Michigan	6,098.3	47. Memphis, Tenn.—Ark.—Miss.	5,597.1
		32. Yakima, Washington	6,092.3		
14. Saginaw, Michigan	6,617.1	33. Tampa—St. Petersburg, Fla.	6,064.2	48. El Paso, Texas	5,569.9
15. Denver-Boulder, Colorado	6,584.6	34. Flint, Michigan	5,938.9	49. Baltimore, Maryland	5,545.6
16. Sarasota, Florida	6,584.1	35. Seattle—Everett, Wash.	5,924.9		
17. Gainesville, Florida	6,575.8	36. Anaheim—Santa Ana—Garden Grove, Calif.	5,889.4	50. Vallejo—Fairfield—Napa, Calif.	5,483.4

Burglary

1. Las Vegas, Nevada	2,639.1	12. Fort Lauderdale—Hollywood, Fla.	2,144.2
2. Daytona Beach, Florida	2,634.1	13. Santa Cruz, California	2,123.2
3. Phoenix, Arizona	2,509.6	14. Portland, Oregon	2,081.1
4. Ann Arbor, Michigan	2,417.2	15. Orlando, Fla.	2,051.4
5. Sarasota, Florida	2,407.8	16. Gainesville, Florida	2,050.4
6. Fresno, California	2,383.8	17. Stockton, California	2,031.4
7. West Palm Beach, Florida	2,243.2	18. Tampa—St. Petersburg, Fla.	2,024.2
8. Albuquerque, New Mexico	2,231.0	19. Santa Rosa, California	2,022.2
9. San Francisco, California	2,205.6	20. Baton Rouge, Louisiana	2,018.7
10. Riverside—San Bernardino, Calif.	2,190.4	21. Atlanta, Georgia	2,003.8
11. Los Angeles—Long Beach, Calif.	2,187.6	22. Denver—Boulder, Colorado	1,996.4
		23. Sacramento, California	1,995.0
		24. Anaheim—Santa Ana, Calif.	1,942.8
		25. Saginaw, Michigan	1,936.1

Top 10 states

1. Arizona	6,703.9
2. Nevada	6,632.1
3. California	6,304.9
4. Florida	5,960.3
5. Colorado	5,495.8
6. Michigan	5,489.4
7. Oregon	5,297.1
8. Washington State	5,089.9
9. Hawaii	4,958.8
10. Alaska	4,943.3

Rape

1. Memphis, Tennessee	64.6
2. Tallahassee, Florida	63.6
3. Las Vegas, Nevada	62.2
4. Little Rock, Arkansas	57.7
5. Albuquerque, New Mexico	57.0
6. Los Angeles— Long Beach, Calif.	55.0
7. Jacksonville, Florida	52.9
8. Orlando, Florida	51.0
9. Denver-Boulder, Colorado	48.8
10. Santa Cruz, California	47.1
11. Daytona Beach, Florida	46.8
12. San Francisco, California	44.9
13. Ann Arbor, Michigan	
14. Norfolk— Virginia Beach, Va.	44.7
15. Fayetteville, North Carolina	43.3
16. Detroit, Michigan	43.2
17. Pueblo, Colorado	42.7
18. Savannah, Georgia	42.5
19. Atlanta, Georgia	42.4
20. Charleston, South Carolina	41.4
21. Riverside— San Bernardino, Calif.	41.2
22. Gainesville, Florida	41.0
23. Muskegon, Michigan	39.8
24. Killeen—Temple, Texas	39.7
Jackson, Michigan	39.7

Aggravated assault

1. Columbia, South Carolina	552.3		14. Flint, Michigan	409.4
2. Miami, Florida	530.7		15. Baltimore, Maryland	407.5
3. Greensboro— Winston-Salem, N. C.	502.3		16. Fayetteville, N.C.	406.4
			17. Tallahassee, Florida	403.9
4. Lafayette, Louisiana	491.9		18. New York, New York	401.5
5. Baton Rouge, Louisiana	469.0		19. Los Angeles— Long Beach, Calif.	400.0
6. Waco, Texas	452.5			
7. Peoria, Illinois	442.3		20. Charlotte, North Carolina	390.2
8. Wilmington, N.C.	435.0		21. Pueblo, Colorado	387.3
9. Orlando, Florida	433.1		22. Albuquerque, New Mexico	385.3
10. Gainesville, Florida	428.2			
11. Jackson, Michigan	426.4		23. Corpus Christi, Texas	380.4
12. West Palm Beach, Fla.	417.8		24. Ann Arbor, Michigan	365.2
13. Kalamazoo-Portage, Mich.	414.1		25. Little Rock, Arkansas	363.4

Larceny-Theft

1. Phoenix, Arizona	4,394.2		13. Bakersfield, California	3,761.4
2. Ann Arbor, Michigan	4,264.3		14. Stockton, California	3,703.2
3. Daytona Beach, Florida	4,130.6		15. Yakima, Washington	3,696.8
4. Fort Lauderdale— Hollywood, Fla.	4,120.3		16. Santa Rosa, California	3,649.2
			17. San Francisco, California	3,643.0
5. Reno, Nevada	4,119.6		18. Champaign-Urbana, Ill.	3,631.9
6. Modesto, California	3,977.9		19. Fresno, California	3,553.3
7. Tucson, Arizona	3,895.1		20. Santa Cruz, California	3,495.7
8. West Palm Beach, Florida	3,838.8		21. Gainesville, Florida	3,477.2
9. Kalamazoo-Portage, Mich.	3,829.5		22. Sarasota, Florida	3,475.2
10. Eugene, Oregon	3,779.1		23. Albuquerque, New Mexico	3,468.7
11. Saginaw, Michigan	3,778.8		24. Melbourne-Titusville, Fla.	3,433.8
12. San Jose, California	3,772.2		25. Spokane, Washington	3,433.2

Murder

1. Atlanta, Georgia	21.8	10. Detroit, Michigan	19.3	19. Saginaw, Michigan	16.9
2. New Orleans, Louisiana	21.6	11. Fort Myers, Florida	18.8	20. Gary—East Chicago, Indiana	16.8
3. Waco, Texas	21.6	12. Memphis, Tennessee	18.7		
4. Jackson, Mississippi	20.8	13. Macon, Georgia	18.2	21. Shreveport, Louisiana	16.7
5. Santa Cruz, California	20.3	14. West Palm Beach, Florida	17.8	22. Fort Lauderdale— Hollywood, Fla.	16.7
6. Savannah, Georgia	20.1	15. Atlantic City, New Jersey	17.8		
7. Jacksonville, Florida	19.8	16. New York, New York	17.5	23. San Antonio, Texas	16.6
8. Biloxi-Gulfport, Mississippi	19.7	17. Gainesville, Florida	17.4	24. Stockton, California	16.3
9. Lakeland—Winter Haven, Fla.	19.5	18. Asheville, North Carolina	17.0	25. Columbia, South Carolina	16.1

Most California officials refuse to publicly admit that their area has a high crime rate and evince surprise at the Crime Index figures showing California third in the nation in crime and in the top ten in every category except murder. One notable exception is Santa Cruz Police Chief Supervisor Charles Scherer, who states that "we are located in the most scenic place in the West Coast, the weather is real stable, don't get extra hot or cold and attracts all sorts of people, and we were referred to a year or so ago as the crime capital of the world." Scherer confesses that there is ample reason for the designation; Santa Cruz has produced three mass murderers in the last two years. In late 1972-early 1973 one man killed five people, and in 1974 two men, acting independently, killed a total of 27. One of the '74 killers murdered 11 and the other killed 16 women. "He butchered the girls after killing them," says Scherer of the woman killer. "There was sexual assault after death in most cases, and he spread their remains all over the county." All three are now in jail, but, according to Scherer, the climate continues to attract "all sorts of people," with the current major problems being armed robbery and burglary.

Indeed, all of the "Sunshine Crime Belt" is a growth area, with thousands of new residents arriving daily. The resultant lack of social stability further contributes to the crime problem. Lt. Preston Hobbs of the Las Vegas Police Department notes that "people who live side by side for four years will not know each other, and when someone goes in and removes the TV or the whole house all they say is, 'I guess those people are moving.'"

But, in spite of the high crime rates, there is a general

absence of fear of crime in the Belt, a fact which, in itself, makes citizens more susceptible to victimization. "In Phoenix," notes Mike Sophy of the attorney general's office, "there is not a noticeable fear of crime. People do not talk about crime as they do in the Northeast and, unlike the East, they are not afraid to go out of their homes after dark." In nearby Albuquerque, which was the nation's crime capital in 1971 and 1972, Bob Fentor, director of public information for the police department, finds "a more casual style of living and less a feeling among citizens that they are in the midst of crime. They feel that Albuquerque is a safe city." More and more "Sunshine Crime Belt" police departments are finding themselves in the position of having to try to actually create fear in an effort to bring the crime rate down.

Though the Northern urban centers certainly have their fair share of crime—New York leads in robberies, for example, and Boston in auto theft—the only cold weather area with as much crime as the Belt region is the Ann Arbor-Detroit-Saginaw area of Michigan. Ann Arbor Mayor Jim Stephenson is at a complete loss to explain his town's status, as are local police officials, though others variously blame the area's large student population, its seasonal auto industry, it's large unemployment rate or the large number of local gun owners.

But with that solitary exception, crime is most prevalent in more pleasant climes. The existence of the Belt hardly matches our beliefs about crime in this country, but it has been there for years, and there it will likely remain.

The only question that remains is which area within the Belt will be the crime capital when the next Crime Index is released late this year. Phoenix police, for their part, are sanguine about their city's prospects of retaining the title. "We'll probably lead the list again" says a public relations official for the Phoenix Police Department. "I can't see anyone beating us."

We want your advice.

Any anthology can be improved. This one will be—annually. But we need your help.

Annual Editions revisions depend on two major opinion sources: one is the academic advisers who work with us in scanning the thousands of articles published in the public press each year; the other is you—the person actually using the book.

Please help us and the users of the next edition by completing the prepaid reader response form on the last page of this book and returning it to us. Thank you.

URBAN BANKRUPTCY AND THE SCHOOLS: A VIEW FROM THE BOTTOM

The educational systems in many of America's biggest cities are teetering on
the brink of total collapse. Time-honored methods of governance are inadequate,
financing systems a cruel joke. Here the chancellor of the largest school district
in America states the problem in stark and compelling terms and suggests
the only solution that makes sense: nationalization of school finance.

Irving Anker

*IRVING ANKER is chancellor, New
York City schools. This article is drawn
from his acceptance speech when he was
given the New York Academy of Public
Education's Medalist Award in May 1976.
The award has been presented to an
outstanding educator each year since
1935. Recipients have included Nicholas
Murray Butler, James R. Killian, Francis
Keppel, Norman Cousins, and James E.
Allen, Jr.*

The operative word in any statement
about education in this turbulent year is
survival. There is a special irony that in
the year of its Bicentennial this country,
which pioneered universal, free public
education, is in retreat from its historic
commitment to education. We don't
always remember that free public education was a fundamental milestone of our
democratic heritage and a commitment
of the *national* government, written into
the Northwest Ordinance in 1787, extended by the Morrill Act of 1862, and
secured in a dozen major pieces of
legislation in this century.

The great campaign against the
American public schools reached its
zenith in the sixties. Public education
was under siege. The presses could
scarcely keep pace with the jeremiads
being ground out by instant experts,
many of them with their own private
agenda. The titles were necrophiliac:
Our Children Are Dying and *Death at an
Early Age*. The language was intemper-
ate: The schools were "murdering" our
children; the teachers were "killers of
the dream"; the classrooms were sterile
and joyless or, at the very least, indiffer-

ent and neglectful. There was even talk
of educational genocide. *Burn the
Schools: Save the Children* was a book
title that became a slogan. The school
was the malevolent villain. Poverty,
crime, drugs, unemployment, malnutri-
tion, slums? The school was responsible.
And the solution — straight out of *Alice
in Wonderland* — was "Off with their
heads! Abolish the schools." It is an
irony of history that George Counts's
challenge of the thirties, *Dare the
School Build a New Social Order?* was
in the sixties turned upside down so
that the public schools were accused of
creating the inequities of our society. Is
it not a further irony that in the process
the urban public schools, which with all
their flaws could be a major instrument
for providing upward mobility for the
disadvantaged, were weakened as vehicles for the very poor?

We are living a self-fulfilling
prophecy. Forces set in motion by the
irresponsible rhetoric of the sixties are
now being accelerated by the fiscal
circumstances and political climate of
the seventies, when education is ex-
pendable but rubbish collection non-
negotiable; when education can be
trimmed, constricted, even withdrawn,
but other public services remain relatively sacrosanct. The public outcry against
cutbacks in education was a whimper
compared with the roar of outrage
which welled up at the suggestion that
an equal share of the economies might
have to be absorbed by other public
services.

Jerry Brown, the youthful governor
of California, has not only put out the

word that New York City has got to go,
that cities are obsolete, if not super-
fluous, but the dismantling process
seems to have gotten under way. Felix
Rohatyn, chairman of the Municipal
Assistance Corporation, is on record as
recommending that the voucher system
be revived because New York can no
longer absorb the cost of financing
public education. He recommends that
the responsibility of providing free public education, free schools for all children, be shifted from the community to
the individual. Imagine the implications
for a city like New York if the voucher
system became the currency of education. It would mean total polarization:
Children would be segregated by class,
by economics, and of course by race. It
would spell total abrogation of our
commitment to integrated schools, and
it would inevitably reduce the public
schools to the status of pauper or
welfare enclaves.

On Monday, April 19, the *New York
Times* carried two front page stories
which are of special significance not
merely for New York City but for cities
all over the country. One story dealt
with an eloquent sermon delivered by
Episcopal Bishop Paul Moore, Jr., at the
Cathedral of St. John the Divine. The
bishop threw down the gauntlet to the
city's corporate leadership in a stirring
challenge directed to large companies
which are abandoning or planning to
abandon the city. He cautioned that
desertion would result in a chain of
social disorders that would affect the
suburbs as well as the inner city; that in
a complex, interdependent metropolis

there are no islands.

The bishop characterized the abandonment of the city by big business as "immoral, a betrayal of basic moral values." When they leave (Union Carbide, Vita Foods, Bond Bread, among others), unemployment rises, particularly in black and Spanish-speaking areas, where it now nears 50%. Among black people in those areas it soars to 80%. Educational, social, and health services are cut back because of diminishing tax income. "The struggle for the city's survival is the struggle for the soul of America," he warned.

On the same page of the *Times*, an analysis of U.S. census figures revealed that New York City's white middle-class population declined by more than 600,000 between 1970 and 1975, doubling the rate of decline in the previous 10-year period. These figures do not reflect the percentages in the public schools, which now have climbed to approximately 67% black and minority enrollment overall. Maybe Governor Brown is right. Cities of America — which have been the matrix of commerce, industry, finance, government, the arts, education, research, major health services — are on the decline. Everywhere in this country middle-class people are forsaking the city for the suburbs, taking with them money and values, and taking their talented, energetic, and productive children. Moreover, business is taking its jobs and its opportunities, leaving the brutality of the inner city to the poor, the minority, the isolated, the alienated, and the angry. The cities are left with an eroding, inadequate tax base and an insufficiency of services where more are needed, blocking traditional access roads to opportunity. In a recent *Time* magazine cover story on our changing cities, George Steinlieb of Rutgers University's Center for Urban Policy Research was quoted as saying, "We have no experience in shaping decline; no graceful way of shrinking a city. We don't know what to do with people left in a city where there are no job opportunities."

Maybe we should find out. We need to harness the best minds, the most creative thinking, the most imaginative strategies, and the most intensive planning to put New York City back on its feet. We must admit that the democratic process implies accountability for good government which New York City citizens and their public officials cannot ignore. Admonitions about thrift and balanced books are not in themselves effective ammunition against the desperate problems facing New York City. A city which has seen its economy decline to the point where it continues to teeter on the brink of default is in desperate trouble. A city where the educational system was the model for the country, the launching pad to middle-class stability for the poor and the dispossessed, is now telling its minority poor that there is no room for them in its economy — or in its society. A city that has lost 500,000 jobs since 1969 is in dire trouble.

Our situation is not unique. We have lots of company in large cities from Los Angeles, to Newark, to Detroit, Cleveland, Milwaukee, Kansas City, and Chicago. There are others. The Kerner Commission warned that the United States was heading toward becoming a nation of two discrete societies. We are nearing that unhappy day now. Certainly our large city schools are becoming segregated institutions, isolating the minority poor and giving the lie to our proclaimed national objective of integrated education for our children.

The poverty of the inner cities is primarily the result, not of wanton waste, random profligacy, or even open-handed generosity, as some have suggested. It *is* the result of many factors. It might help to place some of them in historical context. The move from rural areas to the cities is as old as the Industrial Revolution itself. When industry flourished, the city was a magnet for cheap labor. Opportunities were abundant and requirements simple: a strong back, willing hands, and the spirit to endure. The lures were subsistence pay and the persistent vision that the end result would be a better life for the next generation. Public education would be the touchstone for a fulfilled life, if not immediately, at least for the children. And for many it was. But today's sophisticated technology, combined with a declining economy and what the sociologists call "the successive ecology" of the cities, has created a very different labor market. Jobs for the skilled are dwindling; jobs for the unskilled are almost nonexistent. Poverty has become a consuming and devastating local problem, but it is a national responsibility. The people who flock to the cities and flood the welfare rolls come from all parts of the country, from all parts of the world. Leading economists urge immediate and fundamental reform of the welfare system, with federal instead of state/city responsibility for a problem that has drained off city and state resources in a self-defeating cycle, creating generations of dependent rather than productive citizens.

The dual system of housing which isolates the minority poor in increasingly tight islands of color and deprivation has recently been challenged by a Supreme Court decision in Chicago. The decision is expected to have some impact on housing patterns, but immediate changes are unlikely. The flight of the middle class has ringed the inner cities with a stranglehold of white suburbs — remote, apart, wholly separate from the stark poverty of the city. Local legislative bodies have been powerless to deal with this problem. It must be dealt with on a federal level if we are to reverse the trend of continuing isolation of the minority poor in the large cities.

The influx of illegal immigration — estimates range as high as 500,000 in New York City alone — with its wake of social and cultural collisions, is not a local problem; immigration, both legal and illegal, is a national problem, which has been left for the major cities, notably New York, to deal with.

Drugs, which have been maiming our young of all social classes, is a national, even an international, problem.

The tentacles of crime, which have reached into every recess of the inner city, have assumed national proportions, requiring major infusions of social as well as financial help from the federal government.

And selective regulations, which mandate "integrated" schools in areas where integration is no longer possible because of the clear and visible racial imbalance of the extended community, and which blandly ignore immediate suburban communities, where black and white educational systems exist side by side, totally separate and totally unequal, are destructive and inequitable.

It is these factors which increasingly menace the financial, social, and moral well-being of the big cities — and of the educational system which must survive if the cities themselves are to survive.

Time-honored methods of school governance are totally inadequate and outmoded against the crushing problems which are battering educational systems in all the large cities in 1976. We have reached the point where the financing of education can no longer be handled primarily from local revenues, particularly in large cities. The property tax, which has been the mainstay for educational revenue, is not calibrated to register the needs of the population. It does, in fact, often decline as the economic level of the population declines and as needs increase. School financing in this country is one of the persistent anomalies of modern America. Although we have a tradition of an open society, of upward mobility for all citizens, regardless of racial origin and accidental geographical location, we continue to provide more and better educational services to children who live in advantaged suburban communities.

In democratic countries throughout the world — Great Britain, West Germany, the Scandinavian countries, and Japan, for example — educational financing is a national or state function. Local school district or city funding is peripheral. In Great Britain, which has a national system of government, education receives 65–75% of its funding from the national government; the local regional councils, which in many cases extend well beyond a single city, finance the remaining 25–30%. In Japan, financial support to schools in cities such as Tokyo comes overwhelmingly from the national government. In West Germany, with a federal system somewhat like ours, finances come primarily from the state government. Hence the problems of educational funding are national or state issues, and they are not tied to urban crises, as they are in American cities like New York. I do not advocate the abandonment of local control. I do advocate a scrupulous reexamination of alternatives to the present method of school finance that will free the cities from the imminent disaster of a bankrupt school system.

We have a tradition in America that education is primarily a state not a national function, and that the state in turn expects local school districts to assume the burden of school financing, with partial, and often minimum, state aid. Although the national government does not have a constitutional responsibility for educational finance, it does have a historic tradition of federal commitment to public education, as I have already noted. For most of our 200 years of existence the system has worked, and for the most part it has worked well. Education has been free, it has been open, and it has been, if not the holy grail, a high road to mobility from one economic and social class to another, a fact which makes this country unique.

It is time to rethink even a venerable tradition. Given the American dynamic following World War II, the thronging to the cities of multitudes of minority poor, with neither the resources nor the skills to cope with the technology of industry and the pressures of big-city living, we are moving relentlessly to two societies. Gunnar Myrdal, in his brilliant and prophetic book *The American Dilemma*, wrote the scenario. It was confirmed in the Kerner Report, and our own Mr. Rohatyn has warned that no city can exist "half suburb and half slum." The question then becomes whether this uniquely American system of financing and school governance can continue to meet the needs of the future, even of the present, if we are to continue to offer an unconditional guarantee of equal educational opportunity for all of our children.

The question has been raised in many forums — in the courts of California, *Serrano* v. *Priest*; in the Supreme Court of the United States, *San Antonio Independent School District* v. *Rodriguez*; in New Jersey; and now in New York.

It is with a view toward righting such blatant inequities that the City of New York has recently joined with Buffalo, Rochester, and Syracuse as intervenors in a suit initiated by the Levittown School District to challenge the discriminatory payment formula of the state's public education aid statute. Similar situations prevail in other cities and states of the U.S. To solve them we need state and federal governments willing to face the fact that we are a society, not a group of isolated governmental units. We need a government of problem solvers, not of buck passers.

To Americans there are no problems without solution. In a generation, we have unlocked the secret of the atom, placed men on the moon, and put cable television in every motel room. I am supremely optimistic about the future of this country and, yes, the future of our educational system even in this city, even in this bleak and dismal moment in history.

There used to be a sign in a tailor shop I frequented as a boy. It read: "The difficult we do immediately. The impossible takes a little longer." Education is as much the art of the possible as is politics. It's the possible we're working on — and even that takes a little longer these days. But we've all got too much invested in it to stop now.

Mass Transit for the Few

"Who benefits, who pays" is the issue in transportation planning.

Peter Marcuse

Peter Marcuse is chairman of the Division of Urban Planning of the Graduate School of Architecture and Planning at Columbia University. He was president of the Los Angeles City Planning Commission when many of the events described in his article occurred.

Everyone knows by now that mass transit is cheaper, quicker, less smog producing, less energy consuming, more useful to the poor, and more equitable racially than the automobile, and that mass transit preserves open space and reduces sprawl. Everyone knows that, were it not for the greed of the automobile manufacturers, the highway lobby, and the real estate developers, we would have good mass transit in every big city in the country today.

Exception and Explanations

Except in Los Angeles. Twice within the past two years Los Angeles has deliberately rejected chances for a major new mass transit system by turning down referenda proposals to levy a 1 percent sales tax to pay for such a system. Everyone of course knows why.

Los Angeles is the automobile town, par excellence; Angelenos have an undying emotional attachment to their cars. Whatever the divorce rate among real sexual partners may be, the wedding to the car as sex surrogate will never be dissolved in Southern California. Neither cost nor sprawl nor gloom of smog will stay the Angeleno from the fulfillment of his or her appointed rounds by automobile; neither will skyrocketing gasoline prices, Environmental Protection Agency regulations, congestion, nor the shocked disapproval of the rest of the nation in concert. The defeats of the transit sales taxes in November 1974 and June 1976 were still further proof of this irrational attachment of Angelenos to their cars, regardless of the advantages of the obviously superior alternate modes of transportation offered to them.

For those observers less given to psychological hyperbole, the more mundane explanation of the 1974 and 1976 votes in Los Angeles is simply that the highway lobby won again, a not surprising development in one of its strongest bastions. Or is it possible Los Angeles voters knew something that "everybody" else did not?

There is prima facie evidence against these two explanations. As to the highway lobby explanation, it was the president of a major national oil company (Atlantic-Richfield) who spearheaded the citizens committee that campaigned *for* passage of the first sales tax measure, and the Automobile Club of Southern California was among its many supporters. As to the auto-fixated irrationality explanation, it at least raises some interesting questions to note that the prospective capital cost of the proposed system equals four times the city's total annual operating budget for 1974 plus enough to buy every family in the city of Los Angeles a Honda Civic—and with its use instead of their regular car, smog, congestion, and dislocation would be far less than what the mass transit system would produce.

Or look at these figures, innocently included in an appendix to the report of the citizens advisory committee which supported the 1974 referendum: the average cost per day of the proposed system would be 73¢ to someone using it, compared to an average incremental cost for the same trip to someone using his or her car of 60¢—so that even for someone using the system, it would not pay to do so unless he could actually give up ownership of a car by doing so. And less than one person out of twenty-eight was expected to use the system!

Perhaps what needs explanation most is not why these proposals were defeated, but why they were developed and progressed as far as they did in the first place. Common sense seems to belie them, and expert opinion is certainly far from being as unanimous in support of mass transit (and particularly fixed-rail mass transit) as many laymen think, and in fact makes only very modest claims for the usefulness of high-technology systems. As J.R. Meyer, J.F. Kain, and M. Wohl conclude in *The Urban Transportation Problem* (1965), "It would be sensible to experiment with ...buses before committing large sums to rail rapid transit installations."

Yet not much experimentation has taken place in Los Angeles. Why not? The key to the answer may lie in who would have benefited from the 1974 proposal and who would have paid for it. Because of the much greater detail available on the 1974 than the 1976 plan, it will be the major focus of my discussion.

The Proposal

In 1974 the consultants recommended—the countywide

Southern California Rapid Transit District (SCRTD) never took a firm position on their proposal, but used it universally in propaganda to show what the voters could gain if they approved the referendum measure—a 242-mile fixed-guideway system, the first 145 miles of which alone were estimated to have an ultimate capital cost of between eight and ten billion dollars. It would be, in terms of costs, the single largest public works project ever undertaken in the history of mankind.

It was further intended to purchase one thousand new buses for the system over a period of three years; to acquire the rights-of-way for the fixed-guideway system (fixed-guideway will probably mean what the technicians call a high-capacity steel-wheel-on-steel-rails system, like the Bay Area Rapid Tranist (BART) system in San Francisco and like—but not too like—New York's subways, but the options of which technology to use were supposed to be still open), do the engineering, and build it during the next ten years at a rate to be determined by the availability of federal funds; and to subsidize its operations sufficiently to preserve a uniform 25¢ fare until 1976.

Early Rapid Transit

The plan came at the end of years, actually decades, of planning for rapid transit in Los Angeles. Although most people do not know it, in the early 1900s Los Angeles had an excellent mass transit system: the Big Red Cars of the Pacific Electric, a comprehensive streetcar system, and the trains of the Los Angeles Railway, with a total of 1,146 miles of track in use by 1926. Their evolution is a clear microcosm of how transportation systems developed under free enterprise in the growing cities of the industrial United States.

At first—in the 1890s—the electric streetcar was the chosen instrument to improve transportation. Through the 1920s it thrived, expanding ridership and miles of track and contributing to growth and real estate profits simultaneously in suburbs and downtowns. The automobile, when it first appeared, contributed to exactly the same results, and was in fact—in cities like Los Angeles—boosted by the same interests that supported the streetcars.

It was only when the auto and the streetcar interfered with each other that conflict between them surfaced. Expansion of automotive use entailed widening of streets downtown; streetcar tracks were a nuisance there and at intersections, and the slow-moving cars impeded auto traffic. Where they could be accommodated on the same streets as cars they were tolerated, but expansion downtown was resisted.

As investment in the auto mushroomed and the infrastructure devoted to its use became both more sophisticated technically and much greater in size, the streetcar became less and less economical. Finally, with a coup de grace administered directly by automobile-related interests—in the Los Angeles case General Motors, Standard Oil, and Firestone Rubber—all remaining lines were bought up and abandoned. The last of the Big Red Cars disappeared from Los Angeles on April 8, 1961. With poetic irony County Supervisor Baxter Ward, designer of the 1976 mass transit proposal, called his plan "The Sunset Coast Line—Route of the New Red Cars."

Automobile Investment

The scale of investment in the auto in Los Angeles today almost beggars the imagination. The freeway plan adopted in 1958 calls for a system of between six- and twelve-lane high-speed, limited-access, grade-separated freeways covering the county with a four-mile grid pattern. It would have consisted of 1152.6 miles when completed. Up to 1974, 463.2 miles had actually been built; and, in fact, with its use Los Angeles was one of the more accessible cities in the country.

While figures for all cities are not available, Los Angeles clearly ranks well both in the reduction of commuting time and the size of the area over which residential opportunities are thus made available to the average commuter. The 31 mile per hour average speed during peak hours is one of the highest in the nation. In fact, according to Sam Bass Warner in *The Urban Wilderness* (1972), the "distribution of automobiles and freeways gives the Los Angeles employee the widest choice of job opportunities ever possible in an American city."

Including all roads and highways and auto-related land uses, one-third of the Los Angeles urban area and two-thirds of its central business district are already given over to the car. Residents of the county spend over five billion dollars per year in private costs to support their habit, not to mention over one-half billion dollars more a year in direct public costs—without even counting the cost of air pollution, congestion, etc.

Studies and Referenda

But voices from another quarter were arguing the question of the continuing need for certain types of public transportation even as the freeway system was being built. Both the quarter from which the voices came and their approaches to the alternate transit possibilities presaged the subsequent referenda campaigns.

It was the Los Angeles Chamber of Commerce, a downtown-oriented business group, that first sent a rapid transit proposal to the state legislature in 1948. When the Los Angeles Metropolitan Transit Authority was founded in June 1951 as a planning agency, its assignment was to study a monorail system going from the central business district to the San Fernando Valley (the newest suburbs in Los Angeles) on the one end and to Long Beach on the other. While it found no funding available for that system, it also concluded that an all-bus system was not feasible.

Study followed study in steady succession (twenty-one separate major ones and countless minor ones between 1925 and 1968), all recommending regionalization of planning and operations and development of some form of mass transit system; otherwise, a 1965 study argued, "failure to achieve peak-hour transportation mobility could, in 1980, prevent as many as 225,000 employees from suburban areas from reaching jobs in the Core resulting in a loss annually of $1.5 billion.''

SCRTD, the present rapid transit agency, was established by the state legislature in 1965 to take over existing public bus lines and become a regional transit planning as well as operating agency. In 1967 it recommended a sixty-two-mile rail commuter system, and pushed it to an eighty-nine-mile system costing $2.4 billion in 1968. The sales tax to finance that proposal was put on the ballot in November 1968; it was defeated by a vote of 55 to 45 percent.

It is revealing that the proponents of the transit proposal defeated in 1968 raised $458,000 in ten weeks for the campaign for its passage. Forty-two per cent of their money came from firms having interests in close proximity to proposed stations; 36 percent came from those who would have a direct interest in the construction of the system. Only 22 percent of the proponents' funds came from sources without obvious direct financial interest in the outcome of the vote. It is also revealing that 78 percent of those people voting against the measure, in a subsequent survey published in *Consumer Reports* (March 1975), reported that an important reason for their opposition was that ''it would serve the few at a cost to everyone.''

Undaunted, SCRTD decided to try again. It used as its model BART in San Francisco, then launching its much advertised, brand new fixed-rail system. Both its executive director and its ''director of planning and marketing''—an odd but significant combined title—came from BART, and BART cars were featured in its publicity. With county- and state-authorized local tax funds and grants from the Federal Urban Mass Transportation Administration, it retained consultants to devise a new and more salable plan. They began work in the fall of 1972, and in less than one year developed a 116-mile system to cost $6.6 billion after escalation of costs. Shortly thereafter, in the summer of 1974, that proposal was extended to a 242-mile, $8-$10 billion plan; and it was that plan that the voters had before them when they voted ''No'' on the sales tax ballot proposition in November 1974.

The defeat of the proposal surprised many observers. It had massive support, including four of the five county supervisors and Mayor Thomas Bradley of Los Angeles, a political figure of national stature. In addition to the political leadership, a wide assortment of interest groups and civic associations supported the ballot proposition: the *Los Angeles Times*, major radio stations, the League of Women Voters, the Chamber of Commerce, the Automobile Club of Southern California, the Sierra Club. The president of Atlantic-Richfield led the Citizens Advisory Committee on Rapid Transit.

Ridership Estimates

In SCRTD's publicity the system looked very good indeed. With it, SCRTD contended, the people of Los Angeles would be able to ''go where they pleased, when they pleased, quickly, comfortably, and inexpensively, without enduring delays, pollution and congestion.'' Beneath the rhetoric, however, is a single major issue, half technical, all political. The technical part is what the ridership of the proposed system would be. The political part—which transportation planning often likes to ignore—is who gains and who loses from the system. The technical question leads us quickly to the political one.

The single most startling figure appearing in all the thousands of pages of consultants' reports on the proposed high-speed system is the prospective ridership: it amounts to only between 6 and 8 percent of all trips taken in the greater Los Angeles area, and many of these will be trips now being taken by bus. The total number of people expected to switch from cars to the new system after it is completed is only 3.5 percent, and the total reduction in car trips is even lower than that figure (since cars contain more than one occupant on many trips). Indeed, the Los Angeles traffic engineer estimated publicly that if average occupancy could be changed from the present 1.2-1.3 persons per car to 1.6, there would be no need for any rapid transit. And according to the consultants' figures, even 1.4 persons per car would do it!

These ridership figures are disturbing indeed, for it is ridership estimates more than anything else that determine whether any kind of new system ought to be built at all and, if it is, what its capacity ought to be. Even with SCRTD's consultants' ridership estimates, given a 25¢ fare as the county requested, the system will operate by 1990 at an annual deficit of over $335 million. That fact, of course, was not enough to deter SCRTD; its reports suggested that Uncle Sam would foot the bill for the deficit, and, if he does not, Aunt California, via subsidies or grants of taxing authority to the district, would. At worst, the system would simply be built more slowly. But, given these ridership estimates, alternate modes of transit may be perfectly adequate to handle a smaller number of riders; and the Federal Urban Mass Transit Administration, which provided much of the funding for SCRTD studies, has in fact insisted that evaluation of alternate transit modes be undertaken.

But even these low ridership estimates are subject to serious question. Their history provides a transition from the technical to the political part of the story. A high-speed, high-capacity fixed-guideway system can carry between 25,000 and 64,000 passengers per hour past any given point. Comparable figures for alternate transportation forms are: light-rail system, 12,00-25,000; buses on freeways, 6,000-12,000; and automobiles on freeways, 2,200-2,800 vehicles per lane.

In the initial round of ridership estimates for each corridor along which lines were projected, four corridors showed a demand for over 20,000 trips per hour. These estimates were based on a massive 1968 study of transportation needs done by the Los Angeles Regional Transportation Study (LARTS). By 1973 the population projections on which the LARTS study were based had been changed dramatically; instead of a projected 1990 population for Los Angeles County of 8.6 million, the estimates were reduced to 7.7

million. In addition, there were major problems in handling the 1968 data—all of which had been placed on computers at that time—because the new studies used different geographic areas, changed other assumptions, and wanted different kinds of results. To compound the problem, the key personnel who had programmed the computers in 1968 were no longer with LARTS, and many aspects of what they had done remained a mystery to the 1974 round of computer programmers.

In any event, SCRTD's consultants went back to try to refine their figures between Phase II and Phase III of their $1.2 million study in 1974. The 3.5 percent figure, which represents 1.8 million riders per day, was a result of their Phase II effort. What happened when they went back to reexamine their computer-based results in Phase III can best be phrased in their own terms:

> The main consequence of these new data . . .is that the required system capacity is substantially reduced. Rather than needing a "large" line-haul solution it now appears that an "intermediate" solution would suffice.

In other words, the figures show that the big system SCRTD had been talking about for all these years was not needed! And what conclusion to draw?

> A conclusion, due to the significant variation of the results of the different model runs, is that patronage estimation for a new system is an uncertain art at best.

And what to do next? The answer is simple: if the data fit, wear them; if they do not fit, manipulate them—which is exactly what the consultants did.

When professionals begin to manipulate data, talking about the "realistics of everyday life" and substituting "common sense" for the results of literally hundreds of thousands of dollars worth of computer printouts and data analysis, questions are bound to be raised about the objectivity of the professionals; and indeed such questions were raised. Unfortunately SCRTD left itself wide open to such questions.

Downtown Interests

The consultants SCRTD had hired were not new to Los Angeles. Several of them had been working with SCRTD for many years, and had helped develop the earlier high-capacity system proposals. While they might be assumed to have some preexisting commitment to such a system going into the new study (which was supposed to evaluate its necessity), there was at least an argument that their prior experience in Los Angeles would be beneficial to their work.

But several of the consultants had also worked and were still working for a group called the Committee for Central City Planning, Inc., a business group composed of downtown real estate, commercial, and professional interests pushing for a major urban renewal program in downtown Los Angeles. In the study they completed for that committee they projected a glowing future for downtown, but one very much

dependent on improved access. Without this improved access congestion on the freeways, on local streets, and in parking spaces would have precluded major development downtown. The more transit lines that could reach downtown, of course, the better.

Eight months after that study was completed the same consultants were hired by SCRTD to advise SCRTD whether a high-capacity rapid transit system was needed in Los Angeles and, if so, where the lines should go. Not surprisingly they recommended such a system, with five separate lines going to the central business district. In their timing program both the priority lines led along the most heavily traveled corridors right to their downtown clients' backyards. Conflict of interest? Not by the planning profession's current code of ethics. Poor judgment by SCRTD? Some people felt so.

Downtown interests, in fact, are major potential beneficiaries of a high-capacity system, and they know it. The citizens advisory committee was chaired by Thomas Bradshaw, the somewhat maverick and progressive president of the company with the largest new skyscraper on the downtown scene; that the company happened to be an oil company made his chairmanship more piquant, but not less subject to suspicion. The downtown focus of the system can be seen from the detailed figures on projected ridership: the highest percentage of trips served by the system would be those going downtown, and in fact these corridors are the *only* ones for which the argument for the need of a high-capacity rather than a medium-capacity system or mere buses could even be made.

Who Rides and Who Pays?

The literature of SCRTD did try to make the argument that non-central business district users—the poor and the minorities, the elderly and the young, in general the "transit-dependent"—would use the system extensively. Their argument was made by superimposing RTD routes on a map showing where the transit-dependent lived. The fit looks good; QED, says SCRTD, the system serves the poor. But the implicit assumption is that, given the location of transit stops in low-income communities, the transit lines will go where low-income people want to go. In fact, that assumption is not true in most cities, nor is it true in Los Angeles.

A study for one of SCRTD's consultants pointed out that most transportation demands within the southeastern area of Los Angeles (in which Watts is located) were for trips within the area, for which the high-speed, commuter-oriented RTD system was not useful, and that the jobs available in the central business district, for which the system would have been useful, generally did not match the skills of the residents of southeastern Los Angeles.

In short, the ridership benefits of the system would have gone, by and large, to the white middle and upper class, white-collar employees, executives, and professionals commuting to work downtown from suburban residences. Real estate, commercial, and development benefits would likewise have gone disproportionately to property owners and businesses in the downtown area. These conclusions are all consistent with the findings from what are by now a substantial number of studies of transportation patterns in other cities here and abroad.

And who would have had to pay for these benefits—disproportionately the poor, blue-collar workers, property owners and businesses away from transit stations, and non-riders. The sales tax, the basic financing mechanism the authorization of which was on the ballot, is of course a regressive tax, even though there are exemptions for food and prescription medicine in California. Even the prorefendum citizens advisory committee's funding subcommittee expressed itself as "deeply concerned with the regressivity of the sales tax." The 25¢ fare for all rides (recommended by Mayor Bradley and endorsed by the County Board of Supervisors) is likewise regressive on a long-distance system. A graduated fare charges according to the length of the trip; with a flat fare the lower-income, short-trip, inner city passenger subsidizes the higher-income, long-distance, suburban commuter.

Employment and Physical Problems

The shift from buses to high-technology fixed-guideway transit is also a shift from a labor-intensive to a capital-intensive system, in other words, how few employees are needed to run it. SCRTD did not try to hide this fact. In an area with an unemployment rate of over 8 percent, and much higher in low-income neighborhoods, such an approach did not sit well; when it is remembered that a large percentage of SCRTD's present bus drivers are black, the grounds for resentment are obvious.

The physical problems caused by construction of freeways and highways are well known, and in many places they have virtually halted all such construction. They include dislocation of families, destruction of homes, division of communities, noise, fumes, and visual eyesores. With the possible exception of fumes, each of these problems also accompanies construction of mass transit facilities.

A 150-foot right-of-way was assumed for the Los Angeles system; within it the configuration might at times—according to the SCRTD—be aerial, subway, or at grade. Subway, of course, would only be downtown; in residential areas at or above grade was most likely. Two thousand three hundred dwelling units were estimated to require taking within the right-of-way alone; the effects on the areas immediately adjacent to it cannot be either predicted or quantified, but they are certainly negative rather than positive from the point of view of those people living there.

Land Values and Land Use

Property owners and businesses away from transit stops are also likely to suffer. After all, since it is clear that with a fixed-guideway system land values rise sharply near its transit stops, and most sharply where transit lines intersect, it is also clear that they will tend to fall elsewhere. There is only so much demand for land in the region; if more of that demand is concentrated in one place, raising prices there, prices in other places will decline.

SCRTD's own consultants knew this fact; in a transit study for another region they commented that "the estimated new development of higher property values will be redistributed from the region to transit-oriented areas." But no studies were ever done by them or SCRTD to show where those declines will occur, how extensive they will be, whether they will affect single-family homeowners as well as business-zoned properties, whether they will completely offset the effect of increased property values elsewhere, and so forth.

In fact, SCRTD's handling of the issue of the effect of their proposed system on land values and land uses was repeatedly criticized as the biggest single technical weakness in their consultants' reports. Clearly the location of land uses does shift when a major new transportation facility is built. The direction of change is pretty well known: areas that are made more accessible develop to a higher intensity, and those people using them are enabled to live further away from them than before. Experience with highway construction as well as with mass transit lines bears out these expectations. Thus the higher densities result at some parts of the sytem, typically at transit stops, highway exits, and at the end of the routes.

In the areas opened for faster access by the new system new development takes place and sprawl increases. The more radial the system, the greater the build-up of densities and property values at its typically downtown hub; the longer the arms of the system and the faster the travel on it, the greater the incentive to sprawl. Whether these results are desirable for Los Angeles is a matter that should be subjected to real debate.

Whereas SCRTD's consultants were quiet on the issue of land values, SCRTD's publicity department was positively misleading. One of their brochures, for instance, stated that "not only will transit help to revitalize declining neighborhoods and business districts, it will materially increase property values," and cited the increase of property values in post-mass transit Boston as an example.

Not only were corresponding declines in property values ignored, but so was the fact that the increases that do occur are not net benefits but have to be paid for by someone in the form of higher rentals or higher purchasing prices. SCRTD's own earlier consultants admitted this fact in discussing the costs and benefits of the 1968 mass transit plan, observing that the effects of mass transit on property values should be counted not as a net benefit or a net cost but rather as an internal transfer within the economy. Furthermore, the consultants wrote, "it is important to note the value of such property appreciation since it represents equity earnings to a sector of the society—the present property owners."

No discussion of these issues is to be found anywhere in the SCRTD consultants' reports. In fact, not only was the desirability of such land use consequences not discussed, but it was assumed as a part of the very technical data that become the chief argument for the consultants' recommendations. Patronage projections are the key issue in determining the appropriate type of transit, as we have seen: over 25,000 trips per hour requires fixed-guideway high capacity, 12,000-25,000 requires medium capacity, and so on.

How do you calculate the likely patronage along a given corridor in 1990? You make assumptions about the location and intensity of land uses, most importantly residences and jobs, in 1990. But how do you know the location and intensity of land uses in 1990? You look at what the city plan projects. How did the city plan know what to project? It made assumptions about the rate of growth and the patterns of transportation in the future. And what assumptions did it make about transportation? Why, a high-capacity fixed-guideway system, of course! So the entire process is circular.

Technical problems such as this one may of course happen by mistake, or out of ignorance, or because time was not available or money provided to explore the issue. If it were the latter reason, why the money was not provided would have to be examined; plenty of money was available for less important studies. That it was not because of ignorance is clear: three years before the Los Angeles study was formally begun, a principal in one of the consulting firms was already pointing out that

> a major benefit of rapid transit is the production of high land values in the concentrated central districts possible only with this mode [high-capacity fixed-guideway] of urban transportation.

Why then was there no discussion in the SCRTD consultants' reports of the extent of these increased land values, who benefits from them, and whose land values are correspondingly diminished?

Alternative Financing Plans

The uneasiness raised by the question is heightened when put in the context of alternate means of financing the program. The recommended sales tax is regressive. There are other possibilities; one of them in particular, the special assessment district, seems to combine real progressiveness with a strong element of justice so as to make it a prime candidate for serious attention. Under some special assessment district proposals an additional tax is levied on land in those specific areas where land values are in fact increased because of the construction of the rapid transit system. Most such proposals simply levy an additional tax on property within a certain radius of transit stops. Thus those people who benefit most directly are also taxed most directly.

Other possibilities for a public recapture of the benefits of its own investments also exist: excess condemnation, public development corporations, capital gains taxes, real property transfer taxes, and the like. Still other possibilities for financing might well be both more progressive and simultaneously contribute directly to reinforcing the policy objectives of a mass transit system: peak hour road user charges, for instance, or "congestion tolls," such as suggested by William Vickrey, would both provide revenues and discourage rush-hour commuting by automobile, thus increasing utilization of mass transit.

Yet these alternatives were never explored by the consultants. Their obligation to dual clients makes the ommission that much more awkward, especially since it is clear that the concept of special district benefit assessments and the utility of a real estate transfer tax on property whose values appreciate in a post-mass transit situation were known to them from a previous study conducted for the Twin Cities metropolitan area.

The need to explore broad alternatives was not universally neglected, however. The Southern California Association of Governments (SCAG), composed of representatives of local and county governments in the six-county Southern California region, for instance, was concerned. SCAG's technical analysis of the Los Angeles plan recommended concentrating on speeding up trips of between three and eight miles duration with an intermediate-capacity shorter-haul system, rather than facilitating longer commuting trips with a high-capacity line-haul system.

SCAG's argument was that facilitating means encouraging, and long-distance commuting trips ought to be *discouraged* in the interests of energy conservation, reducing net travel time, and promoting efficient land use patterns and discouraging sprawl. The city's own Planning Commission raised many of these same questions with SCRTD, but was constrained from pursuing them in view of Los Angeles Mayor Bradley's position.

Bradley's Position

The mayor's position was essentially that the transit sales tax should be passed as the beginning of the effort to rationalize Los Angeles's transportation system. In his 1973 election campaign Bradley had stressed mass transit as a key issue, and had promised to lay the cornerstone of a new system by December 1, 1974. He could thus not easily repudiate the idea of a streamlined, new fixed-guideway system which in most people's minds—although not in his—was synonomous with mass transit.

On the other hand, his own staff's studies increasingly led him to the conclusion that short-term, community-level, low-capital-improvement types of programs (bus improvements, mini-buses, jitneys, dial-a-ride service, etc.) were the top priorities for mass transit, and made him increasingly doubtful about the public benefits of the high-capacity fixed-guideway system to which SCRTD seemed committed. City staff were also extremely critical of SCRTD's technical work, which resolved very few of their doubts. The conflict came to a head when the mayor recommended—and the Los Angeles City Council approved—a proposal for short-term bus and other improvements and an eighty-mile fixed-guideway system, and SCRTD approved a 242-mile system.

Rather than be put in the position of publicly disagreeing with SCRTD, and thus appearing to be negative and obstructionist on the very issue on which he had so positively campaigned two years before, Bradley attempted to postpone the resolution of his differences with SCRTD until after the vote but to assure adequate bargaining power at that time. His plan was twofold: (1) he persuaded SCAG to adopt a resolution supporting the transit sales tax but recommending that SCRTD not spend any funds for capital improvements until further criteria suggested by SCAG had been met, and (2) he convinced the state legislature to give him a veto power over any construction done by SCRTD within the city of Los Angeles, the heart of the SCRTD proposals.

SCRTD opposed the Bradley-backed bill, but it passed the legislature on September 24, 1974, six weeks before the slated referendum. With passage of the bill Bradley aggressively embarked on a well-publicized campaign supporting the sales tax.

Defeat

But fate intervened to upset all these carefully laid plans. The rate of inflation, already high, continued increasing during the fall. Unemployment and the threat of a recession turning into a depression were constantly in the headlines. Ford's economic summit conferences brought home the uncertainty at the highest levels about the country's economic future. And, incredibly, SCRTD allowed its negotiations with its drivers and mechanics for a new contract to break down three months before the election, precipitating a sixty-eight-day strike that completely shut down all SCRTD transit operations during the critical preelection period.

The voters rejected the sales tax in November by 56.7 to 43.3 percent. Interestingly, the city of Los Angeles itself voted for the proposition by a 54 percent majority. The city with the highest favorable vote was Compton, just south of Watts, with a large black population and a black mayor, which gave it a majority of 71 percent; and the second highest majority (61 percent) was racked up by Beverly Hills. South Gate and Bell, on the other hand, gave it the lowest votes of any incorporated areas; they are both heavily blue-collar areas and somewhat, but not much, further from proposed transit stations.

Whether the defeat was the result of the fear of inflation, a generalized taxpayers revolt, distrust of SCRTD's capacity either to manage an existing transit system or plan a new one, or of displeasure with the plan itself and its means of financing, is not certain. No doubt all these factors played some role. The public opposition to the plan came, by and large, from two sources: a fringe taxpayers group that wrote the argument against the measure that appeared—in accord with California law—on all ballot materials, and who argued that any additional taxes were bad; and from representatives from communities not well served by the proposed routes, who argued that they should not be forced to pay for a system from which they did not benefit. Few of the underlying technical or policy issues raised by SCRTD's proposals were extensively publicized. But in a sense most of these issues were in the air and contributed to the generalized distrust of the SCRTD proposal.

Second Attempt

The 1976 plan was even more ambitious, although much less detailed. It was a countywide plan, the brain child of

Baxter Ward, an energetic member of the county's five-member Board of Supervisors. It contemplated a 232-mile heavy rail network following rights-of-way along existing freeways, rail routes, and the Los Angeles River (the latter already flowing in its own concrete channel for much of its course). The cost was to be $5.8 billion in 1976 dollars, according to Ward's projections; the city of Los Angeles's Technical Committee estimated twice that amount, and Stanford Research Institute used a $16 billion figure including costs of financing if bonds were to be used. Other estimates went as high as $20 and $22 billion. The assumption was that no major federal aid would be available, a wise assumption in view of the skeptical attitude of the federal government toward the whole idea.

To bring the resultant staggering local expenditures even remotely within the range of reason, the plan provided for completion of construction somewhere around the year 2011 and "pay-as-you-go" financing from a 1 percent sales tax. While the number of communities to be served was greater than that in the 1974 plan, the estimates of ridership in the 1976 proposal were below—about one-half—those urged in 1974 because of the long-distance heavy-rail characteristics of the plan. Its details were left wide open at the time it went to the voters.

Second Defeat

If rapid transit lost decisively in 1974, it lost disastrously in 1976; the vote was 60 percent against Supervisor Ward's plan. In 1974 the interests that had most to gain from the plan supported it vigorously. Professional opinion was obtained that presented the 1974 plan with a thorough (if flawed) veneer of technical respectability, and it was a reasonable political conclusion that the support for mass transit which helped elect Mayor Bradley would prevail also when mass transit appeared directly on the ballot.

The serious possibilities of 1974, however, turned almost to farce in the 1976 rerun. Those interests most directly affected had no serious hopes for the referendum; they did not participate in the formulation of the plan and supported it reluctantly. Professional involvement was minimal. One consulting firm, brought in from Philadelphia, put itself on a questionable limb by saying with "no reservations whatsoever" that the plan was "operationally feasible" at the same time that another consultant was estimating that an annual operating deficit of over one-half billion dollars would occur ten years before the line was even completed.

In addition, in 1976 the political leadership was heavily divided. The proposal badly split the always factional County Board of Supervisors, Mayor Bradley's support was pro forma, and the Los Angeles City Council voted against the plan by thirteen to two. Cal Hamilton, the city's planning director, did little to help himself or the proposal when, following the mayor's lead, he suddenly supported it—having previously consistently signed Technical Committee reports criticizing virtually every detail and every figure in it. The plan's defeat was assured one week before the vote when the county assessor released figures showing the inevitability of a tax increase on real property for the following year.

Lessons

What are the lessons of this history? For the politicians it suggests that obtaining sound and independent technical advice, and listening to it when received, should be essential ingredients of decision making. But both in 1974 and 1976 the technical people most involved opened themselves to the criticism that their professional judgment was either directly influenced by the interests of the clients who were paying them, or indirectly influenced by their reading of the desires of the political leaders under whom they served. Perhaps the Los Angeles events should also teach the professionals the extent to which their own standards of conduct need to be reexamined.

Neither the politicians nor the planners proved themselves capable of solving Los Angeles's real transportation problems. Whether it was the technical difficulty of the issues, the human failures of the individual actors, or the unresolved conflict of real interests that accounts for the failure is a moot question. In any event, the process actually followed in Los Angeles hardly measured up to the ideal of enlightened and democratic planning, regardless of what its outcome ultimately was.

The lessons for Los Angeles are equally painful. Angelenos will have to live with the city they have built—or which the free enterprise system, unbridled land speculation, and development practices have built for them. They will not have a downtown like New York, Chicago, or San Francisco. On the other hand, their plan for multiple centers, for the growth of smaller communities around smaller downtowns, may be closer to implementation, and the net amount of traveling they may end doing may in fact be reduced. Their hope for the control of smog must remain with smaller cars emitting fewer pollutants, and with less drastic transit improvements and auto disincentives—as it always has.

A new effort for improved bus and other non-fixed-guideway mass transit improvement will be needed. Studies are beginning to show, without exception, the feasibility and cost-effectiveness of a regional bus system with limited freeway improvements to facilitate its operation. Highway and downtown interests, having no alternative, are likely to converge in supporting such a plan. A victory for bus rapid transit may thus emerge out of the fixed-guideway defeat. And county residents will only pay a 6 percent sales tax on their purchases, instead of 7 percent, thus saving $200 million per year.

For mass transit planning the lessons are equally clear, although they may be read less often. They challenge the orthodoxy that streamlined high-capacity, high-speed transit systems, using all the latest technology, are universally either more desirable or more desired than smaller-scale, more down-to-earth proposals like better buses or smaller cars. They suggest that land use and land value questions are very relevant to proposals for construction of massive fixed-guideway transit facilities. They raise questions about the usefulness of technical reports and the objectivity of technical consultants. They show that Congress's action in approving, for the first time, federal subsidies for transit operating expenses as well as capital improvements may ultimately be of as much help to cities like Los Angeles as to cities with heavy existing investments in fixed-rail systems like Chicago or New York.

And they prove that the issue with mass transit planning, as with most other public questions, is still "who benefits and who pays?" A mass transit system can be immediate bread-and-butter transportation for the masses, or it can be luxury transit for the few, paid for by the many. The latter is the way Los Angeles voters saw SCRTD's proposed system twice within the past two years.

To prevent the Los Angeles fiasco from recurring, future studies of transportation alternatives—and indeed of any technological choices—must be explicit in addressing the question of benefit and payment. Political and social analysis should become as indispensable a part of transportation decision making as origin and destination studies or studies of technology are today.

READINGS SUGGESTED BY THE AUTHOR:

Gakenheimer, Ralph. *Transportation Planning as Response to Controversy: The Boston Case.* Cambridge: MIT Press, 1976.
Hamer, Andrew. *The Selling of Rail Rapid Transit.* Boston: Lexington Books, D.C. Heath, 1976.
Wingo, Lowden, Jr. and Harvey S. Perloff. "The Washington Transportation Plan: Technics or Politics." In *Readings in Urban Economics,* edited by Matthew Edel and Jerome Rothenberg. New York: Macmillan, 1972.
Zwerling, Stephen. *Mass Transit and the Politics of Technology: A Study of BART and the San Francisco Bay Area.* New York: Praeger, 1975.

The Urban Fiscal Crisis

A short-term manifestation of institutionalized decline

Edward S. Herman and Richard B. DuBoff

EDWARD S. HERMAN *teaches at the Wharton School, University of Pennsylvania.* RICHARD B. DU BOFF *is a professor of economics at Bryn Mawr.*

Most of America's large cities have been suffering from deep-seated, cumulating disorders for decades: spreading blight and slum conditions, expanding pools of the chronically unemployed, increasing crime and insecurity, and a steady exodus of business and the more affluent. The urban "crisis" is now sufficiently long-standing that it must be regarded as an American institution; so cherished that no national commitment has ever been made to cope with it with any of the dedication applied to sending a man to the moon or waging war in Vietnam.

The current fiscal crisis is the short-term manifestation of our institutionalized urban decline, as city managers try to grapple with forces over which they have very little control. Their problems have been exacerbated by inflation, by militant and effective bargaining on the part of proliferating state and municipal unions (4.5 million of the 11.6 million state and local government workers now belong to unions or educational associations), and by recession-induced increases in welfare obligations. At the same time, there have been tightening limits and, more recently, downward pressures on revenues. The inevitable financial squeeze has raised the specter of default, which in turn has driven up borrowing costs of state and local governments (SLGs) or rendered their bond issues virtually unsalable—adding further to their fiscal difficulties. The most conspicuous short-term effect (and probable impact) over the next two or three years, however, is not a large number of defaults but a radical pruning of outlays and services in circumstances that call for more rather than less.

The process of retrenchment is well along across the country, with payroll reductions and diminished outlays for welfare, education and public works planned from Florida to California, from Medford, Oregon (pop: 33,900) to Greater Boston (pop: 3,386,000). New York City, of course, has already absorbed wholesale reductions of workers on the City payrolls, as well as hikes in taxes and transit fares—although financier Felix Rohatyn, chairman of the Municipal Assistance Corporation and a principal architect of the financial "rescue" attempt warns that "the pain is just beginning . . ." In coming years New York will have to undergo "the most brutal kind of financial and fiscal exercise any community in the country will ever have to face."

The social implications of this frank declaration may be glimpsed from some proposed cutbacks for 1976: outlays for New York City parks down 67 percent from 1975, roads and highways down 43 percent, schools down 30 percent, culture and recreation down 22 percent, plus a $600 million slash in capital expenditures (no new schools will be started). Of course these cuts, which come on top of earlier, 1975 spending decreases and personnel layoffs, may eventually be self-defeating. Such measures are bound to have a negative multiplier impact, beginning with a furloughed city employee who buys less food and clothing, fewer city purchases of supplies from firms which must then retrench, and so on. New York City's unemployment rate—11.7 percent, or two-fifths above the national average—will undoubtedly rise, taxable incomes will fall, and the budget crisis may stand no closer to being resolved. In the nation at large the fiscal crisis of SLGs is exerting a deflationary effect that may not be fully understood in Washington.

The contention that the urban fiscal crisis is a product of municipal "mismanagement" is a diversionary tactic. New York City certainly has engaged in some questionable budgetary accounting practices, and its budget is also inflated by an inefficient use of manpower and by compensation levels (especially pensions) slightly in excess of that found in comparable corporate employment. But the urban decline and fiscal crisis are not confined to New York City. The inability of the cities to meet the demands being placed upon them represents a complex of political decisions as to where

The cities .. are turning into the repositories of the poor, the blacks and other victims of a society whose labor markets are shaped by the initiatives and requirements of private profitmaking.

the social surplus is to be allocated, which "excesses" are tolerable and which are not. In its own way, the federal government has been incomparably more wasteful than New York or Detroit over the past 20 to 30 years. Federal resources allocated to socially negative boondoggles, most often Pentagon-inspired, have set a standard for waste unduplicated by SLGs; and this huge resource drain, plus heavy reliance by Federal Reserve monetary managers on tight money and high interest rates to combat inflation, have made it drastically more expensive for SLGs to finance their needs through the bond market. An irresponsible federal government can get away with *its* mismanagement because of a greater taxing capacity, control over the Federal Reserve and the money supply, and its resultant ability to support with ease a volume of debt almost twice as large as that issued by the aggregate of SLGs.

The urban fiscal crisis is a reflection of national priorities on resource use and, more fundamentally, an intensifying struggle over income shares. The cities, and especially the urban cores of the northeast and midwest, are turning into the repositories of the poor, the blacks and other victims of a society whose labor markets are shaped by the initiatives, and requirements, of private profitmaking. As whites flee the cities, blacks continue to move in, and the latter now comprise one in every four city dwellers (against one in six in 1960). New York City, for instance, lost 1.6 million whites to its suburbs between 1955 and 1975—and gained 1.5 million poorer blacks and Puerto Ricans. Median family income in central cities was 105 percent of nationwide family income in 1960; it dropped to 94 percent by 1974. Of all Americans living below the federally-defined poverty level, 27 percent resided in central cities in 1960, 37 percent in 1974. The income-generating base of core cities declines as white families and businesses move outward. Any effort by municipal governments to ward off budgetary disaster by increasing taxes simply accelerates the exodus of the better-heeled taxpayers. Income, and power, are shifted toward the suburbs and ex-urbs.

Nationally, the same trends are being played out on a broader, regional plane. Kirkpatrick Sale's *Power Shift* hypothesis (see *Commonweal*, November 21, 1975) appears to be supported by the most recent data on personal incomes and taxable property. The military-industrial-oil-leisure complex sections of the country have been growing more rapidly than the older regions. Between 1960 and 1974, the share of aggregate personal income going to the New England, the Middle Atlantic, and the East North Central states (Ohio, Indiana, Illinois, Michigan, Wisconsin) dropped from 50.2 to 46.1 percent, or by 4.1 percentage points. The corresponding gain accrued mainly to Georgia, Florida, Arkansas, Louisiana, Texas, Oklahoma, Arizona, New Mexico, and California; from 1960 to 1974 their combined share of the nation's personal income rose by 2.5 percentage points, from 23.7 to 26.2 percent. Per capita incomes remain lower in these southern and western "rim" states, but, with the exception of California, they have been increasing faster than per capita incomes in the older northern and eastern states. Similarly, while per capita assessed property values are still lower in the cities of the southern and western states than in the northeastern and north central states, between 1961 and 1971 they doubled in the former while increasing only 56 per cent in the slower growing states.

Recent national administrations have encouraged, and taken political advantage of, these trends. Lyndon Johnson channeled significant portions of defense and space contracts into his native Texas, and the Nixon "revolution" was a form of "southern strategy," whose basic ingredients were bigger and better military budgets, a thinly-veiled resort to racist voter appeals, and a not-so-benign neglect of the poor and urban blacks effectuated by a ruthless trimming of what little remained of the modest "Great Society" programs of the 1960s. The latest installment in the continuing dismantlement of federal welfare programs is the decision by the Ford administration to cut manpower training funds—during a period of compelling need for them—in 14 of the 15 largest municipalities in the country. On January 8 the Labor Department acknowledged that there had been a significant drop in funding of these job training programs for the nation's inner cities. Only San Diego is slated to receive more funds over the next year.

Military spending provides a still more important example of how political conservatism and resource allocation interact to penalize the older urban agglomerations and reward the "sunbelt" states. A recent *New York Times* series states that in 1974 the latter managed to collect $13 billion more in federal expenditures than they paid in federal taxes, whereas nine Northern states suffered a net loss of $20.5 billion. It seems clear that the Pentagon is the source of most of this redistribution, the sunbelt states getting almost 50 percent of military-research funds, over 40 percent of prime military contracts, and the benefits of federal funding of 140 military installations, more than the rest of the country combined. Even transfer payments moved disproportionately in the same direction, with two out of three military retirees living in the sunbelt and drawing billions in retirement pay.

A decision at the federal level to spend money on the military thus leads to a specific geographical pattern of job opportunities that benefits particular areas and bypasses and damages others—the latter including the Northeast and Northcentral states. The symbiotic relationship between the beneficiary states and the military establishment has been self-reinforcing, strengthening conservative political tendencies, which helps sustain large national military budgets and channel them into this friendly terrain. Military expenditure is also a job-loser overall. A hypothetical trade-off for the years 1968-1972 between military spending and civilian outlays, constructed by a Lansing, Mich., public-interest research group, found that a reallocation of the Pentagon budget to civilian uses would have created about 840,000 additional jobs. The older states and cities thus suffer from both an overall job loss and an unfavorable regional pattern of federal resource allocation. This has not prevented sunbelt representatives from opposing "bail-outs" and other forms of aid to troubled Northern cities on the ground of alleged regional inequities.

Meeting State and Local Needs

It is generally known that government outlays (federal plus SLG) have grown faster than private expenditures over the past several decades. Less well known is the importance, and relatively more rapid increase, of SLG spending. SLG purchases of real goods and services, as opposed to transfer payments, increased some ten-fold between 1950 and 1974 (federal purchases grew six times). And while total outlays of the federal government are higher than those of SLGs (in 1974: $299 billion versus $206 billion), actual purchases of goods and services by SLGs substantially exceed those of the federal government ($192 billion, against $110 billion in 1974). A good part of the federal increases—and nearly two-thirds of its total outlays—have been in the form of transfer payments: programs like old age pensions, medicare, or scholarship grants that exert no public sector claim on current output, as would be the case with federal or state construction of mass transit facilities, or the purchase of a typewriter, or the services of a municipal garbage collection agency.

One significant federal transfer item is grants-in-aid revenue sharing to SLGs, which increased by $39 billion from 1950 through 1974. But by far the biggest federal transfer expansion has come through social security —reflected in a rise of transfers to individuals of $90 billion between 1950 and 1974. This might appear to be a notable contribution to human welfare, and con-

The federal government has been preoccupied with the 'larger picture' in a way reminiscent of Dickens' Mrs. Jellyby devoting life and resources to the faraway natives of Boorioboola-Gha.

servatives have pounced on it to prove the adequacy (or excess) of federal support for the "welfare state" and the reasonableness (or insufficiency) of expenditures for national defense. A transfer payment, however, does not directly affect resource allocation; it merely redistributes income from one sector of the private economy to another. What is more, social security transfers have been closely tied to social security payroll taxes, possibly the most regressive of all major taxes imposed in the United States today. This tax has been increased seven times in the past ten years to pay for enlarged benefits, on the fiction that all recipients of social security at one time or another contribute to an insurance fund that will cover their subsequent benefits. In fact, with Congress inclined to adjust benefits upward to offset price inflation, this "fund" is perennially in deficit, and outlays from it will increasingly be met out of general tax revenues on some sort of ad hoc, year-by-year basis. Confining the stipulated revenue source to the old payroll tax represents a political trade-off, in which the national administration agrees to step up benefits for the elderly and sick so long as the funding comes mainly from the pockets of ordinary low- and middle-income citizens in the traditionally regressive mode.

In 1970, 4.8 percent of the first $7,800 of a person's income was taken as a payroll tax; in January 1976 the rate was up to 5.85 percent of the first $15,300, whether the worker in question earned $5,300 per year, or $153,000. (President Ford proposed a further increase starting in 1977—to 6.15 percent—in his State of the Union message of January 1976.) The resultant higher tax yields have in effect permitted the role of the (mildly) progressive corporate and individual income taxes to decline; federal income tax rates have been cut three times since 1964. In 1960, 67 percent of Washington's budget receipts flowed in from individual and corporate income taxes, 16 percent from social security contributions. By 1975 over 30 percent of federal receipts came from social security, while the combined income taxes produced only 56 percent. The social security payroll deductions are especially burdensome to younger and lower-paid workers, who must pay immediately, and on their first dollar of earnings, half of the total 11.7 percent payroll tax rate—with benefits to accrue in the distant future. Since the employer's half of the payroll tax is probably passed on to the public via lower wages and higher prices, the tax is far more onerous than the regular income tax for the bulk of American families.

Compared to total transfer spending, which climbed by nearly $140 billion, federal expenditures made directly for goods and services went up by $91 billion during 1950-1974. Of this total, $65 billion (71 percent) took the form of greater *military* outlays; only $26 billion was allocated to increasing non-defense expenditures. This lopsided expenditure pattern prevailed during a quarter-century of exceptionally rapid economic growth. America's population grew from 152 million to 211 million (39 percent), secondary school enrollments doubled, real gross national product more than doubled, and real per capita personal incomes rose 85 percent. Our postwar growth surge greatly enlarged demands for ordinary public services (sewers, schools), but it also generated an ever larger demand for offsets to the negative by-products and "spillover effects" of modern free market expansion. Modern technology, and above all the continued spread of the automobile, have had a severe impact on the city and its environment in the forms of increased congestion, pollution, waste disposal problems, the uneconomic sprawl into the suburbs and a decline of public transportations systems. The profits from this growth were, of course, "internalized"—private business firms made them and disposed of them as they saw fit. The social costs of growth have been largely externalized at the expense of the public at large.

The statistics cited above show how very little the federal government did to alleviate the urban-focused burden of growth: it increased its nonmilitary services at the rate of little more than $1 billion per year from 1950 to 1974. The thankless task of meeting the demands of the civil society fell chiefly to SLGs. Their growth-related outlays on schools, highways, police, fire, sanitation, parks and recreation, and water supply jumped from $14.2 billion to $109.7 billion in 1973—almost eight-fold. Per capita expenditures of SLGs rose five times over this period.

The federal government has been preoccupied with the "larger picture," in a way reminiscent of Dickens' Mrs. Jellyby devoting life and resources to the faraway natives of Borrioboola-Gha—totally disregarding her household, in a pitiful state of neglect and resentment. (At least Mrs. Jellyby and her friends were harmless to the natives; they knitted woolen underwear for them rather than supplying them with M-16 rifles.) The irony is that many novel federal programs from the New Deal through the Great Society were begun because of the ineffective performance and corruption of local government and the essentially sound belief that only a public body with the resources, and the capacity for taking a unified national view of costs and benefits, could deal with the demands of unemployment, urban decay, pollution, and the deterioration of regional transportation networks. This view was—and is—valid, but since the Second World War the federal government's role has become largely one of a military entrepreneur.

There is no economic growth factor inherent in national defense outlays: increases in population and per capita incomes do not call for a larger nuclear deterrent or conventional forces. Barring war, defense expenditures *ought* to fall relative to gross national product; but, as a percentage of a steadily rising GNP, military spending has grown from 1 percent in 1936 to 4.2 percent in 1950 and 5.6 percent in 1974 (a calculation based on a highly conservative definition of "national defense expenditures"). And for much of the most recent period military outlays averaged above 7 or 8 percent of GNP.

These outlays, however, are determined by "noneconomic" factors. One is the perceived requirements of U.S. corporate business and the ruling elements of both major political parties for armed forces capable of protecting, and enlarging, America's sphere of economic interests, which is the most extensive in history (see Du Boff and Herman, "Corporate Dollars and Foreign Policy," *Commonweal*, April 21, 1972). A second factor is the power of interlocking vested interests within industry, labor, the universities and the military to command resources and jobs. The federal government was the natural focus of a coalescence of both these factors once the critical decision was taken by the Truman administration that a high level of arms spending would henceforth be necessary to deter "Communist aggression." Furthermore, it should not be surprising that since the late 1940s the primary Keynesian tool for imparting fiscal stimulus to the economy to counter slump and stagnation has been military spending. On several occasions the executive branch has stepped up the defense budget in the face of impending recession, a policy sure to gain quicker acceptance than, say, a countercyclical proposal to initiate a large-scale program of low-cost housing and urban rat control. The upshot is that the "military-industrial complex" has been able to divert to its own ends 61 percent of the increase in federal purchases since 1950.

The Power To Owe And Tax

The federal government has broader constitutional freedom of action than state and local authorities both in raising revenue and in issuing debt. And it has long since preempted the most fertile revenue sources, leaving the lower level government authorities in a position of fiscal inferiority. SLG tax and debt powers were tightly constrained by law during the 19th century, and again in the 1930s, in response to periodic SLG defaults—eight states defaulted in the recession of 1837 and some 20% of SLG issues were in default during the 1930s—and out of fear of the recklessness that often characterized 19th century local government financial practices. Through time, and with burgeoning SLG needs, many of these restrictions have been relaxed; but the process is far from complete, and now it encounters among the electorate a hardening of resistance to any new taxes whatsoever.

Passage of the 1913 constitutional amendment allowed the federal government to levy income taxes. Washington soon took up the option, and by the late 1920s personal and corporate income taxes had become the mainstay of the federal fisc (displacing customs duties and excise fees). By 1974, 59 percent of federal budget receipts were accounted for by taxes on income and another 30 percent by social security taxes. With given rates, rising personal and corporate incomes yield increasing tax revenues; so that the general revenue of the federal government is derived mainly from a progressive tax rate system strongly responsive to economic growth. Most of this lucrative direct tax harvest is then utilized by Washington to develop its military establishment.

SLGs on the other hand have been dependent upon property, sales and excise taxes. These made up 78 percent of SLG tax revenues in 1950, a proportion that was only marginally reduced during the long economic boom that followed. Despite greater recourse by SLGs to income taxes in the postwar period, 72 percent of SLG tax revenues still came from the traditional property-sales-excises sources in 1973. Not only are such taxes regressive, they are less sensitive to economic growth than income-based taxes—which means that rates must be sharply escalated if they are to produce more revenue. States and municipalities have done just that over the past decade, but at the cost of much dissatisfaction and opposition. At present any further hikes in the traditional taxes would appear to be limited by business community threats to move away, to areas with "more reasonable tax burdens."

The gap between the financial capacity of SLGs and the service demands on them had become so wide by the 1960s that the federal government was gradually forced into the picture indirectly via increasing grants-in-aid, revenue sharing and a certain number of direct federal programs. Total federal aid to SLGs was up from $11 billion in 1965 to $46 billion in 1974. This 1974 total includes general revenue sharing payments of $6.1 billion, urban renewal funding of $1.2 billion Medicaid payments of $5.8 billion, EPA subsidies of $1.6 billion (mainly for the construction of waste disposal facilities), and public assistance payments of $5.4

billion, among other outlays. These are substantial sums, and it may seem ungenerous to cavil about their adequacy. Still, they must be considered in the context of the huge demands being imposed on SLGs.

The $46 billion aid total of 1974 is far less than the *increase* in SLG outlays for education since 1950 (over $60 billion), and barely exceeds the direct (unassisted) outlays of SLGs for health and welfare, which grew from $6.2 billion in 1950 to $44.6 billion in 1974. Federal aid to education, far and away the largest SLG expenditure, has been extremely modest—the $46 billion SLG aid total of 1974 includes $1.7 billion for primary and secondary schools, which is less than 5 percent of SLG outlays for local schools. Even in the field of health and welfare the more substantial assistance of the federal government has typically matched SLG contributions, and in the context of mounting demands SLGs have had to foot an enormous bill.

Under the impact of regional and class conflicts of interest, and log-rolling accommodations, federal aid has also suffered from a tendency to spread benefits widely rather than concentrating on points of need. We have seen that taxable assessed property values have increased more rapidly in cities of the sunbelt states, while at the same time they have required fewer or less expensive municipal services than many of the older declining cities. In 1972-73 the cost of municipal services per person was $141 in growing cities, $240 in declining cities, and $637 in New York City. Federal aid has responded to differences in need, but a significant proportion of federal resources have been allocated on other bases.

Principles & Possibilities Of Reform

The technical problems of relieving the urban crisis are difficult, but theoretically manageable. The *political* problems are severe—and may even be unsolvable in the immediate future. The federal government has the revenue capability, but it lacks the social purpose: its eye is currently on Angola and its purse strings have long been loose only for national "defense." SLGs have the responsibilities for civil society—by default—but neither the resources nor the breadth of political scope and vision, given the fact that modern urban problems are national in a literal sense.

One proposed solution to the urban crisis is metropolitanization, i.e., the consolidation of all the fragmented communities of metropolitan areas into single political-fiscal units. Some cities (Indianapolis, Phoenix,

Houston and Dallas), have found it possible to take this route, extending their jurisdiction into the expanding suburbs by systematic absorption. But they are the exceptions. As a solution to the more deep-seated urban malaise, this route presents several difficulties. First, it would still not improve the overall fiscal capacity of SLGs relative to the federal government. Secondly, it would still not encompass a large enough territory to capture all important spill-over effects and to preclude inter-area competition. Finally, the fragmentation process (suburbanization and the escape of those able to do so from the problems of central cities) has created conflicts of interest among local political units that make voluntary consolidation ever more difficult. Consolidation could be forced or encouraged by state and federal authority, but it offers no ready panacea for the urban crisis.

The most promising route to solutions almost certainly involves an expanded role for the federal government. Only Washington has the operating scope to take into account spill-over effects, and it has the resources —tax capability and debt issuing powers—to meet urban needs. A 20 percent reduction in national defense outlays, which might well *enhance* national security, would provide an excellent starter. It would allow the federal government to take over entirely the public assistance budget of SLGs, and to begin investing in public transportation systems and urban reconstruction. A restructuring of federal taxes to allow more room for state and local taxes would help—especially closing the gaping loopholes for the affluent and terminating the use of the regressive payroll tax to finance social security. Revenue sharing, tied more effectively to need, can also be a useful short-term expedient for allowing SLGs to participate in the superior tax resources of the federal government. It was used by Nixon, not as a supplementary sharing device but rather as a substitute for federal responsibilities simultaneously terminated. (For Reagan and Ford, also, federal cutbacks and "consolidations" of programs are thinly veiled attempts to reduce social expenditures under the rhetorical guise of "decentralization" and reducing the "burden" of government.)

At bottom, the real problem is that the American socio-economic system does not readily respond to mere human need, even at home, that cannot be geared closely to the private profit-making process. The breakdown of the 1930s and the burning of the cities in 1967 could elicit national programs, but usually patchwork in planning, under-funded and petering out in the absence of renewed crisis. One of the few federal programs with massive funding over an extended period has been highways—i.e., one in which a powerful congeries of auto and oil companies, real estate and construction businesses, and building trades unions provided a critical support base. Comparable funding has never been available for metropolitan and interurban transport systems (in 1974 federal aid for highways totaled $4.5 billion; for mass transportation, $348 million).

In our Bicentennial year Gerald Ford sees it as a political plus to recommend a big boost in military spending and a slashing of social outlays on a wide front; and Edmund Muskie's political sensors lead him to pledge a "tough spending ceiling" and to admonish us against the delusion that problems can be solved "by simply throwing federal dollars at them." Altering this picture will require mass organization arising out of grass roots interests and purposes, prepared to combat the overwhelming impact of corporate enterprise on national priorities. Establishing such organizations, *de novo*, or via a stunning transformation of American trade unionism, should rank high on the public agenda for the 1970s.

Business Prospects in the Inner City

"The inner city is the worst place to do business in the U.S., and is unlikely to get better."

Richard N. Farmer

*Professor of International Business,
Indiana University, Bloomington*

THE REDISCOVERY of poverty in the mid-1960's led to rediscovery of small business prospects in the inner city. This new interest was tied up with new interest in minority rights, since the inner city also has a large black and Chicano population these days. Investigators discovered that there was indeed a minority business sector, more or less alive, but certainly not well, concentrated largely in retail service establishments of the mom-and-pop sort. Since encouraging capitalism attracted two disparate groups—the black activists and the conservative banker types—it seemed logical and even humanitarian to support minority business efforts.

So, for 10 years now, we have seen fairly extensive efforts to help out minority firms—and, after 10 years, very little has happened. The percentage of business done by minority enterprise is perhaps the same, if not a bit less, than it was 10 years ago, and no minority-owned giant corporations have emerged to threaten or support the business mainstream. The few well-managed large minority firms have done about as well as the rest of the economy, and a handful of million-dollar-level new minority firms have emerged. Minority business development has been interesting, but hardly world-shaking, especially after several billion dollars of expenditures have been made in helping out. Like most other grandiose projects designed to achieve equality, support of minority enterprise, at best, has achieved very little.

Inner-city business support is an example of trying to do things with all the wrong premises underlying support attempts. Dreamers and planners think up schemes, and even get them financed, but, unless we have a realistic idea of what is actually going on, the dreams fail. What went wrong here?

Problems of the Inner City

The inner city is the worst place to do business in the U.S., and is unlikely to get better. On the demand side, population is steadily falling, which makes it tough for firms catering to individual consumers; income levels per capita are very low, which makes things worse; and most consumers, as their incomes go up, either leave the inner city or find more attractive options, such as supermarkets and suburban shopping centers. We have seen a lot of efforts to encourage ghetto residents to buy black, but such appeals fail quickly when consumers can find better products at lower prices elsewhere.

The inner city is also a very high-cost place to do business. Exploding crime rates, particularly burglaries, create costs which inner-city businessmen must bear. The cramped physical layouts of most inner-city neighborhoods means higher distribution costs, since large trucks can not get to the stores to make mass deliveries, even if the stores were large enough to buy in truckload lots, which they typically are not. Old buildings burn easily, which leads to higher insurance rates.

Where minority capitalists have ventured into other fields, the inner-city structure also creates high costs. Contractors have to wrestle with high crime rates, lack of skilled labor, and low levels of construction investment in the smaller types of projects where a good man can learn. A small firm can not handle the multi-billion-dollar projects, except to be a subcontractor on one piece of the total action. Manufacturers can try to make ancient, multi-story factory buildings viable, which is difficult. The mainstream manufacturers abandoned these 20 or 30 years ago. Black-oriented companies, selling insurance, newspapers and magazines, cosmetics, or undertaking services, do well, but they are trapped with smaller markets determined by the very nature of their services and products.

Throwing Money at Problems

All of these problems were obvious to any astute observer in 1965 or 1970, but politicians and activists felt that something had to be done. So, we began our usual type of reformist efforts, which attacked the symptoms, but not the causes. Ask any businessman what he needs and the answer is always the same—money. Everyone has a cash shortage. Moreover, it was and is easy to make a good and correct case for the fact that minority businessmen were unable to obtain capital easily, so the obvious answer to all problems was to provide cash. We now have the Office for Minority Business Enterprise, new efforts by the Small Business Administration, private efforts (mainly quite small) by private banks, and considerable foundation money tossed into the minority capital pool. For a while, anyone who claimed to be a small minority businessman could get at least a few thousand dollars with no collateral and no questions asked, and some gifted con men managed to do a lot better than that. Usual loan standards, of course, did not apply to these needy firms.

In the end, the result was exactly what might be expected. Most of the cash was lost, and much of the rest was tied up in slow receivables. Organizations got a few million dollars, announced grandiose plans, lent out all available resources, and then sat back and waited for results. With all cash tied up in dubious ventures, it did not take long for the organization to lose all its clout, since it could not finance more. The beginning concept of revolving loan funds got bogged down in losses, and, after a year or two, such organizations gradually drifted to impotence. The inner city fumbled on, without much happening that was economically important.

Mistaken Premises

Examination of such experiences suggests several mistaken premises. The first was to believe that capital is the key to everything. However, not only is the inner city a terrible place to do business, it also is a place where managerial and technical skills are in very short supply. Saying that I can build an office building is easy—knowing how to actually do it is quite another thing. Given low training and experience levels, it is not surprising that many inner-city firms promised a lot more than they could deliver.

A second assumption which has created much trouble is the Egalitarian Thesis that all businessmen are the same. If all are in trouble, then it makes sense to give each his or her fair share. In practice, this led to some very sharp and potentially great companies getting a bit of cash, while incompetents and outright crooks also got the same amounts. It seems offensive in the white mainstream to even infer that some blacks are less capable than others, but, as in all groups, this happens to be true. If public programs assume the opposite, particularly in such a tricky and complex field as business, then the results of any program will be dismal. Good people can not get enough capital to make a difference, while incompetence will waste most of the assets.

Four out of five small firms fail in the first year, and black-owned firms are no different from white in this regard. Public programs and socially oriented ones are in trouble on this point, since it seems unethical to find the winners and give them all the cash. Yet, the winners will be the ones who provide the economic gains and employment, not the losers.

A third assumption which no one notices, but which turns out to be crucial for inner-city businessmen, is the fixed-in-place syndrome. It is typically assumed that the best place to be is where one is. Hence, the inner-city firm being supported is implicitly expected to stay put, in its dreary economic environment.

Actually, any firm or individual with any economic aspiration has every incentive to get out of the inner city—the economic and even social climate is so much better out in the mainstream. If a sharp black entrepreneur succeeds in retailing in the inner city, his next best move is to start some stores in the suburban shopping centers, where the money is. A good black contractor should get out and make bids on the lush projects in the suburbs, while the black manufacturer should buy or lease a modern low-lying industrial plant out in the new industrial park at the fringe of the city. A few (very few) successful black firms are doing this, and they are likely to be the big winners in the next 20 years. Ironically, however, they will merely be well-managed firms in the mainstream that just happened to be owned by blacks, not inner-city operations. In the end, when the black-owned firm succeeds, it loses its color. The capable black owner/manager sounds just like any other successful businessman.

People leave the ghetto too. Literally thousands of highly motivated, intelligent blacks have been trained in business in the past 10 years, and over 90% of them work for mainstream white firms since the pay is better and the risks are smaller. Good black and Chicano technicians can find very good jobs with large companies, thanks to fair employment efforts, and General Motors is a lot better employer than most small black firms.

So, after all the hoopla, excitement, and activity, we are about where we were 10 years ago. Not much has happened and, given these mistaken premises about what is going on, not much will happen. The inner city will continue to become more depopulated, the mama/papa stores will struggle along marginally, and economic development through minority enterprise development will not deliver the goods. This is too bad, since there is, in fact, a pool of very competent minority businessmen around who just might become very important.

Realistic Strategies

Here and there we can find a few organizations that actually do get something done. The reason they work well is because they have a hard-nosed, realistic view of what the problem is and, as we might expect, they violate all three premises noted above.

If we want results, we should first recognize that smart people can get money. Most smart people can be brought up to this level by some tough education, which involves mainly finding out how the *man* runs financial rationing systems. This means, in practice, lots of tough micro-financial work. Banks like to see good accounting, cash-flow projections, budgets, and other evidence that the borrower just might know what he is talking about. A good loan proposal for a half-million dollars can run 50 pages or more and involves more technical accounting and financial work than most minority businessmen know, but they can be taught.

Second, smart businessmen find business where it is, not where romantics want them to be. If this means getting out of the inner city, then the smart people will get out.

Third, and perhaps most importantly, successful programs have learned that you bet on the favorites, not the long shots. If your goal is to develop minority firms quickly, it is easier to find the 10 best companies now (out of several hundred, perhaps) and try to double their sales. If these minority firms were good enough to survive and prosper in the inner city, they should be good enough to grow very fast. Few programs have seen this point, which means that they are not very effective, but those that have have prospered. This strategy means giving those who have still more, which makes it unfair, unegalitarian, immoral, and all that. All you can say for it is that it works. Most businessmen, even those who survive, are unable to grow very much, but a few winners can. They tend to be the ones who already have their Cadillacs, but, if they double in size, they will hire more people, expand incomes more rapidly, and generally get the kinds of economic development minorities so desperately need.

All through the 1960's and to date, the poor have gained a bit, but the rich have gained more, so that the gaps between the two groups have widened. Efforts to narrow the gaps, while based on very nice ethnical principles, apparently just do not work too well economically. Programs designed for growth become a low-level dole, allowing people to eke out some precarious existence, while, unfortunately, penalizing those who just might be able to do something about the situation. Until we do some very clear thinking about what we want to do and why, it is highly unlikely that very much will happen.

Thoughts on a Bicentennial City
Boston Desegregation
Joseph Featherstone

This is the second year and second phase of court-ordered desegregation in Boston. Phase I, in the fall of 1974, touched off demonstrations, boycotts and bloodshed. Cool weather brought a lull to the racial violence that flickered through the streets last summer. With the exception of South Boston High, which remains in turmoil, most of the city's schools are relatively quiet. Attendance figures have climbed steadily. Resistance to busing continues strong in white neighborhoods, particularly the Irish enclaves of Charlestown and South Boston. Groups opposed to busing, such as ROAR (Restore Our Alienated Rights) have been subdued. Near the high school in Charlestown, mothers have staged marches against busing, prayed and sat in the streets. At night white youths throw rocks and bait the police. This school year, supporters of desegregation, or at least obedience to the law, are better organized in the city. The city's leaders, who have equivocated on busing, now stand foursquare against violence. A desultory mayoral campaign has resulted in the reelection of Mayor Kevin White. The legal technology for enforcing desegregation has expanded into a formidable machine: city, state and metropolitan police, units of the National Guard, federal marshals, the FBI, officials from the Justice Department, have all entered into play at one time or another. A teachers' strike came and went without shattering the tense calm. A relative quiet reigns, but a lot of people are very scared.

Meanwhile Bicentennial visitors arrive in town to see the sights—Bunker Hill memorial is just across the way from Charlestown High—and pay tribute to the 200th anniversary of our republic.

US District Court Judge Arthur Garrity has issued a very complicated desegregation plan. Besides busing, it involves new districts, a large city-wide magnet district with special programs to draw students from the neighborhoods voluntarily, and a complex series of advisory councils to monitor the whole operation. The judge is making an unprecedented effort to link desegregation with improvements in education. It remains to be seen how much he'll accomplish. His notion of pairing schools with businesses and universities still has to be worked out. The distinguished array of institutions of higher education around Boston stays aloof from schools; strangely enough, it is not clear what crack universities can offer the city's schoolchildren. Apart from student assignments, the most visible effect of the judge's planning is the presence in the system's 162 schools of more black and Spanish-speaking teachers. Boston's students are 52 percent white, 36 percent black and 12 percent other minorities, such as Spanish-speaking children and Chinese. Desegregation here, as elsewhere, has sharpened each group's awareness of grievances: Spanish-speaking parents worry that it has thrown bilingual services into confusion, and some Chinese parents conducted a boycott to resist busing.

Judge Garrity has in many respects taken temporary possession of the school system. No one supposes that a federal judge should be doing this, yet the situation is not of his making. It results from the fact that for many years both the school administration and the school committee have deliberately segregated black schoolchildren, maintaining what is in many respects a dual school system. The school administration is a mainly Irish hierarchy that looks back to better days; its inbred loyalties have produced a style of professionalism even more pathological and vacuum-sealed than that of other big city systems. The Boston School Committee, though it often speaks the genuine concerns of its constituents, has been a scandal.

A new school committee has recently been elected. With the election, the committee lost two opponents of desegregation. The voters elected three moderates and one staunch foe of busing. One of the moderates, Kathleen Sullivan, got more votes than any other candidate for any city office, which some take as a mark of the voters' recognition that the old school committee had taken them for a ride.

Whatever the future of the new committee, the present mess is in large part the work of the old. Three of its members profited politically and in more direct ways from the city's prolonged school crisis—one is under indictment for misuse of school funds—and thus had a vested interest in keeping trouble alive. On the eve of the second phase of desegregation, for example, the old committee fired William J. Leary, the capable school superintendent who supervised Phase I. They replaced Leary with Marion J. Fahey, who promptly began appointing as functionaries in the school system figures known as fund raisers for school committeemen. (Local Boston practice is to shake down employees of the school system for political contributions.) As the desegregation crisis came to a head, Fahey busied herself getting rid of the new district superintendent of the magnet schools, John Coakley. Coakley's offenses were two: he worked hard and in good faith planning desegregation, and he publicly refused to go along with the custom of donating to the political campaigns of school committee members.

The new school committee may change this sort of thing. And Judge Garrity may have performed a real service in opening up new channels in the city's moribund educational politics. Citizens and parents have started to participate in the newly activated district councils and advisory groups. Whatever happens, it seems likely that the administration and the new school committee are going to get more attention from parents and people active at the school level, which will be a big change. It is also clear that the teachers' union, which has supported desegregation, will play a larger role in shaping school policies.

In the short run, though, a question remains whether the school administration will desegregate in good faith. On alternate days, Judge Garrity plays philosopher king or Brer Rabbit confronting the tar baby. If he stays above it all, he can't be sure that anything is happening; if he steps in, he's engulfed, handling everything from pupil assignments to purchases of walkie-talkies. He has considered putting the school system into some form of receivership, and it may come to that. (He's already done that at one school.) The imperviousness of the administration and the small, dangerous wiles of the politicians only make up a fraction of the city's problem, but they give it a particularly local twist. Social forces outside the schools, years of conflicting demands for compensatory education and desegregation, the fears of the whites, the bitterness and frustration of the blacks, have all gone to creating a war no one can win.

The Bicentennial is on many people's minds. The contrast between its ideals and the frightening actualities of the present, and between memories of recent decades of relative peace and the present turmoil, all feed a sense of loss. There is something elegaic in the air, as when Judge Garrity writes in the past tense, "Boston became the bridge not only to liberty but to the ideal of the free, universal and inclusive public school." The anti-busing people speak a nostalgic language of rights and redress for the wrongs of an oppressive government. Black activists and the lawyers for the NAACP are fighting for rights, liberty and an ideal of schooling, although they don't have much to be nostalgic about. To the worried whites and blacks who are not activists, people who live in very similar three deckers and projects, there doesn't seem all that much to celebrate.

It is a bad time; many feel it to be the worst of times. The memory of the bitter ethnic and religious wars of the past is fading, and people have forgotten that

Boston's history in the 19th and 20th centuries is a story of chronic, sometimes violent conflict. The struggles between Yankee Protestant Republicans and Irish Catholic Democrats formed the major fault line, but successive cleavages opened up as each set of older groups faced each wave of newcomers: Italians, French-Canadians, Jews, Portuguese and now blacks and Puerto Ricans. Blacks go back a long way in Boston, but their numbers were small until the 1950s. Within the memory of many citizens, Roxbury was a mainly Jewish section of town; it is littered with abandoned synagogues. Now the older ethnic quarrels take second place to race, without, however, disappearing.

Our pleasant legends about schools in the past lead us to ignore the fact that they, too, were involved in the wars. These days a number of what are sometimes called "revisionist" historians are looking into the past of institutions like schools, prisons and asylums. The revisionists have only a mood in common; the mood is skeptical. They peer at the motives of the founding fathers of such public institutions, and find them more mixed than many of us think. American traditions of reform and institution-building have a dark side, it turns out. It might interest Bicentennial visitors who come across the statue of Horace Mann to know that Mann cuts a rather different figure in the historians' accounts from the public figure portrayed in earlier boosterish histories of public education. He begins to look more like Melville's monomaniacal Captain Ahab than the benign figure of reform legend.

In a sense, Mann and the founding fathers of many of our urban institutions were obsessed by what we now call the crisis of the cities, which has been going on much longer, at least in the older Eastern cities, than we generally imagine. Boston's schools in the 1830s and 1840s were a first venture in what we now speak of, rather grandly, as the framing of social policy. They were one facet of a complex institutional response to modernity, part of a whole array of institutions designed to redress the imbalances generated by unchecked economic growth and technological change.

From the beginning, city schools were perceived as an answer to problems generated by industry, technology, divisions of labor and new impersonal urban institutions. The reformers hoped they would take up the slack for other, supposedly failing older institutions, such as the family, the village and the church. They intended schools to renew a sense of community in cities where community was felt to be collapsing. Building common schools was a real achievement in cities whose inhabitants found it very difficult to act collectively. Nineteenth century civic reformers found it hard to wrest services such as water, sewers and even police forces from a profoundly individualistic culture given over to a frenzy of capitalist enterprise. In the chaotic cities whose slums appalled foreign visitors like Charles Dickens, schools were sometimes the only collective and communal enterprise Americans seemed able to agree on.

Modernity made Americans strangers to each other in two ways whose consequences we still live with. First the industrial revolution made strangers out of country and village people who were going to have to work in factories, new realms of social distance and divided labor. And second native Yankees confronted a flood of alien immigrants. Richard Titmuss once said that the central question of social policy is what people in modern societies are willing to do for strangers. In America the crucial fact about industrialization is that it coincided with immigration. Americans were doubly strange because they belonged to different social classes and because they were drawn from different countries and races.

The reformers who faced this twin urban crisis tried to make the schools into what one historian aptly calls "cultural factories"; they were supposed to right imbalances, restore lost community and keep order. Schools were also part of the social machinery with which the Yankees attempted to deal with the threat the strangers posed to their rule. Among other functions, schools served as poverty programs to shape up the children of successive waves of strangers.

In reacting against the legends that paint education as the pillar of democracy, the revisionists show the power of the American love-hate relationship with schools. Once, implausibly, schools were thought to be all-powerful agents of social good. Now, in the revisionists' hands, the old legend gets turned on its head and the schools sound, equally implausibly, like malevolent elite conspiracies against democracy. (An echo, perhaps, of the curdled nationalism that imagines sin to be uniquely American.) The revisionists generally think of themselves as radicals, yet they usually write elite history, in the sense that they concentrate on the motives of the Yankee reformers. They tell the story as a melodrama in which elites work their wicked will on the passive immigrant masses. We still lack an adequate history of what ordinary people made of schools, but there are bits and pieces of a more complex and interesting story at hand. It is significant, I think, that the first articulate rationale for public education in places like Boston and New York came from the working class political parties whose vigor so impressed Karl Marx. Where the elite reformers stressed the role of schools in promoting social order, the workers argued that the citizens of a republic needed education to preserve their liberties against the threats of power and privilege. (Early on, workers were less enthusiastic about the high schools, which seemed to them to benefit the middle class.) You would not gather from the revisionists that immigrant outsiders themselves placed a high value on education, and badly wanted schools to do their part in helping raise literate children. Nor would you gather that immigrants wanted schools

to Americanize their children—only on their terms, and not those of the Yankee elites. But they did.

The reformers did want to impose their values on the children of Boston's strangers. Yet to desire is not to succeed. The dreams of social and cultural control through schools often turned out to be pipe dreams. The truth is that big city schools rarely worked well, for good or evil purposes. Throughout much of their history, for example, they have not been able even to catch up with the numbers of immigrant children whose parents clamored to enroll them. Schools excluded the poorest and most unruly of what were called "the dangerous classes." They enrolled the children of the deserving poor, when there was room.

Being radicals who are skeptical of today's politics, the revisionists tend to ignore city politics in the past, which is a great mistake. For while politics in the past, like politics today, is often a charade and a comic opera, it is also important. Our city history is not a tedious melodrama in which the elite villains have always had their way. It is the story of conflict, in which the "masses," far from being passive, fought back. It is among other things the story of how ordinary people acted on their own behalf, battling with some successes and some defeats against narrow definitions of what it is to be American. Often, as Diane Ravitch has shown in *The Great School Wars*, conflicts over city politics and institutions like schools were the arenas in which the hopes of the immigrants confronted the fears of the Yankees.

Thus the schools stood in an ambiguous relationship to the city's strangers. An extraordinary consensus emerged as to the value of schooling but, like the larger ideological consensus of American society as a whole— the common agreement on the sanctity of private property and the Constitution—it masked profound conflict over who would define the purposes and content of public education and whose definition of America it would serve. (The awkwardness of those Bicentennial TV programs about our past derives from the fact that a central issue has always been who would be included as one of "us.") The growth of the Catholic parochial schools—still a critical, if generally ignored part of Boston's educational scene, enrolling just under a quarter of the city's schoolchildren—was a response to the Protestant nativism preached in the public schools. The creation of separate Catholic schools marked an extreme of religious dissent from bigoted versions of the American consensus as great as that of black separatists and community control advocates in recent years.

When schools insulted outsiders they fought back; the result was the school wars that Diane Ravitch chronicled for New York. (Boston's wars remain to be described.) Sometimes elites and reformers won, as in the successful effort to centralize the big city systems whose rigidities plague us today, and sometimes immigrants and outsiders won, as in the establishment of ward and neighborhood systems, the hiring of immigrant teachers, or in the capture of city hall and the machinery of local government. As the fortunes of the wars shifted, power was reshuffled and to different political jurisdictions; and as they won or lost, cycles of separatist and integrationist political impulses touched the outsiders.

It is at this point in the story that blacks, sensing that historic parallels are about to be drawn, demur. Such parallels have a heavy symbolic weight these days. Blacks insist that their story, the record of their oppression, is different. And these days, many of the social historians agree. In his admirable book, *The Other Bostonians*, Stephen Thernstrom has talked about the various strangers who struggled for a living in 19th and 20th-century Boston. Many things he describes are novel and fascinating: the high rates of social and geographical mobility belie our picture of the past as more stable than today. (To read historians like Thernstrom is to find out that urban malaise was probably never less than it is today; in many periods it looks decidedly worse.) Thernstrom asks why different immigrant groups rose from the bottom at such very different rates, the Irish and the Italians who now predominate in Boston being slower than many others. The reasons are complicated: a mix of history, culture, religion, previous city experience and a good many other factors that Thernstrom and others have yet to explain. The historic position of blacks is striking. In a city of rising immigrants, their place lay squarely and permanently on the bottom. They are the only group that for a long sweep of Boston's history looks like a permanent proletariat, certainly the only group in American life requiring a national political movement to begin to alter its historic status. In recent decades, Thernstrom cautiously concedes, their status has changed somewhat. From World War II on, a combination of prosperity and political activism did produce gains. For this period, Thernstrom guesses, it might be possible to draw some parallels between blacks and other groups. Most of the time the parallels don't hold.

Nineteenth century blacks in Boston and elsewhere struggled first for families and churches, then for freedom, then for schools. It seems to be an axiom of educational history that strangers and dissenters—those barred from formal educational institutions—must put all the more stress on informal ways of passing on their culture and tradition, such as families, synagogues and churches. The struggle for families, the social historians are showing, was far more successful than the social scientists who speak of the legacy of slavery and black family pathology generally realize. The long struggle for access to formal schooling came next. It is partly a consequence of this history that faith in education tends to be even stronger among blacks than among other groups. In point of cold statistics, education did not serve blacks all that well. Schools often kept them out, North and South; the

separate education they did get was radically unequal, and premised on racist assumptions. Educators offered them a secondhand version of somebody else's idea of practicality and vocationalism. Many blacks got schooling without making gains in other realms. Thernstrom points out that the low standing of Boston's blacks is not explained by a lack of education. In 1950, for example, Boston's blacks had more education than the Irish, Italians and French Canadians, yet were lower in occupational status.

It is tempting to conclude from this that the traditional black preoccupation with access to schooling was misguided, a diversion from more fundamental issues. But that would be a mistake, I think. Blacks inherit more than their share of American faith in schools; but in the past this was less grounded in naive idealism than in a shrewd assessment that schools were the only game in town that would let them in, albeit on condescending racist terms. Schools kept blacks out and oppressed them, but they also served as havens, turfs and sources of jobs. The reasons for black separatism have been truly complex. (Reasons for white support of black separatism have been fairly simple.) There is a complex, dialectical quality to the whole story: segregated churches, for example, led to the spiritual autonomy of black Protestantism, and segregated schools and churches provided a base for those who, at different points in the story, led the attacks on slavery and segregation. The old dialectic between integration and separation has deep roots in the history of Boston's black community. The fascinating doubleness of the tale lies in the fact that the intentions of white society have never wholly controlled the use blacks have made of the racist institutions offered them.

Schools were the way up for black leaders and professionals, and they seem to have become more important in today's professionalized world of credentials and degrees. One crucial fact presses on the whole school situation today in Boston, illuminating another difference between immigrants of the past and the urban poor today: the lack of adequate work. It was not education that lifted most people in most groups—although some did use the schools to rise—but jobs. The immigrant kid who left school became a worker; black students who leave today are part of the unemployed dropout problem. When all the long, moralizing analyses of group character and social pathology are rehearsed, the difference in the past between those who were able to climb out of the dangerous classes and those who weren't probably boils down to the availability of steady work.

Schools in the past, as today, were arenas of conflict; they were, as they are, more accessible to outsiders than most other institutions. The same ambiguous quality—the legitimacy conferred by access—that pervades the American political system suffuses the history of education. Politics and the politics of the

3. URBAN PROBLEMS

schools have mediated the symbols of ethnic, religious and, in recent times, racial conflict. It's exasperating to see the way the ethnic, religious and racial agenda has consistently overshadowed the pursuit of economic justice and a redistribution of power. The responsiveness of schools, like the responsiveness of politics itself, has certainly worked to defuse class conflict. The revisionists and neo-Marxists are quite right to point out that in many ways the traditional focus on politics and education is a poor substitute for fundamental economic change. The school wars never challenged the mainly economic values and priorities of the society; and thus in many respects schools have been marginal to the main business of the American past, which was business. And in classic form, the historic dilemmas of the schools reflect the problems of all social service institutions in an unequal, competitive capitalist society. The egalitarian promise conflicts with the realities of inequality.

Yet to the historic actors the symbols involved in urban politics and school wars have been fundamental, sometimes worth dying for. Religion, ethnicity and race overlay and complicate the class politics of American cities. What makes the educational history of Boston terribly complicated is the fact that to the participants, the poor and the working class, as well as the elites, the central fact about American life was the diversity of its peoples, and not the existence of clear-cut, homogeneous, counterpoised social classes.

This urban history has left a legacy (of strengths and weaknesses) that affects life in the city to this day. The main strength is the historic leverage that successive groups have been able to use to their own advantage. In fighting back, the strangers used the mechanisms of American city politics, including school politics, to force the culture to adopt a wider and more pluralistic definition of itself. Each group has taken over political tradition, the language of rights and the machinery of local politics and reworked them to its own purposes. The result, for all the bigotry that has surfaced in Boston today, is a more pluralistic society than many 19th-century Americans would have thought possible or desirable. (Because the central Boston cleavage pitted Yankees and the Irish against each other for so long, Boston's rather weak civic culture has been much more of a late-comer to urban pluralism than cities where a diversity of groups emerged earlier.) To describe all this is not to say, in the words of the banquet orators, that the system was sound. There was nothing automatic about what happened. It was not an abstract, benign "system," but people acting on their own behalf who changed things. Ruling groups never sent out engraved invitations to outsiders; strangers forced their way in.

One legacy from this past is a style of politics that stresses symbols. From the standpoint of jobs and bread and butter economics, it can look like a politics of

shadows, devoid of substance. In an earlier Boston the Irish working class was captivated by symbols of national and religious identity. These were never empty symbols. They were the sort of symbols by which, all over the world, people live and die. Yet the power of symbols made the Boston Irish here, as in Ireland, vulnerable to shadow politics; Irish and Yankee elites in Boston often worked out symbolic accommodations at the expense of the Irish poor. Now the symbols are racial, and once again they seem quite fundamental, but a certain lack of substance remains. "Ireland will get her freedom, and you will still break stones," Yeats had his Parnell say to the cheering workman.

A history of school and city wars created in the long haul a more pluralistic, tolerant and egalitarian city culture than that of the past. It never produced anything quite like the legendary melting pot, but the city historian Sam Bass Warner, Jr is right to argue in *Urban Wilderness: A History of the American City* that elements of a common urban culture emerged. Working class voters in Boston and other cities may be far ahead of the country's leadership in recognizing the need for basic social change guaranteeing people jobs, homes, schools and adequate medical care. The way the present symbolic fight over the schools diverts everyone from such egalitarian goals gives one a sinking feeling that even the winners, if there are any, will end up breaking stones.

The history of the school wars got forgotten. In part it was forgotten because after the 1920s, when the main features of the present centralized and professionalized school systems were in place, it became plausible—though never entirely convincing—to think of schools as the apolitical province of neutral experts and professionals. Second and third generation immigrants forgot their parents' fight. For several decades, there was relative peace. The school machine ticked quietly. The revisionist historians are right to point to the enormous significance of the organizational changes that took place. Whatever else the progressive educational reformers left us—and their legacy is an ambiguous mixture indeed—it is clear that they were cementing professions and bureaucracies that have often taken on a life of their own. And it is clear that the world they built is very different from the highly political world of the 19th-century schools. Yet, as we are finding out in a new era of school wars, schools are still a very political matter. The present politics of education is so complex precisely because it represents a fusion of older political styles, traditions and institutions, with the professionalized realm of bureaucracies, experts, courts, unions, national educational policies and statistics. Some would argue that the new professionalized order has totally usurped the old, making a mockery of the democratic machinery of local school governance. There is a good deal of truth in this: Judge Garrity's constituency of lawyers and other federal judges is not the same as the constituency that just elected Mrs. Louise Day Hicks to the Boston city council. And yet the political role of the schools in Boston today—as the arena of confrontation between the city's older groups and new—does bear a resemblance to the role of the schools in the less complicated and professionalized past, just as the battles over community control in New York City bore an eerie resemblance to earlier school wars. Much has changed; there is no doubt that in many areas of education there is a growing chasm between the machinery of local democratic governance and the highly professionalized, often national forces that play on the schools. But some things remain the same.

Historically, symbols of religion and ethnicity and race take precedence over those of class. This is true today in Boston, where many people have the feeling that what is going on in the schools is largely symbolic; the have-littles and the have-nothings are set to fighting over bones without any meat on them, while the haves look on and shake their heads. Class emerges when people speak resentfully of the elites who send children to private schools and make decisions about busing.

The common culture of Boston is plagued by two historic weaknesses that run from the past to the present. One is the continuing acceptance of the legitimacy of a society run as a lottery with big winners and big losers. The ready acceptance of enormous differential rewards for the privileged has crippled the culture's egalitarianism. The egalitarianism of American life is real, but it easily turns into what Richard Hofstadter once called an equality of greed, rather than fraternity. This is why the fitful Populist impulse of this society is so vulnerable to entrepreneurial radicalism, slogans and reactionary styles of populism that attack everything but corporate privilege and the enormous disparities of wealth and power. Reactionary populism has a particular susceptibility to the second great historic threat to urban culture: its racism.

The acceptance of gross inequality and racism both frame the current crisis, which involves another set of strangers. Once again the symbols are crucial, and far from empty, yet there is not even any guarantee of solid improvements in education, let alone in the economic status of either working class blacks or whites in the city. Beyond teaching staffs, schools do not have all that many jobs to offer. They cannot create new jobs or break down the walls of residential segregation or repair existing housing, or build new homes. They can give blacks in the city the exact amount of symbolic and educational leverage they have won through the history of the court decisions in the 21 years since the famous Brown case, but at a potential political cost and a potential sacrifice of real Populist possibilities to reactionary Populist demagoguery. Boston is twisting in the ambiguous momentum this society has taken since the Brown decision.

Things appeared less complicated in 1954. When the Rev. Oliver Brown tried to enroll his daughter in an all-white school three blocks from home in Topeka, school authorities instead bused her to an all-black school 21 blocks away. The Rev. Brown sued, and ultimately the Supreme Court declared that separate schools were inherently unequal and therefore a violation of black children's constitutional rights under the Fourteenth Amendment. The Brown decision and its successors struck crippling blows to the Southern system of dual schools. The struggle for desegregation in the South led to many regional and national gains for blacks.

Contrary to what much current defeatist thinking about education says, schools can act as powerful instruments of social change. Not by themselves, of course, but in alliance with other social forces. The Brown decision shows this. Together with post-war prosperity and the civil rights movement, the events touched off by the Brown decision led to the destruction of many historic obstacles to equality, altering the terms of the country's most enduring dilemma, the relations between the races. Brown helped sweep away the legal underpinning of the South's Jim Crow system. It was part of a whole series of modernizing forces that transformed today's South into something very different from a one-crop, single party region gripped by poverty and racial oppression. The federal civil rights acts—particularly the voter registration laws— are altering the political face of the region. Southern public education is now more integrated than Northern education. In some parts of the South, as politicians like Reuben Askew and Jimmy Carter have noted, the school issue has disappeared. And North and South, the black middle class—especially new professionals and white collar workers—has expanded. American society is far less monolithically racist than it was. Yet the Brown decision and the civil rights movement that both prompted it and fed on it were failures, too, in important respects whose consequences we are living with today. Neither changed the lot of the poor all that much. Schools in the North are still very segregated, and some of the larger Southern cities are resegregating along patterns familiar in the North. (At the time of the Brown decision no large city had a majority black population; the vast folk migration of rural Southern blacks to the Northern cities was still underway.) Everywhere in the country residential segregation has increased; the trend toward increasingly black cities and mainly white suburbs continues.

Thus the balance sheet on Brown, like that of the civil rights movement in general, has to be complex. Sometimes you hear it summed up in an argument between the generations. "Remember how bad things used to be, how far we have come," the old timers say. Against which the young insist: "Look at how bad things still are." Both have a point.

White Flight and School Resegregation: Some Hypotheses

Research on the human motives behind resegregation is unbelievably sketchy.
But Mr. Wegmann believes "racism" is a minor factor. If he is right, direct governmental intervention to improve school quality and safety — and to reduce social-class differences — will pay off handsomely. The alternative is two societies, one black and one white, neither understanding or trusting the other.

Robert G. Wegmann

ROBERT G. WEGMANN is associate professor of educational sociology, University of Houston at Clear Lake City. He is a former member of the Milwaukee Board of Education. This article is a modified version of a longer and fully documented chapter in Daniel U. Levine and Robert J. Havighurst, eds., Desegregating Big-City Schools, *a National Society for the Study of Education paperback to be published this spring by McCutchan. Mr. Wegmann acknowledges his debt to many researchers on whose work the article is based. Readers who wish a pre-publication copy of the fully documented paper may write Wegmann at the University of Houston at Clear Lake City, 2700 Bay Area Blvd., Houston, TX 77058. Enclose $1.*

As the recent debate between James Coleman and his critics has made clear,* desegregated schools exist within a multitude of contexts, and each of these contexts influences what does or does not happen in the school. There is an ongoing process of suburbanization which surely would have occurred if there were no racial minorities, but which in fact disproportionately involves the white middle class. There has

*James Coleman, "Racial Segregation in the Schools: New Research with New Policy Implications," *Phi Delta Kappan*, October, 1975, pp. 75-78; Robert Green and Thomas Pettigrew, "Urban Desegregation and White Flight: A Response to Coleman," *Phi Delta Kappan*, February, 1976, pp. 399-402.

been a major downturn in white birthrates which is now causing, in most school districts, a loss of white enrollment quite unconnected with desegregation. Longitudinal studies of school desegregation are complicated by the fact that school attendance areas and school district boundaries change over time. Comparisons with city census data can be difficult because many school systems have boundaries not conterminous with city boundaries. Further, there are minority groups other than blacks in most school systems. Some authors add these other minority students to the white population when analyzing white flight, others do not. Despite these problems, the available research on white withdrawal from desegregated schools does reveal some reasonably clear patterns.

Two Initial Distinctions

Before examining these patterns, however, it is particularly important to note the degree to which issues of race and class are consistently confounded when studying school resegregation. Blacks and most other minority groups are, of course, disproportionately poor. The poor do not do well in school, and schools where the poor are concentrated are no more attractive to minority-group parents (especially middle-class minority parents) than they are to white parents. The schools in communities such as Richmond, Virginia, are reported to be experiencing "black flight" as they become increasingly black and poor; they are just as unattractive to the black middle class as to the white middle class. Similarly, some 10,000

black students in Washington, D.C., are in private schools. What is often called "white flight" is, in fact, a class phenomenon as well as a racial phenomenon.

Further, it is useful to make a distinction between withdrawal and nonentrance. The phrase "white flight" tends to suggest that white students were attending a school, the school was integrated, and then white students found this undesirable and left. In fact, reported drops in white attendance in the first year of school desegregation really refer to students who never showed up at all. It wasn't that they experienced desegregation and found it undesirable; rather, they declined to try the experience in the first place. Some of this decline in white enrollment may consist of students who formerly attended a given school; but part may also consist of students who, in the absence of school integration, would have moved into a neighborhood but now have not done so.

In addition to nonentrance into the neighborhood served by a particular set of schools (elementary and secondary), there is also the issue of nonentrance into a particular school. Schools are particularly susceptible to nonentrance, not only because there are private and parochial alternatives but because the transition from elementary school to junior high, and from junior high to senior high (each school often serving a wider attendance area and having a different reputation and racial composition), repeatedly presents parents and students with the decision to enter or not enter.

Issues of Quality, Safety, and Status

Surprisingly, little research seems to be available on the motives that lead parents to avoid desegregated schools. Such discussions as are found center on three areas: parental perceptions of school quality, parental perceptions of student safety in the desegregated school, and parental concerns about social status. In view of the very limited data, however, any conclusions about the relative importance of these concerns (or their actual impact on the decision to withdraw from a desegregated school) must remain very tentative.

Neil Sullivan, the superintendent of schools who presided over the desegregation of the Berkeley (California) public schools, describes the main fears of white parents when school desegregation is proposed as fear for their children's safety and fear that educational quality will be lost. Concerns about educational quality do seem widespread; national polls show that a fourth of the public believes that the test scores of white students decline sharply in desegregated schools. Although such declines do *not* generally occur, the quality of research in this area leaves much to be desired.

Parental perceptions of student safety may also be involved in decisions to reject desegregated schooling. Black and white students bring differing perceptions of each other to the desegregated school. They may exhibit different behavior patterns and ways of handling conflict and hostility. Rumors can fly as latent parental fears are triggered by incidents which would otherwise be ignored. In some cases, of course, inner-city schools in our major cities are *not* safe, and physical attacks, shakedowns, and threats are real occurrences. What seems to be involved in some of these situations is the fact that, though desegregated, these schools are not truly integrated. Though black and white students are physically present in the same school, the degree of friendship, understanding, and community can be very low.

Finally, just as some individuals do not wish to live in a neighborhood with members of a group whose social status they view as below their own, some parents who do not have specific concerns about educational quality or safety as such may still object to having their children attend school with stu-dents from a lower social class. Desegregation generally brings not only an influx of black children into the white child's environment, but also an influx of lower-class children into a middle-class environment.

Although parental concerns about educational quality, safety, and status may be present no matter how the desegregated situation comes about, the available evidence suggests considerable differences in the likelihood of a school's resegregating and the process by which this may occur, depending on whether the racial mix in the school is a reflection of the neighborhood served by the school or whether some level of government has intervened to bring about school desegregation quite apart from the situation in the surrounding neighborhood. The resulting racial and class conflicts as well as patterns of flight and nonentrance (should these occur) can work themselves out in markedly different ways.

I. Neighborhoods and Schools In Racial Transition

Atlanta has been judicially cited as having a great deal of white flight from its school system, so much as to render further attempts at integration futile. The system, once majority white, was 69% minority by 1970. The minority population of the city as a whole, however, also went from 38% minority in 1960 to 52% in 1970. (It is routinely the case that the proportion black in a city's school system is well ahead of the proportion black in the general population.) Hence the change in the racial make-up of Atlanta's public schools took place within the context of a general change in the racial make-up of the entire city (witness the fact, for example, that Atlanta now has a black mayor). Indeed, all of Coleman's findings as he *initially* presented them must be considered to have happened within the context of the changing neighborhoods of large central cities, since a check by the *New York Times* revealed that there was no court-ordered busing, redistricting, or other "forced" integration in any of the 19 cities initially studied.

These changes in central-city racial balance are of considerable magnitude. According to the U.S. Commission on Civil Rights, enrollment in the 100 largest school districts (which have half of the nation's black pupils) dropped by 280,000 students between 1970 and 1972. Since there was a gain of 146,000 black students during this same period, the data suggest a very considerable loss of white students. Some of this loss, of course, can be attributed to a drop in the white birthrate and to other factors. Nonetheless, it is clear that whites with children are disproportionately likely to live in suburban areas. According to the U.S. Census Bureau, 60.1% of the white population (age 18 and over) of metropolitan areas lived in the suburbs in 1974; but 66.6% of the school-age whites (ages 5 to 17) were to be found in suburbs. Note that this is the opposite of what one might expect, since the poor are more likely to live in the city, and are also more likely to have large families. Of course, this situation need not be totally attributed to problems with schools; suburbanization would no doubt be going on if there were no racial minorities in the U.S., and suburbs hold special attractions for families with school-age children for other reasons. The data suggest, however, that schools do play a part.

The most obvious fact about the neighborhood context of school racial proportions is the very high degree of residential segregation that characterizes every U.S. city; there are only a few stable interracial neighborhoods in American cities. Some of this segregation is due, of course, to differences in income level, but rather convincing data show that economic factors account for only a small part of the concentration of blacks in the central city. According to the Census Bureau, blacks constituted only 5% of suburban populations in both 1970 and 1974, despite the fact that a majority of metropolitan residents now live in the suburbs rather than the central city.

Thus while it is important to understand how the process of school and neighborhood resegregation proceeds, it is initially necessary to point out that one fundamental fact cannot be ignored: Given constant density, a growing minority population staying within the central city will inevitably produce an increasing number of segregated neighborhoods and segregated schools.

Interracial neighborhoods are commonly found on the fringes of the black ghetto. What is striking as one reviews studies of the process of racial transition in these areas is the degree to which white *nonentrance* is much more involved than white flight as such. This is not to deny that some individuals move from racially changing neighborhoods specifically to avoid an interracial setting. The fundamental pattern, however, seems to be one of blacks moving short distances into racially mixed neighborhoods, while whites fail to compete with them for the available housing. One study in Milwaukee found that only 4% of a sample of black movers selected housing more than 10 blocks beyond the original ghetto neighborhood. At the same time, beyond 30% black occupancy, the number of new white housing purchases fell off sharply. Other data indicate that this is a common pattern; neighborhood racial change apparently is less a matter of invasion than of retreat. So long as blacks seek to occupy housing on the fringes of the ghetto while whites avoid it, racial change is inevitable. Such neighborhoods then go through a transition from a white to a black housing market.

The School and Neighborhood Change

The research on the school's role in the process of neighborhood change is sketchy, but suggests much. A study in Milwaukee found that in interracial neighborhoods the proportion of blacks within the school is consistently higher than the proportion of blacks within the school attendance area. And schools, like double beds, enforce a certain intimacy. One can ignore a neighbor down the street; it is harder to ignore someone sitting beside you in the classroom. The school, moreover, is a social institution which serves as the focal point for much community interaction.

Parents, students, and schools may or may not be ready for racial integration. To the extent that they are unprepared and fearful of racial change, the schools can become a focus of discontent. And the schools are, indeed, often unprepared and fearful of racial change. A study of riots and disruptions in public schools indicates that such disruptions are most likely to occur in schools with 6–25% minority population and lacking an integrated faculty — precisely the situation found in most urban schools as the neighborhoods they serve begin the process of racial transition.

The available research suggests that school and neighborhood have a recip-

rocal relationship, with the school seemingly more sensitive to racial transition. To consider what is happening to the racial make-up of the urban school outside the context of the racial make-up of its school attendance area and the changing racial proportions of the entire school district is to risk serious misunderstanding.

Any consideration of the "tipping point" controversy might most profitably occur within this framework. Various authors, including myself, have referred to a point where white departures accelerate or at least become irreversible, leading shortly to a neighborhood or school's becoming all black. References to this concept can be found in several school desegregation suits. A careful examination of racial change in Milwaukee's schools over the eight years for which data exist convinces me that, though there are occasional "surges" of white departures in individual schools in changing neighborhoods, the more common phenomenon seems to be a relatively steady pattern of black entrance combined with white departure and/or nonentrance. Schools do not "tip" by themselves. They resegregate because there is a growing black population which has to go *somewhere*, and which is being steered by a dual housing market to transitional neighborhoods; simultaneously, white buyers avoid these same neighborhoods, anticipating that they and the schools which serve them will shortly be resegregating. Thus it now seems to me that tipping is not a particularly useful concept to describe the changing racial proportions of schools, because it ignores the contexts within which resegregation takes place and tends to imply that there is no such thing as stable integration — which is not true.

Class Levels and Neighborhood Change

One additional variable which may be closely related to school resegregation is the social-class level of the white population in the changing neighborhood. One study in Detroit found that the moving-order of white households is markedly affected by family income, with the more prosperous families moving first; racial attitudes were irrelevant. Indeed, the disorders which have sometimes accompanied court-ordered busing seem to be concentrated in working- and lower-class areas, perhaps because these groups are more

prone to physical expressions of their frustrations, and perhaps because, unlike the middle class, they cannot easily afford to move quietly away.

Taken as a whole, the research evidence indicates rather strongly that, so long as in-migration and natural increase provide a growing minority population, it is most unlikely that the process of school "desegregation" in these changing neighborhoods around the fringes of the inner city will be anything but a temporary situation. Without government intervention to provide a stable level of integration in these schools, and simultaneously to provide adequate, safe, and desirable living opportunities for minority citizens in areas other than those immediately surrounding the inner city, the process of resegregation cannot but continue. In some cases (such as Inglewood, California), this process has passed the boundary of the central city and is continuing on into the suburbs.

II. School Desegregation by Governmental Action

The second broad type of school desegregation develops when the local school board, the executive branch of either federal or state government, or the courts intervene to bring about the desegregation of previously segregated schools. In the South this has occasionally meant changing from a dual to a unitary — but still neighborhood — school system, particularly in small towns. In many Southern towns of any size, however, as in many Northern areas, segregated neighborhoods are large enough so that students must be transported if school desegregation is to be accomplished.

School resegregation may or may not occur in such situations. White Plains, New York, which began busing students to desegregate its schools in 1964, did a follow-up study in 1970. White students were doing as well or better academically than before integration, black students were doing better, and there had been no white flight. Pasadena, California, on the other hand, recently completed a four-year follow-up study of its experience with school desegregation. Achievement levels of students throughout the district have dropped significantly. Simultaneously, white enrollment has declined precipitously, from 18,000 in 1969 to 11,000 in 1973. Although much of this wide-variation in the consequences of school desegregation may be attributable to the particular characteristics of individual cities and school districts, there do seem to be some general patterns.

Racial Proportion and Class Effects

Studies dating back to the period immediately after the 1954 *Brown* decision indicate that resistance to desegregation is closely related to the proportion of black students in the schools. Just as resistance to school desegregation seems to mount as the proportion of black students increases, so apparently does the likelihood of some white withdrawal. There was less than a 1% additional decline in white enrollment after busing began in the 18%-black Kalamazoo (Michigan) school system, but an additional 4.7% decline in white enrollment in the 38%-black Pontiac school system. A similar relationship between the proportion of blacks and white flight in Mississippi has been reported, with particularly heavy withdrawal from majority-black schools. In Nashville the number of whites in one school declined from 560 to 268 when busing to a 40%-black inner-city school began; the white decline in a similar school was only 15% when students were to be bused to a school which was 20% black. (There was an additional factor, however; the former students were to be bused through high school, while the latter were to be bused only for one year.) In a major research project in Florida, the proportion of whites withdrawing to private schools was found to have a 30% black "threshold" beyond which white withdrawal increased, as well as a close connection to white family income.

The impact of the proportion of blacks on white withdrawal may not only be a matter of the proportion itself, but also of the difference in social-class level between black and white students. Memphis, Tennessee, and Jackson, Mississippi, for instance, are often cited as particularly striking examples of white withdrawal from desegregated schooling. Shortly after the Memphis busing order, white enrollment in public schools fell by 20,000, while the number in private schools rose by 14,000. Memphis lost 46% of its white public school students between 1970 and 1973. What is striking about white withdrawal from public schools in Memphis is that it occurred in a

situation where the black school population was both large (54% even in 1968) and unusually poor. According to 1970 census data, 35.7% of black families in Memphis were below the poverty line, compared with only 5.7% of the nonblack families. By one estimate, Memphis is second among the major cities of the nation in poverty, with 80% of it found in the black ghetto.

A similar example can be found in the case of Jackson, Mississippi. The Jackson school system, 55% white before mid-year desegregation, lost 9,000 whites and dropped to 40% upon desegregation; 1,500 additional whites left in the following year, dropping the proportion of whites to 36%. Half of all the white pupils in Jackson now attend private schools. Here again is a combination of high proportion black and extreme poverty. According to recent census data, 27.3% of the black population in Jackson are high school graduates, compared to 77.5% of the nonblack population; and 40.3% of the black families are below the poverty line, compared to only 6.3% of the nonblack families.

Just as the social-class level of minority students involved in school integration may be important in determining the presence and extent of racial instability, so may the social-class level of the white students. One study of white withdrawal to private schooling in the Charlotte-Mecklenburg (North Carolina) school district found that income alone explained 54% of white abandonment of the public schools after integration. Thirteen new private schools have opened in Charlotte-Mecklenburg since the 1969 desegregation order. The Florida study already mentioned found that rejection rates for white students assigned to schools more than 30% black were 4% for low-income students, 7% for middle income, and 17% for high income. It is important to note that though such losses did not represent a very high percentage of the public school population (only 3.6% overall), they can deprive the public schools of a disproportionate number of students from the most affluent part of the community.

The available data suggest, then, that the proportion and social-class level of minority students, the social-class level of the white students, and the cost and availability of schooling alternatives are among the variables which may have a significant relationship to whether or

how much white withdrawal may be expected to occur if there is government intervention to desegregate formerly segregated public schools.

III. Concluding Comments

The relationship of one aspect of desegregated schooling to white withdrawal has not, so far as I know, been formally investigated, yet it seems to me to be at the heart of the whole issue: To what extent is the racially mixed school truly integrated? Are the students merely physically co-present, or are they relating to one another in an environment of mutual understanding and respect?

Anyone who has spent any time in racially mixed schools, especially high schools, knows that students in these schools can be as distant from each other as if they were on separate planets. Blacks sit in one part of the cafeteria, whites in another; ditto in classrooms, assemblies, athletic events. Some social events may even be held separately. Indeed, there is evidence that school desegregation may actually *increase* feelings of racial identity. And yet, although a number of studies have investigated interracial attitudes in desegregated schools, the literature contains few reports of programs which foster interracial cooperation and understanding. Yet it should be obvious that schools were never organized to help people understand each other, and there is no evidence that bringing students from different racial, class, and neighborhood backgrounds into them will automatically lead to understanding, appreciation, and friendship. Though some good studies have been done on the relationships among interracial friendship, self-esteem, and academic accomplishment, almost nothing is available that could serve as a blueprint for the school administrator trying to decide what to do tomorrow in order to overcome the racial, class, and cultural gulfs that are so frequently a part of racially mixed education. The answer to this dilemma may contain the key not only to the control of white flight but to the survival of our national commitment to school integration.

Summary and Conclusions

The issue of white withdrawal from desegregated schools is an unusually complex one, and the research done to date has not been equal to the task of explaining all that is involved. Trying to understand this complicated phenomenon is much like trying to put together a giant, confusing jigsaw puzzle with many of the pieces missing. For almost every pattern there seems to be a contrary instance. The available research is characterized by many data gaps, unanswered questions, and unverified assumptions. Nonetheless, the following tentative conclusions seem justified:

1. Whites do not necessarily withdraw from desegregated schools. Some schools maintain a high level of integration for years, some change slowly, and some resegregate very rapidly. Others may experience some white withdrawal followed by stability, or even by white reentrance.

2. Racially mixed schools located in areas bordering the inner city present some markedly different patterns of resegregation from schools located in school districts which have experienced districtwide desegregation. It is important not to extrapolate from the one situation to the other.

3. In situations where there has been no governmental action to bring about desegregation, white withdrawal seems to be linked more than anything else to the underlying demographic consequences of increased minority population growth. This growth takes place primarily in neighborhoods located on the edge of the inner city, as area after area "turns" from black to white. The schools "turn" more quickly than the area generally, and play a significant role in making this process relatively rapid and apparently irreversible. Stable school integration seems to be a necessary if not sufficient precondition for stable neighborhood integration.

4. Decisions on where to purchase a home or where to send one's children to school are made not only on the basis of the present situation but on estimates of what is likely to happen in the future. The belief that presently integrated schools and neighborhoods will shortly resegregate is a major barrier to attracting whites to integrated settings.

5. Little formal research has been done on the motivations behind white withdrawal from desegregated schooling. Worries about the quality of education, student safety, and social-status differences may be among the

chief causes. To the extent that this is true, it could be expected that, other things being equal, school integration would more likely be stable and successful when combined with programs of educational improvement, in settings where concerns about safety are adequately met, and when programs of which parents can be proud are featured.

6. School desegregation ordinarily creates situations which have the potential for both racial and class conflict. The degree of white withdrawal to be expected when there is governmental intervention to desegregate schools may vary, depending on the proportion of minority students who are being assigned to a given school and on the social-class gap between the minority and white students.

7. White withdrawal from desegregated schooling has widely varying costs in different settings. Moving to a nearby segregated suburb, moving outside a county school district, attending a parochial school, attending a private school, transferring to a segregated public school within the same system, or leaving the state are examples of options which may or may not be present in a given situation. Each of these options, if available, will have different costs for different families, just as families will have varying abilities to meet these costs. So long as school desegregation is feared (or experienced) as painful, threatening, or undesirable, it can be expected that the number of families fleeing the desegregated school will be proportionate to these costs and to their ability to pay these costs.

8. Although there is a certain degree of racial mixing in many public schools, there may also be a notable lack of cross-racial friendship, understanding, and acceptance. Superintendents in desegregated districts tend to describe racial relations as "calm" or characterized by few "incidents." Few claim that they have attained anything like genuine community, nor is there much indication that extensive efforts are being made toward this end.

Some Policy Implications

Given the incomplete nature of research on white withdrawal from

desegregated schools, policy implications are perhaps better stated as personal opinion rather than as "proven" by the available research. The suggestions given below are so offered.

1. A thorough, national study of school resegregation is needed. Scattered case studies and sketchy national data are not enough. Unless the public schools of this country are going to continue to contribute heavily to the development of two societies, one white and one black, neither understanding nor trusting the other, white withdrawal from desegregated schools needs to be better understood — and avoided. It is significant that the available research is found in journals of law, political science, economics, education, geography, sociology, psychology, and urban affairs. Any such study would have to be a significantly interdisciplinary effort.

2. Although it may be true that government intervention to desegregate schools has in some instances precipitated white withdrawal, it is equally true that the lack of any positive government intervention in the so-called "changing neighborhoods" surrounding the inner city has been responsible for continuous and ongoing resegregation. In discussing problems of school desegregation in major metropolitan areas, it is desirable to separate the discussion of what to do about inner-city schools from the special problems of resegregating schools on the fringes of the ghetto. If the steady growth of the ghetto is to be arrested, it must be done in these areas. A comprehensive approach to fostering racially stable and integrated neighborhoods and schools would go a long way toward removing the present connection in the minds of many Americans between school desegregation and eventual resegregation.

3. Finally, there is a great need to emphasize the *quality* of school integration and to develop and communicate practical approaches to overcome the cultural and class barriers between the races. The available evidence does not suggest that, if one can just get black and white students into the same building, the rest will take care of itself. It will not. School integration worthy of the name will only come about as the result of conscious, deliberate effort.

Nobody Gets Indicted for Killing a Neighborhood

Denis Hamill

In the '30s Columbia Street was the Hester Street of Brooklyn, a great bawdy, boisterous bustle of shouting, shoving, shopping, street peddling, and saloons. Ice and coal and fish and dry goods were sold from wooden stalls, handcarts, or horse-drawn wagons. Men shouted the daily price of fresh fruit and vegetables; great big homemade cheeses hung in store windows next to thick ropes of handmade sausages; organ-grinders had their monkeys panhandling to the beat of jolly Italian tunes; peppermint-stick barber poles lured the men in need of a shave; kids shoveled up the horse dung to be used as fertilizer for the fig trees, grape vines, and tomato plants, and soccer balls were boomed through the streets.

Mothers hung from windows and called in Italian accents for their children to come in for dinner, as their husbands walked the two blocks home from the waterfront with longshoreman's hooks clamped over their shoulders. The smell of fresh bread and rich pastries drifted from the all-night bakeries while the men drank vino and played cards, and the women sewed at small tables in front of their homes. It was the kind of place Jacob Riis would have loved to have photographed. It was a place bursting with life.

"At one time there was no greater hub of commerce in New York," said Salvatore (Buddy) Scotto, a community activist and civic ombudsman on a recent visit. "But today it is dying a very horrible death. The city let it die. What a rotten shame."

To see Columbia Street now is like watching someone die from a slow-working poison. There are ghostly patches of vacant stores, clumps of soggy litter, and knots of idle men and women. The gutter is a dilapidated mash of crumbling asphalt, pot holes, and sudden bumps. Huge trenches dug as sewage lines gape uncompleted. The rainwater and garbage in the trenches breed monster-sized rats and giant mosquitoes. The buildings on the block are rotting like neglected teeth. Huge cracks run up their sides. The structural foundations, made of wood and resting on mud-fill, are giving way because of the depth to which construction crews have dug the sewage trenches. Huge timbers brace the structures against collapsing to the sidewalks. One person has already been killed in a building collapse. His death is being investigated by Brooklyn District Attorney Eugene Gold. All work has come to a halt since that investigation was first called in December and further complications have lengthened the delay. No district attorney has ever investigated the death of a neighborhood.

This neighborhood known as the Columbia waterfront area, near Red Hook, is roughly bounded on the north by Atlantic Avenue, the Brooklyn Battery Tunnel on the south, Buttermilk Channel on the west, and the Brooklyn-Queens Expressway on the east.

The death of this neighborhood can be attributed to multiple causes, among them what Jack Newfield calls "the permanent government," that seedy band of power holders in the city who appear always to have been here and who never seem to go away. In this case the Brooklyn Democratic machine must be charged with prime responsibility.

Three major doses of poison are responsible for the neighborhood's death.

The first was administered in 1946 when Robert Moses built another highway out of the city and called it the Brooklyn-Queens Expressway. As Robert A. Caro tells it in *The Power Broker: Robert Moses and the Fall of New York,* Moses rented a penthouse suite in an old hotel overlooking the expressway route as it was being built.

" 'And I'll tell you,' " Caro quotes a friend of Moses at the hotel as saying, " 'I never saw RM look happier than he did when he was looking down out of that window.' "

"The BQE was the first thing to send the neighborhood into decline," Buddy Scotto said. "I was just a kid then, but I remember the sour effects it had on the area."

Within months the prosperous working-class area surrounding the intersection of Union and Columbia Streets started to degenerate. Commerce was badly affected because of the design of the BQE. The highway served as a kind of moat between the Hicks Street side of the neighborhood and the Columbia Street side. Pedestrian overpases were spaced several blocks apart, often too distant for the shopping convenience of the working people and the elderly on the Hicks Street side. Traditional Columbia Street trade was now going to the more accessible Court Street shopping area.

After completion of the BQE, property values tumbled on the waterfront side of the neighborhood. But still the community survived. Families who had come to this neighborhood after being processed through the maze of Ellis Island were not going to let a highway make them move. It was a tough, hard-working Italian neighborhood that was also *safe.* It now had such geographically profound borders that it existed as an almost autonomous hamlet within the city. There was common respect and trust, and transients rarely passed through their world. People stayed, too, because there was still plenty of work on the nearby waterfront in the '50s. It didn't matter if property values went down, the neighborhood was the kind of turf that was warm and familiar and worth fighting to save.

For a long time they did a pretty good job of it. There was an unwritten law that you shopped only in the neighborhood. If you patronized your local merchant he would stay, and as long as he remained the neighborhood still had some value. Commerce, safety, self-respect, and a sense of community pride was all that was needed to maintain life. Some places like Cioffi's Pastry & Cake Shop had a citywide reputation. The Boston Fish Market was there for over half a century and drew customers regularly from New Jersey and Long Island and the rest of Brooklyn. And the Lattacini Barese Italian deli on Union Street had customers ordering homemade cheese from as far away as Texas.

But in 1964 the neighborhood absorbed a second dose of bureaucratic venom. Abe Stark was then Brooklyn's borough president and he, with the help of several urban planners, came up with a proposal to turn the entire neighborhood into a containerport to meet the needs of the new highly technological methods of loading and unloading shipped goods. It was called the Abe Stark plan, and with the urging of community activists like Buddy Scotto the plan called for the total revitalization of the Gowanus Canal area: a thorough cleanup of the canal, and the construction of new housing to the west of it and an industrial park to the east. The displaced shops from Columbia Street would be relocated along the new cleaned and sweetened banks of the canal like a Brooklyn version of San Francisco's Fisherman's Wharf. The idea was that the neighborhood would then be incorporated into Carroll Gardens, bounded on both sides by industry to which the local residents could walk to work. The containerport and the new factories would rely on the working force of the neighborhood for their labor. It was a hell of a piece of urban planning.

But it didn't happen. There was plenty of money around in those days so funding was clearly not the problem. Some residents of the Columbia street area balked at the plan, but it was not a majority protest. No, the plan found its greatest opposition in the Brooklyn Democratic party whose county leader then was Stanley Steingut. He and the powerful local district leader, James Mangano, shuddered at the thought of losing an assembly district. If the plan went through it might be beneficial to the people but it would be a drain on *their* political power base.

So the pols came up with their own plan. They claimed the neighborhood did not have to be completely demolished in order to build the containerport. It was suggested that all the land from the waterfront up to 100 feet east of Columbia Street would be used as a containerport. That way all the stores on Columbia Street would remain and a one-block-wide strip of housing from Hamilton Avenue to Atlantic Avenue would remain intact.

From a politician's point of view this made sense. It made the International Longshoremen's Association (which was much more powerful then) happy. It made

those who were against moving their homes and businesses happier. And the politicians themselves maintained the assembly district, their power base, and patronage. This made them the happiest.

But from a planner's point of view the idea was ludicrous. How could anyone expect a single row of homes to last when they would be so closely walled in by the BQE on one side and the containerport on the other? Those houses and stores would last as long as a morsel of cheese between two famished rats.

To begin with, the containerport would call for the use of some 5000 heavy-duty trailer trucks per week in order for the containerport to show its worth. That meant that 5000 trucks and the traffic from the BQE would make the air unbreathable. It meant the decibels would reach deafening levels. It meant the new traffic would hinder the already existing deliveries to the small shops and would discourage those who traditionally came to the neighborhood to shop by car. And it also meant the continuous vibrations from the trucks would shake loose the foundations of the surrounding houses, most of which were 100 years old and supported by wood. (Right now, houses are being condemned on Hicks Street because of the structural damage caused by the rumble of traffic on the BQE along.)

The plan shuffled back and forth through the bureaucratic maze until it went into limbo. In 1971 architects and planners from Pratt Institute called for the containerport to veer off into Red Hook, thus reducing the amount of land to be carved out of the Columbia waterfront area. The idea was to save more housing, and it won the support of Assemblyman Mike Pesce and of Ramon Regueira, who, until his recent death, represented an organization called LaCasa Neighborhood Service Center, a local antipoverty program dealing with the needs of the growing Hispanic population in the area around Columbia Street. That plan is also in limbo, although it has the eager backing of the ILA and the Port Authority.

Ever since the 1964 announcement that the neighborhood was going to go through *some kind* of major transformation, a cloud of condemnation has hung over it. Few property owners in the area have made major investments in their buildings because the future is so uncertain. Many of the century-old structures have begun to decay. Their proximity to the water has added to that erosion.

The third and fatal dose of urban malignity was prescribed for the Columbia waterfront area in May 1975. The month the city began digging the trenches for sewage along Columbia and President streets. These sewage lines were part of a massive $350 million operation called the Red Hook Interceptor Sewage Project. South Brooklyn badly needed this project because the sludge being dumped from the area was raw sewage. The Gowanus Canal alone was receiving the wastes of some 250,000 people daily, which gave it a putrid smell of national reputation. The raw sewage in the canal only moved after rainfall forced it into the overflow discharge basins. If it did not rain the sewage lay there, festering. (According to Buddy Scotto, a test of those waters has revealed that live cholera, typhus, and typhoid breed freely in the canal.)

So the feds earmarked $350 million for treatment plants on the condition that the city and state come up with matching funds of 12½ per cent each. The city pleaded poverty, of course, but so eager were the trade unions for this new work that they have offered to put up their pension funds to buy MAC bonds in order to pay their workers. The federal EPA is investigating the legality of this offer.

The construction firm of Mascali Zindler and Copat won a bid of $10.37 million dollars for the Columbia Street leg of the massive project. They began digging in May 1975. They were still digging on December 4 when a man was killed in a building collapse at 21 President Street, bringing on the Gold investigation and halting the work.

Since then the Department of Water Resources has further delayed the digging for a modification of the original plans. They have now decided to shorten the sewer and reroute it slightly. This, of course, has to be approved by the city, and it took Commissioner Charles Samowitz until August 17 to get a consensus from the Bureau of the Budget, the Corporation Counsel, the Board of Estimate, and the Comptroller's office on the renegotiation of price with the contractor and extended money needed to redesign the sewer so that further structural damage to surrounding buildings will not occur.

"I really wish it wasn't this complicated," Samowitz said on August 17. "I'm not the city. I'm a small part of it. But I will go on the record as saying construction will resume in the next couple of weeks."

There have been many promises by many people in the past. No one in the neighborhood believes them anymore. Since August 17, some work has resumed on a small section of the project near the water, but work on Columbia and President streets is at a standstill for several more weeks at least, because, according to Samowitz, the city and the community are still negotiating the question of structural underpinnings for the buildings there.

In the meantime, the partially completed trenches on Columbia and President streets remain open sores. On the night Hurricane Belle walloped the city, the trenches filled to near capacity. A gondola would have come in handy to move through the neighborhood. The shored-up buildings could be heard creaking and swaying as the punishing winds hurtled off the harbor. Rats slithered through the night, plump and healthy, terrified by the assault of the storm. The rain slobbered down the eerie streets, and inside the Italian deli, Joe Balzano served steaming cups of espresso in miniature cups and smoked cheese sandwiches as he talked about what he has had to live with for this past year and a half since the first municipal shovel broke ground.

"When I first heard of this digging operation I didn't like it," Joe said. "I go to all those meetings they hold. I hear this man, Councilman Tom Cuite, talking about how this is gonna be such a wonderful thing. He tells me, and I

remember perfectly, that they are gonna only dig down 20 feet. I remember saying to him, 'Excuse me, Mr. Cuite, I know I'm just a cheesemaker, and I'm not an architect, but these buildings down here are old and near the water and I think maybe all this digging is gonna make them fall down.' "

Majority leader of the City Council Thomas Cuite assured Joe that nothing of the sort would happen; this was a very carefully thought out plan, he said. Then they dug 40 feet down, and Joe's worst fears came true when his neighbor on President Street was killed.

Tom Cuite responds to reporrters the same way he responds to his constituents. Not at all. This reporter called him five different times in a four-day period for a statement on the Columbia waterfront problems. He never returned a single call.

Assemblyman Mike Pesce is another person who has had trouble reaching the powerful councilman.

"I have told my constituents over and over that they must pressure Cuite," Pesce told this reporter. "Stanley Steingut doesn't respond to me in Albany because I'm not in his pocket. Mayor Beame doesn't like me because I exposed him in Albany to the assembly during the fiscal crisis as being a man who doles out patronage, no-shows, freebies, and then comes asking for money.

"As a member of the Democratic machine Cuite doesn't like me either," continued Pesce, who along with Frank Barbaro and Joe Ferris are the only three assemblymen in Brooklyn who do not receive lulus. "I called Cuite three times at one point and got no return calls. I finally told one of his cronies that if he didn't call an emergency meeting about the Columbia Street problem I'd expose him in the press, on TV, anyway I could. Almost immediately I got a call. He was frantic. He called the meeting. Every elected official in the district showed up. A spokesman from the mayor's office was there, a representative from police, health, sanitation, you name it."

At that meeting, and several that followed, the citizens of the community insisted on knowing what the city intended to do about the problems, and they listed them: 1) the open trenches—they wanted them at least temporarily filled so traffic could move; 2) the damaged buildings—who is gonna pay and how much; 3) sanitation—ever since the trenches were dug the garbage trucks have disappeared, and people throw their garbage into the trenches; 4) ruined businesses—who is going to compensate those people who lost their livelihood because of the digging and structural condemnation?

The meetings were a sham. Nothing ever resulted from them. Even the sanitation department has failed to resume regular garbage collection.

Other independent local representatives, like State Senator Carol Bellamy, are powerless without the help of the men of real power.

"This area is the largest blemish of my political career," Bellamy said recently. "It is one of the greatest outrages in the city. I throw up my hands every time I look at it. I have tried everything within my power to do something about it, but nothing seems to work. I just hope something can be done soon. The city must act now before it is too late."

James Musico from the President Street West Block Association hopes so, too, because he sees greater dangers ahead.

"Right now we have a verbal agreement from Deputy Mayor John Zuccotti that the city will reimburse us for some of the damage," Musico said. "But we're saying, that's not good enough. We're saying we don't want the city to fix up President Street unless they are also gonna make Columbia Street like it used to be. Without Columbia Street there isn't no President Street. Hey, if I wanted to live in the country I'd move to Staten Island, right?

"And let me say one more thing there about the United States of America, the greatest country on the face of the earth. Why is it the only time you get anything done in this country is when you threaten violence? I go and I ask the city, 'Hey, come on, why don't you fix things up? Fill in the trenches. You know what I get when I ask them nice like that? *'Nungotz!* That's what I get. But if we take a few of them guys and dump them down the hole, they'll start filling in the hole. They've been shafting us too long. Someday soon this neighborhood is going to explode."

The question of whether or not the containerport will ever be built should be answered right now. If it is not going to be built, then the citizens of the Columbia waterfront will start sinking some of their hard-earned money into their homes and businesses again. They cannot be expected to live on the borders of uncertainty.

Some of the people in the area feel the containerport will never be built but the rumor of it will be used as a ploy to discourage local residents so they will evacuate the area. Once these working-class people are gone, they fear the real estate investors will rush into the area and build high-rise luxury buildings—like nearby Brooklyn Heights, an outpost for the rich on the banks of the world's greatest port, overlooking the Manhattan skyline and Governor's Island. They point out that one such real estate speculator is already in the area. His name is David Goldman. People in the community regard him as a slumlord who has at least 20 apartment buildings in the section, uses them for welfare dumping, a device as effective as block-busting. Guys like Goldman could make a mint in the Columbia waterfront if the working class were to pack up and leave.

The city must also assume complete responsibility for all structural damage done to the buildings because of faulty planning over the years, especially the moronic plan for the sewer trenches. The people who have lost their livelihoods because business suffered from city blunders should also be compensated for their losses.

Basic city services like sanitation should be brought to a standard appropriate to 20th-century living. The trenches must be quickly finished and filled. The streets must be newly paved. New housing to replace what has crumbled must be built.

These things should be done right away. But instead the city has forced neighborhood people to resort to filing a class action suit. This could drag on for years in the bloated courts where hack-appointed hacks grow old in black robes.

Some landlords in the area have been forced by the Buildings Department to vacate their buildings. They have received no income since the vacate orders, yet the city still expects them to pay regular real estate taxes on the property. Pesce tried to reason with the city, asking it to accept a token $1 per year until the buildings begin to make money again. The city gave him a flat no for an answer. Some of the vacated buildings are slated for demolition. The city expects the landlords to pay for the demolition even though the damage has been caused by the city. More businesses are planning to close down. Several buildings have already been torn down.

This is the area Arthur Miller wrote of in *A View From the Bridge.* Soon the only view will be vacant lots. Columbia Street is fast becoming more worthless than Baltic Avenue on a Monopoly board.

The reality right now is that most of the city's power is in the hands of unaccountable bankers. The banks have redlined Columbia Street. But we still have a governor from Brooklyn who used to drink in places like Monte's. In the last session, Carey helped defeat a bill that would have outlawed redlining. Maybe that's because he has lost touch with his roots and hasn't visited places like Columbia Street lately.

Meanwhile men like Joe Balzano sit and wait, hoping for some small act of attention.

"I dunno," Joe said as he waited on a customer and nibbled on his own cheese. "Like I say, I'm just a cheesemaker, but I still think there is something a great city like this one can do for a good neighborhood. Don't you?"

Is it shameful to be poor?

In 1940, nearly half the people in the United States lived in substandard housing. By 1970, that figure had been cut to 7.5 per cent.

Substandard housing is defined as structurally unsound, in need of major repairs, or without plumbing facilities. Although definitions have changed somewhat over the years, the improvement in the nation's housing stock is unquestioned. Overcrowding (defined as one or more person a room) was at a similar low level in 1970.

Housing, however, remains a major problem. Although the U.S. population increase rate was low in the mid-1970's, the post-World War II baby boom was producing increasing numbers of families, each needing a separate home. Inadequate housing still exists, and older units need repair or replacement.

The housing situation is worst for single people and for large families (six or more people). Finding adequate housing is most difficult for the poor—urban and rural. Also, in the 1970s, with a shaky economy, tight money market, stricken housing industry, and a federal government determined to cut back on social spending,

finding an affordable place to live is becoming increasingly difficult for middle-income people as well.

The housing industry, of course, is interested in profits. Posh urban developments for the wealthy and suburban housing for middle and upper-income groups earn builders more money than shelter for those with less money—unless they are subsidized.

Since the 1930s, the federal government has taken steps to provide housing for lower-income groups. But critics say many of these programs have had less than satisfactory results. The government has spent millions and millions of dollars, builders have become wealthy; and the poor and those with moderate income are still looking for someplace decent to live.

Lifelong debt, architectural mediocrity, cramped units, backward technology, suburban sprawl, class animosity, and desperation for the poor are among the major problems mentioned by housing consultant Charles Abrams.

In his book, *The City is the Frontier,* Abrams wrote, "The many federal housing programs launched since

Unchecked urban growth produced the boring gridiron pattern of some suburbs

1934 did achieve gains—when billions are lent and spent, some money is bound to turn into houses. But the fruit of each effort always left a blemish. . .

"With all the formulas for building and subsidizing housing, we have not yet struck upon a good device for clearing slums and rehousing the slum dwellers, improving the shelter of large families, migrants, skidrowers, the poor, and the elderly. We have failed in the very areas where the needs and justification for government aid is greatest."

While no one has the answer to the nation's housing problems, major difficulties in existing government programs can be identified.

Despite the rhetoric of government housing programs, it is considered shameful to be poor in America. Slum clearance and housing for lower income groups have been hampered by a sometimes subconscious, sometimes overt, tendency to blame and punish the poor for their plight.

As Jacobs writes, "Generation after generation stick to the same foolish ideas about slums and slum dwellers. The pessimists always seem to feel that there is something inferior about the current crop of slum dwellers themselves and can point out supposedly dire differences that distinguish them from previous immigrants. The optimists always seem to feel that there is nothing wrong with slums that could not be fixed by housing and land use reform and enough social workers."

The result of these opinions is the view that something must be done to or for the poor. It is considered too simple to say that the problem of the poor is that they don't have enough money.

This kind of thinking prevented any government action until the Depression when, as Abrams put it, "many among the 13. million unemployed found themselves homeless or crowded into slum flats, it seemed illogical as well as impolitic to assert that all these people could be criminal, filthy, and inebriated."

The other major difficulty in federal housing programs has been the schizophrenic split between a desire to support the free enterprise system while at the same time propounding government regulations. It might well be better either to have the government directly build and manage housing or to provide housing allowances directly to the poor to be applied in the general housing market.

The 1937 public housing program and the 1949 Urban Renewal Act were relatively minor in economic terms but were politically important. Economically, the major federal housing thrust came in the lending programs of the Federal Housing Administration (FHA), the Veterans Administration (VA), and the Federal Home Loan Bank Board.

But until recently funds from these programs were directed toward middle-income groups and were funneled mainly to the suburbs. This imbalance remains, although efforts have been made to use such funds for the benefit of urban and rural poor.

Because of the efforts to depend on the private sector, fortunes have been made from government housing

As cities grew, farm land disappeared

programs. In his book *Mortgage on America,* journalist Leonard Downie writes:

"Uninhabitable slums, exploited suburbs, chewed-up countryside, poisoned air and water, high taxes and declining public services, inflated land and housing prices, economic and racial segregation—these symptoms of the spreading cancer in urban America are recognized by almost everyone. Yet there are those who look at the sprawl and decay of our cities and see in them golden opportunity: the opportunity to make big money, often very quickly, and to protect from taxation the money they already have.

"These people are land speculators, developers, builders, realtors, landlords, bankers, and other real estate investors of all kinds. . ."

Downie and other critics contend government agencies and programs have played a large role in perpetuating discrimination against Blacks and other minority groups, in making slum housing a profitable business for landlords; in encouraging blockbusting and the racial, economic, and class divisions which mark American life; and in fostering the suburban sprawl which has both undermined the nation's great cities and scarred its open lands.

Most housing experts do not support the idea of direct federal housing construction and management. But critics such as Charles Abrams do contend that more forceful federal action, as a backstop to local and private efforts, could have produced better planning and environmental controls.

Because government housing and redevelopment programs are neither all-powerful nor nonexistent, they often constitute, in Abrams' words, a "half-measure," and he sees three major difficulties growing out of that paradox.

● An overemphasis on slum clearance along with a lack of provisions for those whose homes are thus demolished.

● An almost exclusive reliance on the speculative profit motive for the clearance of these slums and the rebuilding of slum neighborhoods. This means there may be no help for areas and people who need it the most.

● A tendency to focus on housing and slums to the exclusion of other urban ills such as poverty, education, racial friction, and the erosion of economic resources. Efforts to mount an integrated attack on these problems as in the much-touted Model Cities program were undermined by congressional logrolling and the efforts of local political power groups.

Where the role of government is most direct, in public housing, the results have been disastrous. It is here where contempt for the poor is most clear. The worst of this program's results can be seen in the high-rise public housing projects that dominate whole areas in most of the nation's major cities. Unfortunately, such projects were considered socially and economically valid at just that period when the greatest amount of public housing was being built.

Oscar Newman, New York architect and city planner, outlines the rationale for and problems of such public housing projects:

"The distinctive form of highrise publicly-assisted housing is immediately recognizable. The barren, red-brick towers stand out as prominent landmarks in all our cities—well-built monuments to a half-hearted attempt at benevolence. It would be unjust, however, to suggest that the politicians, bureaucrats, planners, and architects responsible for these projects were callous or maliciously motivated. The end result of their efforts may now appear inadequate and irrational, but they were well-intentioned."

Newman notes that public housing is often "seen as housing of last resort." And he adds:

Four million people live in federally subsidized low-middle-income housing, for them there is effectively no choice to exercise on the housing market. The same factionalizing of our society which is expressed in middle and upper-class withdrawal has, moreover, infected the design and structure of their environment. The stigma of poverty and minority group membership has been stamped onto public housing. It has been made to appear as different as possible from its surroundings; it has been marked off as clearly as if by quarantine."

A typical high-rise project was Pruitt-Igoe Homes in St. Louis. Huge towers, surrounded by open space, Pruitt-Igoe was considered a showplace when it was built: It was new, it was clean, it replaced noxious slums, and it was plain. The blame placed upon the poor for their economic status is often translated in housing into grim, prison-like buildings—there should be no frills.

In 1972, authorities dynamited several of the Pruitt-Igoe buildings. There was nothing else to do with them. They were unsafe, filthy, and hateful. Even the most desperate poor avoided being sentenced to live there.

The dynamite explosions had wide repercussions. One writer noted: "They blasted the subject of housing design into the public consciousness. It took the violent and necessary act of destruction of part of a public housing project that had become an obscenity of American life to make it clear that we have been doing something awfully wrong."

Those who need public housing are those for whom the high-rise projects are least suited. Large families with many young children are unable to supervise and protect their children from the 23rd floor. Frills that authorities avoided providing in public housing included locks on the outer doors of the buildings, adequate elevator service, safe play areas, maintenance, and security.

The design of these projects has a strong psychological effect on residents and outsiders alike. Oscar Newman expressed it this way:

"Society may have contributed to the victimization of project residents by setting off their dwellings, stigmatizing them with ugliness; saying with every status symbol available in the architectural language of our culture, that living here is falling short of the human state."

Newman points to problems with interior design as well. Cinderblock walls, institutional colors, heavy-duty fixtures—all were chosen to avoid upkeep problems. But Newman says they add to the stigma: The "ostentatious" use of theoretically vandal-proof materials seems to encourage attempts to destroy them.

Of course, the residents of these projects knew about the problems long before the experts would acknowledge them.

In St. Louis it took dynamite to draw attention to the misery of Pruitt-Igoe. In Chicago, the 1970 murder of two city policemen focused widespread attention on the Cabrini-Green housing project.

Suddenly, authorities acknowledged the problems.

Public housing in New York City

MAINTAINING THE IMAGE

The American tendency to blame the poor for their poverty has many unfortunate results, among them public housing designed, as architect and city planner Oscar Newman explains below, to keep the poor "in their place:"

"By gentleman's agreement, public housing must never approach the luxurious in appearance, even though it may cost more per square foot. It must retain an institutional image. Unfortunately, this practice not only 'puts the poor in their place,' but brings their vulnerability to the attention of others.

"Parallel to this, and much more devastating, is the effect of the institutional image as perceived by the project residents themselves. Unable to camouflage their identities and adopt the attitudes of private apartment dwellers, they sometimes overreact and treat their dwellings as prisoners treat the penal institutions in which they are housed."

Meetings, reviews, and press conferences were held. George Romney, then secretary of Housing and Urban Development (HUD), flew to Chicago to inspect the project. Cabrini residents set up a tour for him and developed a long report calling for conversion of some apartments into child care, health, and other needed facilities; improved security; job training and employment of project residents for necessary social services; relocation within the community; and a voice for tenants in the management of Chicago Housing Authority (CHA) projects.

The tour planned for Romney was lengthy because the people wanted to show him all the problems: the lack of recreational facilities for the large number of children and young people, the squalor of the buildings, the hazards to health and safety. But the secretary would only stay half an hour. Romney got a taste of the life,

No one wanted to live in Pruitt-Igoe. . . .

**. . . so the only solution
was to demolish the project**

however, when the elevator carrying him and his group to a typical apartment was stuck for several minutes.

There were few immediate results. CHA residents now can elect members of building, block, and central advisory councils. In 1974, Chicago received a federal grant to finance some of the improvements demanded four years earlier.

One thing has happened in the wake of these revelations. The government has stopped building these high-rise projects for low-income families. Some areas were more advanced than others. Minneapolis, for example, has long barred high-rise projects for families. The towers are built for low-income elderly people whose needs can better be served in high-rise projects. Families are placed in townhouses or small apartment buildings.

But the high-rises left their mark. Resistance to any type of public housing has been fierce in neighborhoods throughout the country. Suburbs have attempted to ignore the problem of providing subsidized housing. City housing authorities have found it difficult to build any kind of units in any but the poorest neighborhoods. In Chicago, individual aldermen used de facto veto power of project construction in their wards. Therefore, units could be built only in the poorest, almost always Black, wards.

The American Civil Liberties Union filed suit against this practice in 1966. In 1969, a federal court judge ruled in favor of the ACLU. The Chicago Housing Authority appealed. Construction was halted, and the delay reinforced when the Nixon administration froze federal housing funds in the early 1970s. In 1974, a federal appeals court upheld the lower court and took the ruling even further, ordering desegregation throughout Cook County, including the suburbs.

Despite the standstill in the early 1970s, attempts were being made to develop new answers to the housing problem.

Financing remains a major bar to adequate low and moderate-income housing. Nevertheless current government attempts at meeting the problem are in a sense broader than before—and also less grandiose.

New, experimental programs include homeownership, direct housing subsidies to the poor, government-assisted construction of units to house all income levels, and attempts at renovating or preserving current housing stock instead of wholesale demolition. Large-scale, high-rise, low-income projects are not being built.

Optimism, however, is guarded. Oscar Newman wrote in his 1973 book, *Defensible Space,* "In many respects, the decision to house the poor and the old together in large public housing ghettos followed naturally. For one thing, no middle-class community really wanted the poor around. A housing program committed to the use of many, small, in-fill sites located in middle-class neighborhoods was, and still is, unthinkable. Large sites at the periphery of existing urban ghettos were the only solution in the past and are likely to remain the only solution."

One trend involves letting the poor in on a widely held American dream: home-ownership. Actually, single-family homes have been the focus of much government housing activity but only for the middle class.

According to Charles Abrams, "From President Hoover to President Johnson, federal objectives in housing have stemmed primarily from an interest in homeownership or in the building industry. As President Hoover said to a conference of housing experts in 1931:

"To possess one's own home is the hope and ambition of almost every individual in our country, whether he lives in hotel, apartment, or tenement. . . . Those immortal ballads, Home, Sweet Home, My Old Kentucky Home, and The Little Gray Home in the West were not written about tenements or apartments. . . they never sing songs about a pile of rent receipts."

The latest experiment in this area is "urban homesteading," a result both of progress and failure. In the late 1960s and early 1970s, abandonment of urban property became widespread. A survey by the National Urban League defined abandonment as:

"When a landlord no longer provided services to an occupied building and allowed taxes and mortgages to go unpaid."

Abandonment, along with demolition, meant that a

quarter of a million housing units were lost in New York City alone during the 1960s.

The Urban League charted the process in this way:

"The first step in the process is the decline in neighborhood socio-economic status. Step two is racial or ethnic change in a given area. Step three is characterized by property speculation and exploitation: this is the time when the block-busters, the illegal subdividers, the contract sellers, and the tax scavengers are hard at work. Step four is disinvestment, which commences with under-maintenance and culminates in mortgage default and tax arrears. Step five is the desertion of the area by the middle and working-class elements of the population and the emergence of the 'crisis ghetto.' At this state, we see a marked increase in female-headed families and in crime rates and a concomitant decrease in family income, years of schooling, and male employment. Step six is the end of the game—abandonment."

Another source of abandoned property consists of homes and buildings purchased by individuals with mortgages subsidized by the Federal Housing Authority (FHA). Ironically, an earlier attempt to aid low-income people by getting the FHA to move away from its middle-income, suburban bias, produced wide-spread default by those unable to keep up the payments or disgusted by the condition of shoddy homes whose condition they thought had been guaranteed by the federal government. Considerable scandal has revolved around that FHA program.

Faced with a need for housing, a cutback in construction, and a mushrooming supply of abandoned property, officials developed the concept of "urban homesteading."

Hearkening back to the 1860s' land rush when the federal government threw open wide territories to those who would settle in the west, officials hoped to lure settlers to the new frontier: the city. An article in the Journal of Housing gives this description of urban homesteading: "A house or land would be given to any qualified family or applicant, provided they agreed to: (1) rehabilitate the existing building to meet property and building codes or build on the land and (2) occupy the unit for a prescribed time. After this period, title to the property would be transferred to the occupant and the property would then be taxed by the municipality at its full valuation."

If successful, this would be the best of two worlds. It would provide housing for the needy while putting abandoned property back on hard-pressed city tax rolls.

But, having been stung by would-be solutions before, experts were cautious. For one thing, much of the abandoned property involved defaulted loans—in other words, there was money owed to banks, or savings and loans, or various government agencies. Getting rid of all the redtape so homesteaders do not face old debts is complicated. Then, too, many of the structures are in

poor condition and do not meet city building codes—and it's illegal to occupy such buildings. Probably most difficult is the question of rehabilitation.

As the Journal of Housing put it, "To permit poor people to place all of their hope and money into rehabilitating a vacant house, considering the stringent building and housing codes and the allotted time and to subject them to failure, may be immoral and unjust, serving little purpose.

"There are practical problems of placing upon low-income families the responsibilities for being general contractors, even in a self-help project. Home improvement contractors, and those in the specialized, licensed trades—heating, plumbing, and electrical—are expensive and the know-how and coordination needed for effective production are difficult."

With sufficient safeguards, however, urban homesteading could be a useful tool in broadening the housing supply.

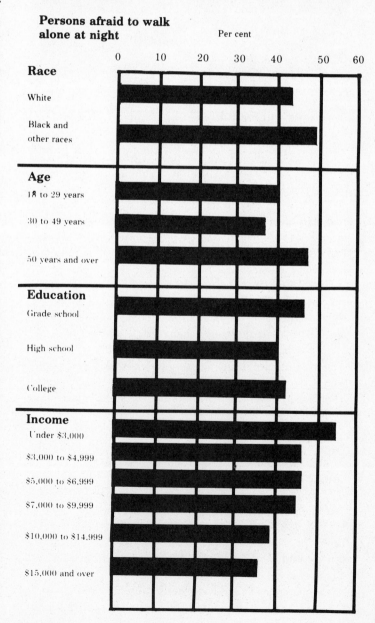

Persons afraid to walk alone at night

A similar desire to retrieve existing housing and stabilize neighborhoods involves what Jacobs calls "unslumming."

As one New York City planner said, "Why is it just occurring to us to see if the slums themselves have some of the ingredients of a good housing policy? We are discovering suddenly. . . that slum families don't necessarily move when their incomes go up; that independence in slums is not stifled by paternalistic management policy; and finally (incredible!) that slum people, like other people, don't like being booted out of their neighborhoods.

"The next step will require great humility. We will have to admit that it is beyond the scope of anyone's imagination to create a community. We must learn to cherish the communities we have; they are hard to come by. 'Fix the buildings but leave the people.' 'No relocation outside the neighborhood.' These must be the slogans if public housing is to be popular."

Neighborhoods have been "unslummed" without government assistance. Sometimes, as in parts of Chicago's north side in the mid-1970s, "unslumming" happens because upper-middle-class professionals discover the conveniences and amenities that made a now-deteriorated area popular in the past. Old buildings are rehabilitated; new stores and services move in, lured by the more affluent residents; and the neighborhood is suddenly fashionable.

It has been done by the not-so-rich too, but not as easily because low and middle-income families find it far more difficult to obtain funding for this type of activity.

Part of the problem is a practice called "red-lining," in which lending institutions, and sometimes government agencies, "write off" an area and refuse to make loans to the people who live there even though area residents may deposit their savings in these same institutions.

In 1974, HUD announced a pilot program to help people in such neighborhoods get funds for renovation and rehabilitation. The program, based on a successful Pittsburgh experiment, provides a high-risk lending pool that will advance funds in areas "red-lined" by traditional lending institutions. The program is designed to involve local residents in planning and policy decisions.

An experiment, launched under the Nixon Administration, sought to avoid all direct government involvement in housing by providing direct grants. Twelve cities were chosen for an experiment in which low-income families were given direct subsidies so they could secure housing on the open market. In a related program, the subsidy goes to private landlords who rent or lease to low-income families.

In 1974, HUD Secretary James T. Lynn defended direct grants as necessary to make sure "the federal role in housing is drastically changed."

URBAN BEGINNINGS

The history of cities can be traced back to ancient cultures, such as Mayan and Incan, and to many places, from China to Mesopotamia. In all those civilizations, cities were places of change and progress. That is why the history of ancient Europe is that of Rome and the Greek cities.

Cities, therefore, shared the fate of Rome; and when Rome declined, so did cities. Their role as the hubs of culture and learning passed to monasteries until a resurgence of cities in Italy in the 11th Century.

The importance of great modern cities began in the 13th Century, where the dynamic life of the Middle Ages was centered. The giant city of today is a product of the Industrial Revolution, which introduced large-scale manufacturing.

However, the watchdog General Accounting Office (GAO) issued a report calling for further experimentation before any expansion of the direct-grant program. The GAO said the experimental sites were not typical of American cities because they had far more high-quality housing available. And the GAO said studies of rent subsidy programs in the U.S. military and in several European countries show the usual result is higher rents.

Some public and government housing has been successful. Included are some relatively small projects built in Chicago before the rush to high rises. Others are newer, built by private developers under programs which gave them low interest rates and appealing tax exemptions.

James Fuerst, director of the graduate studies program at Loyola University, listed several factors leading to successful projects, with the foremost being good location and design. Others are:
● The total size of the project should be limited to 150 to 350 units.
● Only a limited number of large families (or three or four-bedroom units) should be put in one project, probably under 10 per cent.
● The number of families receiving public assistance admitted in any one project should be limited.
● A good management firm must be chosen.

Yet another experiment, this one under the auspices of the Illinois Housing Development Authority (IHDA), will provide low-interest construction loans to developers in exchange for their agreement to lease up to 20 per cent of the new units to poor families receiving federal rent subsidies.

3. URBAN PROBLEMS

Irving Gerrick, IHDA director, announced the first such agreements in 1974. These loans are to go to two luxury apartment buildings to be built on Chicago's wealthy Near North side. While mixed-income-level developments, including upper-income groups, have been successful, this is one of the first to include only the very rich and the very poor.

How to provide adequate housing at affordable costs has become even more important in recent years as increased prices and a tight money market have widened the gap between what is needed and what is available.

In 1974, government statistics indicated the average cost of a house had risen to $40,000. According to a popular rule-of-thumb, a person must earn at least $15,000 or $20,000 a year to afford this. But the median family income in 1971 was well below that—$10,250. The median for whites was only slightly above that figure, but the median for Blacks and other minorities is far lower, under $7,000.

To be eligible for public housing in Chicago an individual can earn no more than $4,800 a year; a family of 12, no more than $10,000. These figures hover around the official poverty level. But 4.5 per cent of all Chicago residents live in public housing—a total of 153,000 people. That is more than the population of Rockford, the state's second largest city. There is a waiting list of nearly 10,000, and still others are eligible, but have not applied.

Even those with income near the median may be eligible for subsidized moderate or middle-income housing. Such units may in fact be the only housing they can comfortably afford.

With this type of need it is obvious that no one program will solve the problem. Many approaches are needed; and cooperation between the public, private industry, and government at all levels is essential.

The quality of life in metropolis

The quality of life in 18 metropolitan areas, as determined by the Urban Institute of Washington, is shown on this chart. The best rating is numbered 1, with the numbers going upward to the worst, which is numbered 18.

METROPOLITAN AREA By 1970 population	Unemployment	Poverty	Income level	Housing	Health	Mental Health	Public order	Racial equality	Community concern	Educational attainment	Citizen participation	Transportation	Air quality	Social disintegration
New York	9	9	4	17	9	1	18	1	18	14	9	1	10	7
Los Angeles/ Long Beach	18	15	3	10	2	17	11	3	17	11	3	7	8	3
Chicago	2	5	5	13	18	3	14	6	15	2	7	13	16	1
Philadelphia	7	9	14	9	17	13	6	9	10	8	13	2	15	N.A.
Detroit	17	3	1	5	12	15	17	8	7	5	13	8	14	N.A.
San Francisco/ Oakland	16	17	2	14	2	18	13	2	13	7	2	16	1	5
Washington	1	2	8	11	5	7	15	7	16	18	1	10	3	6
Boston	4	1	17	18	6	10	3	N.A.	12	2	6	15	5	4
Pittsburgh	14	12	13	3	11	11	5	5	2	2	13	3	17	N.A.
St. Louis	10	13	12	8	10	4	9	11	6	11	17	14	18	2
Baltimore	5	11	16	4	15	14	16	4	14	14	18	9	11	N.A.
Cleveland	12	7	9	15	8	16	10	12	1	9	9	6	13	N.A.
Houston	5	17	11	1	16	12	12	10	11	16	9	17	5	N.A.
Minneapolis/ St. Paul	14	4	6	6	1	5	7	N.A.	5	1	3	11	2	N.A.
Dallas	3	16	7	2	14	6	8	N.A.	9	16	3	4	3	N.A.
Milwaukee	10	5	15	16	4	8	1	N.A.	8	5	7	4	11	N.A.
Cincinnati	7	14	10	7	7	9	2	N.A.	3	11	13	12	9	N.A.
Buffalo	12	8	18	12	13	2	4	N.A.	4	10	9	18	5	N.A.

"WHAT IS THE CITY?"

Cities have always produced admirers and despisers. "What is the city but the people?" asked Shakespeare, and other writers of various eras have tried to answer that very question.

Cicero (106-43 B.C.), enemy of Julius Caesar and Marc Antony and the greatest Roman orator, expressed his opinion by saying, "Socrates was the first to call philosophy down from the heavens and to place it in cities."

Likewise, Simonides (556-468 B.C.), a Greek lyric poet, said, "The city is the teacher of the man." Simonides' contemporary, Themistocles, an Athenian statesman, agreed: "Tuning the lyre and handling the harp are no accomplishments of mine, but rather taking in hand a city that was small and inglorious and making it glorious and real."

Many centuries later, John Milton, 17th Century English poet, wrote:

"Tower'd cities please us then
And the busy hum of men."

A generation later, however, the English poet Byron took a different view:

"I live not in myself, but I become
Portion of that around me: and to me
High mountains are a feeling, but the hum
Of human cities torture."

That view was shared by Matthew Arnold (1822-88), English poet and critic, who wrote:

"Calm soul of all things! make it mine
To feel, amid the city's jar,
That there abides a place of thine,
Man did not make, and cannot mar."

And while American Poet Walt Whitman (1819-92) was saying, "A great city is that which has the greatest men and women," Charles Dudley Warner, American editor and author, commented, "The thing generally raised on city land is taxes."

The most philosophical comment, though, may have come from Horace (65-8 B.C.), one of the greatest of Latin lyric poets, who wrote: "In Rome you long for the country; in the country—oh inconstant!—you praise the distant city to the stars."

4. Urban Social Policies

Social policies deal with critical issues that disturb the well-being of many individuals. A problem is recognized and defined and a solution is proposed. Since urban social problems are complex and difficult to clearly define, the social policies that evolve are likely to be complicated. Often the proposed solutions generate intense debate and conflict.

Social scientists have been invited to participate in social policy debates. For example, school desegregation generated considerable attention from scholars interested in this specific educational policy. It was assumed that scholarly objectivity could determine what desegregation policies were most effective. But many factors—different perceptions of the problems upon examination and the difficulty of measuring the outcomes of conflicting social goals—influence a given policy. In spite of this, it is recognized that disciplined, rational inquiry about urban conditions will continue to require the skills of social scientists to examine the issues, to explain the dynamic conditions which operate in a given context, and to present possible alternatives.

Social policies are usually directed at specific ends, but the unintended consequences of a given course of action sometimes have strange effects. Several federal programs designed to assist the city have resulted in unexpected outcomes. Since our skills in program evaluation are limited, it is difficult to foresee these effects. At the same time, new programs often have competing goals or vague statements of purpose. Often new policies are implemented without adequate resources, hastily developed in response to political pressure from outspoken groups. The articles in this section illustrate these processes in specific policies and in particular urban areas. Some of the debates are about *how* to resolve issues while others center on jurisdictional concerns—who will direct city matters, the city itself or the national government. Other issues concern financing reform, making better use of urban land, and managing welfare problems.

Concerning the material presented in this section, several questions might be considered. Who benefits and who loses if a policy is successful? How has the social problem been defined? What social, economic, and historical factors have influenced the social policy? Does a social policy accomplish what it is supposed to achieve?

171

A
Marshall Plan
for Cities?

Norton E. Long

*Norton E. Long is Curators
Professor of Political Science at the
University of Missouri, St. Louis.*

THE nation's mayors, meeting in Chicago, have sent their plea for aid to the President-elect. Unfortunately, although they indicated what they would like the nation to do to help the cities, they appear to have remained silent concerning what the cities are prepared to do to help themselves. A review of our foreign-aid experience may help to clarify some of the problems of mounting a program of domestic municipal aid on a comparable scale. For example, a Marshall Plan for cities has frequently been advocated, notably by the late Whitney Young. However, the idea has been little more than a catchy slogan to symbolize big federal dollars and contrast our willingness to aid in the recovery of Europe with our grudging support of our own cities. Consideration of the Marshall Plan and the reasons for its success and the failures of our programs elsewhere than in Europe has much to offer those seriously concerned with structuring a federal aid program with any real promise of achieving for our cities what the Marshall Plan did for the nations of Europe.

Since a major proposal of the mayors was to establish an urban-development bank similar to the World Bank, one might have hoped that they had at long last come to recognize the necessity of restoring the viability of the local economies of the cities. If there is one thing our foreign-aid experience should have taught us, it is that we can only help those who are ready, willing, and able to help themselves. Failing this, what results is a welfare program that merely postpones the day of reckoning and deepens dependency. The first point about the Marshall Plan, usually completely disregarded by advocates of a similar plan for our cities, is that it was designed to restore the war-ravaged economies of European nations. It was a program of investment to replace entire industries, not just a program of income redistribution and maintenance to restore and sustain a standard of public and private consumption. It was only concerned with maintaining consumption until its major investments revived the economies of the European

"A Marshall Plan for Cities?" by Norton Long, from THE PUBLIC INTEREST, No. 46 (Winter 1977), pp. 48-58 ` 1977 by National Affairs, Inc.

nations and restored them to self-sufficiency. No comparable plan for restoring the local economies of our cities to self-sufficiency has been envisaged, let alone formulated. Indeed, there is little or no understanding of cities as entities with local economies that must produce as well as distribute, and redistribute the wealth that permits public and private consumption. We must conceptualize these local economies and ask why some have become inadequate to meet the demands and genuine needs of private and public consumption.

A second point that is highly relevant to a federal program for cities is that the individual countries under the Marshall Plan were responsible for making the integrated plans for the recovery of their economies. These plans were not dreamed up in Washington, though the United States government had some voice as the banker for the program. It is impossible for Washington to make plans that meet the individual requirements of thousands of more or less unique local economies. The narrow interests of the Washington bureaucracies, their state and local counterparts, and the forces that they represent could scarcely, if ever, cooperate in the formulation of an economic plan for a city, or subordinate their concerns in the unlikely event that such a plan were adopted. And given the realities of the other pressures at work, the interests of suppliers, unions, and other producers would overshadow those of the local inhabitants.

Our experience with plans and planning has been depressing, for the most part. To a large degree, planning requirements in federal legislation have produced expensive busy work, clearance problems, and empty ritual. For example, some serious purposes were at least originally entertained in the proposal requirements of the Model Cities program, but the cities lacked the capability to formulate appropriate proposals. The resultant widespread use of consulting firms thus negated the very reasonable assumption made by the Department of Housing and Urban Development (HUD) that a city whose staff could not formulate a proposal could not be expected to carry it out. Despite the seeming wisdom of HUD's position it proved practically impossible to maintain. But this lesson appears to have been lost on those who need most to profit from it.

The federal government cannot depend on the cities to make competent plans for the revival of local economies. Their failure to use revenue-sharing funds in a serious way to begin restoring local economies indicates what might well be the fate of larger funds. Only recently has serious work in urban economics begun. Conventional municipal finance has remained innocently unaware of the relationship between fiscal solvency and the state of the local economy. Cities haven't even started to keep ledgers acknowledging that, like countries, they must pay for their imports with exports, and what they cannot pay for they must either produce themselves or do without. City expenditures are treated as pure "merit consumption," and not as investments of scarce resources that, to some important degree, must generate a return if they are to be sustained.

4. URBAN SOCIAL POLICIES

The federal government must help cities develop adequate conceptualizations of their local economies to facilitate competent plans for improving them through appropriate investments and other measures. Washington must also assist in the training and supply of competent staffs to do this economic analysis. In addition, it must exert continuous pressure, without masterminding, to insure that resources are not dissipated, but employed in ways that hold genuine promise of aiding fiscal recovery. The cities should be assisted and pressed to plan for their economic recovery; at the same time, they should accept and demand the responsibility of coordinating the appropriate federal programs—in health, housing, education, manpower, law enforcement, and the rest—in a concerted effort to improve the local economies.

Only when federal policy descends to the concrete context of the local community can we measure both its intended and unintended effects. The local communities are the socioeconomic cells of the larger body politic. Only when these cells are healthy can the nation be healthy; a nation of sick cities is a sick nation. We therefore have to regard them as functioning social organizations, a view largely ignored by macroeconomics and census data alike. Because cities and local communities do essential sociological and economic work, we must come to grips with them both as testing grounds for policy and as building blocks of a sound national political economy.

The problems of restoration

The experience of the Marshall Plan should also indicate the differences as well as the similarities of the economic problems involved. The economies of many of our cities have been ravaged, but not by war; and while our cities have experienced quite palpable physical devastation, for the most part it has not resulted from shelling by an organized enemy. Most important, as we discovered when we extended foreign aid to the underdeveloped countries, the economies of the European nations were already going concerns that only needed tiding over to restore them to health. Unfortunately, this was not the case with the underdeveloped countries, nor to an important degree is it true of troubled cities.

Although crime, vandalism, and riots are far from unimportant, physical devastation accounts for only some of the problems besetting city economies. The relatively straightforward task of physically rebuilding Europe under the Marshall Plan was quite different and far simpler than the task of restoring our cities. The contemporary analogue of the wartime destruction of the European economies is the disinvestment in industrial and residential areas that manifests itself in empty, blighted, gutted, and abandoned factories, office buildings, warehouses, lofts, houses, and apartments. The reasons for this disinvestment have to be faced if the process is to be halted and reversed. The single most important explanation is profitability. For many reasons, the costs in many cities have become far out of line with those prevailing elsewhere. Hence the search for profit entails disinvestment in existing industry, as well as the failure to attract new investment. The mayors will find that federal low-interest loans will not by themselves produce any fundamental change, and will in fact simply mask the problems they are designed to cure.

A variety of factors account for this adverse cost differential, which affects whole regions. The Northeast in general and New England in particular have suffered the loss of manufacturing jobs; within the region, the decline has been particularly severe in Connecticut, the Hartford area, and especially the city of Hartford itself. We know some of the environmental reasons for high regional costs—for example, energy shortages. But there are additional and more important cost differentials that cannot be charged to such adverse factors as geographical resources. Alice Rivlin's study of the fiscal plight of New York City pointed out that a large number of the welfare population could have been employed if New York had the kind of jobs available in South Carolina. What the Rivlin study did not discuss was why those jobs had relocated to the South. The study accepts this condition as a fact of nature rather than an avoidable and possibly reversible self-inflicted injury.

It is odd that with the vast migration of low-skilled Southern blacks and Puerto Ricans to Northern cities, there has been little or no recognition that they would need precisely the kinds of low-pay jobs we have been driving out. We have lived in a kind of dream world with respect to both housing and jobs. We have used conveniently deceptive labels like "slum landlord" and "substandard employer" to avoid facing the hard truth that, except for token exceptions, poor people will get the quality of housing that the market can provide, and low-productivity labor will also suffer the constraints of the market. No one except the real-estate industry asks how a landlord could make a profit renting standard housing for substandard rents to people with substandard incomes; no one asks how an employer could avoid bankruptcy paying high wages to low-skilled employees. Yet these questions must be confronted and answered if we are to solve the cities' economic problems, rather than avoid them with self-serving rhetoric.

As Bennett Harrison and others have maintained, our policies have tended to subsidize the "dual labor market." There is reason to believe that we have been busily driving out the lower half of the primary labor market—jobs in textiles, the garment industry, foundries, brick kilns, and the like. Welfare has acted as a kind of tax by making these jobs unattractive, even though the annual wage they generate is considerably higher than welfare payments. What results are local economies with great gaps between the well-paying jobs of the primary labor market and the other work alternatives found in the secondary labor market. The latter provide only dead-end, intermittent, high-turnover work with marginal employers in low-profit, low-capital enterprises.

The wages of social disinvestment

There are important social and psychological consequences for the individuals and communities afflicted with these employment problems. As Freud pointed out, the job is the most important factor integrating the human personality. Where it provides little or no respect for oneself or others, the effect is debilitating, especially where there are no other institutions adequately performing the same function. The loss of meaningful participation in the mainstream economy has resulted in neighborhood decay, social disorganization, crime, vandalism, blight, and housing abandonment—all the phenomena of crisis associated with the ghetto. A seemingly cancerous process leads to the rapid destruction of sound housing and stores in neighborhoods populated by those trapped on welfare or in the secondary labor market. Their incomes are inadequate to maintain their properties. The constant moves to evade paying the rent not only force properties into rapid obsolescence, but also undermine neighborhood attachments and social control, and result in a turnover of school populations that signals educational failure.

Frank Kristof has shown how the destruction of sound housing in New York City has outpaced new building. He argues persuasively that the city and state rent-control policies have had a perverse and destructive effect on the housing stock and the poor, the intended beneficiaries. But despite all this, Kristof is forced to admit that other cities unburdened by rent control are also losing sound housing because of spreading social disorganization. The destruction of our cities' housing capital through blight and abandonment is only the most visible symptom of the crisis of the ghetto. But despite the obvious concern for those who flee, if this process is to be halted and reversed, the most serious concern must be for those who remain—the victims and agents of social decay.

Constitution Plaza in Hartford and Pruitt-Igoe in St. Louis symbolize the failure of the brick-and-mortar approach to urban problems. HUD and the cities have been far more interested in physical rather than social structures, in physical rather than social capital. But gleaming central business districts surrounded by festering, crime-ridden, spreading slums, plagued by drug addiction and unemployment, bear witness to the truth that cities do not live by brick alone. A committee of the National Academies of Science and Engineering was asked to recommend a program of urban behavioral research to HUD. Even the engineers were emphatic that our knowledge of technology far exceeded our understanding of the social conditions necessary for its application. Despite all this Operation Breakthrough was the major HUD effort.

Cities without citizens

To understand this persistent and seemingly perverse concentration on bricks and mortar, it must be realized that the unions, construction industry, real-estate industry, banks, insurance companies, architects, planners, federal bureaucrats, politicians, and media all have something to gain, even from building uneconomic monuments. We have not yet learned to put together an equally powerful coalition to strengthen social structures, whose building materials rarely provide remotely comparable profits or other rewards. But once again, our foreign-aid experience is instructive.

Outside of Europe, foreign aid frequently led to elite enrichment, black markets, military hardware, inflation, and misdirection of resources. Many of our federal domestic-aid programs have had similarly sorry results. In effect, we have created systems of perverse incentives that stimulate investments as tax gimmicks rather than producing jobs, that co-opt indigenous leaders and foster neighborhood disintegration. We have bred municipal inflation and undermined productive local economies—in the name of benevolent intentions toward cities, the poor, and the minorities.

The federal government has generated harmfully unrealistic expectations without recognizing its incapacity to fulfill them. In the judgment of Anthony Downs, the Johnson housing goals, which were never formally abandoned, would have required a national effort in housing comparable to waging World War II—an effort that, if made, would have had disastrous effects on other social needs. As another example of unrealistic expectations, the Department of Labor was recently quoted as asserting that "the typical family of four requires $15,500 a year to maintain a moderate standard of living." The Department of Labor did not say how untypical such an income was, or what level of GNP the nation would need to permit the typical family to have that income. The impression leaps to many an impressionable mind that wages under $15,500 should be regarded as untypical, and hence substandard. As another example, labor leaders in St. Louis were aghast when they learned that top companies in the city were paying only $9,000 a year—with the city fathers and the media, they have been busily putting the axe to three fourths of the city's jobs as substandard. But neither they nor the federal government has ever bothered to find out the actual distribution of wages. Nor are they in the least concerned with what the businesses they have been driving out can afford to pay in wages yet remain competitive.

In a piece entitled "Should Every Job Support a Family?" (*The Public Interest*, No. 40, Summer 1975), Carolyn Shaw Bell argues that although a fair number of jobs will support a single person above the poverty line, far fewer will offer similar support to a single-earner family of four. A recent study of incomes in New York City found that multi-earner families had the best chance to be above the poverty line. Thus, strange as it may seem, it hurts rather than helps the poor to drive from the city those jobs that will not support a family of four. A realistic appreciation of the actual array of wages and the wages different employers can afford to pay indicates that a genuine concern for the welfare of the poor would lead to a strenuous effort to expand the employment opportunities of all family members, including the aged, the young, and the handicapped. It is a curious benevolence that limits the existing options of the poor while providing no superior alternatives. Yet such has been the direction of union and liberal policy, and of many business conservatives as well. Perhaps the practices of the American farm family rather than the affluent are a better guide for improving the condition of the poor.

Unfortunately, the values that only the affluent can afford dominate our thinking about what should be done by those whose circumstances make such values an insupportable and even disastrous luxury. The poor cannot afford to emulate the rich. Idleness may be attractive for the jet set but it can become a nightmare for the poor. The rich can afford individualism, privacy, and the indulgence of an anarchical libertarianism in their personal lives, since they are securely supported by a corporate order. The poor must help themselves; they cannot afford the luxury of either purchased privacy or purchased security. Despite the claim that the police and the legal order will provide security for the poor and the working class, we know this to be a liberal myth. Neighborhoods police themselves. The liberal who does not blink at the use of union muscle to produce a closed shop decries as fascistic any attempt to produce a closed and physically secure neighborhood. Organizations are good for unions and corporations, but a powerful territorial organization is anathema to police and civil libertarian alike. Our dominant liberal ideology denies the necessity of social control and acts to denigrate and undermine it where it exists. In practice this is to preach social disorganization in the guise of defending liberty and individualism, and to recommend flight as the only realistic remedy—for those who can afford to flee. But society dissolves without a normative structure with motivated, committed citizens.

For some time we have supposed that we could operate cities without citizens by treating legally franchised, casual voters as if they were a functional equivalent. We are beginning to learn that the normative order on which our cities depended in the past was not the product of their formal governments but of the many informal governments of their ethnic neighborhoods. They provided the social control for the working class and the poor, not the Irish cops, whose relation to the city resembled nothing so much as that of the Mamelukes to medieval Cairo. These neighborhoods —cooperative social organizations founded on a normative order, social control, and trustworthy leaders—are the social capital truly analogous to Europe's war-ravaged industries. The halting and reversal of the processes leading to their destruction, and the provision where possible of viable substitutes, are what an effective federal aid program for cities should be about. Such a plan would have as a major goal changing the present federally sponsored system of perverse incentives that contributes so much to the cities' woes. William Skinner, the eminent Stanford anthropologist, has shown how the overseas Chinese maintained their informal governments and their family structures under the most hostile environments for thousands of years. It is only now, with the corrosive influence of American cities, that the Chinese family is breaking up.

The road to the "reservation"

After this bleak picture of decay and disintegration, people want to ask for a solution. There are no easy answers, but there are indications of the form a solution will have to take, in neighborhoods and institutions that are resisting and even overcoming social disorganization, and recreating local social structures. This is the kind of capital a Marshall Plan for cities will have to help build and, just as importantly, prevent from being subverted and destroyed. In St. Louis, the famed Italian Hill and the St. Ambrose Church—recognized even in the Soviet Union—offer an excellent example of what Gerald Suttles calls a "defended neighborhood." The Hill is a working class neighborhood of 30,000 to 40,000 residents in tiny houses on small lots; almost anywhere else it would have become a slum. After visiting the other attractions of St. Louis—the Arch, Busch Stadium, and Pruitt-Igoe—visiting foreign officials were brought to the Hill to see one healthy, hopeful part of the city. Here, in an old, low-income neighborhood, the houses are well kept up, the streets are clean, people help each other, the kids are well brought up, the streets are safe, and housing values are stable and rising. This is an example of the kind of social capital an urban Marshall Plan would seek to create, if possible, and maintain. But when these foreign visitors asked at a neighborhood party what the city, state, and federal governments had done for the Hill, the answer was, "Not a god-damned thing." There was a short addendum: "Yes, the federal government, the city, and the state drove a super highway right through the neighborhood and we had to fight like hell to get [Transportation Secretary John] Volpe to build a bridge to keep the neighborhood together."

The Hill is often dismissed because it is both Italian and Catholic, two factors that supposedly make it unique. The example of the Italian Hill does not show that such a neighborhood can be created amid adverse conditions out of the unpromising material of most city slums. But the experience of the Muslims and the Puerto Rican evangelicals provides ground for hope that even there trust and order can be brought into being. Perhaps this seems surprising only because we have forgotten that the early Christian church was a kind of guerrilla government ministering to slaves, outcasts, and even criminals in the rotting structure of the Roman Empire. Clearly such a force provides stronger political medicine than the laissez-faire, civil-libertarian individualism our Republican and Democratic parties are prepared to administer.

The question is whether the city can halt its present path toward becoming an "Indian reservation"—a poor house, with a set of suburbanized keepers (cops, school teachers, welfare workers, and other municipal bureaucrats), that surrounds a central business district protected by barbed wire—with anything less than a renewed social structure of committed citizens. Failing that, the path toward the "reservation" is the line of least resistance and greatest gain for those having a vested interest in what our brick-and-mortar and welfare politics represent. Can a coalition of black, Puerto Rican, and ethnic neighborhoods be built to support a city leadership that can master the brick-and-mortar coalition in the interest of the city's inhabitants? Can such leadership program both the local and the federal vested interests to restore a viable community political economy? These questions can only be answered by those who must fashion concrete answers out of the materials of their cities. What such leaders can do is to demonstrate that they understand the nature of the job and the form answers will have to take, and that they will make the lifelong commitment required to turn their cities around.

A Marshall Plan for cities will need much more than sunshine patriots. We have learned that the new states of the world require nation building. We have to learn this also applies to us: Our cities and their citizenship require renewing, as well as brick and mortar. This will require city builders whose job is as important as the nation builders of the new countries. In fact, the rebuilding of our cities is the rebuilding of our nation—though, incredibly, we do not realize it. Until we do, a Marshall Plan for cities is likely to come, however disguised, as an act of federal compassion or guilt or worse, as an intervention through the masterminding of an urban Vietnam, rather than as a diagnosis of our collective condition and a concerted, pluralistic effort to put the nation's economic and spiritual house in order. The mayors will find that seriously addressing the problems of our cities requires a politics of civic and moral reconstruction that far transcends central-business-district renewal, mass transit, low-interest loans, or the shifting of the burden of welfare to the shoulders of the federal government.

Facelift for Detroit

Roger M. Williams

DETROIT has become everyone's favorite example of a dying city: the place where urban problems have converged to wipe out the achievements and values of twentieth-century America. Although accounts of Detroit's demise have been exaggerated as well as premature, the patient is indeed very ill. Many thousands of houses and apartment buildings lie abandoned and often gutted. Stores and hotels have closed downtown to follow the white middle class into the suburbs. The violent-crime rate is among the highest in the nation's cities, and the heroin problem is second to none. Unemployment runs around 14 percent—almost 40 percent for black teen-agers. Gangs of youths terrorize neighborhoods, parking lots, and even expressways, where, for a period last summer, they preyed on stalled motorists.

It is understood among businessmen that in such a situation everybody tries to cut his losses and pull out smoothly. Nobody expands or builds anything new. Yet downtown Detroit today is the site of the most expensive real estate development in the world—arguably the most expensive in history, if you figure that slave labor built the pyramids. The project is Renaissance Center, a colossal group of office buildings, shops, and a hotel that has risen on the barren banks of the Detroit River. The cost of construction is $337 million, and every dollar of it is private money. Thus the center is billed as proof of private enterprise's concern for Detroit and, by extension, for all of urban America.

In that sense, at least, Renaissance Center has more importance as a symbol than it does as an actuality. Boosters already are proclaiming it the symbol of the "new Detroit," a concept that has been struggling to gain credibility for the past several years. The name itself was chosen to suggest the city's emergence from a dark age. (Ironically, the deposed emblem, called "Spirit of Detroit," is a statue of a crouching man who could be rising to his feet or sinking to his knees, depending on one's view of him—and of his city.)

Whatever the merits of Renaissance Center as symbol, architecture, or homage to the gods, it will be judged most critically for its impact on beleaguered Detroit. Henry Ford

II, the driving force behind the center, admitted as much when he proclaimed the project "primarily a catalyst to make other things happen." By "other things," Ford and his associates mean the physical regeneration of downtown Detroit and the spiritual regeneration of the whole city.

That is a very large order, and many observers are skeptical that it can be filled. How, they ask, can a flashy real estate development solve the urban problems that abound in Detroit? What significant impact can it have on unemployment, white flight, the decay of downtown? What impact of any kind can it have on crime, housing abandonment, heroin addiction, and the hostile, hopeless feeling that pervades vast segments of the city's population? If the answer is, "Very little," aren't the renaissance centers of our time—the "megastructures" mushrooming in American cities—expensive baubles that divert attention and money from the real problems?

Before I talked to the Renaissance Center people, the theorists as well as the day-to-day managers, I was pretty sure those questions were better than the answers to them would be. Now I am not at all sure. While Renaissance is no panacea, a good case can be made for it. The case goes beyond the essentially negative "What the hell else might work for a place like Detroit?" It goes to what may well be the critical element in restoring the health of the cities: attracting middle-class whites to live in them again.

THERE are several explanations of how Henry Ford came to build Renaissance Center. One has it that he wanted an achievement to cap his career as one of America's premier industrialists; another, that he was mortified by his brother Billy's decision to relocate the Detroit Lions football team, which Billy owns, in suburban Pontiac. Ford's own explanation is persuasive. He says that leaders of Detroit's would-be regeneration persuaded him to do it—shamed him, in a sense—by pointing out that he had already helped adjoining Dearborn, headquarters of the Ford Motor Company, by constructing the huge Fairlane project there. They pointed out, too, that although the company no longer has operations in Detroit, its well-being is inextricably tied to that of the city.

Renaissance Center, then, was principally a balancing of obligations and interests by Henry Ford. "Mr. Ford realized that the suburbs can't be the financial and cultural base for a metropolitan area," says Wayne S. Doran, president of the Ford real estate subsidiary that put together the Renaissance deal. "The city has to fill that function. He realized also that the other suburbs had been draining population and business from Dearborn itself. Certainly, with both the Dearborn and Detroit projects, he was protecting his own economic interests. But he was protecting a larger interest as well—the economic well-being of the whole region." Once Ford determined that Detroit had to be helped, he summoned the help. As Doran says, "He's not the kind of guy who lies back."

Henry Ford's helpers turned out to be 51 major corporations, each with a substantial economic stake in greater Detroit. Among them are names that have made the city world-famous: General Motors, Chrysler, American Motors, B. F. Goodrich, Firestone, Bendix, Gulf & Western, TRW. The corporations amassed $37.5 million in equity capital—with Ford, GM, and a couple of others contributing $6 million each—to start the project. They purchased 33 acres of Detroit River frontage. And they hired Atlanta architect John Portman, developer of Peachtree Center, Embarcadero Plaza, and other spectaculars, to design the biggest, most stupendous urban megastructure ever seen.

Portman produced a very Portmanesque design: a cylindrical 73-story reflecting-glass hotel surrounded by four octagonal 39-story office towers and, eventually, a half-dozen or more lower buildings. The cluster is interconnected by enclosed walkways and a four-story pedestrian mall that will house shops, restaurants, and so forth. The hotel, named the Detroit Plaza, opened in March, and two of the office towers have been accepting tenants for several months. It is all properly awesome and futuristic, with 1,000-feet-a-minute elevators and small suspended cocktail areas called "pods"—although to this layman's eye the pitted, dun-colored natural concrete makes as dull an interior here as it does in other Portman buildings.

The center has not had a smooth road financially. Cost overruns on construction were so large that Henry Ford, aided by Mayor Coleman Young, had to go back to the investors for almost $100 million more. While the hotel has had excellent advance bookings (downtown Detroit is short of first-class hotel space), the office buildings and retail shops have done only modestly well. Local sources say office rentals were lagging badly until Ford decided to move 1,700 of his own employees from Dearborn into the center, where they will occupy an entire tower. The retail-space purveyors are trying to secure big names from the fashion world, especially some from Western Europe, to give the center chic. Although that seems logical, it is also risky: in Atlanta's Omni complex, such classy shops as Gucci, Lanvin, and Rizzoli have fared poorly; their sophistication and prices outpace the local market.

Without question, the center has transformed a substantial section of the riverfront and raised hopes for the rest of it. Through the shortsightedness typical of city fathers and their professional planners, Detroit's side of the river had become little more than a junkyard, a collection of dilapidated warehouses, obsolete factories, and parking lots. Now Detroiters realize that the river and its north bank (because the river twists, Detroit is north of Windsor, Ontario, on the south bank) are among the city's finest natural assets.

But no one knows how far inland, to the core of Detroit and its problems, the blessings of Renaissance will radiate. In the immediate vicinity, across busy Jefferson Avenue, there are signs of new life. Blue Cross–Blue Shield has expanded the complex that serves as its Midwest headquarters. An architect who was ready to leave the area has instead renovated one old building and transformed another—a former flophouse—into a branch of a well-known Grosse Pointe restaurant. Retail and service establishments will follow in an effort to capitalize on the spillover business from the Renaissance offices and hotel.

Farther into the city there are other examples of rejuvenation, although it becomes difficult to attribute them to the center. Woodward and Washington avenues, once Detroit's proudest thoroughfares, are stirring after years of sliding downhill.

Mayor Young, an early supporter of candidate Jimmy Carter, has not yet seen his support repaid with Carter administration largess. Nonetheless, Young's skill at dealing with the Washington bureaucracy has attracted more federal dollars than Detroit has ever received before. The feds have agreed to fund a "people mover" system, a roof for the Woodward Avenue mall, and part of the mayor's current pet project, a sports arena. In all, $2 billion worth of construction is now under way in the city.

That Detroit should require this kind of resurrection is ironic. As the birthplace and home of the automobile industry, it has symbolized the successful material side of the American way of life. Detroit not only helped to create the American dream, it lived that dream to the fullest. Until withered by urban blight, it was a melting pot where southern blacks and Appalachian whites could and did come to make, in its factories, more money than they had dreamed possible. Nor was Detroit a gritty, turn-of-the-century manufacturing town. It was a green city, with broad boulevards, a high proportion of single-family home ownership, and its share of creditable cultural institutions.

Several things combined to change this happy picture. Detroit's mighty industrial base became shaky and increasingly vulnerable to the vicissitudes of the national economy. Seeking to take advantage of the nationwide flight from the cities, Detroit's suburbs mounted effective campaigns to capture the people who worked downtown and, with them, their jobs. Detroit lost 100,000 residents in the 1960s and another 100,000 from 1970 to 1975, as the suburbs flowered with apartment and office buildings. While the towns of Southfield and Troy were the most successful raiders, almost every district with a few trees and no poor blacks scored at the expense of the city. Among the major companies that pulled out of downtown were S. S. Kresge and Bendix. With them and many smaller firms went confidence in and commitment to the city.

Poorly managed government programs exacerbated the problem. The program run by the federal Department of Housing and Urban Development during the early Seventies was so bad that today HUD is a dirty word in Detroit.

The very companies that built modern Detroit contributed heavily to its decline. For example, the Big Three auto makers have until recently failed to support public transit, preferring to see their Motor City choke on private vehicles. (In the process, almost half of downtown became parking lots.) Office construction stagnated, and the owners of "Class A" buildings maximized their profits instead of modernizing to meet the increasing competition from the suburbs. Detroit's conservative banking community stunted whatever speculative growth might have taken place. "You must have overbuilding if a city is to grow," says Henry Hagood, a black Detroit developer, "but the banks demanded that everything be sold or rented in advance before they'd put up money."

Robert McCabe, president of Detroit Renaissance, a civic group, readily admits that the city has suffered from establishment neglect. "The captains of industry were making it big then," McCabe says. "Who thought of problems? That's one reason we were so shocked by the 1967 riots." Those highly destructive riots set off a rush of government-funded social programs that may have eased ghetto problems but did nothing to revitalize the city as a whole. Both the image and the reality of Detroit continued to deteriorate.

Enter Henry Ford II, a refreshingly informal tycoon known around Detroit as "Hank the Deuce." Ford and the corporate executives to whom he appealed had seen enough "people programs," as they were called in the high-flying days of the Johnson administration. "We wanted a brick-and-mortar operation that would start important *physical* things happening," says McCabe, whose organization was a spiritual godfather to Renaissance Center. "We had to become competitive again in the local and national markets. And we wanted to do that the way we knew how—through private investment."

Ford has been criticized for not spreading the $337 million around Detroit in a series of smaller projects. His answer is that he wanted a project with a certain catalytic effect and that any number of routine buildings would not produce that. As McCabe puts it, "We wanted to build something with the kind of critical mass that would make people say, Something's really happening in Detroit. In the trade, that is sometimes called 'J.C. architecture' because it triggers the exclamation, 'Jesus Christ!'" John Portman not only designs J.C.'s, he also believes that city revitalization requires the creation of "total environments" rather than of standard structures that fulfill only one or two basic needs.

"You can't make people come into or stay in the city," Portman told me recently. "You have to create the circumstances that will attract them." These days that means convenience, pleasing surroundings, style, and, increasingly, physical safety. Portman's total environments provide these. Even when he talks about "putting people on their feet again, so they can walk to work, to church, to the drugstore," he means walk *within* a single urban complex.

Critics have called Renaissance Center a Noah's Ark for the white middle class. They note the easy access for motoring suburbanites, the on-site underground parking, and the cluster design—with formidable abutments on the side facing downtown—that accentuates the fortress feeling. Other than explaining the abutments (they house the huge heating and air-conditioning units), Portman simply shrugs off the charge: "I'm glad the center offers a sense of security. Let's

face it, cities, and certainly Detroit, have at least the image of being unsafe places. To reverse that, we have to give people city environments where they feel safe."

Police statistics demonstrate that downtown Detroit is actually one of the safest sections in the city, but it takes a long time for this news to penetrate to the suburbs. One can hardly spend a day in the city without hearing stories of suburbanites who won't come downtown or who haven't been there for years and are proud of it. A wave of youth-gang violence last summer increased suburbanites' fears sharply.

In selling Renaissance Center, its promoters play up the security of the place while pointing out subtly that the suburbs themselves are none too safe these days. Gazing out a window on the top floor of the center, a Renaissance representative told me how pleased businessmen from Chicago and New York are to come upon this vista: "You don't really see the ghettos from here. They're not obtrusive the way they are in those other cities."

Although Renaissance salesmen have not yet persuaded any companies to forsake the suburbs, they have signed up a number of downtown firms that probably would have relocated there. The center has compiled quite a record of making off with the major tenants of other downtown office buildings. To the building owners' protests, Renaissance replies rather piously that this is the price of progress and, rather sensibly, that the suburbs were "raiding" downtown office buildings long before it entered the competition.

The competition is not on even terms because the entire center is, in effect, an in-house project of the auto industry's extended family. Of the 51 investor companies, only a dozen or so have no readily identifiable connection with the industry. The rest, as suppliers or bankers to Henry Ford and the other auto makers, are subject to the wishes of and pressures from the purchasers of their products. So, too, are a high percentage of the tenants who have taken office space in the center.

Beyond this is the question of whether a project of Renaissance's magnitude could be brought off without a big daddy who has economic muscle and lots of IOUs to cash. Perhaps in no other city could a Henry Ford muster this kind of extended business family for this kind of undertaking.

The least mentioned element of Renaissance Center—housing—may turn out to be the most important in terms of the future of Detroit. Phase two of the scheme contains plans for high-rental apartments in adjoining buildings. "You have to establish [Renaissance] as a job site first, then hope people will want to live near their jobs," Portman explains. "We worked in reverse at Embarcadero Center, putting in the apartments first. We had a hard time renting them, and that was San Francisco, not Detroit."

Yet several Detroiters with whom I spoke insisted that if Renaissance had apartments, they would be renting right now. There is evidence to support their claim. What little good downtown apartment space remains is fully rented, with waiting lists common. Henry Hagood says that his middle-income downtown apartment buildings are full and that whites represent a steadily growing proportion of the tenants; about half of these whites have moved in from the suburbs. "Builders are crawling all over Detroit now," Hagood adds. "Everybody's looking for sites." In addition, old houses in Detroit's in-town neighborhoods are selling better than they have for many years. They hold a fresh appeal for young couples whose alternative is to pay at least twice as much for a run-of-the-mill ranch house miles from anything but suburban sprawl.

To the west of Renaissance Center, industrialist-financier Max Fisher is attempting to do what Ford and Portman have put off doing, that is, build apartments on the riverfront. Fisher is about to break ground on a 2,500-unit high-rise that will be the first major apartment building constructed in central Detroit in two decades. "If it goes, it'll mean a lot to this town," Hagood says. "Even if we can get well-to-do whites interested in coming back in, at this point there's almost no place for them to live."

Recognizing the importance of such housing to Detroit, the Michigan legislature recently passed a bill that provides a 12-year moratorium on taxes on improvements made on land used for housing projects in the city. Without a break of this sort, developers would find the speculative ventures that Detroit now badly needs much too risky to undertake.

If America's cities are to become stable, they need people who will live in them by choice, not, like the poor, because they are captives. Without such people, a city has too little vitality and spirit, as well as too small a tax base. New York, for all its fiscal problems, is healthier and more vital than many of the cities whose residents deride it—because it remains a place where people choose to live.

Detroit's predicament grows out of two deep roots. One is the plight of its poor. Optimistic predictions notwithstanding, Renaissance Center will do little for them; that is a job for government, through large-scale, imaginative programs, sensitively administered. The second root is the attitude of the middle class. As long as middle-class whites and increasing numbers of their black counterparts choose to live outside the city and avoid it whenever possible, Detroit cannot recover.

When suburbanites come to Renaissance to work or shop or eat at a restaurant, even if they come by armored car, their irrational fears may begin to dissipate, and they may discover the numerous advantages that any major city holds over any suburb. That is a far from certain prospect, but it is Detroit's best hope.

Joseph Scrofani

IDS Building, Minneapolis, Minnesota

Gerald Brimacombe/Black Star

The Case Against Urban Dinosaurs

William G. Conway

William G. Conway, an urban affairs consultant, was formerly associated with Atlanta's architect-developer John C. Portman.

AS CONTEMPORARY wisdom would have it, the future of the American city depends on megastructures— those huge but slickly sophisticated commercial real estate projects that have been springing up in American cities for the past decade. Tax-starved mayors, along with the owners of dwindling downtown business establishments, persist in their claim that these giant renewal efforts are all that keep their cities from irreversible decay.

The truth is, however, that the megastructure guarantees neither the investment of its owners nor the future of the city. Far from lending strength to downtown areas, these complexes create little more than a suburban island in mid-city. The hope had been that the architectural behemoths would be the most promising of the creations thus far produced by the boom-bust cycle of real estate speculation. But it is the cycle itself, together with the size and complexity of the projects, that spells financial trouble for megastructure owners. Plagued by cost overruns, the overbuilding that accompanies speculative fever, and onerous finance charges, more and more owners are turning over control of their projects to the out-of-town financial institutions that made them possible in the first place. The size of the structures keeps financial institutions committed to the projects after owner troubles ensue.

Trailing in the wake of financial concerns has been the unforeseen dilemma these edifices impose on their host community: building them stimulates inflation—and thereby further agitates the deterioration of the central city, which further divides the poor from the middle and upper classes.

But what of the much touted benefits of the megastructures? They were intended as more than profit-making ventures for their investors: they were supposed to revive the central city. Generally, they draw people to the city no more successfully than they attract revenue.

It is understandable why mayors and businessmen would cling to anything that promised to stop the decentralization of downtown. The dwindling of population, retail trade, and jobs erodes the tax base. Those citizens left behind make bigger and bigger demands on the public treasury.

Billions have been spent in the United States to stem this flow from city to suburb. But despite the full-page ads and megastructural magnificence—or perhaps because of them— the exodus continues. Minneapolis, for example, after two decades of hard-selling of the city—including the IDS building—has lost more than a fifth of its population. In Atlanta and Los Angeles, both of which boast a great many of the mammoth complexes, researchers discovered that downtown patrons are usually "captive" central-city employees and transients.

Why? Because the megastructure enshrouds the creator's visions of a controlled environment. It respects neither the texture nor the geography of its surroundings. From the street, which the megastructure normally blind-sides with the exception of a grand entrance or two, the unrelieved boredom of whatever material is in vogue reveals the designer's hostility to the cities he professes to save.

Removed from the heights of their angular abstractions, we on the ground can bear witness to a few of the things the megastructures and their apostles have done to our cities. As Paul Goldberger, architecture critic for *The New York Times*, wrote recently about Renaissance Center (Detroit's answer to its severe case of the urban blues): "The . . . towers are set on a multi-story base, which turns a massive wall to the rest of the city. . . . It wants to stand alone, and fails to do the crucial thing that all good urban buildings do—relate carefully to what is around them."

Renaissance Center has so far cost $330 million, more or less. It is removed from and creates a barrier to most pedestrian movement, except for those inside, who enjoy the mazelike and private-cop-supervised rigors of what Goldberger calls the "conceptually . . . suburban development." Visitors to these projects are never in the city. They, and these projects, could be anywhere.

Meanwhile, in reaction to the street crime and sales erosion that these projects were supposed to end, department stores and jewelers are abandoning downtown—in Detroit, Baltimore, and elsewhere—for the suburbs, where cash registers tend to be open more often than they are closed.

Peter Wolf, in *The Future of the City*, writes that if the big-base megastructure trend continues, the existing city will be "closed out," and "the already perilous decline in the amenity offered by public spaces within the city" will be accelerated. The street, as the traditional organizer of urban life and design, will be replaced by enclaves.

ATLANTA exemplifies the curse of megastructuralism. The five huge architectural jewels in the South's queen city are transforming her crown into fool's gold. This reverse alchemy is laying waste the downtown areas *between* the megastructures. In so doing, it obeys the laws of economics now ignored by the projects' sponsors and by the city officials who clamor for more megastructures without first knowing the effects of those already constructed.

In 1960, Atlanta's "first class" office space was spread among 40-odd buildings, and much of this prime office space was centered near the heart of the business district, Five Points. Land values decreased rapidly as the distance from this intersection increased. Property ownership was fragmented; downtown lost the lead in office space and retail sales to the suburbs. Enter the megastructure.

It all begins with the land; and megastructures require acres in zones where property is measured in square feet. With one exception, the land acquired for Atlanta's renewal projects is on the fringe of the business district, between the peak of the land-value "pyramid" and its base. The focus of the center has thus been blurred. Other major acquisitions, for projects that may be abandoned, have also been made. The result is a previously unknown concentration of property ownership—at some distance from the traditional center—and the creation of several new and absurdly inflated "value pyramids."

Property in the vicinity of the $250 million Peachtree

Allen Green/Visual Departures

View from the ashes—" 'It fails to do the crucial thing . . . relate to what is around it.' "

Center that traded for less than $10 per square foot in 1960 cannot be purchased for less than $50 per square foot this year. The pattern is repeated around the other acquisitions. If inflation this severe were experienced by the economy as a whole, it would be crippling. In downtown Atlanta, it has been most destructive to the small firms that hoped to incubate their calculations of prosperity in the warmth of large, accessible markets and cheap space. The cheap space is gone, and so are many of the small firms.

Big employers are also beginning to feel the pinch. The distributing firm of Beck and Gregg, one of downtown Atlanta's larger employers, has quietly declared its intention to leave for more efficient quarters. St. Joseph's Hospital has put its property on the market for $75 per square foot and is building new facilities 15 miles from downtown. Either to be closer to a better-trained labor force or to reduce costs, the South's largest bank, The Citizens and Southern National Bank, along with many insurance companies and airlines, has removed some computer operations and many office functions with high clerical requirements.

If only because of the real estate taxes they pay, the sponsors of megastructures acquire certain enduring political influence. The economic weight and the burden-sharing of the new real estate pyramids are not calculated in the environmental impact statements that breeze through city hall on the wings of political ambition. But in forgoing such concerns, the sponsors of these projects have permanently altered the social and economic ecology of downtown.

At the behest of megastructure owners, city officials plead with state and federal governments to build new highways and to install new anti-crime lights for the owners and their tenants—who, more often than not, no longer live in town and are even afraid to go there unless they can park within the walls of the megastructure. The well-lighted streets empty when they go home. Nevertheless, requests for rapid transit, people-movers, and other capital-consuming projects follow. The city, of course, tries to meet many of these demands, spending to its limits. Meanwhile, the needs of the under-served are relegated to lower and lower priorities.

"Every bank and insurance company with money wanted to get a piece of the developer's action in Atlanta," said a bank officer whose department placed over $100 million in real estate loans there during the Sixties. "We were under unbelievable pressure to get the money out, despite the fact that we had an inexperienced staff and only passing familiarity with the markets." A colleague, pondering his moribund portfolio of megastructure investments, commented that "lenders were too quick to elevate architects and developers from the status of manufacturers of space to visionaries."

The visionaries have secured more than one billion dollars from the lenders in the past 15 years. While that sum was being invested in downtown Atlanta, employment there remained almost steady—in the range of 80,000 jobs. And while "upward" shifts in the composition of employment occurred, the changes have not been sufficient to justify the hot-market monuments to hope.

Atlanta and many other cities now have a surplus of office space that can be expected to last five to seven years. The average size of new office buildings has trebled. Seven projects account for over half of Atlanta's downtown office space. After three years of leasing efforts, the megastructures' shopping arcades are little more than half full. Tenants are complaining. As for hotels, Donald Ratajczak, Atlanta's leading economic forecaster, has said that the city built three (averaging 1,000 rooms apiece) when it needed only one.

The dismal economic performance of these projects has put the lenders squarely in a role they do not relish. Lenders are now actively involved in the financial administration of four of Atlanta's five megastructures.

Economies of scale are an important tenet of the developers' faith. Build one more big one, believers say; revitalization is around the corner. But if Atlanta builds another, its promised land of urban salvation may be populated solely by the megastructuralists and their bankers, waving to each other through see-through floors, elevated from the parking lots and abandoned blocks that await the next vote of confidence in downtown.

A block north of Peachtree Center is a group of buildings once leased by firms that designed stores, did printing, fixed teeth, sold books, served cheap food, repaired cars. These firms have been replaced by one of the few tenant types that will not be admitted to the megastructures—porn shops. The new tenants will pay whatever rent is asked. They are now the object of outbursts of civic virtue and midnight raids.

The property near Omni International is not as expensive as the stuff up on Peachtree Street. It is much emptier, though. Marietta Street, connecting the Omni with Coca-Cola's world headquarters, wends its way through a series of largely unoccupied industrial structures that for years housed several key employers of those Atlantans who lived near the center of the city. These buildings now provide shelter for ·itinerant winos while they polish off shared pints of scuppernong before heading out to huddle in the next building down the block. The land the winos stand on sells for $20 per square foot, compared with $5 per square foot for the industrial property in a suburban zone that has increased its employment 630 percent in the past 15 years.

Two other concentrations of small businesses, close to or at the center of downtown, were removed primarily for aesthetic considerations. Most of these firms provided a variety of goods and services to bus riders who, because of the route structure, transferred nearby. But in the past three years, the buildings containing many more than 200 of these establishments have been torn down by the wrecker's ball.

On one site, a sterile park now gives photogenic prominence to the bank from which flowed the funds that purchased the parkland. The other site, presently a fenced-in pit, is comically straddled by a five-and-dime, the only retail tenant on the block that has a listing in Standard and Poor's. Gone is the bebop and diddy-wah from the record stores, the fragrance of the peanut stand, the harsh colors of the Day-Glo socks hung amid the sundries of no name. When the city's mass transit system is completed, this land will be the site of yet another plaza on which some developer will be granted "air rights" to build yet another rebuttal to the "Towering Inferno."

The customers that frequented the now vanished establishments were the people who, in the words of Central Atlanta Progress, an establishment-backed planning group, caused "racial imbalance on the streets," from which the megastructures were supposed to be a refuge. The stores themselves once offered goods and services not found on North Michigan Avenue or Fifth Avenue or Rodeo Drive, elite streets that the megastructures attempt to emulate in their self-contained, monocultural ambience.

Atlanta, which in the premegastructure era billed itself as "the city too busy to hate," is now hyperbolically "the city without limits." Perhaps there is still time for that city, and for the other cities that have fallen under the spell of the megastructure shamans, to demonstrate that it is not "too big to care" about the essential destructiveness of these lumbering urban dinosaurs.

Ten Ideas to
Save New York

Jack Newfield and Paul DuBrul

Can New York be saved? Is it too late? Are there specific government programs and policies that can still make a difference?

We want to think so. There is nothing inevitable about the life cycle of cities. No one is predicting the death of Paris, Amsterdam, or London, and they are much older than New York. Neighborhoods like SoHo—one filled with light industry, now a thriving residential and artistic haven—have been regenerated, so why not other communities in the city? Italian, working-class Belmont, in the Bronx, has preserved its vitality, so why not other neighborhoods?

To begin with, any agenda for the restoration of New York must start from a national vision. New York City by itself does not have the power, or the authority, to alleviate unemployment, print currency, control interest rates, tax its suburbs, or receive an equitable share of federal economic assistance. And federal programs are essential to any long-term solution to the economic predicament of New York.

America, as always, seems in jeopardy of becoming two nations: a wealthy, growing, satisfied Sunbelt in the South and Southwest, and an impoverished, withering, bitter slum belt

stretching across the northeast quadrant.

Since the Depression of the 1930s, many national policies have nourished and encouraged the prosperity of the Sunbelt at the expense of the Northeast. The Highway Trust Fund and national transportation policy subsidized Houston, Phoenix, and Los Angeles with interstate highways but starved the New York subways and the Northeast's rail corridor. Farm-subsidy programs, like cotton-price supports, helped speed the introduction of mechanized farming in the South. But this threw hundreds of thousands of unskilled agricultural laborers out of work and forced them to migrate to the alien cities of the North, where they applied for welfare.

The geometric growth of the national-defense budget has also been a significant factor in swelling the new economy of abundance in the Sunbelt. The fifteen states from Virginia to California contain 38 percent of the nation's population but receive half of all the defense expenditures, including military installations and bases. The fifteen states from Maine to Minnesota hold 44 percent of America's population but get only 31 cents of each military dollar. New York State ranks twentieth in defense-contract payrolls.

The Sunbelt has received dams, soil banks, agricultural extensions, land-grant colleges, and a favorable tariff policy. But Nixon and Ford allocated comparatively little for urban reconstruction.

Thus, for a generation the federal government has been redistributing wealth and power, not from the rich to the poor, but from the Northeast to the Sunbelt. The first step toward reviving New York City has to be an end to this policy, which discriminates so severely against the northeast quadrant. For 30 years the national government has deliberately funded and favored the South and Southwest. This was a justified and successful investment strategy. But today, this strategy is unfair and unnecessary. Now a period of compensatory development and legislation is required to save the entire northeastern United States from urban death.

Here are our recommendations:

1. Federalize Welfare; Enact National Health Insurance

For fiscal 1976 — 1977, New York City had an expense budget of $12.5-billion. Of that sum, 12.1 percent went for welfare and 14.7 percent for Medicaid. New York is not likely to become a viable economic organism until all, or most, of this dual burden is lifted by the federal government. Federalizing the cost of welfare and a fiercely administered system of comprehensive national health insurance would help solve this problem for New York and would benefit other deteriorating municipalities at the same time.

A federal assumption of welfare costs seems reasonable, since poverty is a national responsibility and many of New York's poor arrived in this city as internal American migrants, life in other parts of the nation being unbearable. Many varieties of national health plans are up for consideration;

while none is perfect, the Kennedy-Corman bill seems the best attainable version. Any system would have to be sensitive to the potential for waste and to the need for quality care.

2. Create a Federal Urban Bank

In fiscal year 1975 – 1976, debt service represented 16 percent of New York City's expense budget, and in 1976 – 1977, that figure rose to 19 percent. (For 1977 – 1978, the projected debt service, including MAC bonds, is $2.3 billion.) Debt service today is the single largest expense for New York City—bigger than welfare, bigger than Medicaid.

The best way to alleviate this crushing burden would be to create a federal urban bank that could sell New York City securities, and other cities' paper debts, at lower interest rates than is now possible. The idea of such a bank, which was first circulated in a memo by union-pension-fund consultant Jack Bigel in February, 1975, is based on the concept of using the power of the federal government to create a new market.

An urban bank would be a federal agency that would buy municipal debt at reasonable interest rates. It would issue its own bonds to the public in order to raise revenue, which, in turn, it would use to purchase municipal debt. New York City would be able to recall its outstanding debt, issued at interest rates as high as 9.4 percent, and reissue it to the urban bank at a lower interest rate.

In addition to providing fiscal relief to local governments, an urban bank could be a mechanism for tax reform. If fully implemented by the federal government, it would remove municipal bonds as a tax shelter used by trust departments of banks, bond departments of brokerage houses, and a small number of rich people.

An urban bank, according to Bigel, would save New York City "a minimum of $210 million a year" and "would allow the city to borrow again for current needs."

3. End Redlining by Savings Banks

Direct methods for dealing with the perfidy of redlining are available. The state legislature should enact a law that would mandate savings banks—and insurance companies—to invest at least 50 percent of all their new mortgages in neighborhoods that are now denied credit. Also, at least 75 percent

of all the mortgages given by the city and state employee pension funds should be within the city or the state.

We cannot permit a savings bank to prosper on deposits from a neighborhood by investing that money in a shopping mall in Dallas or a sewer system in San Diego, to redline the community of its own depositors, and to close the local branch when the neighborhood begins to decay. We cannot forget that banks are creations of the chartering power of democratic government. Banks must behave in the public interest, and in the interest of their depositors. If they don't, they should lose their charters and the right to make money with our money.

4. Get Tough on Crime; Make Punishment Certain

In some ways crime may be New York's deepest and most intractable disease, because effective remedies seem so problematic. We know that crime is driving taxpaying families and businesses out of the city. We know that the crime rate is rising each year. A month does not go by without some hideous homicide in the city: an elderly woman beaten to death in her apartment for pennies, a young woman walking her dog stabbed to death in Central Park, a shopkeeper shot to death by a junkie in Brooklyn.

The fear of crime has become a prison for many citizens of the city. Many old people subsist on the food neighborhood children will buy for them because they are afraid to venture out alone into the street. In the South Bronx, on the Lower East Side, in Times Square, hunting gangs of what former Bronx Police Commander Anthony Bouza memorably called "feral youth" terrorize people.

Liberals and radicals have often been reluctant to face the crime problem squarely. (In 1968, Eugene McCarthy equated any mention of crime with a covert appeal to racist voters, not realizing how concerned minorities were about their own safety.) In no other area is what we think we are supposed to think more at odds with what we do think, if we are honest about our experience and our real feelings.

We believe that in the short run, one effective remedy against violent street crime is swift punishment and significant penalties for those found guilty.

In the fall of 1976, a nineteen-year-old named Ronald Timmons was arrested in the Bronx after he was caught beating and robbing an elderly woman. He was released on $500 bail because the judge did not have legal access to Timmons's confidential juvenile criminal record. This juvenile record included seventeen arrests and an accusation of murdering a 92-year-old man in 1972. Timmons immediately jumped bail. The confidentiality of juvenile records seems to us less important than the prospect of a murderous youth roaming the street. We also believe that fifteen-year-olds in family court should be fingerprinted and photographed and treated as adult offenders.

Most penologists agree that certainty of punishment is probably the most likely deterrent to crime. But there is no certainty of punishment today. Most violent juveniles know that the first couple of times they are arrested, they will simply be recycled back onto the street by the family court. Also, the median lapse of time in New York between arrest and trial is six months; this should be reduced to 60 or 90 days.

We have to agree with Harvard Professor James Q. Wilson, who argues in his book *Thinking About Crime* that harsher penalties against persistent violent criminals discourage the marginal criminal from predatory offenses. Wilson believes that some portion of the criminal population is not indifferent to the likely risks and rewards of this occupation, and if the mathematical odds on serving three years for a violent mugging increased, then the criminal would think twice.

Our belief in swift, sure punishment, however, does not mean we have any sympathy for the extreme remedies conservatives promote, like capital punishment, Rockefeller's drug law, or other notions based on *severity* rather than *certainty* of punishment. All we are saying is that liberals have been too slow to recognize that there is some value in prison terms for recidivist violent criminals. And that freedom from fear to walk the street is also a civil liberty that needs protection.

A fifteen-year-old who commits a homicide should be treated as an adult. A nineteen-year-old who is convicted of a second violent robbery should go to prison for four or five years. Many of the teenagers who commit violent crimes may be psychotic, in the sense that they have no feelings of guilt and may not know right from wrong. There are no existing facilities in which to treat such offenders adequately. Certainly the prisons and juvenile facilities offer scant programs geared to rehabilitation. But, nevertheless, we think that even without hope of rehabilitation, those guilty of violent crimes should be incarcerated, just to separate them from, and to protect, the rest of society.

All this said, prison reform and rehabilitation should be high-priority goals and probably together are the best preventive method to combat violent crime. But our experience is that private organizations like the Fortune Society have been more successful in accomplishing individual rehabilitation than any of the agencies of government, especially in the realm of therapy and self-image.

History has chosen to remember its most brutal cultures by their prisons: Stalin by the Gulag; the Nazis by Auschwitz and the other concentration camps; the South Vietnamese under Ky and Thieu by the tiger cages; the Chilean junta by the prison ship *Esmeralda*. And America by Attica.

We have visited Attica, Clinton, Greenhaven, and the Tombs when it was open. There can be little question that these New York prisons, like so many others, cause rather than cure crime. Men come out of prison ten times more bitter and antisocial than they were on entering it. They meet potential crime partners and learn more subtle criminal skills in prison. Prison reform—including job and psychiatric counseling and conjugal visits—is imperative. So is removal of all the licensing provisions that now discriminate against and deny employment to ex-offenders in more than 50 different job classifications.

In the long run, the causes of crime remain unemployment, racism, lack of education, and drug addiction. But poverty is only a reason for crime, not an excuse. The enormity of the crime problem demands a simultaneous attempt at finding immediate, short-term remedies. Otherwise we are setting the stage for a demagogue to exploit and manipulate our fear.

Stricter, swifter criminal sanctions, especially against the hunting juvenile gangs, is a distasteful, simplistic solution whose time has come.

5. Rebuild the Railroads; Restore the Port

Incredible as it may seem, New York City is the only major American city without direct rail-freight access. Freight cars destined for New York from the West must be routed north to Albany, where they cross the Hudson and travel south, a ridiculously circuitous route. The Institute for Public Transportation (IPT) estimates that this raises the cost of each carload by $198 and adds two to three days to an average trip. It adds $100 million a year to freight charges for New York, according to the institute.

Until a few years ago, rail freight crossed the Hudson on an ancient wooden bridge at Poughkeepsie, and the additional cost to shippers was about half what it is today. When the bridge burned down, it was supposed to be replaced by new construction paid for with state transportation bond moneys, but the financial crisis has kept the bonds from the market. Actually, there is no reason to use either the Poughkeepsie or the Albany route, since an existing rail tunnel crosses the Hudson and enters New York directly, at 34th Street, right behind Penn Station. Railroad companies used to claim that this tunnel was too small for freight cars and could be used only for passenger cars—a charge that enabled them to extort extra payments for "lighter" cars (i.e., cars placed on barges and floated across the river). (This was a classic ripoff by the railroad robber barons and gives a good idea of why the privately owned railroads went bankrupt.) But, as IPT director Robert Rickles has shown, the railroads artificially "shrank" the tunnel by raising its roadbed by three feet. While this effectively barred larger freight cars, the Hudson tunnel is still actually larger than the existing Detroit River and St. Clair River tunnels, which provide freight service for Detroit.

Limited direct freight service for New York City could thus be resumed immediately, and larger, piggyback trailers could soon be accommodated if the tunnel track bed were lowered three feet to its original level. Rail freight destined for the city, Westchester County, Long Island, and the bedroom communities of Connecticut is currently unloaded in New Jersey and transferred to trucks. Yet severe traffic congestion costs New York businesses at least $100 million each year. Restoring rail service would reduce traffic congestion and pollution in New York City and its suburbs by 2,000 trucks a day. It would also mean the equivalent of a $200-million tax cut for shippers and their customers. More important, it would permit the industrial development of hundreds of acres of vacant and unutilized land adjacent to the rail lines, and the intense development of existing land in and above rail yards. This is New York's richest development frontier.

The Carter administration is committed to upgrading the Northeast's rails generally, something its truck-oriented Republican predecessors carefully avoided. This will be a major shot in the arm for the entire region, and an especially hopeful sign for the Port of New York. In the last five years, the port has lost 20,000 jobs. Much of this loss has been because of a continuing revolution in ocean shipping—the containerization of cargo so that it moves from a truck bed or freight car directly into the hold of a ship without extensive unpacking and repacking. New York has lagged behind other ports in establishing the new facilities needed for this technology.

With improved rail links to dockside, however, and with the completion of at least two container ports (whose construction was arrested by the fiscal crisis), this trend could be reversed. A third container port should be constructed in the Hudson River at 34th Street, adjacent to the Penn Central yards now designated as a possible site for a white-elephant convention center.

All of these projects should be undertaken by the Port Authority of New York and New Jersey, an immensely wealthy monstrosity that grew rich servicing the automobile instead of dealing with the development of the port and mass transit—its original mandate. The Port Authority is run by a handful of bankers and Wall Street lawyers who have used its resources for the pleasure of bondholders and banks, not for the people of the region. The authority's defiance of governmental demands is one more example of the astounding power of New York's collective elites over the elected government. It is a mockery of democracy.

High on any construction agenda for the Port Authority should be the completion of a new rail tunnel under the harbor (actually begun and then abandoned in the 1920s) which would link Staten Island with Brooklyn. This would provide a direct route for rail freight and mass transit from Long Island to New Jersey and would finally tie together the five boroughs in a coherent transit network. The facility could be built for $1 billion and would pay for itself in ten years. Since the Arab countries alone are expected to purchase $163 billion in American-made goods in the next five years, ocean shipping from a port like New York should experience a vast renaissance. But the Port Authority stands as the major obstacle to New York City's getting its fair share of this commerce.

6. Abolish Some Real-Estate Tax Exemptions

Because of tax exemptions, 40 percent of New York City's property is untaxed. A decade ago it was only 33 percent, and now the value of this tax-free real estate has risen from $15.6-billion to a current assessed value of $25 billion. Tax-exempt property includes land and buildings owned by religious organizations, universities, foundations, hospitals, charitable organizations, the state, the federal government, the Port Authority (including the World Trade Center), and foreign governments. If all the tax-free real estate were taxed, the city coffers would gain more than $2 billion in revenue each year.

Our view is that at least a portion of the tax exemptions are unwarranted and should be withdrawn. For example, income-producing buildings owned by universities and hospitals should be taxed. They receive essential city services like fire and police protection, and garbage collection—and they should be taxed at the normal rate.

The definition of religious organization has been imaginatively applied, so that the properties owned by the Reverend Moon's Unification Church, by the scientology church, and by exotics, mystics, and swamis yield no taxes at all.

The Chrysler Building, owned by Cooper Union for the Advancement of Science and Art, valued at $22 million, pays no real-estate taxes. St. Patrick's Cathedral and its land are worth $25-million, but no taxes are collected. Apartment buildings owned by voluntary hospitals and used by their staffs are tax-exempt. State-owned buildings, valued at $44 million, pay no taxes. Columbia University's academic plant is valued at $264 million, and this wealthy and politically influential institution is tax-exempt. The Boy Scouts and the YMCA also have broad tax exemptions.

Many of these tax exemptions were given in a better economic climate. New York City now cannot afford to have $25 billion of its most precious asset—real estate—off the tax rolls.

In February, 1971, Richard Lewisohn, then the city's finance administrator, urged the state legislature to allow the city to tax the Port Authority on the basis of gross rents from leased property. Lewisohn said that on such a formula, the Port Authority would pay the city annual real-estate taxes of $66-million instead of the ludicrous $2.6-million "in lieu of taxes" payment made to the city in 1970. The bankers and brokers who control the surplus-rich authority ignored Lewisohn's prophetic proposal.

At this point in New York City's history, we think every real-estate tax exemption should be reconsidered case by case. The Port Authority, state and federal governments, and affluent private institutions should be compelled to pay their fair share. The World Trade Center and Columbia University can surely afford to pay real-estate taxes.

Experts estimate that the city might recover between $300 million and $500-million a year if all the obviously unworthy, political, and frivolous tax exemptions were abolished.

7. Municipalize Consolidated Edison

High utility rates are damaging the economies of all the states in the northeast quadrant. The worst offender of all is the Consolidated Edison Company of New York. The time has come, we think, to go to the root and institute a series of takeovers of utilities, starting with Con Ed.

As might be imagined, the legal mechanism for a public takeover is cumbersome, but far from impossible. (The small upstate city of Massena has recently rejected the giant Niagara Mohawk monopoly and set up its own public power system.) New York City and Westchester County would have to schedule simultaneous referendums, at which time the people would be asked to vote for condemnation of Con Ed's properties. Such a vote is likely to pass. PASNY—the Power Authority of the State of New York—could then be instructed by the legislature to operate the Con Ed system (it already operates two plants originally built by Con Ed) while the courts decide how much the stockholders are entitled to receive as a condemnation award. The money to pay off the stockholders could be financed by 40-year PASNY bonds (the agency has an excellent credit rating), which would be insured by revenues derived from the sale of electricity, natural gas, and steam.

Public operation would result in an immediate reduction of 20 percent in electric rates. Half of this would come from abolishing the profits now artificially granted the company, the other half from a combination of cheap power that would be available to city residents as part of the PASNY system and absolution from some state and federal taxes. The utility could be required to continue making payments to the city equivalent to current property taxes, as is the common procedure in other jurisdictions with public power agencies.

These are conservative estimates of the benefits that would accrue from public takeover. Studies have indicated that public power is far more efficiently administered than private power. Lavish executive salaries and stock options, gratuitous public relations and advertising, wasteful overstaffing would be abolished, saving a minimum of 10 percent in costs to consumers. Most Con Ed consumers would be grateful to have their electric rates frozen; public takeover offers substantial reductions in rates and, probably, improvements in service. Marginal businesses that have been hardest hit by rising electric bills would be the major beneficiaries, and New York City would have another critical selling point to attract new jobs and industries. Even the stockholders would get a good deal: They could write off their losses, if any, on their federal tax returns.

8. Save Rent Control to Keep the Middle Class

Rent control is often poorly understood by its supposed beneficiaries and totally misunderstood by key outside decision-makers like Senator William Proxmire, who went out of his way during New York City's crisis to denounce rent control in total innocence of the facts. Rent control helps the middle class, not the poor. It is not a mechanism for prohibiting rent increases; rather, it is a system of perpetual rent increases. There are actually two rent-control systems, each of which once related to separate categories of apartments (prewar and postwar), but which have now become so jumbled from various efforts to weaken the whole idea that one building will have apartments covered by each system separately.

One group of tenants covered by the "maximum base rent" (MBR) system receives annual rent increases of 7.5 percent; another group, known as "rent stabilized" tenants, receives increases of 8.5 to 13.5 percent annually depending on the length of lease they sign (one to three years). (We have had to use average increase figures for "rent stabilization" because there are now *two* systems in that category, and we choose not to risk our sanity, or yours, by going into further detail.)

The essence of all this is that landlords are given a guaranteed profit (8.5 percent of the "rule of thumb" resale price of their property) and constant protection against inflation. If their profit rate ever falls below this guaranteed minimum, they can apply for "hardship" increases, in whatever amount is necessary, to reach the 8.5 percent. Few landlords apply, despite

their cries about rising operating costs, because the majority are making much more than the minimum profit.

The tenant, on the other hand, is guaranteed only that the rate of increase will be regulated. Rents in New York are rising faster, with rent control, than in any other city without it. And average wage increases have consistently fallen below the minimum 7.5 percent rent increase in recent years. As a result, the average New Yorker finds himself paying a bigger and bigger portion of his paycheck for shelter. On the average, the working poor pay 35 percent of their total income for rent.

The landlord lobby has thrown up a series of straw men in its attempts to abolish rent control. The simple reality, of course, is that they would reap windfall profits if they could charge whatever they chose in a market where there are almost no vacant apartments. But it would be a short-lived victory. Tens of thousands of middle-income families, who want desperately to stay in the city, can do so only when rents are held to an acceptable level. Many of these families have been forced to send their children to private schools and must now shoulder the added cost of tuitions ranging to $2,000 per student each year. They are locked into their existing housing because as soon as an apartment becomes vacant its rent is allowed to rise to whatever price the landlord chooses. (After this first rental, future increases are then "stabilized.") These people remain not for economic reasons—they could probably live more cheaply in the suburbs —but for cultural, social, and psychological reasons. Make the economics unworkable and they will be gone for good.

We have no illusions about expecting any industry to forgo short-term profits for the long-term social good. Even the banks, which must of necessity think in longer time frames than one year's balance sheet, are determined to destroy rent control in New York because it stands as a beacon for the rest of the country. Demand for new rent-control statutes has grown as inflation has bit deeper and deeper into urban America. This is why the death of rent control appeared so early on the agenda of the Rockefellers, Rohatyn, Simon, etc. It is crucial to their overall plan for the national economy.

9. Rehabilitate Housing to Preserve Neighborhoods

We feel that almost all housing ex-

penditure in New York for the foreseeable future should be poured into renovating and restoring existing housing. The era of overconstruction of luxury housing was an epic blunder.

Obviously, rehabilitation makes good sense. Most of the city's worst slums, like Brownsville, Bedford Stuyvesant, and many parts of Harlem, were once thriving middle-class communities. The brownstone houses that prevail in these areas are prized as architectural gems when found in other parts of the city. (By the same token, almost all of the Lower East Side, Williamsburg, and parts of the South Bronx is covered with the rightfully despised old-law tenements, which were outlawed for human habitation at the turn of the century. Ironically, many of these warrens stand fully occupied today, while far superior housing elsewhere has succumbed to either landlord greed or the torch. This can best be explained by looking at the corrupt definition of "slum clearance" created by Robert Moses and his clubhouse cronies.)

Saving existing housing is cheaper. An apartment can be fully modernized and upgraded for $20,000 (the construction unions recently agreed to accept below-scale wages for remodeling work, although labor is only one third the cost of any building project), while a new apartment can't be built for less than $45,000. Rehabilitation saves not only money but energy; the type of work done tends to be far more labor- and skill-intensive than the energy-intensive task of digging excavations, pouring thousands of tons of cement foundations, etc.

Perhaps even more important, rehabilitation saves neighborhoods. It should be clear by now that we believe that strong, coherent neighborhoods with their own special institutions and strengths are the backbone of any city. In recent years, we have seen New York City's neighborhoods dying, first building by building, then block by block. Yet in each of them some kernel of strength, some seed for a better future—a shopping street, a church, even a park—still stands. Now we must go back and wherever possible reverse the pattern of decay—building by building and, if necessary, block by block. (It is the rejection of the value of saving distinct neighborhoods which underlines the antipeople, technocratic essence of the "planned shrinkage" approach to the city's problems.)

One of the best places to start this process of rebuilding is with the thousands of buildings already owned by New York City itself. Rehabilitated, they could either find buyers or be sold directly to tenants as low-cost co-operatives. The city would get some of its money back when it most needs it, and at the same time blight could be arrested.

The funds for this undertaking must come directly or indirectly from the federal government. One way is to expand FHA insurance guarantees to rehabilitation lenders.

10. End Waste, Ripoffs, And Legal Graft

Over the last several years, uncountable millions of dollars in public funds have been wasted or stolen in a series of scandals involving nursing homes, welfare, Medicaid, methadone clinics, day-care leases, summer lunch programs, antipoverty corporations, manpower-training programs, the monumental waste at the Board of Education, the Yankee Stadium $75-million cost overrun. At the same time, audits by the city and state comptrollers have discovered waste, laxity, inefficiency, and various abuses in almost every agency of city government, from the concession contracts awarded to vendors by the Department of Marine and Aviation to rental leases signed by community school boards. Moreover, as we have demonstrated, the taxpayers lose money through political favors like interest-free bank deposits, reduced real-estate tax assessment, patronage jobs, and city leases with private landlords.

In general, we believe, with Louis Brandeis, that sunlight and publicity are "the best disinfectant." We believe that merit, accountability, and disclosure are three principles that can help clean up a municipal government and party structure that thrive on legal graft.

Some of the specific reforms we have in mind to foster frugality and integrity in government include:

☐ Truly competitive bidding on all city contracts and leases above a nominal amount should be instituted. Disclosure of all equity partners in companies doing business with the city should be required.

☐ Members of the Board of Estimate should be disqualified from voting on projects involving anyone who has contributed more than $500 to their last campaign.

☐ No member of the state legislature should be allowed to represent a client before a state regulatory agency. This practice was an element in the nursing-home scandal, and the legislature has twice defeated efforts to abolish this conflict of interest.

☐ Lobbyists should be required to disclose and itemize publicly all their expenditures and all their contacts with members of the legislature.

☐ Party and legislative leaders like Pat Cunningham, Stanley Steingut, Vincent Albano, Meade Esposito, and John Calandra should be compelled to withdraw from their law firms, insurance companies, and banks that do business, even once removed or indirectly, with city and state government. Party leaders should be salaried; in the long run, this will probably save the taxpayers money.

☐ Every level of government should hire more auditors. When the nursing-home scandal broke open in 1974, the state of New York had fewer than twenty auditors on the payroll, with responsibility for auditing for more than 2,000 health-care facilities.

☐ There should be independent professional selection committees for all engineering, architectural, and construction contracts let by the city.

☐ We need merit appointment, by independent screening panels, of all judges, including state supreme court justices.

☐ There should be a permanent statewide prosecutor for all Medicaid-related fraud. Joe Hynes, the special prosecutor for nursing homes, obtained 78 indictments of nursing-home owners, administrators, vendors, and public officials between January, 1975, and December, 1976. He identified $30-million in fraud he believes can be recovered. And his legal jurisdiction does not include private hospitals, Medicaid bills, methadone clinics, or health-related facilities.

The future is unknowable. With Antonio Gramsci, we are pessimists of the intelligence, optimists of the will.

They have done their worst to us—the banks; Nelson Rockefeller, Lindsay, Beame, Nixon, Ford, and lesser politicians; the muggers; the Sunbelt; the permanent government. Our services have been cut. Cops and firemen are unemployed. People are dying in municipal hospitals for want of a bed or a night nurse. Our children are not learning, 50 to a classroom. The upward mobility that came with a free college education is gone. Democracy is diminished.

But we are still standing. We are still here. We are survivors.

These ideas, these remedies offered, will not become law easily or quickly. We cannot trust our leaders to do all this just because it is logical, or necessary, or promised.

The most important lesson we have learned, as political citizens, is this: Reform—change for the better—comes only when movements of common people rally around an idea and create new leaders from the bottom up. Movements of ordinary people, acting out of self-interest, can write law. The moral authority of exemplary action can change lives.

Leaders sell out. Leaders get tired. Leaders get killed. But movements of our countrymen stopped the Lower Manhattan Expressway, passed the Voting Rights Act of 1965, ended the Vietnam war.

From Rosa Parks starting the Montgomery bus boycott to Frank Serpico exposing police corruption to Charlie Rosen leading the Co-op City rent strike, common people saying *Enough!* have transformed consciousness and altered history.

Restoring a City: Who Pays the Price?

In Washington D.C.'s real estate market, it's well-to-do against the poor. Their city's elected council is caught in the middle, and the issues aren't all black and white.

Carol Richards and Jonathan Rowe

CAROL RICHARDS is a journalist and free-lance writer who is currently a graduate student in urban and regional planning at George Washington University. **JONATHAN ROWE** is on the staff of the Committee on Finance and Revenue of the District of Columbia Council, and is joint author of *Tax Politics* (Pantheon Books, 1976).

Block by block, private developers in Washington D.C. are converting decaying homes into elegant townhouses. Some see this restoration movement as a godsend, for it promises both to upgrade the city's housing stock and to expand the tax base. But there is another, less rosy side to the neighborhood rehabilitation: it has caused rampant speculation in residential property.

Housing prices, already among the nation's highest, have been driven even higher. And the overall effect is to force the city's poor out of neighborhoods they've lived in for years. Government urban renewal programs in the late 1950s and 1960s disrupted poor neighborhoods in much the same way. This time, however, there are no federal funds to relocate the homeless.

In a kind of reverse blockbusting, speculators comb neighborhoods on foot and by telephone just ahead of the restoration movement, making attractive cash offers to owners. If the owners refuse to sell, the more persistent speculators call in building inspectors who order expensive repairs on the old and dilapidated homes. Homes are bought and sold the same month, week, and even day for profits of up to 100 percent and more.

Often the speculators never even take title to the property but instead sell their purchase contract to a third party, a process called "flipping." (The term also is used to describe quick turnovers generally.) Between October 1972 and September 1974, 21 percent of all recorded sales of row and semidetached homes and flats in Washington involved two or more sales of the same property (80 percent within ten months of each other). Sixty-nine percent of these sales were in five neighborhoods. Moreover, many speculative transfers are not recorded.

Aside from the displacement caused by rehabilitation, the spiraling of home prices has its own dislocation effects. Tenants are sometimes evicted because they cannot afford the rent hikes that go hand in hand with the new landlord's high purchase price and increased property taxes. Since property tax assessments are based largely on sale prices of nearby properties, homeowners face tax increases whether or not their own properties have been improved; these higher taxes also are passed on to renters.

Some speculators turn the tax woes to their own advantage. At a city council hearing on property tax assessments, a woman who lived on a street on which seven homes had been sold in two years testified that speculators had knocked on the doors of the remaining homeowners saying, "I understand your property taxes have gone up. Do you want to sell?"

Speculation is not new to the District of Columbia. Original District planner Pierre L'Enfant fought to keep land speculators from disrupting his plan for the orderly development of the city's neighborhoods. He was fired in the process. In this century, speculation and restoration started with Georgetown in the 1930s, went to Capitol Hill in the 1960s, and to Adams-Morgan, Mt. Pleasant, and other neighborhoods in the 1970s. In each case the pattern has been similar. In 1930, half of Georgetown's population was poor and black; now the neighborhood is rich and predominantly white. But it wasn't until the 1970s that community opposition in the District galvanized into resistance, or that the city itself had the power to do anything about speculation.

In 1974 Congress granted the District a measure of home rule,

Reprinted by permission from *Working Papers for a New Society*, Vol. IV, No. 4, Winter 1977 Center for the Study of Public Policy, Inc.

including its first elected government in 100 years. The 13-member elected city council has been faced with the problem of speculation and displacement of its constituents on the one hand, and the District's financial and housing problems on the other hand.

Washington has an acute housing shortage. The city's vacancy rate is less than 2 percent (anything under 5 percent is considered an "emergency" by HUD). In 1975, one estimate put the District's housing need at over 91,000 units. Much of the existing housing is in disrepair, with nearly half of the units over 35 years old. If these houses are not soon restored, they could be lost to the city forever.

When the redevelopment industry comes before the council and says it produced 3,000 units of housing during the preceding year, it is little wonder that many officials look on with approval and hope. And given the shortage of public initiative or funds to support low-income housing, it's hard to refute John O'Neil of the Office and Apartment Building Association when he says, "It's not a choice between houses for poor people and houses for rich people. It's a choice between houses for rich people or no houses at all."

Jobs and economic growth are also at issue. "Rehabilitation in D.C. has been estimated to create $30 million worth of purchases of services and materials each year and to employ in excess of 5,000 persons," says James Banks of the Washington Board of Realtors. If the bulk of these outlays actually went to District — and not suburban — businesses and employees, they would give a considerable boost to the D.C. economy. Then too, the fiscally hard-pressed city will benefit from the increased property tax assessments. Government and industry officials hail the new townhouse owners as "tax providers" (as opposed to the

poor people they replace, who are labeled "tax consumers" because of their heavy use of public services).

Taxing flippers

On April 1, 1975, D.C. city council members David Clarke and Nadine Winter put a speculation bill before the council. Following the example of legislation in Vermont, Ontario, and New Zealand, they sought to curb speculation by taxing the profits of speculators. Their bill was a simple tax on short-term buying and selling of rowhouses with no deductions permitted for rehabilitation or other expenses. It was seen as a one-year stop-gap measure to allow the council time to develop a longer term solution.

Although the District is commonly perceived as merely a bland federal enclave, it is home for about three-quarters of a million people, who live in well-defined neighborhoods and who have a high degree of community consciousness. Clarke, a lawyer in his early thirties, was spurred to action by the speculation in his ward, which includes the Adams-Morgan neighborhood, one of the few racially mixed areas in the city. Cosponsor Winter represents the heavily speculated Capitol Hill.

Because it was a tax bill, the speculation measure was referred to the council's Committee on Finance and Revenue, which is chaired by at-large council member Marion Barry. During the sixties, as head of the D.C. SNCC office and leader of the fleeting but feisty Free D.C. movement, Barry had been a chronic pain to the established powers, leading a boycott of the bus system and disrupting the Cherry Blossom Festival.

Now Barry is a leading D.C. Democrat and one of the home rule council's more influential

m[...]
i[...]

mo[...]
the sp[...]
essary. W[...]
tax bill grew[...]
new measure n[...]
lation, but req[...]
dealers in residentia[...]
cording all transfers of [...]
property; registering vacan[...]
erty; disclosing the seller's pu[...]
chase price and costs to buyers of residential property. The bill also strengthened the tenant's right of first refusal under the District's rent control law by providing cash damages to tenants when their landlords fail to honor this right.

Barry, who says, "I like the tough ones," soon found himself in a crossfire gritty even by his own standards. On the one side were the District's real estate and financial interests, probably the largest private industry in town and a major supplier of campaign contributions in D.C. elections. On the other side were community organizations from neighborhoods most directly affected by speculation.

The Adams-Morgan Organization (AMO), probably the most militant, had already picketed weekend showings of rehabilitated townhouses, had splattered paint on billboards announcing luxury condominium conversions, and had even prevented the rehabilitation of an entire block. The anti-speculation tax was the rallying point these groups had been waiting for. They were joined by their professional public interest allies such as Ralph Nader's Tax Reform Research Group. Included were some of Barry's early supporters, along with activists who in general feel entitled to a special claim on his loyalties and

pectations of his
change.

anizations moved
orm a community-
ation task force. The
put out a pamphlet
Our Neighborhoods for
or citywide distribution,
all the council members,
roduced a draft antispecula-
bill. Perhaps the crest of this
ivity was the council hearings in
une 1975 when the coalition put
on an impressive display of community support. Ministers, the
teachers union, the Association of
Black Social Workers, even the
Afro-American Police Officers,
all testified in favor of a tax on
speculation. And a coalition-
produced slide show on speculation upstaged the hearings.

The real estate industry was
somewhat slower to react. Most
directly affected by a speculation
tax would be the "flippers" who
buy and sell houses without improving them, and the "redevelopers" who buy old houses and
repair them in varying degrees.
(Often the same people do both.)
The flippers and redevelopers were
perhaps the last unorganized segment of the real estate industry.
They are clever business operators
whose office addresses are often
tawdry mail drops in low-rent
areas. They take pride in being
"self-made" and genuinely feel
that they are making a contribution to the city. "We're taking
blights off the market," George
Panagos, a long-time D.C. speculator and redeveloper, told the
Washington Post.

In pre-home-rule days, these
real estate operators had done as
they pleased. Most lived in the
suburbs and were little aware of
the intensity of community feeling
against them. The Clarke-Winter
bill took them by surprise. Within
a month of the bill's introduction,
however, they had formed a $100-
a-head Washington Residential
Development Coalition (WRDC)

and retained as lobbyist Chester
Davenport, a politically connected
black lawyer who was President
Carter's transition man on
housing and transportation and
whose firm was the city's bond
counsel. (The industry's con-
tingency plan was to switch to
a noted white litigator if the issue
went to court.)

Choosing sides

The developing conflict raised
issues beyond the immediate question of whether rehab should be
encouraged. Political and even
moral dilemmas arose as well.
Foremost was the issue of race. In
the District, "rehabilitation" is
code for "black removal." When
the *Post* real estate ads tout a
neighborhood as "fast moving"
and "up and coming," they mean
that poor blacks are moving out
and better-to-do whites (and some
blacks) are moving in.

Questions of justice aside, black
removal is politically ominous for
the newly elected council members
and mayor. The people being up-
rooted from their homes are their
constituents. The young white
townhouse owners who move in
have different loyalties and little
or no local memory. A sign of
what may lie ahead appeared in
the recent annual elections for the
Adams-Morgan Organization executive board: the white owner of
a hip new neighborhood bar called
Columbia Station, a symbol of
"Georgetownification" to many
activists, took one of the offices.

It is not just a matter of politicians nervous about their seats,
however. Home rule has a highly
charged emotional meaning for
many D.C. residents and especially for blacks. The 100 years
of congressional rule dominated
by peevish white Southerners such
as former House District Committee chairman John McMillian of
South Carolina is to them parallel
in kind if not in degree to South

Africa's minority regime. Even
today when such otherwise respected senators as Lawton Chiles
(D-Fla.) and Thomas Eagleton (D-
Mo.) drag D.C. officials before
their District Committee hearings,
the occasions embarrassingly resemble whipping day at the plan-
tation. The measure of home rule
granted thus far, partial as it is,
still symbolizes the eventual
overthrow of a colonial power.
Speculation, however, jeopardizes
this dream by eroding the dominant black majority.

The predicament is that not all
of the District's 80 percent black
population is poor. A solid middle
class and pockets of affluence also
exist. And at least some of the affluence stems from real estate. In
the past, blacks had gained a
measure of success in derivative
activities such as brokering. As the
market for homes in the city has
heated up, they have begun to buy
and rehab properties on their own
behalf. As the newest entrants in
the field, they are the most vulnerable. An antispeculation tax could
knock them out, while merely in-
conveniencing the established
white entrepreneurs whose deeper
pockets, larger inventories, and
firmer credit lines enable them to
maneuver around it.

In addition, although most
black renters and homeowners
may resent the effects of speculation, at least some of the homeowners feel otherwise. They are
delighted at the prospect of selling
their home for a pocketful of cash
or of having their neighborhoods
upgraded while their own property
appreciates in value.

As a result, stereotyped class
and race roles have been confounded on this crux of self-
interest. While poor blacks and
their white activist allies come
before the council demanding action against the speculators, the
black entrepreneurs demand just
as righteously to know how a
black elected body can even consider taking away the piece of the

action they have laboriously, and against great odds, won.

Redeveloper Don Grey, an earnest young black with a large Afro, begins his testimony at council hearings with a reminder that he assisted Barry while the latter was head of SNCC. Beatrice Reed is the forceful president of the Washington Real Estate Brokers Association, an organization established by black brokers about 15 years ago in reaction to discrimination by the white-controlled Washington Board of Realtors. Reed makes speculation sound like black power. "We blacks will never rule this city," she tells a community forum in the auditorium of an old Baptist church near the 14th Street riot corridor, "until we *own* this city. That's what power is all about — *ownership*. What I do is helping my brothers and sisters to own their homes. And until we all do that, the whites will control us."

Long-time black residents in the audience had applauded and nodded in agreement as earlier speakers had torn into speculators. Now they applauded Reed too. Liberation means different things to different people and even to the same people at different times.

Not all the black real estate entrepreneurs are happy about their role in the speculation controversy. Being portrayed — rightly or wrongly — as the antagonists of their own people is only one reason. Even more important is their relation to the white entrepreneurs. Although the newly organized WRDC is overwhelmingly white and suburban, its leaders pushed efforts to include blacks. Blacks have gone along primarily because their livelihoods are at stake. But they are sensitive to being used as showpieces by the white speculators. Finding themselves in that role is just the latest in the endless series of frustrations that have attended their efforts to

To the suburbs

Like other U.S. cities, Washington D.C. has lost much of its middle class to the suburbs. The 1974 median family income in the District was about 35 percent lower than the median for the metropolitan area as a whole. And the District's suburbs vie with it for jobs, tax dollars, and services. When the city, to balance its budget, removed its business tax exemption for lawyers, doctors, and other professionals, the suburbs leaped like piranhas with newspaper advertisements and direct mail solicitations urging those affected to move their offices from the city.

Further, congressional representatives of the suburban districts succeeded in tacking an amendment onto the D.C. Home Rule Charter prohibiting the District from taxing the income of the 266,000 suburbanites who commute to the city every day, making it virtually the only comparable jurisdiction in the United States that lacks this power. This prohibition costs the District close to $200 million a year (an amount that would just about cover the cost of its police and fire departments).

The suburbs attracted 90 percent of the job growth in the metropolitan area between 1970 and 1974. Private investment in housing also followed the highways and shopping centers. In 1973, 90 percent of all loans made by the District's savings and loan associations went to the suburbs.

earn a dollar in a way routinely accessible to whites.

The issue before the council became still more complex when the redevelopers' rebuttals made them appear less the phalanx of evil than they had first been portrayed. The expensively restored townhouses in the inner city neighborhoods had received most of the public attention, but the bread and butter of many D.C. rehabbers — especially the larger operators — were more modest improvements to properties farther from the urban core. A WRDC official testified at council hearings that of 1,500 units sold by its members the previous two years, the average price had been $24,500 and 90 percent of the purchasers had been black D.C. residents. According to the WRDC official, over 70 percent of the properties had been vacant at the time of acquisition. "I've sold two houses over $40,000 in the last two years," says WRDC president Jerry Lustine. "And most of my houses go to blacks."

Also, at least a few realtors and speculators were quietly attempting to help tenants them-

selves. Nathan Habib, a puckish, cagey man commonly labeled a "slumlord," has been selling off his properties to his tenants and "taking back the paper" (that is, financing them himself) without even requiring a down payment. In the Shaw area, a young broker named Richie Jones has been finding alternative housing in the community for tenants displaced by his transactions. He has also been trying to keep speculators out of the area by dealing directly with homebuyers. "We get better rapport in the community by giving the homebuyers the real price" instead of a price jacked up by a speculator, he says.

While a few good apples cannot redeem a whole barrel, such examples tempered the good-guy, bad-guy melodrama that was important to the antispeculation cause. At the same time, the council's own posture was weakened on several counts. For one, it bears the cross of the D.C. government's own land acquisition activities, which have resulted in large-scale evictions and thousands of boarded-up houses concentrated in poor black neighborhoods throughout the city. "There are blocks and blocks of vacant land here and the government keeps buying more," says Joyce Chestnut of the Shaw Project Area Committee. "The speculation bill does nothing about government speculation, and the government is the biggest menace." This is perhaps the only point on which the industry and community groups agree. "It's criminal," says WRDC president Lustine. "The D.C. government should clean up its own house before picking on us."

More squarely laid to the council is the District's rent control problem. A poorly written, poorly administered law has provided steady ammunition to the real estate industry and has given any public intervention in the real estate market a bad name. Council members are wary of getting burned a second time. Furthermore, the District's precarious budget makes this an unfortunate time to propose slowing down a rehabilitation trend that will improve the tax base. (The city's tax base is expected to grow by less than 5 percent a year between now and 1980, while its expenditures will increase by 9 to 12 percent.)

These complications have left their mark on the bill, especially in its treatment of rehab. The original Clarke-Winter bill, by treating both flipping and rehab with equal severity, amounted to a straightforward one-year moratorium on redevelopment. Faced with heavy industry lobbying, the opposition of the mayor, and the reluctance of his fellow council members, Barry gradually modified this approach. First, he broadened the deductions for rehab expenses. Then he softened the tax rates on rehab. The emphasis shifted from stopping the redevelopment process to restraining excess profits and generating revenues to provide low and moderate-income people with homeownership assistance. Finally, when his fellow Finance

Committee members balked at even this modified approach, Barry had to scrap the tax on rehab entirely, along with some other provisions.

Competing causes

Even stripped down, the Barry bill is significant. His staff has found no other jurisdiction that requires the recording of all transfers of residential property (including contracts flipped to third parties) or that licenses dealers to the degree the bill does. And no urban area in the United States levies a tax on short-term buying and selling (without improvements) of residential property — let alone a tax in which rates go as high as 75 percent. The tenant's right of first refusal, and the disclosure of the seller's purchase and rehab costs to homebuyers are also trend-setting measures. Yet compared to what it set out to do, the bill is barely half a loaf in the eyes of its original supporters.

Will the bill, if passed, do anything about the displacement of tenants and low and moderate-income homeowners? The best answer now is, "Probably, to a degree." By curtailing flipping, it should deter the drastic price increases that impel the new landlords to raise rents, and that put houses out of reach of tenants and low and moderate-income persons generally. "I could have bought this place myself if they gave me a chance to buy it at the original price," said one black woman on a heavily speculated street on Capitol Hill. "But nobody offered it to me. And I sure can't pay what it's going for now."

In addition, by deterring flipping-induced price increases, the bill should restrain property tax assessment hikes, which will relieve the plights both of tenants who end up paying the tax in their rents, and of homeowners whose budgets are geared to property tax

bills at prespeculation levels. A damper on flipping, moreover, should slow down the rehabilitation-displacement process somewhat, since it is the rapid churning over of properties that breaks them loose for redevelopers and creates a momentum that spreads through the neighborhood. It is nevertheless true that a property may be flipped several times without the tenants being evicted. Rehabilitation, however, means eviction. With rehab alive, evictions will continue.

Would a tax on rehab have stopped such displacement? The real estate industry argued that there are enough wealthy people looking for houses in the District to enable rehabbers simply to pass the tax along in higher prices. Alternatively, the larger speculators could hold houses off the market — perhaps keeping them vacant — for three years, after which time they would be clear of the tax. Then, after rehab, they could charge more to compensate themselves for the holding period. Either way, the real estate industry argued, the result would be a reduction in the number of rehabbed houses coming onto the market and a consequent increase in prices, making houses less, not more, available to low and moderate-income persons. Proponents of the tax argued differently, of course, and it is questionable whether the industry would have lobbied so intensely against the rehab tax if all that was at stake was higher prices for rehabbed houses.

The D.C. council was reluctant to tax rehab for a variety of reasons. The lengthy preparation of an ambitious bill gave opponents both time and openings for attack. Also, the council's principled stands on civil and human rights — a majority of council members were civil rights activists and tolerate few encroachments in that area — do not always translate into similarly progressive economic stands. But most important has been the lack of sustained grassroots pressure. The bill simply has not yet become a highly visible political issue.

The community speculation task force was really a committee of organization employees and leaders. Only one of these organizations — the Adams-Morgan Organization — was genuinely constituent based. The others were United-Fund-supported neighborhood houses and the like. Their proxies were in most cases valid, but they never established the ongoing community support that was necessary to turn on the heat.

As the issue dragged on, the task force wore down — a familiar malady, and fatal in this case. When people left, there was no mechanism for replacing them. The diffusion of the racial issue was also a serious blow. In addition, AMO was so offended by one provision in an early draft — an exemption for moderately priced rehabbed houses — that it went off in a corner and sulked, leaving the lobbying to the speculators. By the late fall of 1976, a week-long series on speculation in the *Washington Post* that would have prompted an angry demonstration at the District Building 18 months before provoked hardly a telephone call or letter to the council.

Among the leaders of the task force were several whites. The role of white activists in the black-majority District is uncertain, and especially so on the speculation issue. For one thing, it is difficult for white activists to invoke the same degree of outrage at black profit seekers as they do when the perpetrators are white. Then, too, white activists themselves play an inadvertent role in the speculation process. Many live in racially mixed, inner-city neighborhoods such as Adams-Morgan, where rents are relatively low and where speculation is booming. Their VWs and white faces calm the jit-

ters of prospective home buyers apprehensive of such threatening surroundings, while their countercultural enterprises create an aura that speculators and realtors can exploit as a lure for affluent people on the search for urban chic. It is understandable that some blacks and Latinos perceive their white activist neighbors as accomplices in the very speculation process they are working to stop.

The irony is that if the antispeculation proposal accomplishes nothing else, it has molded the rehabilitation industry into a political force. A year and a half ago rehabbers were a loose assortment of staunch individualists. Today the WRDC has 250 members, and its tactics on the speculation bill showed a gain in sophistication over the industry's efforts in its first council battle — the rent control bill.

The positions of the two sides at this point compel a question. Should the antispeculation forces have started with a proposal more modest than a tax, which they could have won before their momentum waned? Some think Barry may have erred in expanding the original Clarke-Winter bill. "It would have been wise in retrospect to pass it" as originally introduced, Clarke said recently of his measure.

The industry has not been the only obstacle to the speculation bill. D.C. mayor Walter Washington, a cautious former housing administrator, has been cool to it from the beginning. "But what's wrong with speculation?" the mayor's city administrator Julian Dugas asked Barry with genuine bewilderment.

Nor have the media been very helpful. Their coverage of speculation has been sporadic, especially compared to the recent daily flagellation of a human resources director for putting his relatives on the city payroll. The *Post* did do a fine series on speculation on one

block on Capitol Hill — 19 months after the Clarke-Winter bill was first introduced. Its major contribution until that time had been a column attacking the bill, which appeared a week before council hearings. The author of the column, Maury Seldon, was a paid consultant to the Washington Residential Development Coalition. Yet the *Post* identified Seldon only as a professor at American University.

Then there is Congress, which has kept veto power over all District legislation. Most of the speculators are suburbanites, who get a sympathetic ear from their representatives. Dabbling in real estate, moreover, is common sport among amply paid Congressional staffers, as it is among their bosses. On the 1400 block of Corcoran Street, just off the riot corridor, $20,000 rowhouses are being restored and sold for close to $70,000. The investor is Representative Stewart McKinney (R-Conn.), a liberal House District Committee member and, on most issues, one of the District's best friends on the Hill. McKinney is just one of innumerable examples.

Despite these problems, the speculation issue is by no means dead. Barry intends to introduce his stripped-down bill early in 1977, and community groups, chastened by their setback, are regrouping. Whatever the outcome, a few lessons have emerged. The first concerns the limits of a progressive elected body. The D.C. council is probably as receptive to the idea of a speculation tax as any legislative body in the United States, but without solid constituent support it has hesitated to move. Also, the council members have felt intellectually insecure with the tax. It has not been made clear to them how the tax would remedy the displacement problem, nor what it would do to the real estate market generally, nor — and this is most important — what if anything would arise to take the place of the private speculative market. All sides agree that a tough speculation tax on rehab could doom the city to stagnation if positive housing programs were not wheeled quickly into place. Aside from some vague talk about cooperatives, these programs are nowhere in sight.

Looking nationally, there is a message to the Carter administration in the District's struggle. During his campaign, Carter proposed a shift to rehabilitation as a source of housing for low and moderate-income city dwellers. Community workers in the District report that government-subsidized rehab programs have triggered the speculation and displacement processes in their neighborhoods. Without careful checks on such speculation, Carter's laudable approach could turn into a replay of urban renewal, with federally sponsored removal of poor and moderate-income people. And speculation could substantially drive up the cost to the taxpayers of any rehab programs.

Similarly, the speculation issue has flagged a hazard up the road for the antiredlining campaigns underway in many cities. Bank willingness to lend in a given neighborhood can add fuel to the speculative fires. Where conditions are right — a housing shortage combined with a growing demand for inner-city homes — a reversal of bank redlining policies could result in pressuring out the very residents the antiredlining drives have been trying to benefit.

What is most disjointing about the speculation controversy is the twisted face it has given to some cherished liberal causes. Investment in the inner city was supposed to be a good thing. It was supposed to be a good thing for well-to-do whites to leave the suburbs for the city. It was supposed to be a good thing to restore small-scale and often gracious row-houses and brownstones in the inner cities, instead of demolishing them in favor of high-rise apartments or vacant lots. It was supposed to be a good thing for blacks to gain a piece of the action, as they have been doing in the District's active rehab market. Yet it was also supposed to be a good thing for poor people to develop pride in their neighborhoods, a sense of roots, and to improve their stature collectively from that basis. Urban renewal supposedly taught us the inhumanity of punishing people with displacement when their only crime was that they were not wealthy.

The clash of these competing causes has thus far left the poor the losers. If there is enough social and economic room under current arrangements to accommodate all of our good intentions in one small jurisdiction — the District of Columbia — the way to do so has not yet appeared.

The PUSH Program for Excellence in Big-City Schools

Eugene E. Eubanks and Daniel Levine

EUGENE E. EUBANKS (Michigan State University Chapter) is assistant dean of education, University of Missouri, Kansas City. DANIEL U. LEVINE (University of Missouri at Kansas City Chapter) is professor of education at the same institution. This article is a shortened version of a chapter in Desegregation Policy, Magnet Alternative Schools, and Urban Education *(Daniel U. Levine and Robert J. Havighurst, eds.).*

The Reverend Jesse L. Jackson founded People United To Save Humanity (PUSH) in 1971. It soon became concerned with improving conditions in the big-city public schools. Already, PUSH for Excellence constitutes a large and significant movement which has caught the imagination of many elements deeply concerned about the undeniable erosion of these schools.

As a disciple of the late Reverend Martin Luther King, Jr., Jackson certainly is not unconcerned with integration. Much less is he an opponent of it or a separatist. (PUSH seeks to enroll members from all backgrounds, minority and majority, rich and poor.) But he recognizes that efforts at improvement in big-city schools cannot wait on plans for integration, which all too often have proved illusory, and he believes that much can be done, indeed must be done, integration or no integration. Speaking at commencement ceremonies at Southern University in Baton Rouge, Louisiana, on May 21, 1976, he made this point:

> Integrated education or association represents an opportunity for expansion, but does not represent an automatic change. You must put forth an effort. Whether the teacher is well trained or not, has a Ph.D. or no 'd,' if the student is not willing to learn under either condition, will he learn? . . . The schools presuppose that there must be a will to learn and an urge for excellence.

During the 1975-76 academic year Jackson and PUSH made education their main priority and became active participants in public school reform efforts in big cities all over the country. Jackson traveled to Washington, D.C., Detroit, Los Angeles, New Orleans, Hartford, and other big cities to speak with students, educators, and parents and to lay the groundwork for what he calls "a PUSH for excellence in the public schools." Nationally prominent and respected educators such as Hartford Superintendent of Schools Edythe Gaines, Atlanta School Board President Benjamin E. Mays, Harvard Professor Alvin Pouissant, and California Superintendent of Instruction Wilson C. Riles are among PUSH's educational advisors, and school officials in several big cities are beginning to allocate funds to get the program off the ground.

Jackson's intense round of activity was capped last August at the annual PUSH convention in Washington, D.C., where further plans were developed for a nationwide PUSH for Excellence program, centering in whatever cities it proves feasible.

In Jackson's home city of Chicago, PUSH is working with 10 high schools this academic year. A massive downtown parade was held on September 24 to publicize the effort. Similarly, stadium-sized rallies were held in Hartford and Los Angeles at which students, educators, and interested citizens came together to dedicate themselves to the cause of transforming inner-city schools and neighborhoods.

A movement with this much impact in its early stages clearly is a phenomenon worth the attention of educators everywhere. But the PUSH Program for Excellence is much more than a highly visible groundswell of activity likely to impinge on the professional activities of many educators in big-city districts. PUSH is now an important national organization which is attempting to improve conditions in inner-city neighborhoods through a concerted effort to root out or overcome forces which have made the inner city a difficult place in which to live and raise or teach children. PUSH leaders have developed a coherent and relatively comprehensive ideology. If adopted by schools and other social institutions, it could make a real difference. Programs like PUSH could signal the beginning of a historic reversal of the patterns of deterioration and disorganization which have steadily worsened in big cities throughout the U.S. over the past few decades.

The PUSH Ideology

Jackson's PUSH for Excellence in education is intended to bring the resources of 1) parents and other community residents, 2) teachers, 3) preachers and other community leaders, 4) principals and other school administrators, and 5) pupils together in a common cause. The central concept is "total involvement." Initially, PUSH aims at changing attitudes and motivations of most pupils and other constituents through parental, peer, and other local community influences. "The key to success," Jackson has said, "is the forming of new educational team relationships between parents, preachers, principals, pupils, and teachers, with each performing their respective roles."[1] The program hinges on a renewal of spirit, which Jackson has elaborated on as follows:

> We contend that more fundamental than any material deficiencies in our schools are our spiritual deficiencies. We may need more money spent on education. We probably do need more efficient administration. We welcome new teaching techniques which will make teaching and learning more effective. However, more fundamental than any of these material needs is the need to renew our spirits – to renew our hope in the future, our faith in ourselves, our resolve and determination to overcome, and the restoration of the will to learn. With a renewed and positive attitude, effort and action will follow.[2]

The PUSH program further calls for a return to basic courtesies and respect for authority and authority figures by students and a very intense directive influence by parents and other commu-

Used by permission of the *PHI DELTA KAPPAN*, January 1977. "The PUSH Program for Excellence in Big-City Schools," by Eugene Eubanks and Daniel Levine.

201

nity leaders. Jackson cites massive dropouts of parents as one of the major causes for trouble in schools. He calls for parents to take renewed responsibilities as parents. He makes this statement on achievement in reading:

> We keep saying that Johnny can't read because he's deprived, because he's hungry, because he's discriminated against. We say that Johnny can't read because his daddy is not in the home. Well, Johnny learns to play basketball without daddy.
>
> We do best what we do most, and for many of our children that is playing ball. One of the reasons Johnny does not read well is that Johnny doesn't practice reading.[3]

He advocates the following:

> We need to institute citywide study hours (from 7 p.m. to 9 p.m.) where schoolchildren wouldn't be allowed on the streets and there'd be a total blackout of radio and TV.[4]

Jackson also solicits the support of educators, politicians, the press, disc jockeys, and other persons who influence children and youth: "We want the black-oriented media to find ways to publicly reward achievers. We want the black disc jockeys, who reach more black kids than the principals, to inform and inspire as well as entertain."[5]

According to the position of PUSH, children need adult supervision which provides: 1) motivation, 2) care, 3) discipline, and, sometimes, 4) chastisement. These components are all part of love, and Jackson wants to enclose the child in a love triangle including the home, the church, and the school.

Reminiscing on how his own parents worked closely with his teachers and minister to give him needed guidance in the North Carolina town where he grew up,[6] Jackson maintains that all three institutions must demand respect, achievement, and excellence from the child. Love appropriately demonstrated will secure these outcomes.

Jackson also says, "Children cannot be allowed to play the game of 'teach me if you can catch me.' Children must be taught that they have a responsibility to learn as well as a right to education. Busing is absolutely necessary, but without a will to learn, busing is irrelevant."[7]

Educational Program

Based on the concepts and arguments described above (among others), PUSH proposes the following strategies to improve the atmosphere for learning in the school:

1. Establishing "teams" of students who excel in academics.
2. Establishing "peace brothers and sisters" as monitors and supervisors in classrooms, cafeterias, auditoriums, hallways, and playgrounds.
3. Promoting self-discipline and a sense of order among students.
4. Establishing a citywide council of students who will provide leadership to support discipline and academic excellence and resist drugs, violence, and racism.
5. Establishing, at the secondary level, a system of peer justice whereby many cases of misconduct would be judged and dealt with by students themselves, on the relatively simple premise that people near or at the voting age, and thus presumed competent to judge issues of war and peace among nations, are competent to judge a case of spitball throwing. Such a system, involving a civic function, not only would improve discipline but also in and of itself would have educational value.

Jackson summarizes the reaction he has encountered in arguing for these positions as follows:

> Each time I suggest a program of self-development, they respond with overwhelming enthusiasm. Black teenagers — some of the roughest, most street-wise dudes you will ever meet — respond to that appeal.[8]

The challenge to the schools is as mighty and encompassing as the one to parents and students. It calls for specific action on the part of the schools and teachers, with notions such as the following:

1. Formal opening and closing convocation of schools to enhance the meaning of institutionalized education.
2. Careful and repeated explanations, made to the community, of the benefits of a good education, to help develop a self-confident sense of where we are going and how far we already have come, thanks largely to education.
3. All reasonable efforts to bring the parent to school to pick up report cards, thus promoting formal dialogue and contact between school and parent.
4. Creation of specific incentives for students and teachers to achieve excellence in the classroom. On this point, Jackson says:

> Why have we stopped pursuing excellence in the classroom? We still pursue it on the football field, on the basketball court. High school coaches practice their athletic teams three and four hours a day after school. But are there any reading, writing, and counting teams in our schools?[9]

5. Establishment of rigorous rules of behavior in the halls; new dress codes reflecting modesty and dignity.
6. Removal of the graffiti of despair (as well as trash) from schools.
7. Removal of violent weapons of all kinds from school grounds, even if electronic equipment similar to that used to detect arms at airports must be installed at school doors.
8. Requirements that the parent and teacher meet personally and talk at least once a year, even if this necessitates the teacher's visiting the home of the student.

Another important aspect of the PUSH total involvement concept involves the church. Jackson projects a most active role for the church in the resurgence of education in schools serving low-status populations, particularly low-income minorities. The church must be active and vigorous, he argues, as follows:

1. Reinstitute "the value of God-consciousness as a part of the Cosmic Hierarchy."
2. Religious leaders should communicate and cooperate with educators.
3. Provide platforms and scholarships in religious institutions for recognition of excellence in education.
4. Establish church facilities for studying and tutoring after school and on weekends.
5. Incorporate educational progress and excellence as part of the responsibility of the religious institution.

Jackson's charge to the community can be paraphrased as follows: "Racism knocked you down; racism keeps you down and profits from you being down, so obviously it will not pick you up. The community must initiate the action to get up from the knockdown." Jackson's methods:

1. First, the community must accept the challenge and be willing to do much more than is required by law or rules. It must be willing to sacrifice certain rights voluntarily and put forth a much greater effort than in the past.
2. These responsibilities adopted by the community should be founded upon moral authority and ethics that will complement academic and mental development.
3. "Service" must become a general standard valued and acted upon both by children and adults, and the general rebellion against all authorities must cease.
4. Standards of excellence must be set for all endeavors.
5. State of the community meetings should be held for mass audiences in big cities.

Issues in Carrying Out the Program

An educational and social program as ambitious and encompassing as the one PUSH is now undertaking inevitably raises a number of important issues connected with definition and implementation. Delineating all these issues and analyzing them at length would require several articles, but some of the most important should be acknowledged, if only in a preliminary and summary fashion.

In our opinion, the most important issues involving the nature and potential of the PUSH Program for Excellence in Education include the following.

1. *Can the program succeed if it is so highly dependent on the leadership of its charismatic leader?* Jesse Jackson is not PUSH, and PUSH is much more than Jesse Jackson. Nevertheless, there is little doubt that much of its initial growth can be attributed to Jackson's dynamic and charismatic leadership. Most of the proposals being put forward by PUSH have been advocated before by parents, teachers, and others who have tried to generate motivation for academic learning among socioeconomically disadvantaged youth, though not in a form as clear and comprehensive. Nevertheless, as Jackson himself has admitted, "I'm saying something that mom and dad say all the time, but it sounds different coming from Jackson." This, of course, is one reason why PUSH efforts in specific school districts include assemblies and meetings at which Jackson speaks with students and parents on their home turf.

The PUSH leadership is well aware of the dangers of having their efforts too dependent on one person, particularly since Jackson has been hospitalized several times in the past few years due to pneumonia brought on by exhaustion and overwork. They are attempting to institutionalize their program and are struggling to obtain resources to employ personnel to work on a day-by-day basis. So far these efforts are being rewarded in growing support, but whether they will succeed at a grassroots level when Jackson is not present to provide inspiration and leadership is still an open question.

2. *Can participants in the PUSH program succeed in keeping their roles discrete and effective?* Related to the issue of dependence on inspirational leadership is an important question concerning the degree to which actors in the PUSH scenario can each make their special contribution in a cooperative effort to improve social and physical conditions in the inner city. As mentioned earlier, one of Jackson's main tasks is to articulate what others are not

in a position to say persuasively or even to say at all. For example, Jackson was able to persuade more than 30 unemployed residents of one inner-city Chicago neighborhood to volunteer security and supervision around an elementary school which had become dangerous to attend. Since these people were unemployed, he argued, why should they not make a contribution to their community and the welfare of its young people? His suggestion, coming from educators, probably would have been mostly ineffectual; and political leaders probably would have been very hesitant to offer it at all.

By the same token, PUSH leaders recognize that they are dependent on educators for technical expertise in improving instruction once classroom conditions have become more conducive to teaching and learning. At some point in the change process, community pressure will have to be brought to bear on faculties lacking the leadership, skill, or motivation to take advantage of this opportunity. At that time major clashes may well occur with teacher or administrator unions and other professional associations.

Jackson and his organization apparently are not trying to force such confrontations; indeed, they tend to view confrontations as a relic of the 1960s, now obsolete. They insist that the most important deficiency in big-city compensatory education has been lack of cooperation as equal partners on the part of all interested parties. Academic reform will come about, Jackson told us, "in proportion to the emergence of active participation of the missing elements," i.e., parents, students, community leaders. Nevertheless, it is only realistic to expect that at some point PUSH will face a crisis that may tear apart the coalition it is trying to put together.

3. *Will the PUSH program be perceived as "blaming the victim"?* In the past, a number of programs in education and other areas which have attempted to help improve conditions in inner-city neighborhoods have failed largely or partly because they were perceived by their potential clients as "blaming the victim" for his own troubles. Any program designed to help powerless people help themselves may fail for this reason, because in general people will not participate vigorously in an effort which they think maligns and stigmatizes them.

Jackson and other PUSH leaders are well aware of this problem. They are, after all, on the firing lines encountering it firsthand. About all that Jackson or anyone else can do about it is to make his position unmistakably clear at all

times, frequently reiterating the truth that self-help neither logically nor practically need be equivalent to blaming the victim. With his outstanding oratory and his great gift for synthesizing many important themes and communicating them to the people he is trying to reach, Jackson so far seems to be succeeding in making this distinction. The situation was aptly summarized by William Raspberry in a *Washington Post* article (March, 1976):

> The phrase "blaming the victim"... conveys an important truth about the way America has reacted to discrimination against certain of its citizens.
>
> It can describe, for instance, the process of denying job and promotion opportunities to minorities and then contending that the reason for their economic plight is that they have poor work records and too little ambition.
>
> It might also refer to relegating black children to segregated, central-city schools with all the cultural, psychological, and educational deprivation that implies, and then blaming them for their lack of scholastic achievement.
>
> So isn't the Rev. Jesse Jackson "blaming the victim" when he talks about parental neglect, insufficient motivation, and lack of self-discipline as among the reasons black children in inner-city schools are not performing up to par?
>
> It's a question the Chicago-based director of Operation PUSH gave some thought to during a recent, rambling interview.
>
> There is no denying that black people have been, and continue to be, victims of racism, he concedes. And racism must be resisted on every front.
>
> "But to dwell on it in a negative kind of way is to reinforce in the victims a sense of their own victimization and lead them not to action but only to feeling sorry for themselves," he said.
>
> "I'm not saying we should blame the victim. But I am saying we have to stop victimizing ourselves."

4. *Will "practicing" academic subjects yield anything like the same gains which practice may accomplish in sports and physical exercise?* The PUSH program emphasizes such practice. Undoubtedly improvement in academic performance among socioeconomically disadvantaged students depends on their spending more time, both inside and outside of class, on mastering academic subject matter. Recent research tends to verify this commonsense notion. Unfortunately, however, it is very uncertain whether more practice and study *by themselves* would accomplish much. We need improved instructional approaches, for one thing, to diagnose and overcome the learning difficulties of disadvantaged students. Methods of instruction must be modified so that students are not simply practicing the same mistakes over and over again — as

4. URBAN SOCIAL POLICIES

appears to have happened in many after-school or other "add-on" Title I programs.

Jackson and other PUSH leaders recognize that practice in academics is only a part of the solution to achievement problems in big-city schools. They have seized upon the practice-and-study idea because it is easy for parents, students, and others to understand, and because it represents something concrete that inner-city residents perhaps can begin to work on immediately. Nevertheless, there are dangers in oversimplifying the learning problem in big-city schools to this degree. It is comparable to the trap some teachers have fallen into when they argue, "They can't learn because they are hungry." Some parents have fallen into it when they say, "If kids aren't learning it must be because teachers aren't teaching."

Practice may even prove dysfunctional if it turns out that the wrong habits are being repeated or if students perceive little improvement after practice and become still more alienated. Moreover, overemphasis on this approach makes PUSH highly dependent on the expertness of teachers now in the schools, teachers who presumably will provide appropriate guidance in telling pupils what and how to study.

5. *Is religion too much commingled with the public schools in PUSH's approach to educational reform?* If only on civil liberty grounds, there are serious questions concerning the central role which PUSH advocates for religion and the churches in seeking to reestablish the "moral authority" its leaders believe is prerequisite to substantial academic improvement in big-city schools. PUSH leaders can point out that their program does not require membership in a church or attendance at church services, but the program is built explicitly on commitment to religious principles, and it sometimes is expressed — as at school assemblies — in terms closely reflecting Christian fundamentalism. This may make the PUSH effort at school reform not only vulnerable to legal suits but also repugnant to many potential supporters.

The issue we raise here is really much larger. We live in a scientifically oriented society in which religion plays a lesser part in shaping attitudes and behaviors than it did in previous eras. In this sense our society has become much more "rational" and complex than it was generations ago; indeed, it is partly the complexity of contemporary society which has made big cities almost unmanageable so long as we utilize established political and social institutions and policies. As conditions have deteriorated in big cities, and particularly

in the inner city, we have produced a plethora of "scientific" analyses and reports delineating "systems" approaches. We need more science and technology, these reports implicitly tell us, to solve the problems which some would attribute to science and technology in the first place.

Precisely at this point comes Jesse Jackson, arguing that commitment and love are more basic than science and rationalism in solving educational and other problems. It is not that PUSH leaders reject technology and professional expertise; they firmly assert that it must be supplied by the technicians and the professionals. They do insist, however, that community, moral authority, and motivation based on emotional commitment are prior in importance and sequence to solutions based on science and rationality. Who is to say they are wrong?

6. *Can the PUSH program succeed in the face of urban conditions which strongly militate against the success of any organized effort to help the poor and the powerless?* Perhaps this question is too obvious to be worth asking, but the preceding analysis does suggest that it may be worth addressing briefly, in order to place PUSH in an appropriate historical and social context.

PUSH is attempting to bring about what amounts to a revolution in the way inner-city populations and institutions interact and function, explicitly recognizing that anything short of such a revolution probably will fail in the same manner as many earlier programs. As much as anyone, PUSH leaders are aware that the obstacles they face are nearly insuperable, that they are placing a lot of faith on possibly weak reeds (e.g., active cooperation on the part of entrenched bureaucracies), and that they may be expanding their program too fast and spreading themselves too thin. They argue with much justification that big-city problems in education, social welfare, employment, etc., are national rather than local in origin and scope; only a comprehensive national effort which reaches directly to the grassroots level of the family and the peer group will have much chance to succeed in local neighborhoods.

One may well quarrel with their diagnosis and program, but hardly with their fortitude and dedication in undertaking so enormous an effort. In assessing their chances, we can do no better than offer the following quote from a *Washington Post* article by William Raspberry:

That sense of entrapment in love may have been a good deal easier to achieve in tiny Greenville, N.C. (popu-

lation about 12,000 when Mr. Jackson was born there in 1941) than in the teeming cities where uprootedness and unconnectedness combine to produce the very anomie Mr. Jackson is trying to attack.

To a significant degree, what he is proposing is the establishment of small towns in the city, a series of caring communities in which every adult is parent to every child.

Jesse Jackson is, in short, proposing a miracle. And yet, with a little luck and a lot of focused commitment, it could take hold. Not that thugs would suddenly become young gentlemen and hall rovers instant scholars.

But it just may be possible to reestablish in the classrooms a situation where serious scholarship, mutual respect, and discipline are the norm, and where peer pressure serves to reinforce that norm.

It certainly is worth trying.

Comments and Conclusions

The PUSH Program for Excellence in Education is built on a solid foundation of socialization theory. It begins with the premise that socialization is most successful when the forces which shape a child's attitudes and behaviors operate in a consistent and unified manner to communicate beliefs and understandings essential for success in the society of which he is a part. It emphasizes that parents, neighbors, peers, teachers, church officials, and other adults in the local community who interact personally with children must work together to develop motivation and habits which can enable the child to succeed in the society's major institutions. Community control of schools, Jackson told us, would not contribute much to the improvement of public schools unless it started with "the community controlling the child."

PUSH further emphasizes — more explicitly and perhaps pragmatically than heretofore has been the case — that inner-city youths have been particularly victimized by socialization forces which work at cross purposes: the school versus the streets; parents versus peers. The importance of the mass media — particularly disc jockeys — and of political institutions also are explicitly emphasized in PUSH's diagnosis of the problems which parents, educators, and other socializing agents face in raising children successfully in a modern, big-city environment. The PUSH program thus embodies an excellent sociological analysis translated convincingly into language understandable to lay people.

PUSH's educational program also represents excellent social psychology. It acknowledges that attitudes and behaviors do not change overnight, but it insists that change must begin somewhere, and it recognizes that such changes are not likely to be firmly rooted and pervasive with respect to institutions as central as the school unless they have deep emotional well-springs and involve the formulation, acceptance, and acting out of specific roles in the institution.

Similarly, PUSH leaders clearly are aware that ritual and ceremony can be important or even necessary elements in the design and operation of an institution which needs to win greater commitment and loyalty from people who participate in it. These characteristics are among the most important elements which social psychologists have identified as necessary for a true "conversion" experience, one which marks substantial changes in the ways people believe and behave in society. Insightfully, PUSH leaders are trying to provide a conversion experience sufficiently powerful to generate a different environment in which big-city schools, particularly those in the inner city, can function more effectively than they have in the past.

Most aspects of the PUSH argument have an internal logic which it is difficult to challenge. With respect to PUSH's insistence that low-status and minority citizens must accept responsibility for their own success or failure as well as for changing conditions within their communities, for example, Jackson and his staff vigorously assert that self-help need not and should not be equated with compromise of basic rights and principles; thus they are determined to avoid the pitfalls that Booker T. Washington eventually encountered when he argued in the 1890s that black Americans would have to lift themselves by their own bootstraps.

With equal concern for the logic of their position and the changes that will have to occur if their vision is to become reality, PUSH leaders insist that inner-city citizens somehow will have to establish cooperative relationships with the police and other governmental agencies. Jackson, for example, asserts that crime probably will not be reduced much in the inner city unless and until something is done so that the "community views the police as an extension rather than an occupation." Similarly, the Reverend Frank Watkins argues that inner-city residents have to work and take more responsibility for bringing about improvements in local conditions with respect to recreation, jobs, social welfare services, and other elements that go into "building a society" in which children can grow and prosper; otherwise, the inner city will remain as anomic as it is today. All of these arguments seem to us not only impeccable in their logic but exceptional in their awareness of the range of reform needed in big-city institutions and of the traps awaiting reformers whose arguments are simplistic or one-sided.

The weakest element in the PUSH plan probably involves its relatively slight emphasis on the problems likely to arise in improving curriculum and instruction once big-city schools have been made better places in which to teach and to learn. We are not as skeptical, in other words, about PUSH's societal analysis and overall strategy as we are about its pedagogy.

When PUSH addresses issues of social control and student behavior, its platform is relatively specific, much more so than many other groups which plead for order and discipline in the schools. PUSH proposals for dress codes, periodic community/school assemblies, required homework and study hours, close cooperation with the mass media, and parent participation requirements are refreshing in their specificity and promising in their occasional divergence from "conventional wisdom" about what can or should be done in the public schools. With regard to proposals for change in curriculum and instruction, however, or to analysis of reforms needed in school organization and administration, PUSH is mostly silent. Perhaps this is what one should expect, given the fact that its leaders are lay people who realize they will have to work cooperatively with teachers and administrators if real change is to occur in big-city schools.

Thus PUSH poses an enormous challenge to teachers and administrators in big-city schools. Jesse Jackson told us that he believes teachers do know how to teach if students are attentive and motivated; after all, most teachers have had considerable preparation and experience. "I am confident," he said, "that educators have the technology"; and he also expressed the belief that many administrators have the "presence," the know-how, and the determination to organize their schools for more effective instruction if parents demand and support such changes.

We wish we shared this confidence. Several outstanding educators we talked to in Chicago disagreed with Jackson's general assessment of the capabilities of big-city teachers and administrators. Arguing that educators generally have been negligent, failing to try or to properly implement promising new instructional approaches, they pointed out that most teachers are neither prepared nor experienced in working with methods that might improve academic performance in inner-city schools. Even if students and parents "cooperate" fully with previously harassed and harried teachers and administrators, this says in effect, "the emperor may be shown to be virtually naked."

Our own experience in big-city schools tends to support this latter view. In some of them students and parents have excellent relationships with teachers and administrators, yet little or nothing is done to make instruction more effective than in other schools where relationships are poor. Partly for this reason, we are not very sanguine about the prospects for lasting improvement unless efforts such as PUSH incorporate specific and systematic schoolwide plans for change in curriculum and instruction.

Elsewhere we have described some of the major elements in a serious effort toward big-city school reform as follows:

— Outstanding administrative leadership at every level — principal, middle management, and the superintendency.

— Staff development efforts much larger than in the past, carried out intensively on a school-by-school basis with far greater input from teachers and the community.

— A thorough reorganization of traditional school practices, including scheduling, student/teacher relationships, the grouping of pupils, evaluation practices, and the utilization of instructional methods and materials.

— More provisions for different educational environments for students who cannot function well in regular schools.

— Community resources joined to school resources in order to insure that both are fully utilized.[10]

The PUSH for Excellence program may well signify a tremendous step forward with respect to several of these elements. Clearly, it embodies an unusually vigorous and promising attempt to join community and school resources in the service of big-city school reform. Its leaders are painfully aware of the urgent need to improve the selection and performance of administrators at all levels. They appear abstractly aware that pervasive and systemic change is required with respect to staff development, curriculum, instruction, and other aspects of educational programming. But as lay persons they are passing the ball on such matters to professional educators. If it worries them greatly that professional educators have been fumbling the ball for many years, they choose not to emphasize this belief publicly, asserting instead that community participation will make the educator a better ball carrier.

4. URBAN SOCIAL POLICIES

Thus PUSH has joined the issue. For well over a decade teachers and administrators have been complaining that inner-city students and parents have not been receptive to pleas for cooperation to improve the schools, that negative forces in the inner-city environment have stood in the way of success in school. Jesse Jackson and other PUSH leaders agree, and express determination to make it easier for teachers to work in the classroom. "We don't know how well teachers can teach," Jackson has said, "until we provide a conducive atmosphere for learning. The present atmosphere is like sending Hank Aaron to bat with a popsicle stick, or sending Muhammad Ali to fight with one arm tied behind his back."[11]

If PUSH succeeds in this effort but fails to develop a pedagogy which works in the classroom, that is no mean accomplishment. If educators find that organizations like PUSH indeed have made the inner city a better learning environment but then fail to improve academic performance among inner-city students, that will be a rare opportunity missed, and a great tragedy.

---

1. Jesse L. Jackson, "President's Address," Fifth Annual National Convention, Washington, D.C., July 21, 1976.

2. Ibid.

3. Quoted in William Raspberry, "Racism and Victims," *Washington Post*, March 8, 1976.

4. Chet Fuller, "Govern Thyself," *Atlanta Journal*, March 22, 1976.

5. Jesse L. Jackson, "Give the People a Vision," *New York Times Magazine*, April 18, 1976.

6. Personal interview, August 7, 1976.

7. Jackson, "Give the People a Vision," op. cit.

8. Ibid.

9. Fuller, op. cit.

10. Eugene E. Eubanks and Daniel U. Levine, "Big-City Desegregation Since Detroit," *Phi Delta Kappan*, April, 1975, pp. 521, 522.

11. Jesse L. Jackson, "Moral Crisis in Education," commencement speech at Southern University, Baton Rouge, Louisiana, May 21, 1976.

The New Federalism in Community Development

Victor Bach

VICTOR BACH is assistant professor at the Lyndon B. Johnson School of Public Affairs, University of Texas at Austin.

The new federalism in community development, which emerged with the block grant legislation of 1974, potentially provides new opportunities for strategic local innovation, unfettered by federal constraints, aimed at improving living conditions among the urban poor. Yet the early returns from the program question whether such expectations are viable in the absence of further federal initiatives regarding the urban agenda.

To begin with, the community development block grant program (CDBG), should rightly be referred to as the "newer federalism." Although new federalist precepts are closely associated with the Nixon-Ford administrations, the need to extend local prerogatives in the use of federally funded urban development programs was first recognized in 1966 with the passage of the Model Cities program during the Great Society period. Supplemental block grants to Model Cities efforts enabled cities to undertake locally initiated programs not supportable within the existing menu of federal categorical programs. As a variation on the theme of a changing federalism, Model Cities represented a combined approach of block grants and categorical programs which concentrated federal funds in the more impoverished neighborhoods of the nation's larger cities and attempted to bring about a concerted, comprehensive approach to improving the quality of urban life in a relatively small number of targeted neighborhoods within each city.

By contrast, the newer federalism which came about in 1974 represents a consolidation of the earlier urban programs—urban renewal, Model Cities, housing rehabilitation loans and grants, and others—into a single block grant awarded to local general purpose government in an amount determined by formula, which can be applied to eligible community development activities where and how local powers see fit. The block grant program allows local chief executives unprecedented latitudes in the allocation of federal funds to local program strategies, subject only to conformance with federal constraints on local process, such as citizen participation, environmental clearance, equal opportunity, and the Davis-Bacon Act provisions.

Taken together, the two programs—Model Cities and CDBG—suggest a potential continuum of new federalist strategies toward improving federal-local arrangements concerning the urban agenda. Such strategies might differ on a number of dimensions, among which the most critical is likely to be the appropriate mix of local block grant initiatives and future federal programs which are less flexible in nature. Along this proposed continuum, what more than anything else characterizes the new federalism of the Nixon-Ford period is its exclusive reliance on the block grant mechanism as the engine of local community development activity. What follows is a discussion of several key aspects of the new federalism in community development as currently in practice.

OVERVIEW: THE CD BLOCK GRANT PROGRAM

As legislated, the general objectives of the CD block grant program bear a close similarity to those of the earlier categorical programs it subsumed:

1. Elimination of slums and blight.
2. Elimination of conditions which are detrimental to health, safety, and public welfare.
3. Conservation and expansion of the nation's housing stock to provide a decent home and a suitable living environment..
4. Expansion and improvement of the quantity and quality of community services.
5. A more rational utilization of land and other resources.
6. Reduction of the isolation of income groups through spatial deconcentration of housing opportunities for persons of lower income.
7. Restoration and preservation of properties of special value.
8. Expanding economic opportunity, principally for low- and moderate-income persons.

As a realization of the block grant concept—a "no strings" program which accords a maximum of local autonomy and flexibility in meeting federal objectives—the CD program is somewhat imperfect. To begin with, it is incomplete. A housing assistance component, to subsidize rents and promote housing rehabilitation or construction of units for lower-income families, is an integral part of any comprehensive approach to community development. Yet federal housing assistance is not subsumed in the CD block grant funds; it remains a centrally controlled HUD program. Each city or participating jurisdiction is required to submit a housing assistance plan (HAP) outlining its low-income housing needs and annual goals, along with its plan for utilizing the annual CD block grant. Although the HAP is a potentially useful mechanism for laying the responsibility for the planning of low-income housing on city hall's shoulders, what a city receives by way of housing assistance funds and the types of units that are eligible for subsidy, is largely at the discretion of HUD and often inconsistent with the locally prepared HAP. Some HUD area offices have gone so far as to press localities to alter their HAPs to conform to HUD-set priorities, particularly early in the program when Washington was unwilling to promote the use of rent subsidies for newly constructed or rehabilitated units. Moreover, HUD regulations discourage construction and rehabilitation in so-called minority-impacted areas, thereby limiting the ability of the city to undertake residential reconstruction efforts in ghetto areas even when they are responsive to expressed needs in minority communities. Although a housing assistance block grant to cities is presently under consideration, the present program severely constrains local priority setting for low-income housing assistance.

Although the legislation has as one of its objectives the expansion and improvement of community services—and specifically addresses such needs as employment, economic development, crime prevention, child care, health, drug abuse, education, welfare, and recreation—the act contains a number of restrictive clauses which limit the use of CD block grants for the funding of services. Service provision is limited to subareas of the city targeted for other, more "hardware-oriented" community development activities, and must be in support of such activities. The

support clause is probably a classic instance of legislative obfuscation. How can human services be justified as support to street improvements, sewage development, housing rehabilitation, or facility construction? The result has been to give HUD administrators carte blanche in interpreting what services are eligible or ineligible. Some HUD area offices have adopted an informal ceiling of 20 percent of the annual block grant for services, in accordance with the original Senate version of the bill which was subsequently stricken in conference. Other area offices have maintained a strong antiservices posture, claiming the block grant was intended primarily for "brick and mortar" activities. These federal strings on the program have served to reinforce local tendencies to prefer investment in capital improvements rather than services, and to thwart those cities attaching a high priority to a service delivery strategy for community development. It is not surprising that HUD's first annual report found that only 4 percent of the first-year block grants were being allocated to public services, most of which were continued Model Cities service activities.[1] The overriding hardware orientation of the program has made a misnomer of the term "community development," if by that we mean the comprehensive agenda of urban objectives built into the Model Cities program as well as the block grant legislation.

FORMULA FEDERALISM

Under the community development legislation, entitlement jurisdictions receive annual block grants based on an allocation formula which takes into account population size, the incidence of overcrowding in housing, and the incidence of poverty, and combines the three factors additively with poverty weighted twice. Entitlement amounts from one jurisdiction to another are then relative to their combined index scores. The concept of formula allocation is requisite to all of the new federalist programs in some form or other, and has the advantages of making explicit how much each jurisdiction can expect to receive and of assuring some form of equitable distribution. In the case of the CD formula, the

factors used would seem to be indicative of Congress's intent to develop a need-based distribution conforming to the axiom "to each according to his need."

Well before the CD program was legislatively launched, there were criticisms made by planners both of the adequacy of the overall block grant appropriation and of weaknesses in the formula.[2] Entitlement amounts tend to be particularly sensitive to the population factor because of its high variance compared to the other two factors;[3] this artifact of the formula raises the question of whether population is an adequate indicator or correlate of a jurisdiction's community development needs. Moreover, it was argued that housing overcrowding was an unreliable indicator of substandard housing conditions. In short, the formula has yet to be tested in social scientific terms as a defensible multivariate approximation of local community development needs.

The overall distributive effects of the formula have also been a substantial source of concern. It is generally recognized that if the program continues in its present form beyond its initial three years, after which the "hold harmless" provision phases out, the formula will result in a shift of funding away from the older center cities, despite their relatively high needs and extensive participation in the earlier categorical programs, toward their sibling suburban jurisdictions. In addition, there will be a major regional shift in funding which will penalize northeastern and midwestern jurisdictions and reward southern and southwestern jurisdictions. By 1980, Boston's block grant will have been reduced to one-third of its initial amount, while Houston's will have nearly doubled. In terms of its long-range distributive consequences, the formula has come to be viewed cynically by "loser" jurisdictions and by a number of urbanists as a manifestation of a Nixonian suburban and southern strategy.

None of these potential inaccuracies or inequities in the formula are therefore new to those who have followed the program. But in the wake of New York City's fiscal crisis and in face of the imminent fiscal crises in an expanding number of northeastern and midwestern cities, as well as some states, the potential inequities in the formula—particularly its regressive effects on the nation's center cities—take on a new urgency which was not apparent at the time of the legislation. Never before has the hold-harmless provision, which assures loser jurisdictions of their original pre-block grant funding level for the first three years and a gradual drop to the formula level over the next two years, so exemplified its meaning as it does with regard to the declining center cities.

By relying solely on "state" variables which are intended to reflect the extent of intrajurisdictional community development burdens—population, overcrowding, and poverty—the formula does not take local effort into account. More importantly, it is somewhat regressive in its tendency to reward lesser-effort jurisdictions. For example, both Hartford, Connecticut, and Jackson, Mississippi, have comparable populations within their municipal boundaries.[4] By 1980, once the hold-harmless protection lapses, the formula is projected to allocate a $3.3 million annual block grant to Hartford and $4 million to Jackson.[5] Undoubtedly, the difference in the two allocations is, in part, a reflection of the higher incidence of poverty in Jackson. In 1970 about 19 percent of Jackson's population was classified as low-income as opposed to only 5 percent in Hartford.[6] But when one takes into account that the average monthly AFDC payment in Hartford was $248 compared to a $53 monthly payment in Jackson,[7] the formula takes on somewhat different colorations. Moreover, the city of Hartford's share of welfare costs amounts to $6 million annually (roughly twice its projected block grant); in Jackson, the city takes on no such burdens. The question of whether the formula should favor Jackson is less important than the question of whether federal funds should be allocated by entitlement to support a hardware-oriented development program in a jurisdiction where public assistance does not provide a near-subsistence income to the dependent poor. In short, the formula allocation is indeed an entitlement which places no demands on local effort and which, to some extent, rewards lesser-effort jurisdictions.

Furthermore, the formula is blind to differences in metropolitan complexity

which have a direct bearing on community development burdens, particularly for the center city. Because the formula variables are purely intrajurisdictional in nature, they do not take into account the size of the metropolitan area a center city serves relative to its own population, which in turn determines the degree of infrastructural wear, maintenance, and redevelopment required—streets, public transportation, other public services—and the extent to which the center city can raise local revenues to cover these costs. The fact that Hartford is the center of a metropolitan area with more than two and a half times the population of the Jackson metropolitan area is not reflected in the relative formula allocations. Unlike Jackson, Hartford is an extremely small core city, constituting only a quarter of the metropolitan population, ringed by populous and relatively affluent suburban areas. Like most such cities, it has been subject to a steadily declining tax base as industries and the middle class have evacuated to the suburbs. At the same time, it has had to bear increased public burdens resulting from a large influx of poor migrants from the South and from Puerto Rico. Currently the city is facing major fiscal strains.

The structural characteristics of metropolitan Hartford and the disparities between the center city and its suburbs have earned Hartford a designation as a hardship city, the third hardest-pressed among the core cities of major metropolitan areas.[8] But the metropolitan situation of Hartford is shared, in greater or lesser degree, by a large number of core cities in the North and constitutes a common syndrome of the urban crisis as we know it presently.

> Geographically dispersed large cities compete with one another only in a rather remote and long-term sense. In the short haul, each of them is much more intensively affected by whatever differences may exist in the severity of social problems within its own boundaries in relation to the adjacent suburbs . . . Where the city-to-suburb hardship ratio is high and the central city is most isolated politically (these are related conditions, of course), flight to the suburbs can be expected to be accentuated and the "urban crisis" deepest.[9]

That the block grant formula ignores metropolitan complexity and size, in favor of purely jurisdictional parameters of need, is a major shortcoming in the formula's recognition of the higher community development burdens carried by core cities which serve broad urban areas beyond their own boundaries. More gravely, within the context of the fiscal crises many cities presently face, the program is regressive in its distributive effects. By ignoring metropolitan effects and placing the core city on a par with other entitlement jurisdictions, the formula is a manifestation of a policy of benign neglect toward those center cities in greatest need.

METROPOLITAN BALKANIZATION

Another major concern with community development revenue sharing was that its reliance on local priority setting would lead to further fragmentation of metropolitan planning and decision making in such a way as to retard regional solutions to urban problems such as housing, education, economic development, and guided growth. The regional councils of government, which had been nurtured during the Great Society period, had not resolved the functional and political disparities among sibling jurisdictions, but they had provided a context, however fragile, for a metropolitan dialogue among local governments, had proved to be a useful technical resource for smaller or less sophisticated jurisdictions, and had begun to make some embryonic attempts toward regional planning and coordination in a number of functional areas. One of the more notable starts was the Dayton, Ohio, plan for "fair share" housing which came about through the Miami Valley Regional Planning Commission and which had succeeded in overcoming suburban barriers to the broader metropolitan distribution of lower-income housing opportunities. Other metropolitan areas had begun to follow Dayton's lead.[10]

The CD block grant program gave a clear supremacy to local jurisdictions regarding housing and development initiatives without any simultaneous incentives that would encourage or give teeth to regional cooperation.

Except for a few key legislative provisions, it could be viewed as a prescription for further balkanization. The provision requiring the A-95 review process enables regional councils and participating local governments to comment on individual CD applications and raise issues prior to HUD review and approval. With regard to housing assistance, there are two key provisions that can be viewed as an attempt to counter the potentially balkanizing effects of the legislation. First, all jurisdictions applying for a block grant are required to submit a housing assistance plan, which thereby constitutes a tacit obligation to participate in lower-income housing assistance programs as a condition of the grant. Second, the legislation took pains to clarify the constituency for which a locality was to plan housing assistance: lower-income persons "residing in or expected to reside in the community." Although no legislative guidelines were originally provided as an operational definition of this constituency, the "expected to reside" clause has far-reaching spillover effects across localities if it is taken seriously.

With respect to the issue of balkanization, over the longer haul the results of the program may be far more positive than most of us had reason to expect. On the negative side, the A-95 regional review process has been only as strong or as weak as the regional councils were originally. In that sense, there has been little change for better or for worse. Nor does there seem to have been a consistent substantive review by HUD of housing assistance plans to assure that the "expected to reside" clause has been adequately taken into account by entitlement jurisdictions—suburban or otherwise—that have normally been resistant to low-income housing. This has been most dramatically evident in the suit Hartford successfully brought against HUD which placed an injunction withholding the block grants to seven suburban townships until their applications more closely reflected regional housing assistance needs. Also, HUD presently seems to be reluctant to enforce participation in the housing assistance program as a condition of the block grant.

On the positive side, regions in which there has been a concerted effort toward metropolitan planning have not been substantially deterred by the local determinism of the block grant mechanism. In addition, the urban county component of the program seems to show substantial promise in bringing about more coordinated planning and increased program consolidation among incorporated areas. The entitled urban counties have been fairly successful in securing the participation of smaller incorporated units within the county boundaries. Among the 73 urban counties involved in the CD program each contains an average of about 26 incorporated units.[11] Moreover, such participation seems to be happening at an accelerated rate. Harris County, in the Houston area, was populous enough in its unincorporated area to qualify on its own as an entitlement jurisdiction. By the middle of its first year of implementation, about 30 incorporated units were planning to participate in the county's second-year program in order to receive a share of the CD block grant. The consolidation occurring under the urban county umbrella seems to be a strong and somewhat surprising indication of a debalkanizing effect of the program.

With regard to housing assistance as a key functional indicator of regionalization trends, there is much that looks promising. The consolidation occurring under county-administered housing assistance programs will, at least nominally, open up many new areas to housing assistance that have not had their own housing authorities previously. Moreover, a number of entitlement jurisdictions that have historically resisted federal housing programs have been lured by the carrot of the CD block grant to create housing authorities and participate in the assistance program. In addition, there are some indications that the "expected to reside" clause has catalyzed a degree of coordination among neighboring housing authorities through the vehicle of referral linkages across authorities. That is, a lower-income family looking for housing assistance will be referred by one authority to another, depending on where the family would prefer to reside. If such linkages can be made to work effec-

tively within the context of a program that can deliver housing—and there are doubts that have been cast on the present programs—then we will see the emergence of a model that approximates a metropolitan housing authority. A recently proposed HUD regulation which provides increased funding allocations to coordinated areawide housing efforts will constitute a tangible incentive for more regionally oriented housing assistance programs.

One of the strongest ironies within the new federalism, and perhaps the most positive, is in the leverage it has accorded to center cities to coerce suburban cooperation through the courts. Hartford seems to have set the model for court action that might be taken by other disadvantaged center cities to press for suburban recognition of their own role in helping solve the pressing problems of the center city. Although Hartford's neighboring townships may elect to forgo their block grant entitlements rather than respond to regional lower-income housing needs, there are indications that the suit has helped create a climate of cooperation, however coercive, that hadn't existed before and that might extend beyond housing to other functional areas such as regional economic development strategies that might reduce Hartford's high unemployment rate. Ironically, by providing a legal basis for registering one jurisdiction's objections to another's conformance with federal objectives, the CD block grant may become the long-awaited retractable carrot[12] to encourage regional economic and housing strategies more consistent with the needs of depressed center cities. Unless the suburbs are willing to turn back their block grants, as some will probably do, they will have to deliver more in terms of metropolitan coordination.

THE CHANGING CHARACTER OF COMMUNITY DEVELOPMENT

What emerges at the early stages of the program is a natural layering of the old and new programs as community development undergoes a transition from the previous categorical program structures to the newer, more flexible strategies permitted under the block grant program. On the one hand, a portion of the block grant funds is being used to phase out the categorical programs in an orderly fashion. On the other hand, a substantial majority (63 percent) of jurisdictions with categorical commitments report a shift in their funding priorities away from the categoricals.[13] In short, the program is experiencing considerable shifts in funding allocations which augur a possible change in the character of local community development activity. To make that determination, it is probably best to set aside ongoing categorical commitments and examine where and how the more flexible funds are being allocated.

In the larger center cities which were strong participants in the categorical programs, the changes are probably sharpest. Both urban renewal and Model Cities constituted the lion's share of funding in the pre-block grant period. Although the two categorical programs are very different, they had in common a unitary conception of community development, in that they focused on specified subareas or neighborhoods as units of planning and programming. And they shared a comprehensiveness of vision, however misguided it was at times, as to what the future of these neighborhoods should be. As such, they represented a concentration of federal funds toward long-term neighborhood development in selected subareas, more often than not the most severely declining areas of the city.

The emerging character of local community development under the new federalism is substantially different. The flexibility of the block grant program has resulted in a highly dispersed pattern of community development activity—a "showering" effect involving a dilution of funding and effort across a broader range of subareas and city neighborhoods. Typically, the new pattern is dispersed rather than concentrated, consisting largely of short-term, rapidly visible, "spot" physical improvements and private housing rehabilitation through loan and grant programs.[14] Priorities are being accorded to the more conservable, moderate-income areas, where the lesser degree of deterioration calls for relatively marginal public im-

provements, rather than to the severely deteriorating neighborhoods.[15] In any given neighborhood, the scope of activity is likely to be characteristically incremental rather than the result of a staged plan for neighborhood improvement or conservation over the longer range. Perhaps the best image that captures this pattern is Downs's conception of *triage* as applied to community development[16]—the practice of ignoring those areas recuperating on their own as well as those requiring major surgical intervention, while bandaging the intermediate group as rapidly as possible.

This pattern of dispersed, incremental, selective neighborhood improvements seems to be the overriding characteristic of the new federalist version of community development. In part, it is the result of the prevailing climate of cynicism in federal-local relations. In a period of fluctuating federal commitments and lasting program moratoriums, cities are loathe to commit themselves to longer-range, more comprehensive efforts under federal encouragement for fear that the block grant program may ultimately be abandoned. The recent debate over the continuation of general revenue sharing underlines the reality of local concerns about the durability federal commitments.

In large part, the pattern can be seen as the inevitable outcome of local forces and local process under the block grant program. Under the categorical programs hard choices had to be made in selecting those few subareas that would receive concentrated effort; locally elected and appointed officials could rationalize those choices on the basis of federal constraints over which they had little control. The latitudes for local decision making under the block grant program offer no such rationalization, and there is little incentive and much political risk for local officials who would decide to concentrate funds in a few areas rather than dilute efforts in order to spread program benefits to a wider number of needy areas representing a broader citywide constituency. That local chief executives tend to prefer to keep the community development program within their own offices, rather than delegate responsibilities to city departments or

local redevelopment authorities, is a reflection not only of the responsibilities they bear under the CD block grant program but also of the necessity to maintain close control over a politically sensitive program in which they feel particularly vulnerable.

The most politically vulnerable mayors have probably overseen the program with the greatest care, both with regard to the area distribution of program benefits and with regard to key political parameters of the local planning process. In one city I have closely observed, the mayor consciously chose to appoint representatives to a citizen participatory task force from among citywide public interest groups—e.g., the League of Women Voters, councils of churches, the Urban League—rather than risk taking on the "turf" conflicts he felt would result from area representation. Moreover, the boundaries distinguishing one CD area from another and the staging of the first-year target areas received the close scrutiny of the mayor. Once the first-year application was submitted, a permanent citizen participation body was elected by area representation, and the program has since changed dramatically from a predominant citywide macrostrategy of housing rehabilitation loans and grants to a more neighborhood-oriented program of incremental public improvements, which are listed in the second-year application neighborhood by neighborhood. In addition, a set of funding quotas was developed which determines how much of the block grant will be expended on neighborhood-proposed efforts as opposed to citywide program efforts.

Neighborhood associations and neighborhood-based organizations have emerged with particular force on the community development scene. Among them are ethnic neighborhoods, some of them highly organized, "backlash" working-class communities previously excluded from federal funds under the categorical programs, and often neglected by local public improvement priorities, who are fierce in their determination to get their share of the community development pie, and understandably so. The power of the neighborhood associations, particularly those with strong grassroots support, is in the number of votes they potentially represent. In that sense, they are likely to be strong influences on the program whether or not they are involved in the formal participatory mechanisms.

In this kind of political environment, the dilemma of the mayor is one of achieving consensus and avoiding conflict in the distribution by area of CD funds, while at the same time making it clear that the funds are insufficient to satisfy the needs and demands of each area. The form of political equilibrium that will likely result will involve an agreement on the distribution of CD funds by neighborhood, without regard to specific, substantive program objectives, and a process that will allow communities some degree of autonomy in deciding toward what efforts the funds will be used. Although this process is likely to crystalize most rapidly in those cities with a high degree of neighborhood political organization, what is likely to emerge is some form of decentralized decision making offering a degree of community involvement in priority setting for a limited portion of the block grant funds, while a certain amount of the funds are set aside for citywide efforts at the discretion of city hall.

Many urbanists, myself included, will view the local decentralization effects of the block grant program, in themselves, as a promising development in local process which is likely to have spillover effects beyond community development to other functional areas of city decision making. But the gains in process will be accompanied by a substantially changed pattern of community development activity, one that is more likely to meet the conservation needs of marginally deteriorating areas than the development needs of the hard-core poverty areas.

TOWARD A BALANCED FEDERALISM

In attempting to assess the new federalist aspects of the CD block grant program on the basis of early indications, one might use the simple paradigm: inputs, process, and outcomes. On the input side, there remain substantial concerns whether the aggregate federal funding of the program will be adequate to the needs of the nation's urban communities. Moreover, the formula allocation of block grant funds leaves much to be desired, particularly in the equitableness of its distribution of funds to high-effort, fiscally strained center cities embedded within larger metropolitan areas.

With regard to issues of process, the early indications of the new federalism in action are somewhat more positive. The fears of an exacerbated balkanization of efforts in metropolitan areas seem to have been exaggerated, and some promising trends in the opposite direction have been noted here: the consolidation of program efforts under the urban counties and the potential for increased regionalization of housing assistance. At the local level it seems reasonable to expect that the block grant program will catalyze a more decentralized decision-making process based on consensus-building mechanisms required to make the program politically manageable by city hall. This will accord a degree of community control over the allocation of CD funds, and promote programs more responsive to community priorities, within tight funding constraints, than have been many of the past categorical programs.

It is with regard to community development outcomes that the block grant program is most bewildering. The presumed flexibility of the block grant mechanism is likely to produce nearly universally a low-profile, broad-based, incremental public improvements program which, if it has any coherence at all, will accomplish the conservation of some of the marginally deteriorated neighborhoods of the city. It is less likely to have a major impact on the revitalization of the more impoverished neighborhoods of our cities or to deliver the improved housing, community facilities, and services that residents of these neighborhoods rightfully demand.

In light of the fact that the concentration of funds necessary to bring about substantial improvements in severely declining areas is not forthcoming, it might be argued—in accordance with the triage model—that a local policy of benign neglect toward these areas constitutes the most efficient use of block grant funds. However, if the triage model prevails, it is unclear what the block grant program will ultimately accomplish. For unlike the metaphor of the war wounded from which the term derives, the problems of urban slums are not isolate in nature but epidemic, and are likely to diffuse to adjoining neighborhoods and other areas of the city, perhaps the very areas we would like to believe have been conserved through the CD program. In short, we will not have come anywhere close to addressing our major urban problems through the marginal conservation efforts that are likely to proliferate under the block grant program. If the federal government is seriously committed to solving these problems, it will have to come to recognize the need for a new generation of federal initiatives targeted at the multifaceted problems of our most blighted areas, in parallel with revenue sharing mechanisms that promote community development efforts of a substantially different, though by no means unimportant, character.

The term "categorical" can be applied pejoratively to the brand of new federalist thinking which has posed the question of evolving federalism as an either-or logical proposition, and meted out initiatives for different functional policy areas to either one level of government or to another. The Model Cities program, despite its problematic nature, suggests at least one alternative among a possible continuum of alternative combinations of federal-local arrangements. By relegating community development exclusively to the domain of special revenue sharing and to the vicissitudes of the block grant mechanism, new federalist thinking has categorically decided that local initiatives should govern the pattern of federally assisted community development efforts, and ignored the possible benefits of complementary federal initiatives as well as the values of a continuing federal-local dialogue. Now that the block grant mechanism is in place, this is the time to reconsider parallel federal initiatives for the problems that a local pluralist process cannot easily bring itself to address. Clearly, we need a more balanced federalism which augments local community development under special revenue sharing with a new generation of comprehensive and more responsive categorical programs.

NOTES

---

[1] U.S. Department of Housing and Urban Development, *Community Development Block Grant Program, First Annual Report*, Washington, D.C., December 1975, p.31.

[2] Richard T. LeGates and Mary C. Morgan, "The Perils of Special Revenue Sharing for Community Development," *Journal of the American Institute for Planners* 39, no. 3, (July 1973), pp. 254–264.

[3] Richard DeLeon and Richard LeGates, *Redistribution Effects of Special Revenue Sharing for Community Development*, Working Paper No. 17, Institute of Governmental Studies, University of California, Berkeley, 1976.

[4] In 1970, Hartford's population was 158,000; Jackson's population was 154,000.

[5] U.S. House of Representatives, Committee on Banking and Currency, *Directory of Recipients, Housing and Community Development Act of 1974*, Washington, D.C.: U.S. Government Printing Office, September 1974.

[6] U.S. Bureau of the Census, *Census of Population: 1970*, Volume 1.

[7] U.S. Social and Rehabilitation Service, *Recipients of Public Assistance Money Payments and Amounts of Such Payments, by Program, State, and County*, February 1973.

[8] Richard P. Nathan, "The New Federalism Versus the Emerging New Structuralism," *Publius* 5, no. 3 (Summer 1975), pp. 111–129, p. 126.

[9] Ibid., p. 121.

[10] David Listokin, *Fair Share Housing Allocation* (New Brunswick, N.J.: Center for Urban Policy Research, Rutgers University, 1976).

[11] U.S. Department of Housing and Urban Development, op. cit., p. 11.

[12] For discussion of suburban incentives for lower-income housing development, see Anthony Downs, "Moving Toward Realistic Housing Goals," *Agenda for the Nation* (Garden City, N.Y.: Doubleday), pp. 141–178.

[13] U.S. Department of Housing and Urban Development, op. cit., p. 21.

[14] Ibid., p. 6. In addition, direct observations stem largely from a policy research project currently in process at the LBJ School of Public Affairs under my direction. The effort constitutes a comparative field study of the community development process in six center cities: Baltimore, Md; Birmingham, Ala.; Hartford, Ct.; Houston, Tx.; Kansas City, Mo.; and San Francisco, Ca.

[15] Ibid., p. 30: "There is a greater emphasis on preventing and eliminating blight in the early stages of decay ... Those neighborhoods accelerating into major decline and non-viable, heavily abandoned neighborhoods receive less emphasis."

[16] Anthony Downs, Real Estate Research Corporation, *Recommendations for Community Development Planning* (Monograph based on a study for HUD, Chicago, Ill.: Real Estate Research Corporation, 1975).

5. Urban Futures

The urban future is another area of interest to social scientists. In recent years it has become clear that there is a need for serious planning to bring about a future which will enhance the quality of urban life. Without planned and directed growth, our society may face ecological catastrophe. However, good plans rest upon clearly stated goals and objectives. We are just beginning to understand what choices are open to us, debate what kind of future we want, choose who will direct growth and change; and decide who can mediate the conflicts that are bound to occur.

Ironically, the study of the future has a long history. Philosophers and writers, for example, have already designed utopian communities or described the new world which they envision. In the past twenty years they have been joined by social scientists. By projecting current trends, it is possible to suggest probable development as well as to understand the kind of intervention necessary to change the direction of events. Engineers and architects are also thinking in futuristic terms when they try to visualize new materials and designs to be used in buildings.

The scientific study of human behavior is based upon the assumption that most behavior is patterned and structured. It is possible, then, to predict future behavior that is "probable" or "likely" to occur. Using this approach social scientists assume that urbanization will continue to occur throughout the world and that urban societies will continue to change and adapt to new demands. They also predict that urban issues will continue to produce problems and to improve the quality of life, an effort should be made to solve them.

In thinking of tomorrow it is worth contemplating the qualitative issues at stake. What kind of world do we want? What conditions of today's urban society are likely to influence the future? What options are now available and how can we develop standards to select between them? What are the most serious dangers that we face in determining our urban future?

Alternative Possible Urban Futures

H. WENTWORTH ELDREDGE

Professor of Sociology,
Dartmouth College, New Hampshire

The twenty-first century will witness a considerable variety of urban forms in the West, in the socialist bloc and in developing countries. Multi-group, multi-valued societies should and will offer options in both societal and physical urban living. A spectrum of experimental urban types is developing all over the world and there is much to be learned from these types in their continuous refinement. The author surveys existing and emerging types: those which offer "more of the same" in a surprise-free future, the new towns or cities which provide innovative life styles, and the extreme and intriguing variants which may feed back into the more normal forms. At present the first type looks most likely to persist.

Given the multi-group society of the present USA with widely divergent value systems, overriding democratic values with heavy egalitarian overtones preclude any reductionism to *one national pattern* for societal/physical urbanism. Such a naive, crude, cruel and simplistic perception of "human nature" is not remotely feasible in modern Western nations even though there is a tendency to approach it in totalitaria. The enormous powers of the intellectual, technical, even behavioural and organisation technologies make it possible to "have diversity, choice and to meet human needs" for the first time in history.(*1*) Undoubtedly, we do have some options for our urban futures, despite the energy crunch.

In the "post-industrial society" with its heavy emphasis on the knowledge industry, there is bound to be a multiplicity of variants on patterns already visible in the 1970s. To select a few representative searches for options: *Futures Conditional,*(*2*) guided by that lively ex-engineer turned socio-economist Robert Theobald, is an attempt to imagine various future scenarios for the next thirty years. Paul Goodman early saw *Seeds of Liberation*(*3*) in new thought patterns that would free humanity for building, first better societal futures and later physical structures. The American Institute of Planners launched in 1966 a massive enquiry directed by William R. Ewald Jr. into the next fifty years, budgeting over $1.25 million from a variety of public and private sources. This was a hefty attempt to illumine American (and the world's) professional city planners as to the rich variety of the feasible roads ahead.(*4*) An amazing variety of authors—many exeptionally perceptive—from a wide spectrum of doers and thinkers at least concur to form the clear message that bumbling along with "more of the same" would be hopelessly inadequate. Urban design student Kevin Lynch in "The Possible City"(*5*) stresses that "mobility, access and communication are indeed the essential qualities of an urbanised region—its reason for being". This has been echoed by transportation specialist Wilfred Owen who emphasises the fact that access to activity nodes—jobs, dwellings and recreation—is the key to civilised community development. He glimpses the developing interchangeability of communication (movement of ideas) with transportation (movement of people and goods) which is bound to affect life territory and life styles shortly.(*6*) Even a hard-headed urban administrator, Roger Starr, Executive Director of New York's Citizens' Housing and Planning Council, bewailing the incessant critical attacks on "the city" by Utopian types such as Lewis Mumford, Jane Jacobs, Herbert Gans, Victor Gruen, *et al* knows that the balancing of the multiplicity of values (held by divergent groups *now*) is already an almost impossible task;(*7*) it is bound to be worse in the future as groups multiply and pathways further divide. *Mass society* as "one dead level" seems less likely in the 1970s than it did in the 1950s.

If market choices are to be largely replaced by designed options under a National Urban Policy (NUP), then widespread societal/physical alternative possibilities must be built for multiple present and future life styles. Minimum standards can probably be set; egalitarianism, heavily reinforced—and resisted—by increasingly scarce resources, will be quite likely to create iron maxima, but within these very wide parameters an NUP can offer the citizenry a great variety for numerous versions of an existence of "style and quality". There undoubtedly will be both monetary and societal costs involved in making large numbers of available options, but the resultant stunting of society's rich fabric by dull sameness suggests immediate high societal costs and potential high monetary-costs for the failure to provide such options. Inadequate life styles

 This article first appeared in *Futures*, February 1974, 6(1), pages 26-41 (Guildford and New York, IPC Science & Technology Press).

are a "shaped charge" aimed at urban viability—a rather complex way of stating that insistent frustration leads to tension resulting in the possibility of grim revolution (a most costly societal exercise).

Thus it would appear that one of the most overwhelming tasks of NUP planners is to make readily available rewarding, feasible options in diverse physical and societal forms and combinations thereof.

Traditionally planners have tended to think in terms of multi-purpose or multi-functional cities; this seems a rather narrow conclusion to induce from a long human experience drawn from governmental, religious, recreational, learning, trading and industrial types of cities. The future could see specialised cities with clues elaborated from the above simple list of existent forms with such revised types as: (a) the ceremonial city (Washington, Islamabad), (b) the university city (Oxford as it was), (c) the research city (Novosibirsk), (d) the artistic city (Aspen, Colorado), (e) the fun city or Hedonopolis (Cannes, Miami Beach), (f) communication or media city (see Option 14 below), (g) the museum city (Bruges, Williamsburg, Nara) including Museums of the Future (Mesa City of Soleri), (h) experimental cities of varied types (health, new social relations, communal economic developments), (i) any combination of the above! In fact each venture could be considered as an experiment, (8) and so treated. Actually, sharply differentiated satellite cities in a metropolitan area or sectors or communities within a core city could offer rewarding variations.

Here is a realistic catalogue of feasible, relatively "surprise-free" urban options ahead; it assumes that no major economic, military or eclogical catastrophe will befall the world and its cities in the next three decades. Given multi-group society with divergent life styles and values, holistic planners must offer a wide spectrum of choice. Despite both physical and societal utopianists, it is more than likely that in the year 2000 AD, post-industrial society will be surprisingly like the present only—hopefully—"better". These fifteen options,(9) all pretty standard, are not mutually exclusive and much overlapping is evident; within options there are clearly various sub-options which are not pursued here. Further, the emphasis tends to be on the physical/spatial framework and on location (especially under Type A) which together do not remotely determine societal structuring. Much social diversity is possible within similar man-made physical environments as within similar natural physical environments; the relationship between design and behaviour is not one-to-one. These options are grouped under two categories: Type A—almost certain to continue; and Type B—generally far-out potential environments; no attempt is made to weigh formally the importance of the various options. Certain options clearly occur within the territory of larger urban forms—others are relatively free-standing entities or activity centres. What effects a widespread appreciation of the energy crisis will have on all this is not yet clear.

Type A; Almost Certain to Continue

Option 1. Megalopolis or urban region. This is modern society's fate. Most of the post-industrial urban population (80%?) will dwell in Options 1, 2 and 3. THE PACIFIC BELT (Japan), BOSWASH (Boston to Washington) and RANDSTAD (Holland) are already here. Can such sprawling territorial giantism be redeveloped by opening up "density breaks" (similar to "fire breaks" in a forest) and by the creation of varied activity nodes to restructure interaction and upgrade the Quality of Life (QOL) in such vast agglomerations? These have been defined as "man heaps" by Lewis Mumford, "conurbations" by the English. Obviously there is a multitude of life stlyes possible and existent in megalopolis.

Option 2. Metropolitan Central City (500,000 and up), as a high activity area with "cosmopolitan" sophisticated recreation, jobs and living. The French regional *metropoles d'equilibre* fit this pattern; high-rise, vertically-zoned buildings could serve as an experiment. Both "straight" and "counter" cultures can find room here. This is the locus of high pressure private and public development in the USA as "the city fights back" to lure middle-class population into returning from the suburbs to live and to interact. It means modern office buildings, pedestrian malls and pediment (or higher) walkways with interesting and diverse shops, recreational and cultural facilities—in short the lure of the bazaar which has given variety to urban life. "New Towns in Town" (NTIT) belong here most certainly in an attempt to divide the city into some semblance of meaningful communities (at least at the level of simple services); social development planning will be a must in large sectors of central city. The *metropolis* shades into:

Option 3. Smaller central city (50,000 to 500,000), similar qualities but on a less national and more regional scale. The possibility exists of creating an *entire* community spirit. Town housing, vertically-zoned buildings with possible class and ethnic mixtures. Somewhere between a 250,000 and 500,000 population seems to be presently the critical mass for the full spectrum of city functions. QOL efforts would pay off richly here. The 1970 US Census indicates that cities in this group have continued to grow where Metropolitan Central Cities (Option 2) are levelling off.

Option 4. Small central city or town (up to 50,000), still less national/regional interaction and more on a localised scale. Local realities adjusted more clearly to varied natural environments and with specific functions, such as: the research city; shore city; recreation city; university/learning/information city; mountain city.

5. URBAN FUTURES

Option 5. Satellite cities for Options 2 and 3 to gain the putative benefits of Option 4; closely linked with new communities, but could be upgraded existent towns or cities.

Option 6. Inner suburbs (a subset) for all three major city types (2, 3, 4) must be divided into "communities" (NTIT again) serving various life styles according to economic class, vocational and/or leisure interests, religion, ethnicity, race, etc.—high-rise and low-rise (town houses/cluster housing). There should be a great variety of suburban types to suit various life styles. The USA has its special problem in white/black antagonisms and unless adequate optional suburban space (both integrated or non-integrated) is made available for blacks to leave central city, the ghetto problem will continue. Undoubtedly sub-options whether to integrate or not must be made available to face the hard reality of continuing prejudice. Patently this applies also to outer suburbs and to new towns. Here derelict land can be used as new green space for recreation and relief.

Option 7. Outer suburbs, similar but of a less "urban" character. Varied life styles are stressed by design both physical and societal; a greater attempt through cluster housing to create "community." Some high-rise buildings in open settings are inevitable.

Option 8. Exurbia. Quasi-rural existence of a scattered grain but due to advanced transportation "urbanistic" in quality; not unrelated to "the wired city" and the 1-day work week. Made possible by the electric pump, septic tank and four-whelled drive vehicle; haunt of "hill-billy" types and seclusive "intellectuals". This is high cost scatteration, but an immensely rewarding option for certain personality types—who may be either incompetent, truly creative, or merely hiding from the horrid urban world.(10) Increasingly the haunt of the counter-culture and very suitable for new experimental family/community variants. Alpine recreational resorts possibly fit this category; the seashore has been pretty generally usurped by sprawl.

Option 9. New Towns (or latterly *New Communities*). Building cities *de novo* has held a great attraction for mankind; "leave the messy clutter behind and start afresh" might even be traced back to mobile hunters striking the befouled encampment to move on to virgin areas. New towns are simply dwellings, jobs, recreation, a wide spectrum of services and *controlled* size. Most certainly the current fervor about new cities/towns/communities indicates a deep-seated dissatisfaction with existent urban forms. This is unquestionably the area for widespread experimentation both with physical forms and with societal structure; and a means of ascertaining and developing client desires or choices.

Somewhat oversold as a universal panacea at the moment, the enormous costs for the needed infrastructure of a massive new cities programme to cope with a significant percentage of the expected 80 to 100 million new Americans (35,000,000 new households $\pm$) by the twenty-first century boggles the imagination. To build for 25% only (20 to 25 million persons) would require 2,000 towns for 100,000 inhabitants, each costing between $2-5 thousand million in public and private investment, leading to an over-all cost of $10,000,000 million at least.(11) While undoubtedly much will of necessity be spent in any case to house, amuse and provide jobs for the expected hordes, it is most unlikely that exploiting the vast existing urban infrastructure would even approach such costs—though the possible benefits of thousands of new towns might be of extraordinary magnitude.(12)

Examples of New Towns

Before proceeding further it should be stressed that new towns can consist of

- free-standing independent communities (Brasilia and Novosibirsk Academic City)
- groups of related free-standing functionally divergent communities (Lewis Mumford's ideal)
- satellite communities with high self-employment (London ring new towns)
- extensions of cities; really glorified, quasi-independent suburbs (Long Island Levittowns and Stockholm's semi-satellite cities)
- "New Towns in Town" (NTIT), live tissue grafts to existing internal city structure (Fort Lincoln, Washington, D.C.).(13)

Minnesota Experimental City (MXC), brainchild of oceanographer, physicist, meteorologist, Athelstan Spilhaus, aided by, among others, Buckminster Fuller, urbanologist Harvey Perloff, economist Walter Heller, was to be built by private financing on 50,000 acres, 10 miles north of Mineapolis with a maximum population of 250,000.(14) This is perhaps the most obviously experimental effort to date both physically and societally: downtown will be roofed over; the municipal power plant is to be partially fuelled by garbage; cable TV will approximate "the wired city" (Option 15); farms and factories will be mixed; while people will be housed in megastructures complete with waterless toilets, people-movers and universal computer-managed charge accounts. New city Vaudreuil to house and provide jobs for 150,000 residents is to be built by the French government in the Basse-Seine region outside Paris. It will have the world's first urban centre without noise or pollution (?) and all green zones in the general area are to be preserved, as was announced by President Pompidou. The city's traffic will flow underground; factory smoke is to be carried off by underground conduits—gases being burned at the source; apartments and business buildings to be sound-proofed; with all refuse moved through underground conduits to be used in adding to the city's requirements for central heating. These are merely the most "advanced" examples of a new communities world movement (milennia old) which includes the architecturally striking Brasilia and Chandigarh—and the older Washington, Canberra and New Delhi (the British imperial city stage). The thirty-odd British New Towns are globally renowned; by 1963 probably well over one thousand new towns of various shapes and sizes had been identified.(15) There is a recent 1973 report that there are already 1,000 in the USSR alone.(16) The best known US examples: Columbia (Maryland), Reston (Virginia), Flower Mound (Texas), Jonathan (Minnesota), and Irvine (California)—all privately financed—are in varying degrees innovative socially and physically—primarily in amenities. The semi-satellite cities coupled to the public urban transit system of Stockholm (they do not provide jobs for more than half the resident population) have also attracted world attention concentrating especially on the town centres so reminiscent of American shopping centres without that ugly, naked parking necklace of auto-mobiles. The Dutch have done a splendid job in reclaiming the Zuider Zee for new town development. Tapiola, a tiny gem for only 17,000 persons using adroitly both green and blue (water) space, has cheered the world with the realisation that pleasant urban living is possible. Japan with characteristic zeal plans to dot the hinterland of Tokyo with Quasi-new towns composed of rather barren, high-density dwellings. Tama New Town to house 410,000 on 7,500 acres is the prime example. (Incidentally this is the same acreage as Reston which is designed to house 75,000 with high recreational amenities.) At Tama, tenants, generally middle income, are to be selected by lot and divided into "neighbourhoods", generally convenience-oriented, of 15,000 people. Most dwellers are expected to commute to Shinjuku (New Town in Town) or through it to central Tokyo for work.(17) India is planning a "New Bombay" for a potential population of two million; (18) whether it will be built is another question.

As is well known, Israel has constructed a variety of new towns/new communities: larger ones for port or industrial purposes; smaller for agricultural development often connected with defence(19) under an urban settlement hierarchy system based on Christaller. Connected with the physical siting of population are the renowned versions of communal settlements: the kibbutz and mashav. Thus the twin experimental functions of new communities are exhibited there: technological virtuosity and fresh social patterning. Noteworthy in new community development worldwide is the great variety of fresh

governmental authorities or public corporations invented to get on with the job—where traditional government has been obviously too wooden to do so.

While, for example, the original or Mark I post-war British new towns were aimed in the London region at decanting the central city population, new towns or massively developed old towns both in Britain and elsewhere are now perceived as potentially powerful development nodes furthering national urbanisation policy with high technology, industry, high education, and population distribution.(20) Even Herbert Gans, egalitarian sociologist, believes that treated delicately new communities might possibly make positive contributions to the nasty desegregation muddle here,(21) as will perhaps "Soul City", the Black New Town in North Carolina near Raleigh-Durham under the leadership of Floyd B. McKissick with a planned eventual population of 50,000.(22) Finally, the United States Government is officially dedicated to sponsoring new communities in the Housing Acts of 1970 and 1972. Up to now the action has hardly been impressive; there is no remotely visible over-all strategy for siting or the scale of the total effort.

Option 10. A rural/agricultural setting could now be brought more easily into "urbanistic" living patterns by transportation and telecommunication. European agricultural life has long been town/village centred, contrary to the US mode of isolated homesteads. Clearly an increasing humankind will need more and more food while a (declining) proportion of the population will continue to opt for an agricultural life style. Of course, for some very considerable period there will be islands of "backward" rural culture preserved in Asia, Africa, Latin America and possibly portions of North America. Such areas could offer a rewarding life style for the actual inhabitants and "museums for living" (small residual forms throughout the world) for the denizens of more urbanised habitats.

Type B. Far-Out Potential Environments

These could be either physical or societal—or more likely some combination of both; they might serve as temporary experiences for the many or for the permanent life style of a few.

Option 11. Mega-structures or "mini-cities" have fascinated men at least since the Tower of Babel.(23) Characteristically, there is a Disneyland project copyrighted in 1960 "The Community of Tomorrow" which will be a whole *enclosed* model town for 20,000 persons on fifty acres *only*, to be part of the Florida Disney World. Paolo Soleri has had the greatest visi-bility recently as a highly successful youth-guru with his concepts of giant supra-terrestrial human hives housing up to hundreds of thousands of persons.(24) Soleri has fuzzy, complicated, intuitive, communalistic notions about group life joined to his often cantilevered bridge-like structures which allies him to far-out commune options as well.(25) It will be interesting to see the clients his constructions attract once scale has been attained.

Apparently the term mega- (giant) structure was the invention of Fumihiko Maki of the Japanese Metabolist Group in 1964. *Habitat* by the Israeli architect, Moshe Safdie, prepared for Expo 1967 in Montreal, while financially an initial disaster, has become a much publicised example of this sort of "plug-in", "clip-on" structure;(26) for the record it is turning out to be both a financial and a societal success. Taby, satellite community outside of Stockholm, houses 5,000 people in one group of vast, curved structures, flanked by eight tower blocks containing another 3,000; while in Denmark "at Gladsaxe about 15 miles from Copenhagen, five 16-storey slabs, each 300 feet long, extend in tandem". This latter construct seems to negate the warm humanism of Danish planning; the buildings are factory-made prefabs, site assembled: "These slabs are aligned with formal, rigid, relentless horizontality."(27)

Even mega-structures (human hives) directly in town have been flirted with by responsible officials. In 1966 Governor Rockefeller of New York State proposed a futuristic design for Battery Park City of massive towers for the lower tip of Manhattan, high connective bridges, dozens of apartments with a high pedestrian mall surrounded by other rabbit-warren dwellings on a large land fill totalling 90 plus acres. After lengthy negotiations with the New York City fathers, the plan was realistically toned down into a less grandiose format(28) and is still being re-thought.

In effect though, vertically-zoned buildings with garages and services below ground, retail trade at ground level rising to business offices, to schools and finally to varied dwellings topped by the inevitable penthouse (the higher you go the more it costs?) give promise of things to come. Many of these mega-structures are theoretically capable of infinite expansion or contraction, an eternal meccano set which might be one partial answer to an increasingly mobile society.

Option 12. The Water City Scarcity of usable shore land and possibly usable shallow water (what happens to the ecological balance?) have led recently to large-scale "futuristic" designs for enormous activity nodes on reclaimed land or on stilts in shallow water. Buckminster Fuller advocated this for Japan in Tokyo Bay using his newly-beloved tetrahedron shape as piles.(29) Given oriental population densities and typical minimal family space, the water city/mega-structure idea does not seem out of place now and may be a necessity in the future. Fuller carried his ideas

further in the Triton Floating Community of 30,000 persons with structures up to twenty storeys; these ferro/concrete platforms could be built in shipyards and towed to usable places just offshore of existing coastal cities to be "anchored" in water up to twenty or thirty feet in depth.(30) This project was financed by the US Department of Housing and Urban Development; a trial construction nearly came to fruition in Baltimore harbour. There is a present scheme afloat to develop an artificial island off Tokyo; Kenzo Tange had explored brilliantly the Tokyo Bay project earlier in his *Tokyo 1960* plan.(31) There have been, of course, precursor water cities: Swiss Neolithic Lake Dwellings, Bangkok's *klongs* (canal life); Hong Kong's sampan colony at Victoria; Borneo and New Guinea stilt villages and even Fort Lauderdale. After all, Most of the southern tip of Manhattan Island was once under water. Tange's plan called for a reconstruction of the central city and for a huge expansion in mega-structure form into Tokyo Bay—both linear in form—to take care of a 1980 estimated population of 20,000,000 for the metropolitan area of the Japanese capital!

As a matter of fact, based on research conducted at the Athens Center of Ekistics on the "City of the Future Project", John G. Papaioannou concluded "that floating settlements on different land (mountains, swamps, deserts, frozen soil, etc)(32) some seventy to one hundred years hence with the earth trending toward one world city, Doxiadis' Ecumenopolis.

Option 13. Underwater, underground and space habitations on a scale large enough to be significant. Jacques Cousteau collaborated in the design of a floating island to be built off the coast of Monaco which would have undersea features: ". . . more comfortable dwelling quarters may be floating stably a hundred feet or so below the surface where any wave motion is so damped out as to be unnoticeable."(33)

The habitation-cum-fortress underground house is something new, although underground factories were well known in Nazi Germany and the United Kingdom during World War II as well as the ill-fated Maginot Line. The salubrious atmosphere of huge salt mine caverns could conceivably serve for community experimentation. *Sousterrain* dwellings could have temperature control and construction savings immediately applicable, especially in hot desert areas and quite possibly in sub-Arctic regions. Certainly in central city, burying certain structures and services below ground is already in progress with multi-storey underground parking garages in many cities (Paris, for example) and the increasing use of sub-surface delivery roadways and shopping areas.

The Committee for the Future has as its avowed (and partially endowed) purpose the development of extra-terrestrial space to ease the environmental burden and "the opening of the solar system for humanity beginning with the establishment of a lunar community available to people of all nations". Unlikely as some of these science fiction solutions may appear today, at least they may in time offer recreational locations for future persons searching for new experience.(34)

Option 14. Communes and other societal innovations. Recent new societies in the USA with presumed behavioural innovations are generally the efflorescence of the counter-culture; they are largely and consciously simplistic in technology and are the *nouvelle vague* in societal structuring. Chinese communist "communes" with heavy overtones of directed "togetherness" are quite another thing! Even elementary contact with anthropology and history would suggest that middle class, capitalist, nationalist, habitaions/life styles with certain economic, political, religious, familial, recreational institutions hardly exhaust the possibilities for human arrangements. Nor does a minimal connection with the long story of Utopian schemes and real Utopian communities lead one to assume that it all began with *Walden Two*.(35)

Despite the often jejune aspects of such experimental communal Utopias and the relatively few persons involved in any groups that approach a quasi-organised effort, the present impact is felt no matter how faintly—by a whole generation of American youth (and their foreign imitators) who see an appealing alternative life style to modern traditional Western civilisation. In short, a counterpoint theme, no matter how unsubstantial, has been established; it is already "out there".

Physical communes are in a sense concrete expressions of Utopia, the no-place ideal world, to which the forefathers of most Americans emigrated from their assorted homelands. Once arrived they and their descendants continued to pursue the dream across the wide and once beauteous continent until everything stopped in 1893 (the end of the frontier) on the shores of the Pacific. More extreme seekers for the perfect/ideal life probably founded more Utopian colonies in the New World than elsewhere (although Robert Owen was English and Charles Fourier was French). A catalogue of better known nineteenth-century ventures here would include the celibate New England Shakers (so-called because of their curious dancing/shuffling worship) who early preached "the careful craftsmen"; the Owenites at New Harmoney in Indiana, a socialist/communist community; Brook Farm, a poetic Phalanx with high-minded pretensions in almost anarchist interaction dedicated to "the honesty of a life of labor and the beauty of a life of humanity".(36) The Oneida community believing in "Free Love and Bible Communism" was started in 1847, and still continues in altered form as Oneida Ltd.—successful silver manufacturers. The general theme running through such nineteenth-century experiments sounds familiar

enough today in their search for "freedom", "love" and the escape from crude materialism to production "for use rather than profit". America's penchant for revivalist religious movements such as the Seventh Day Adventists and the Mormons has produced somewhat similar farout societal design. Patently youth culture, unhappily extended well past sexual potency by the lumbering contemporary educational process (and the probable need to keep the masses of young off the job-market in capitalist culture) has become enshrined in the whole counter-culture movement of which the encyclopedic *Whole Earth Catalog*(37) gives some clue of the myriad forms of this "romantic" reaction to industrialism and the search for a "new freedom". The Hippie communes both urban and rural (both benign and evil as some of the murderous, dehumanised monster groups show) possibly number 3,000 in the USA. If each group is comprised of a population of ten (a serious study for environmental purposes found in the Minneapolis area that the twelve communes investigated there had a total of 116 members)(38) the total population of American communes would thus be 30,000 in a nation of 210,000,000 which hardly heralds the Revolution! Even if there were 100,000 such communes, upset is not yet upon us.

Hippie core-values as the extreme example of these minimum physical planning/maximum societal planning variants are an interesting summary of the counter-culture:(39) free, sensually expressive (anti-intellectual), immediate, natural, colourful/baroque, spontaneous, primitive, mystical, egalitarian, communal.

This largely societal option has been introduced here since it is clearly "innovative" and "revolutionary" (often in puerile ways) in its implications for standard society and in its messages to developing lands about the "failures" of industrial society. It could be, however, only the tip of the iceberg of dissatisfaction with the industrial culture of Western society. Minimal space seems to be the *only* physical planning expense involved; the commune people make their own societal plans. Such exotics must not be crushed—even if someone else has "to tend store". The affluent West affords millions of the idle rich, non-producing youngsters, idling oldsters and millions of unemployed; it most certainly can afford a few tens of thousands of experimenters seeking a better life on earth.(40) They might even have something!

Communes, as here defined, obviously do not exhaust possibilities for societal innovation in urban places. A creative systems approach to housing, largely economic, has been sketched,(41) including (a) an executive, professional, intellectual housing centre, (b) new, non-competitive shared-value orientation, (c) "housing as a self-renewing function which adjusts and develops as individuals, opportunities and communities evolve" (no on-site maintenance!), (d) multiple consumer choices,

(e) creation of new credit sources due to housing as a "containerised unit—with registered, computerised bonded and insured controlled units", (f) "Mutual Insurance Fund" to include youth participation and leisure time home-building as inputs with, finally (g) "registered bankable certificates of the units for a house complex" easily exchangeable as a restless population moves above.

Option 15. "The Wired City." With the phenomenal growth of cable television (potentially capable of two-way transmission) added to the almost infinite potentialities of multi-channel electronic interaction through "people's satellites",(42) a non-territorial, high-intensity participatory community fitted to the "post-civilised" or "information society", could await us.(43) Despite piecemeal research, very considerable argumentation, a few limited experiments,(44) and a galloping electronic technology, it seems unlikely that the multiplicity of ordinary (and creative new) functions, which should be possible at considerable energy saving, will be much in operation in even the most sophisticated nations before the commencement of the twenty-first century. The bits of the picture puzzle are slowly being fitted together but they still do not form a whole. It appears that the basic scenario will be a national(46) cable/micro-wave grid of metropolitan networks reinforced or supplanted with satellite connections and eventually lasers; computers serving both as storage facilities and as analysts with display capabilities will be at the centre of this intellectual technology.(46) In the UK consideration is already being given to setting up a national computer grid. In "the wired city" every dwelling will have its typewriter-like keyboard with print-out capabilities and display screen in the home information recreation/business centre (additional home terminals are naturally possible). This equipment will not be cheap and some trained intelligence will be needed to operate such sophisticated gadgetry thus bringing up future questions of equity, egalitarianism and the massive financing and maintenance of such "public services".

Here are some of the bits yet to be assembled in a potential non-territorial, electronic society, partially substituting the transmission of ideas for the transportation of people and goods, and freed to a certain extent from spatial considerations.(47) As transportation expert Wilfred Owen has pointed out:(48)

> The significance of communications as a substitute for transport derives from the fact that while the unit costs of transportation continue to rise as quality declines, telecommunications tend to increase in quality and decline in cost. Distance is important in transportation, but with communication satellites distance is almost irrelevant.

Here is a portion of what "the wired city" might provide:

- *Information storage available by computer/TV*
  national data bank on the total society (with all the safeguards of privacy)
  national library
  national music library
  national theatre/cinema library
  national health records and diagnostic information
  scientific information service
  crime information
  credit information

- *Home service facilities*
  all banking and transactions ("the end of money")
  shopping (plus delivery)
  recreation (passive and active—"anyone for chess?")
  crime prevention
  education in the home for children *and* adults
  automatised cooking
  visiting via video-phone
  print-out news (*The New York Times* nationwide)
  "mail" delivery electronically

- *Advanced societal innovations*
  public opinion surveys
  sampling to replace voting
  "participatory democracy"(49)
  TV surveillance of public (and private!) places
  new industrial/business locations
  new employment patterns (4-day, 3-day, even 2-day work week in a *work place* away from the dwelling)
  new population distribution
  "home visits" by the doctor and specialist
  increased physical and societal design capabilities
  new and powerful techniques for mass behaviour, control and surveillance
  systems design and guided social change(50)

All is clearly not sweetness and light in this future city. What if evil "philosopher kings" should occupy central positions in the national/international network? If "euphoria" characterised the initial reaction to the two-way television, coaxial cable, computer, peoples satellite syndrome, one already sees signs of *alarm* prior hopefully to advanced *protective action* (including active *ombudsman* functions) before the need arises.(51) Finally, for the loyal fans of central city as "the place where the action is", "the wired city" is already posing quite a problem as "people stay away in droves" from downtown especially for evening recreation with simple-minded, axistent TV as one reason.

The US Department of Housing and Urban Development has commissioned a study on the impacts of advanced telecommunications technology on

American cities during the next twelve years(52) which concludes significantly that:

- The advent of telecommunications technology (TCT), while highly beneficial to some segments of society, will prove detrimental to others.
- The positive impacts of TCT will be felt primarily in the middle class suburbs, while the negative impacts will be concentrated in the central cities.
- TCT will not play a highly visible role in the major urban developments of the next 12 years. Unless specifically anticipated by federal and local planning, impacts will not be properly understood and regulated until considerable damage has been done.
- The primary urban impact of TCT will be to reduce the economic viability of the central city by accelerating (though not directly causing) the delocalisation of business and commerce.
- The social impacts of TCT are to be found at least as much in the indirect effects of TCT on the fiscal strength of cities, as in the direct effects of new gadgets on the life styles of individuals.
- The sector most affected by TCT is the service sector, in which processes involving paper transactions are particularly sensitive to technological substitution.
- It is unlikely that the central city population will derive much benefit, in the next 12 years, from such "luxury" applications of TCT as shopping or working at home.
- The most important *positive* impacts of TCT in central cities will be in the areas of technical education (especially in programmes designed to develop job skills among inner-city residents), and routine city services (especially in transit systems, police and fire protection, etc), and remote medical or diagnostic services.

Having explored at some length goals for a good "society" and a rather considerable number of alternative possible urban futures, one is driven to the realisation that quite probably "more of the same" will be the lot of Western urbanism for the rest of this century and probably well on into the next. "Peripheral sprawl will undoubtedly be the dominant form of future urban growth throughout the US"(53) and the Western world. This will probably be true for the socialist nations as well; a degree of urban chaos is predictable for the developing countries as a "genius forecast".(54) It is most likely that there will be no urban systems-break; far-out options will occur only here and there. The standard world projection of *one spread city,*(55) slopping untidily into the next, is all too likely for those nations incapable of the act of will, the intellectual effort, and the *real Politik* ability to direct their growth, as well as sufficient consensus and capital resources to bring about actively planned, alternative rewarding

large-scale variations of the human condition. Superior "intentional societies and ordered environments" still seem just beyond our grasp.(56)

References and Notes

1. Leonard Duhl, "Teaching and Social Policy", *The Bulletin of the Association of Collegiate Schools of Planning,* Winter 1971, pages 4-10.
2. New York: The Bobbs-Merrill Co., 1972. *Teg's 1984* (Chicago, The Swallow Press 1972), a participatory, experimental book on new societal/physical forms by Theobald and J. M. Scott, where, it is claimed, "ego can involve the reader".
3. Paul Goodman (ed.), *Seeds of Liberation* (New York, George Braziller, 1964).
4. *The Next Fifty Years* series commemorated the 50th anniversary of the founding of the American Institute of Planners. Published by the University of Indiana Press (Bloomington, Illinois), it consists of three volumes: Vol. I *Environment and Man* (1967), Vol. II *Environment and Change* (1968), Vol. III *Environment and Policy* (1968).
5. *Ibid.,* Vol. III, page 145.
6. Wilfred Owen, "Telecommunication and Life Styles", *The Accessible City* (Washington, The Brookings Institution, 1972), pages 132-133.
7. Roger Starr, *Urban Choices: The City and Its Critics* (Baltimore, Penguin Books, 1967).
8. John McHale, *Future Cities: Notes on a Typology* (unpublished draft).
9. The urban future could be sliced differently. Cf. Anthony Downs, "Alternate Forms of Future Urban Growth in the United States", *Journal of the American Institute of Planners,* January 1970, page 4. Incidentally, using ten key variables involved in urban development (with several arbitrarily chosen values for each), Downs indicates the logical possibility of 93,312 potential forms of future urban growth! (page 3).
10. Satirised some years ago by A. C. Spectorsky, *The Exurbanites* (New York, Berkeley Publishing Co., 1955).
11. Extrapolated loosely from Walter K. Vinett, *Paper Number Three, The Scenario for Minnesota's Experimental City* (Minneapolis, University of Minnesota, Office for Applied Social Science and the Future, 1972).
12. "Non-metropolitan new cities or expanded communities are not likely to capture any significant fraction of the nation's [USA] future urban growth in spite of their current vogue in planning literature." Anthony Downs, *op. cit.,* page 11.

5. URBAN FUTURES

13. Harvey S. Perloff, *New Towns in Town* (Washington, D.C., Resources for the Future, 1966), reprint.

14. *Time*, February 26, 1973. Sadly abandoned in April 1973—funds ran out.

15. F. J. Osborn and Arnold Whittick, *The New Towns: The Answer to Megalopolis* (New York, McGraw-Hill, 1963), pages 141-148.

16. According to the Department of Housing and Urban Development (*The New York Times*, April 26, 1973).

17. *Information Series 20, HUD International*, U.S. Department of Housing and Urban Development, January 15, 1973.

18. Dena Kaye, "Across the Gateway and Into the Curry," *Saturday Review/World*, September 11, 1973.

19. Ann Louis Strong, *Planned Urban Environments* (Baltimore, Md., The Johns Hopkins University Press, 1971), pages 170-173.

20. Cf. Lawrence Susskind and Gary Hack, "New Communities in a National Urban Growth Strategy," *Technology Review* (February 1972), pages 30-42; also "New Communities," An American Institute of Planners Background Paper, No. 2, 1968.

21. Revised version of a paper presented for the Symposium on "The Human Dimensions of Planning," UCLA, June, 1972.

22. "The Planning Process for New Town Development: Soul City," A Planning Studio Course, Fall 1969, Department of City and Regional Planning, University of North Carolina, Chapel Hill, under David Godschalk.

23. A visually striking book on mega-structures is Justus Dahinden's *Urban Structures for the Future* (New York, Praeger, 1972).

24. Paolo Soleri, *Arcology—The City in the Image of Man* (Cambridge, MIT Press, 1969), in the tradition of "design utopias".

25. See Ralph Wilcoxen, *Paolo Soleri: A Bibliography* Monticello, Illinois, Council of Planning Librarians Exchange Bibliography, No. 88, June, 1969). According to the *New York Times* (Nov. 4, 1973), Soleri stated, "The only way to keep autos out of the city is to build a city without streets."

26. Cf. William Zuk and Roger H. Clark, *Kinetic Architecture* (New York, Van Nostrand Reinhold, 1970). To quote the blurb, "Exciting open-ended planning: proposed and actual structures that are *replaceable, deformable, incremental, expandable, reversible*—even *disposable.*" Italics the editor. Cf. also Peter Cook (ed.), *Archigram* (New York, Praeger, 1973).

27. *The New York Times*, December 2, 1965.

28. *The New York Times*, November 22, 1970.

29. *Playboy*, December 1967.

30. *The New York Times*, November 3, 1968.

31. Kenzo Tange Team, *A Plan for Tokyo*, 1960 (Tokyo), drawn largely from the April 1961 issue (in English) of the *Japanese Architect*.

32. "Future Urbanization Patterns: A Long-Range World Wide View," paper prepared for presentation at the Second International Future Research Conference, Kyoto, Japan, 1970, page 17.

33. *Congressional Record*, November 15, 1965, "Extention of Remarks of Hon. Claiborne Pell, October 22, 1965".

34. 130 Spruce Street, Philadelphia, Pa. 19106. SYNCON is their elaborate physical and intellectual system to relate varied disciplines in a holistic effort to solve primarily urban problems. *Unibutz; Out of this World* (an interplanetary, international kibbutz) was explored at some length in the World Institute Council's *Fields Within Fields* by various intellectuals in 1971 (Vol. 40, No. 1).

35. B. F. Skinner, *Walden Two* (New York, The Macmillan Co., 1948). Cf. W. H. G. Armytage, *Yesterday's Tommorrows: A Historical Survey of Future Societies* (Toronto, University of Toronto Press, 1968).

36. *The Complete Works of Ralph Waldo Emerson*, edited by E. W. Emerson (Boston, Houghton Mifflin & Co., 1904), Vol. 10, 359-360, quoted in Peyton E. Richter (ed.), *Utopias: Social Ideals and Communal Experiments* (Boston, Holbrook Press, 1971), page 129. The examples cited here were drawn from this work.

37. *The Last Whole Earth Catalog* (New York, Random House, 1971).

38. Michael Carr and Dan MacLeon, "Getting It Together," *Environment*, Vol. 14, No. 5 (November 1972). The study was conducted under the auspices of the American Association for the Advancement of Science.

39. Drawn from Fred Davis, *On Youth Sub-Cultures: The Hippie Variant* (New York, General Learning Press, 1971—module).

40. This most certainly is not to encourage elaborate planning provisions for odd groups searching for instant Nirvana through Drug Utopias—a not inconsiderable subset or variant of existant communal experimentation. Cf. Richard Blum, *Utopiates: The Use and Users of LSD-25* (New York, Dodd, Mead & Company, 1963).

41. Julius Stulman, "Creative Systems in Housing," *The World Institute Council*, Vol. 4, No. 2, 1971.

42. For example, ANIK, the Canadian internal satellite.

43. Sloan Commission on Cable Television, *On the Cable: The Television of Abundance* (New York, McGraw-Hill, 1971) is a fairly straight line

projection of more-of-the-same TV pattern only with more choice up to the turn of the century. More imaginative alternative potentials could have been rewardingly explored; the societal planning lead time is shorter than one thinks to cope with the wired city.

44. Jonathan New Town, Minneapolis, Minn.; Tama New Town, Japan; and Washington New Town, County Durham, England.

45. This, of course, could be international as Eurovision has already accomplished for one-way television.

46. James Martin and Adrian R. D. Norman, *The Computerized Society* (Englewood Cliffs, N.J., Prentice-Hall, 1970), page 66.

47. Cf. Melvin M. Webber and Carolyn C. Webber, "Culture, Territoriality and the Elastic Mile," in H. Wentworth Eldredge, (ed.), *Taming Megalopolis* (New York, Anchor-Doubleday, 1967), Vol. I, pages 35-54, which considers the existant professional non-territorial community.

48. Wilfred Owens, *The Accessible City* (Washington, D.C., The Brookings Institution, 1972), page 132. Cf. the hyper-optimistic "30 Services That Two-Way Television Can Provide" by Paul Baran in *The Futurist*, Vol. III, No. 5 (October 1973).

49. *Project Minerva* (Electronic Town Hall Project) has already carried out preliminary exercises in some 803 households of a middle-income high rise housing complex in one of the nation's largest cities" . . . in the comfort of their own homes recently, and aired their views about their security problems during an electronic town hall meeting." Amitai Etzioni, who is conducting the experiment, believes he could carry this out with 40,000 persons. Center for Policy Research, Inc., 475 Riverside Drive, New York, *Newsletter* No. 8, January, 1973, and *Behavior Today*, Vol. 4, No. 10, March 5, 1973.

50. Robert Boguslaw, *The New Utopians: A Study of System Designs and Social Change* (Englewood Cliffs, N.J., Prentice-Hall, 1965). As well as explaining latent capabilities for powerful symbiotic man/machine interaction, Boguslaw wisely explores paranoid possibilities in Chapter 8, "The Power of Systems and Systems of Power."

51. These terms are the main headings for portions of the Martin/Norman book, *op. cit.*

52. Marvin Cetron, *An Analysis of the Impact of Advanced Telecommunications Technology on the American City* (Washington, D.C./Arlington, Va., Forecasting International Ltd., 1973), quoted from the "Executive Summary," pages iv-v.

53. Anthony Downs, *op. cit.*, page 11.

54. Marvin Cetron's terms.

55. *Spread City: Projection of Development Trends and the Issues They Pose: The Tri-State New York Metropolitan Region*, 1960-1985 (New York Regional Plan Association, Bulletin 100, September 1962).

56. Paul Reed, *Intentional Societies and Ordered Environments* (Monticello, Illinois, Council of Planning Librarians Exchange Bibliography No. 320, 1972).

Small Cities and Their Future

James L. Freund

The author was formerly an economist with the Department of Research of this Bank. He is now on the staff of the Board of Governors of the Federal Reserve System.

The ever-mounting economic and social difficulties of big cities continually make page one news. So do the problems of suburbanization. Yet, discussions of the nation's ills often ignore the economic plight of small cities. This "neglect" cannot be traced to a presumption that small cities lack economic importance or have relatively few problems. Over 20 million people live in cities and towns whose populations range from 25,000 to 200,000, and the winds of economic change have whistled up hard times for any number of these communities. The economies of many small towns have contracted along with the general decline in agricultural employ-

ment in their respective regions. Others have suffered with the decline of such industries as coal mining, railroads, and textiles.

While such adversities are not confined to small cities, small cities may find prosperity harder to achieve than large metropolises— and for definite economic reasons. Grasping these forces is the key to understanding the fate of small-town America. On one side of the coin, plants in small cities lack large local markets for their products and often are isolated from regional population centers. On the other side, production costs are often higher in a small city. Lacking the advantages of industrial concentration, high-quality transportation facilities, and a skilled labor force, many small cities and towns find building an industrial base more difficult than do large cities. Likewise, public goods and services — a strong magnet for new residents and businesses alike—can be more difficult and expensive to produce than in many large metropolitan areas.

TABLE 1

POPULATION GROWTH RATES, 1960-70 BY 1960 SIZE OF CITY

Percent Population Change

Size Status in 1960 (Population)	Total, U. S.	South and West Census Regions	Northeast and North Central Census Regions
Nonmetropolitan Cities			
25,000 - 49,999	12.4%	18.6%	6.6%
Small Metropolitan Areas			
50,000 - 99,999	10.9	12.3	8.6
100,000 - 149,999	15.5	20.7	12.2
150,000 - 199,999	15.7	16.8	14.7
Large Metropolitan Areas			
200,000 - 299,999	14.0	16.8	10.4
300,000 - 499,999	15.8	21.5	10.2
500,000 - 999,999	21.5	27.1	13.4
1,000,000 +	14.2	24.8	9.8
Total Population	13.3	17.6	9.7

NOTE: The source of the data was the *1970 Census of Population*, Final Report PC (1)-A1, Table 32 and the *1972 County and City Data Book*. Each city was classified by size according to its 1960 population on the basis of the 1970 definition of the SMSA. Changes in total population for each size class were calculated as percent from 1960 to 1970. The separation of size categories was arbitrary; the results were not greatly changed when groupings were altered.

From *Business Review*, March/April 1976. Reprinted by permission, Department of Research, Federal Reserve Bank of Philadelphia.

Citizens charged with bringing prosperity to their small cities frequently ignore the inherent economic limitations of their municipalities. They also tend to overlook the national and regional economic forces that influence the prospects of small cities. Yet some of these forces could hold promise for the future of many small cities. The workability (and cost) of policies aimed at improving the lot of small cities must be considered in this light.

HOW HAVE SMALL CITIES FARED

Population growth is one measure of the progress of small cities. By this standard, many small cities are doing well. As Table 1 shows, from 1960 to 1970 small, nonmetropolitan cities of between 25,000 and 49,999 grew only slightly less rapidly in percentage terms than the nation as a whole.[1] Small metropolitan areas of less than 100,000 were also below average. Conversely, other small metropolitan areas with between 100,000 and 200,000 population grew at above average rates.

The best performance among smaller cities and towns was registered in growing regions. Growth rates of small, nonmetropolitan cities and small Standard Metropolitan Statistical Areas (SMSAs) in all size categories in the South and the West (Table 1, column 2) outstripped those in the Northeast and North Central states (Table 1, column 3). The most striking example is the case of small nonmetropolitan cities; such places grew almost three times as fast in the South and the West than in the Northeast and North Central sections.

Although regional location strongly influences any city's overall prospects, small cities grew somewhat less rapidly in the 1960s than did large cities *within* the same region. In the South and West, for example, large metropolitan areas registered the most spectacular rates of growth. Growth in the two smallest categories of cities in the Northeast and the North Central regions was well below the combined regions' average and trailed the nation as a whole by a considerable margin.

However, the averages don't tell the whole story. For instance, Table 2 reveals that, despite respectable average rates of growth, small cities were quite vulnerable to population declines between 1960 and 1970. Since small cities greatly outnumber large ones, it might be expected, other things equal, that

small places would be experiencing more declines. However, the *proportion* of cities suffering losses is also strikingly higher among small cities.[2] Almost a third of the small nonmetropolitan cities lost population during the 1960s. (See Table 2, column 1.) Many small metropolitan areas also suffered losses— ranging as high as 18.5 percent for those of 150,000 to 200,000 residents. Although the percentage of small cities declining indicates that such places were more susceptible to decline, the *absolute* number of cities losing population tells the story more vividly. The number of small nonmetropolitan cities that lost population was higher than the total of all metropolitan areas that declined. (These cities constitute 43 percent of the areas observed and 70 percent of the declines.) Further, 70 of the 78 cities that declined had fewer than 200,000 residents. (These areas represented 68 percent of the cities observed and 90 percent of the declines.)

SMALL CITY LIFE: INDIVIDUAL PREFERENCES AND ECONOMIC REALITY

If asked where they prefer to live, far more people would probably opt for a small city or metropolitan area than currently live in these areas. Indeed, many are moving to such

---

TABLE 2

THE INCIDENCE OF POPULATION DECLINE

BY CITY SIZE

Size Status in 1960 (Population)	Percent Cities with Population Loss, 1960-70	Number Cities with Population Loss, 1960-70
Nonmetropolitan Cities		
25,000 - 49,999	30.9%	55
Small Metropolitan Areas		
50,000 - 99,999	14.3	3
100,000 - 149,999	17.5	7
150,000 - 199,999	18.5	5
Large Metropolitan Areas		
200,000 - 299,999	12.8	5
300,000 - 499,999	3.3	1
500,000 - 999,999	3.2	1
1,000,000 +	4.1	1

SOURCE: *1972 County and City Data Book* and *1970 Census*, Final Report PC(1)-A1, Table 32.

---

[1]The fact that small cities did well in relative terms (percentage terms) does not mean that they are gaining absolutely compared to large places. Although cities of 25,000-49,999 population grew by almost the same rate as metropolitan areas of over a million population, the small cities gained 765,325 while the larger category gained 4,665,391.

[2]Because they often rely on a smaller number of sources of employment than large cities, small cities are likely to be subject to higher variation in growth rates in general. Whether the high proportion of declining cities results from this lack of diversification or from inherent economic disadvantages, small cities still have to cope with problems of general economic decline more often than larger cities.

places to take advantage of the agreeable lifestyle. Social and political participation in the affairs of the community is easier and more direct. Residents enjoy less congestion, easier transportation, and a lower population density. Small cities are less likely to have pollution problems and most have good access to outdoor recreation.

If these advantages exist, why has the thrust of economic growth historically been toward large urban areas? Can the nation assure that people who apparently want to live with less hustle and bustle will be able to do so? The answer to both questions lies in the ability of such places to compete with large metropolitan areas in two respects. People must work, so small cities must provide jobs. Many people who might have preferred a small-town setting have left to find better opportunities. Secondly, people value government services such as police protection, schools, and public health facilities. Unless local authorities can provide quality services at reasonable tax rates, attracting new residents and stimulating economic growth will be difficult.

There Should Be No Problem—Theoretically. Many economists would point out that there are mechanisms for assuring that people who prefer small cities are able to live there. If government services cost more in small places, people who really want to live there will pay the higher price. Further, plant location can reflect people's residential choices. Florida and the Southwest have grown largely because families have been attracted by the climate and the lifestyle. Many businesses have followed them. Many scientific and technological firms locate in areas where workers enjoy living in order to attract high-quality personnel without paying them high wages to work someplace they do not like. Lifestyle preferences also can be registered through direct action by workers. Even if all other costs indicate that a plant should locate in a major metropolitan area, workers may be able to offset the higher costs of small-city operations by accepting lower wages.[3]

In theory, these wage and tax adjustment processes can provide for job opportunities and desired public services. In practice, they cannot be relied on to assure prosperity for small cities. Most people are unwilling to make large financial sacrifices to live in small cities; they want "decent" jobs and a normal package of public services at "reasonable" tax rates. Over long periods, migration into an area will stimulate economic growth,[4] but it is rare that spontaneous migration alone makes

an area prosper. Usually migration depends, at least in part, on job prospects, and these, in turn, depend on how profitable a location is for private industry.

A small city may have plenty of clean air, a clear blue lake, and friendly citizens — yet be an unsuitable factory location. Unless an area is so attractive that people will make substantial sacrifices to live there, cities grow or decline on the basis of their existing competitive advantages. The profitability of operating a business in any city depends on two factors: finding customers for the goods and services produced and keeping down the cost of production. On net, size works to the disadvantage of most small towns in both respects.

Can Small Towns Support Big Business? To be successful any enterprise must have viable markets for its products. Many of the firms in any city rely on local residents to buy its products. A moderate-size city obviously cannot offer the same market to a business as Philadelphia, St. Louis, or Boston. For some goods the minimum number of customers necessary to support a profitable operation is small; almost every town can support a drug store, a market, or a service station. Consumer services (such as interior decorating and photofinishing) as well as business services (such as janitorial contractors and advertising agencies) require larger pools of local customers. Even middle-size cities might have difficulty supporting large wholesaling establishments, baking and bottling operations, and legitimate theater.[5]

In short, there are "threshold" levels of demand that must be met to make many locally oriented operations successful; small markets are beneath the cut-off for many products. Since residents must "import" such goods and services from nearby cities, they pay higher prices than if local production were efficient. Further, goods bought from other places create jobs within the supplier's area rather than locally.

Conversely, businesses in small cities can sometimes rely quite heavily upon customers from neighboring regions. These additional customers supplement demand from within their boundaries and support a larger, healthier economy than a city itself could sustain. When population centers are separated by miles of highway, consumers and businesses

---

[3]Some locations may be at such a disadvantage that workers could work for nothing, and it would still be uneconomical to operate there.

[4]For a discussion of the important role population growth plays in economic prosperity, see Jerome Stein and George Borts, *Economic Growth in a Free Market* (New York: Columbia University Press, 1964).

[5]An interesting discussion of the size necessary to support different types of services is by Otis Duncan et al., *Metropolis and Region* (Baltimore: The John Hopkins Press, 1960), pp. 77-79.

located in the surrounding regions gravitate to these centers to buy and sell goods and services. Each population center develops market areas that it services more efficiently than other cities can. Such markets provide economic viability for many of the nation's metropolitan areas and cities in rural areas.

Goods intended for national and broad regional markets form yet another potential source of local jobs. In theory, firms producing these goods could locate anywhere because local customers are not a primary consideration (only a small proportion of auto sales take place in Michigan). Many such plants locate in smaller cities and consitute the backbone of these local economies.[6] This is especially true in resource-oriented industries such as mining, forestry, and agricultural products. While these industries are important, areas that are growing in both size and in average family earnings usually must also attract nonextractive, nationally oriented plants. To do so, they must be able to compete with large metropolitan areas on the cost side of the ledger.

Is It Feasible to Produce in Small Cities? A locale's ability to attract industry depends on many factors totally unrelated to its size. One is the beneficial effect of being in a growing region. Another is the discovery of a new natural resource. A new interstate highway near a city can significantly lower that area's cost of producing goods for national markets. Conversely, a city of any size may suffer because it specializes in a product for which its competitive advantage has faded. This is the case for textile centers in the Northeast and areas depending on employment in coal mines. Changes in tastes resulting in declining markets can affect the business community of large and small cities alike.

The economies of small cities are also affected by their lack of size. Some factors enhance the small city's status as a site of production. For instance, relatively cheap land, lack of congestion, and ease of internal transport all make running a business more profitable. Unfortunately, smallness has other disadvantages. Because local demand is limited, plants tend to be smaller in modest-size cities. Small plants are less likely to be able to take advantage of efficient management techniques and production methods that require large scale operations.[7] A producer in a large city often has the advantage of proximity to many plants in the same industry — for example, there's usually a garment district, a financial district, or food processing centers. Where similar firms locate, specialized business services develop. Legal firms know their unique problems, shippers can adapt to their needs, and subcontractors spring up. In large cities with many firms doing the same work, specialized labor forces can develop. Small-town plants have few of these advantages.

Even if a plant is the only one of its kind in a large city, it has certain advantages over a unit operating in a small city. Business and financial services are usually more sophisticated and extensive in metropolitan areas. For firms in the retail and wholesale trades in large cities, the very concentration of economic activity will often mean exposure to additional buyers that would not be attracted to isolated, small city establishments. Plants in small localities find a less diverse and shallower pool of workers from which to draw. Finally, larger population centers are generally recognized as the environment where new ideas and trends are developed. A firm in a small city often lacks exposure to such developments and, therefore, is once again at a disadvantage.[8]

Meeting Public Needs. Good public services are essential to a healthy community. The efficiency of delivering services and the quality of local facilities are important in determining the quality of life for citizens. Local government operations are also important to businesses. Inadequate or costly services will put firms at a competitive disadvantage. Thus, a key issue is whether small places have any disadvantage when it comes to providing public services.

As in private production, smallness has its pros and cons. Citizens' desires are usually more modest in small cities; public museums,

---

[6]Industries that sell products to the "outside world" are both important to, and a problem for, smaller communities. On the positive side, they typically are one of the most important sources of income for local workers; this income is often spent in the community itself. If a manufacturing enterprise locates in a town, it often attracts firms that cater to its needs and create more jobs. For instance, an automobile plant may attract subcontractors both on the production and product distribution sides. On the negative side, localities tend to depend on just a few such plants. Lack of diversity leaves them vulnerable when these plants experience difficulties.

[7]See Hugh O. Nourse, *Regional Economics* (New York: McGraw-Hill Book Company, 1968), p. 87, for a more detailed discussion of these advantages that economists refer to as "internal economies of scale."

[8]Although the evidence is hardly overwhelming, there is reason to believe that most innovations emanate from large cities. Once they are proven, it is contended, new processes "filter down" to smaller and more remote areas. Two interesting discussions of this process are included in Wilbur Thompson, "Internal and External Factors in the Development of Urban Economies," *Issues in Urban Economics,* Harvey Perloff and Lowdon Wingo, Jr., eds. (Baltimore: The John Hopkins Press, 1968), pp. 43-62, and William F. Ogburn and Otis D. Duncan, "City Size as a Sociological Variable," in *Contributions to Urban Sociology,* E. Burgess and D. Bogue, eds. (Chicago: University of Chicago Press, 1964), pp. 129-47.

social services, and extensive park systems are more typical of large cities. Moreover, many demands are more easily fulfilled. Police protection is less difficult where population is not crowded; maintenance is easier when streets are less congested.

Conversely, small city governments must contend with certain disadvantages. Like business, large government units are better able to take advantage of skilled administrators and specialized techniques. Large scale operations can typically use more efficient equipment. If a fire truck must be bought to protect a few citizens, more people can generally be serviced at little additional cost. Likewise, a small high school might underutilize a specialized teacher who provides services to a few students. In a large unit, specialists could be kept busy.

Economists have not definitely proven whether the costs of government services such as schools, hospitals, police and sewage treatment are substantially higher in small places. It is generally felt that cities of less than 100,000 population may be less efficient in providing most government services; cities over that level apparently suffer no great cost disadvantage for most functions. As for sewerage and fire protection, however, some studies indicate that costs show moderate declines until a city reaches several hundred thousand people.[9]

THE FUTURE OF SMALL CITIES: WHAT CAN BE DONE?

Current or prospective difficulties have caused many small cities and towns to mobilize their resources to attempt to stem the tide of economic decline. Policies are drafted to attack particular problems. Water and sewer systems are built. Roads are constructed. Industrial parks are organized and developed. Wharfs and warehouses are constructed. Local leaders often take out ads in periodicals to trumpet their city's virtues or to offer tax breaks to new industry.

Such policies can sometimes be useful. This is especially true if an otherwise viable town has just one or two problems that can, in fact, be overcome. Occasionally a town has all the advantages businesses need, but market information is imperfect and few executives know about its merits. However, the competitive market works fairly well in the long run, and it is rare that such self-development policies are effective.[10] If a city has remained

small or has declined, it usually is for reasons beyond local control.

There Is Always A Bigger Picture. People concerned with growth of their city or town often fail to realize that local economies do not grow in isolation. A locality's economic health depends on its relationship with neighboring cities. Furthermore, national trends help to shape its position in the contest for a share of national markets.

Any city is vitally linked to other cities in its vicinity with regard to the production of many goods and services. Remember that many cities — especially in rural areas — are central locations to which residents of surrounding areas and smaller towns come to conduct business. These same cities typically rely upon still larger cities for products which can't be produced profitably in the smaller locale. Such hierarchical relations are typical of many activities that create jobs.

While such patterns and relationships reflect efficiencies in production, they leave small places in an awkward position. Towns and cities "low" on the hierarchical ladder become dependent on larger cities. Even if a small city could become less reliant on larger neighboring cities for goods its citizens buy, it still would have to vie with them for businesses that serve national and international markets. In addition to disadvantages inherent in a small city's size, other factors beyond local control will bedevil attempts to improve local economic prospects.

For instance, local officials may want to diversify their town's economic base. But if its only advantage is a skilled labor force in textiles, the community is unlikely to attract an auto assembly plant. While the local leaders may exert pressure to keep an unprofitable railroad spur open, the costs of bringing raw materials to a city that is geographically iso-

---

[9]A review of the literature on the economies of scale in government services can be obtained from Werner Z. Hirsch, *The Economics of State and Local Government* (New York: McGraw-Hill Book Company, 1970), pp. 176-83.

[10]It is understandable that local civic leaders and businessmen in stagnant small cities would not be happy with the market solution to the question of where economic activity should take place. Economists also point out problems resulting from the way things work out. For instance, some argue that when people and plants move into large metropolitan areas, they create costs that others must bear. As large cities grow (especially during periods of rapid growth), congestion and pollution can increase dramatically. The costs of the additional problems fall on everyone — not just the new residents. By making small places more attractive, migration to large cities could be stemmed and such "social costs" could be avoided. Another argument for aiding small cities is that the market solution typically leaves them in an inherently unstable position, and they deserve aid on that account. As suggested earlier, because a small city is usually endowed with only a few industries, its economy is more likely to experience ups and downs. Unlike larger cities, fluctuations in one section cannot be absorbed by others. This vulnerability to extremes of growth and decline can be cited as a reason for public policy efforts at diversification.

lated may continue to discourage local development. Even if the oil crisis rekindles the demand for coal, a city whose resource base is high-sulfur coal may still miss out because of environmental regulations. In short, factors like investment patterns of the Federal Government, the way commerce is regulated, what products are in greatest demand nationally, and the distribution of natural resources influence which places prosper and which do not. Since there is not much local leaders can do to influence such factors, a city's economic fate is largely beyond its control.

A "Balanced National Growth" Policy. The frustration of citizens and their representatives in watching many small cities and metropolitan areas decline or grow very slowly has resulted in proposals for a "balanced national growth" policy.[11] Such a policy, of course, means different things to different people. Most proponents seem to be asking that the large geographic areas of the country—especially those cities and towns in rural areas that have experienced relatively little growth in the last 20 years—share more fully in the nation's prosperity.

If society decides to strive for "more balanced" growth, it makes sense that such a policy be national in scope. Local development planning and public investment certainly cannot hurt the local economy.[12] However, to be successful such a policy must alter the basic competitive forces that have drawn private industrial investment from small cities. As has been mentioned, many of these forces are economic trends which have affected the nation as a whole or are the result of Federal policy.

There are measures that could be used to tilt competitive advantage in favor of small places. Public works and investments could be channeled to small cities on a massive scale. Federal regulatory policies could be altered to make transportation and communication less expensive for small cities. A bolder approach would be a system of taxes on business that would favor plants in small cities, offsetting their competitive market disadvantages.

Any such policy must keep two considerations in mind. First, the magnitude of such efforts must be substantial enough to offset both broad market forces and the inherent disadvantages of being small. Programs exist now that provide local capital, but they are not operating on a magnitude that significantly alters the way markets work.[13] Second, there are costs involved in many such policy suggestions. In some cases it makes no economic difference where an activity is performed. If it is just as efficient to locate a government research facility in a small city as in a large one, it is costless to society to confer the benefits on a small town. In other cases, a policy to achieve a "better" geographic pattern of economic activity may cause efficiency in production to be sacrificed. This means valuable resources are lost to society. For instance, subsidizing a railroad line to a small city may prevent a dying plant from moving to a profitable location elsewhere. Unless the spur can eventually run at a profit and reimburse society for the expense of the subsidy, the money could have been used to meet other social needs.

LOOKING AHEAD

It seems unlikely that a national growth policy will be implemented with enough force to alter the prospects of small cities and metropolitan areas. However, some important national trends now underway could do so. As the nation's population grows, the additional people must be housed. Since the nation's borders are fixed, Americans must look inward for living space. The more rapid the growth of population, the more likely that people will find their way to small places.[14]

---

[11]Typical of new efforts is the Balanced Growth and Development Act, introduced by Senator Hubert H. Humphrey, which would provide a Federal mechanism for long-run national growth planning and consolidate existing development programs, procedures, and goals. Specific account would be taken of the locational impact of all Federal spending. Local planning would also be beefed up.

[12]If a city does grow and the initial problems of smallness are overcome, the advantages become self-reinforcing. As it gets bigger, there is more demand for business services. The resulting growth means more efficient operations for local businesses and more revenues for government. These improvements foster expansion in manufacturing and other "export" industries; this growth also yields tax dollars and further stimulates demand for services. Increased revenues and better government services make private enterprises more profitable and attract people to the town. Such interaction has led many to suggest that once a city reaches a certain size (250,000 population is often mentioned), it has become large enough to be permanently economically viable.

[13]The Economic Development Administration of the U. S. Department of Commerce devotes much of its attention to stimulating long-run economic growth in small cities in rural, depressed counties through infrastructure investment. The budget of the agency averages only about a quarter of a billion dollars a year. Thus, it is dwarfed by other government programs and market forces that affect regional distribution of economic activity.

[14]Even if population growth in the U. S. stabilizes, the population level would continue to rise because of the current mix of population. It is estimated that, even at the "replacement level" fertility rate of 2.1 children per woman, U. S. population will not stabilize until 2037, at a level of 275.5 million persons. For a full discussion of the issue of population growth, see "Zero Population Growth" in the *Monthly Review* of the Federal Reserve Bank of Richmond, September, 1971, pp. 7-12.

5. URBAN FUTURES

A second, and more important, trend may enhance the future of small places. There are indications that an increasing number of people are choosing lifestyles that emphasize small city amenities. For instance, recent evidence for the years between 1970 and 1973 reveals a dramatic shift in population distribution toward small cities. Although the fastest-growing areas were adjacent to metropolitan areas, small metropolitan areas and isolated rural areas grew more rapidly than the nation as a whole and at a much faster rate than previously.[15]

If these trends continue and gain momentum, the market provides mechanisms that can translate them into economic growth for small cities and metropolitan areas. The changing patterns of population would act as a signal to firms as producers and employers. It is a good bet that large metropolitan areas will not lose many of their economic advantages over small cities. But, there is no reason why—if more people show interest in small cities—they cannot overcome their disadvantages and prosper.

Unless such changes take place, many small cities will lose their economic viabilitiy and, perhaps, cease to exist. Others will remain small because they are performing only a minor role in the economic system as it is now structured. The is nothing "wrong" with such a situation. Not all cities can be large and growing.

Policies designed to aid economically lagging small cities and metropolitan areas must recognize such distinctions. Cities need not be large or growing to provide adequate jobs and incomes for their citizens. Efforts can be directed toward increasing the standard of living of citizens in small places that show signs of economic distress. However, programs that are aimed at making such places both "bigger and better" must be applied selectively. Such aid must be grounded on economic realities, not on the feeling of local citizens that every city has a right to grow. The system just does not work that way.

---

[15]See Richard L. Forstall, "Trends in Metropolitan and Nonmetropolitan Growth since 1970," NICHD Conference on Population Distribution, Baltimore, Maryland. Revised, May 1975.

DESIGNING a space community

The extraterrestrial communities that may be built in the future present an opportunity to develop new cultural patterns and new social philosophies. In the following article, an anthropologist discusses some of the social and philosophical issues that will arise as man begins setting up colonies beyond the earth.

Magoroh Maruyama

Magoroh Maruyama is Professor of Systems Science at Portland State University. His address is Portland State University, P.O. Box 751, Portland, Oregon 97207. His latest book, *Cultures Beyond the Earth* (Vintage, New York, 1975, 203 pages, $2.95), co-edited by Arthur Harkins, is available from the World Future Society's Book Service.

The technological feasibility of large, spacious extraterrestrial communities which accommodate from several thousand to a few million inhabitants each has been established in recent research projects. (See THE FUTURIST, February 1976.) Such communities will be highly habitable, with earth-like landscapes including farms, hills, trees, grass and animals. They will run on solar energy and will be constructed with materials mostly from the moon and other astronomical bodies. They will be financially self-supporting and will export solar energy to the earth. Once the first extraterrestrial community is built, the construction of the subsequent communities becomes easier using the first communities as the base.

With the advent of the era of extraterrestrial communities, we have reached the stage of our civilization where we have to think in terms of hitherto unknown cultural options. In the extraterrestrial communities, many of the constraints which restrict life on earth are removed. Temperature, humidity, seasons, length of day, weather, artificial gravity and atmospheric pressure can be set at will, and new types of cultures, social organization, and social philosophies become possible. The thinking required is far more than technological and economic; more basically, it is cultural and philosophical. We will be in a position to invent new cultural patterns and new social philosophies, and then choose material conditions and community design to fit the desired cultural goals and philosophies.

This new vista changes our entire outlook on the future, not only for those who eventually want to live in extraterrestrial communities but also for those who want to remain on earth. In the future, earth might be looked upon as an uncomfortable and inconvenient place to live compared to the extraterrestrial communities. Since a considerable portion of humanity—perhaps even most of it—

may be living in space communities, the meaning, the purpose, and the patterns of life on earth will also be considerably altered. Earth might be regarded as a historical museum, a biological preserve, a place which contains harsh climate and uncontrolled weather for those who love physical adventure, or a primitive and primeval place for tourism. This cultural transition may be comparable to the biological transition when our aquatic ancestors moved onto land or when our quadrupedal ancestors became bipedal and bimanual.

We now need anthropological, psychological, and philosophical thinking which guides technology. We must examine all possibilities thoroughly, choose our goals among the many alternatives available, and gear our technology toward those goals. The purpose of this article is to discuss some of the philosophical, psychological, and anthropological considerations which must be included in the design of extraterrestrial communities.

Heterogeneity is Key to Survival

One consideration basic to the design of extraterrestrial communities

Reprinted from: *The Futurist* A Journal of Forecasts, Trends and Ideas About the Future. Published by: World Future Society An Association for the Study of Alternative Futures, 4916 St. Elmo Avenue, Washington, D.C. 20014.

5. URBAN FUTURES

is the recent shift in the way scientists view the universe. Advances in the study of *mutual* causal processes are making it increasingly clear that the basic principle of biological, social, and even some physical processes is increase of heterogenization, differentiation, and symbiotization. No longer can we assume that the basic state of the universe is a random distribution of events with independent probability in which structures and patterns tend to decay into homogeneity. The homogenistic view places ultimate importance on the search for general rules and universal criteria, believing that there is one "best" way applicable to everybody. In the heterogenistic view, diversity in goals and designs is basic.

Heterogeneity is the very source of growth, enrichment, resource diversification, evolution, symbiotization, and survival. Traditional western logic preaches the ideology of unity by similarity, and regards differences as sources of conflicts. But the new scientific logic is "symbiosis thanks to diversity." For example, animals convert oxygen into carbon dioxide while plants do exactly the opposite, and in so doing, they held each other. The survival of the fittest does not mean the survival of the strongest. On the contrary, it means *the survival of the most symbiotic.* The "strongest" individual or species who destroys others and the environment cannot survive at all.

Heterogeneity also allows for diversification of supplies as well as demands. The richness of life in a tropical rain forest or on a coral reef is due to heterogeneity of species: if all animals ate the same food, there would be a food shortage, and if all animals were not eaten, there would be waste. Even solar energy is used maximally if different organisms employ different means to absorb it.

And obviously heterogeneity increases the probability of survival in unforeseen catastrophes. More importantly, interaction between heterogeneous subpopulations or subcultures increases the speed of biological or cultural evolution.

Therefore, the design of extraterrestrial communities must be heterogenistic. Different communities can be constructed in different forms, suitable for different cultural, social, and biological patterns. And each community must incorporate heterogeneity, variety, changeability, and flexibility.

Several geometrical forms for the physical shape of the space communities have been studied: a cylinder of a few kilometers in diameter; a torus of a few kilometers in diameter and several tens of meters in cross-section; a bundle of narrower parallel toruses; a necklace shape consisting of small spheres; and a pair of large spheres, each of which has a diameter of several kilometers. They have been examined from the points of view of volume, mass, rotational speed, shielding needed, construction costs, etc. There are also some psychological considerations which affect the mental health of the inhabitants. Different geometrical forms of the communities may also influence the types of social interactions and social organization which take place in them.

Solipsism Syndrome a Danger in Space

Some environments are conducive to the state of mind in which you come to feel that everything is a dream, not real. This state of mind occurs, for example, in the arctic winter when it is night 24 hours a day. It is also known to occur in some young people brought up on television as a reality substitute.

Solipsism is the name for this theory that everything exists in your imagination and there is nothing at all outside your brain. As a philosophical theory, it is internally consistent and therefore cannot be disproved. But as a psychological state, it is highly uncomfortable. Just try to force yourself to think for one hour that nothing exists outside your mind. Life is a long dream from which you can never awake. Even your friends are not real. You feel very lonely and detached, and eventually you become apathetic and indifferent.

I lived in Sweden for four years, in the small town of Lund. During the winter, each day consists of six hours of daylight and 18 hours of darkness. You spend most of your life under artificial light. When you go outdoors, you do not see landscape. You see only street corners lit by lamps. These street corners look like theater stages, detached from one another. There is no connectedness or depth in the universe. As theater stages, the universe acquires a very phony quality. This phoniness makes you feel that the whole world is your imagination.

This state of mind can be easily produced in an environment where everything is artificial, where everything is like a theater stage, where every wish can be fulfilled by a push-button, and where there is nothing beyond the theater stage and beyond your control.

There are several means which can help alleviate the tendency toward the solipsism syndrome in extraterrestrial communities:

1. A large macro-geometry, in which you can see far beyond the "theater stage" vicinity is important. Something must exist physically beyond the "theater stage" vicinity and must be overwhelmingly visible.

2. Something must exist beyond human manipulation. You learn to cope with reality precisely because the reality is different from your imagination. If the reality is the same as your imagination, you cannot escape falling into solipsism. In the extraterrestrial communities, nothing should be beyond human control. However, some amount of "unpredictability" can be built in within controllable range. One way to achieve this is to generate artificial unpredictability by means of a table of random numbers. Another way is to allow animals and plants a degree of freedom and independence from human planning. And both types of unpredictability must have a high visibility in order to be effective. This high visibility is easier to achieve in a macro-geometry which allows longer line of sight.

3. Something must exist which *grows.* It is important to feel that the universe is *NOT* static or thermodynamically and informationally decaying, but is self-generating and morphogenetic. Interactive processes generate new patterns which cannot be inferred from the information contained in the old state. It is important to feel that you can personally contribute to something which grows, that in order to do so you must learn reality principles, that the reality often goes in a direction different from your expectation, and finally that what you take care of (your child, for example) may possess more wisdom than yourself and may grow into something beyond yourself. From this point of view, it is important to personally raise children. It is also an excellent idea to grow vegetables and trees with personal care, not by mechanical means. It is also desirable to see plants and animals grow. This, again, is facilitated by a long line of sight.

4. It is also important to have "something beyond the horizon" which gives you the feeling that the world is larger than what you can see. When the five geometrical forms

mentioned earlier are compared on the basis of the four criteria, the circular torus proves to be the most satisfactory. The cylinder and the sphere provide no horizon at all. The bundle torus is rated poor in the first three criteria and the necklace is rated very poor in those same three areas (see table).

Types of Social Organization

There are many different types of social organization based on different cultural philosophies. Let us take three somewhat exaggerated examples, and discuss how each of them may be affected by various forms of macro-geometry.

Type A Community: Hierarchical and Homogenistic. People in this community believe that if there are many ways, there must be one best way among them, and that the "best way" is good for everybody. They think in terms of maximization and optimization. They consider majority rule as the basis of democracy, and competition as the basis of "progress." They look for universal criteria and universal categories which apply to all people and look for unity by means of similarities. Differences are considered as accidental, inconvenient or bothersome, and are ignored as much as possible. Diversity, non-standard behavior, and minority groups are considered abnormal or undesirable, to be corrected by being made more "normal." If some people are inconvenienced by the system which is geared toward the majority, the fault is considered to reside in the "abnormal" people. Because of the belief in the "best way" for all people and in maximum efficiency, all living units are designed alike. Because of the belief that unity is achieved by homogeneity and that differences create conflicts, residents are divided into age groups, occupational groups, etc., in such a way that each group is homogeneous within itself. Similarly, all living units are concentrated in one zone, recreational facilities in another zone, and industrial facilities in a third zone. This allows for a large continuous area suitable for recreational activities which require large space.

Type B Community: Individualistic and Isolationistic. People in this community think that independence is a virtue, both from the point of view of the person who is independent and from the point of view of others from whom he is independent. They consider self-sufficiency as the highest form of existence. Dependency and inter-dependence are looked down upon

as weakness or sin. Each living unit is like a self-contained castle, insulated against others in terms of sight, sound, and smell. Each unit contains its own recreational facilities, and there is no communal recreation area. Within each unit, everything is adjustable to the individual taste. Protection of privacy is a major concern in this community.

Type C Community: Heterogenistic, Mutualistic and Symbiotic. People in this community believe that the basic principle of biological and social processes is heterogenization and symbiotization due to mutual interaction. They consider heterogeneity to be a source of enrichment, symbiosis, resource diversification, flexibility, survival and evolution. They believe that there is no "best way" for all people. They think in terms of choosing and matching instead of maximization or optimization. They consider majority rule as homogenistic domination by quantity, and instead use the principle of elimination of or compensation for hardship which even a single individual may suffer when a decision is made. They consider competition useless and cooperation useful. They think that criteria and categories should be flexible and variable depending on the context and the situation. They look for harmony and symbiosis *thanks to* diversity, instead of advocating unity by means of similarities. Homogeneity is considered as the source of quantitative competition and conflict. Houses are all different, based on different design principles taken from different cultures and from different systems of family structure. Each building is different, and within each building, each apartment is different. The overall design principle is harmony of diversity and avoidance of repetition, as is found in Japanese gardens and flower arrangement. Different elements are not thrown together but carefully combined to produce harmony. People of different ages, different occupations, and different family compositions are mixed and interwoven, but care is taken to place together people who can help one another. For example, old people who love children are placed near families who need babysitters. On the other hand, antagonistic combinations are avoided. For example, noisy people are not placed near people who love a quiet environment.

Now let us consider the advantages and disadvantages of each of the different forms of macro-geometry with respect to these community types.

The cylinder and the sphere offer conditions favorable to Type A and Type C communities, but do not provide enough privacy for a Type B community. The bundle torus and the necklace allow sufficient privacy for a Type B community, but are incompatible with the needs of Type A and Type C communities.

The circular torus form is neutral to all types. This may prove to be convenient if the residents decide to change their community types. Furthermore, the circular torus can be divided into three or four sections, beyond the line of sight of one another, in such a way that different sections accommodate different types of community. This feature may be very important in the first extraterrestrial community, which will not be as large as subsequent ones and which, therefore, may tend to be monotonous.

Gesellschaft and Gemeinschaft

In the 19th century, the German sociologist Tonnies made an important distinction between two types of social systems: *Gesellschaft* and *Gemeinschaft*. There are many differences between the two, but what concerns us here is that it is easy to move in and out of a Gesellschaft, while it is difficult to do so with a Gemeinschaft. Gesellschaften allow for horizontal mobility of people between them. For example, one can relatively easily change jobs between companies or agencies in the United States, while it is more difficult to do so in Germany or in Japan. In this respect, American companies and agencies are similar to Gesellschaften, while German and Japanese companies are more like Gemeinschaften. One of the characteristics of a Gesellschaft is that it can amplify its eccentricity: those who do not like it will leave, and those who like it will stay. It can also easily eliminate non-conformists. Therefore homogeneity tends to increase within a Gesellschaft, though heterogeneity may increase between Gesellschaften. For this reason, a Gesellschaft may become very intolerant toward non-conformists.

There is an interesting relationship between the fact that the U.S. began as a colony of *voluntary* immigrants and the fact that, in the past, American philosophy and ideology have been homogenistic in spite of the heterogeneous population. The U.S. began as a Gesellschaft with a slogan: "If you like our ideology, you are welcome. But if you do not like our ideology, go back to where you came from." Thus began the policy of assimilation, and immigrants were eager to become "standard Americans."

A Gemeinschaft, on the other hand, must deal with non-conformists differently. It must either suppress non-conformists or accept non-conformists. It may become either homogenistically totalitarian or heterogenistic, depending on its policy and philosophy.

An extraterrestrial community may be made either Gesellschaft-like or Gemeinschaft-like. If the migration between communities is too free, each community may become very eccentric and homogeneous within itself, in-

tolerant toward heterogeneity. On the other hand, if the intercommunity migration is too restricted, it may suppress individuals.

Localization and Interweaving

There are two different methods of heterogenization: localization and interweaving. In localization, each of the heterogeneous elements separates itself and settles in one locality. Chinatown in San Francisco is an example. Heterogeneity increases between different localities, but each locality becomes homogeneous. In interweaving, many different elements blend together. This system creates no great differences between localities,

but within each locality there is a great diversity. It becomes easier for the individual to heterogenize himself. For example, a white person may eat Chinese food on Monday, Italian food on Tuesday, learn judo on Wednesday, or become a full-time Tibetan monk. Both localization and interweaving may be incorporated in the design of extraterrestrial communities.

The Problem of Matching

Needless to say, individuals vary in their tastes, abilities, and even in their optimal rate of communication. No culture is "healthy" or "unhealthy" for everybody. Each culture is healthy

---

The debate about man's future in space is increasing in intensity as the Space Shuttle, which will be capable of delivering large payloads to earth orbit, nears completion. By the end of the century, payload delivery costs are expected to be low enough to make space manufacturing facilities feasible. The Shuttle might also be used to transport construction materials and supplies for a large space community into orbit.

If a large space community is built in earth orbit, it now appears likely that the torus design shown above will be selected. This wheel-shaped space community, which appeared on the cover of the February 1976 issue of THE FUTURIST, would be over a mile in diameter and would hold 10,000 people. The community would pay its way by manufacturing satellite solar power stations which would supply cheap and plentiful power to the earth, according to Gerard O'Neill, the leading proponent of large orbiting space communities. (See his article in the February issue.) The torus design is also favored by Magoroh Maruyama because of its psychological impact and its compatibility with a variety of cultural philosophies.

Space experts such as G. Harry Stine claim that the communities suggested by O'Neill represent a very expensive gamble at this time. Stine, in his book *The Third Industrial Revolution* (Putnam, New York, 1975), predicts a bright future for space manufacturing facilities, but he sees a gradual evolution, starting with a compact

module located in the cargo bay of the space shuttle which would stay in orbit only seven to 30 days at a time. A few years later, the first module will be left in permanent orbit. As additional modules are added, the space industrial facility may resemble the artist's concept shown below. Ultimately, space industrial facilities may be much larger than the one shown here.

(See Robert Prehoda's review in the April 1976 issue of THE FUTURIST.)

As the limits to growth on earth become increasingly evident, space may receive more and more attention as a frontier region open to human settlement. Whether space stations or space cities (or some other alternative) will predominate remains unclear.

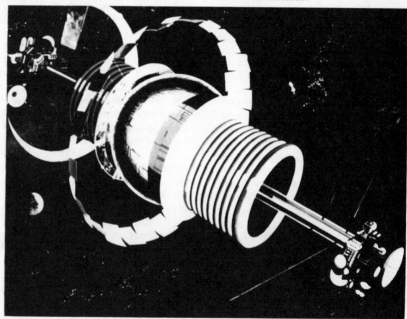

CONCEPT OF A SPACE SETTLEMENT
This is a view of the exterior of a possible space habitat for some 10,000 people. The colonists, members of a space manufacturing complex workforce, would live in homes on the inner surface of a large sphere nearly a mile in circumference which rotates to provide a gravity comparable to that of Earth. The habitat would be shielded against cosmic rays and solar flares by a non-rotating spherical shell made up from the slag of industrial processes using lunar surface material. Docking areas and zero gravity industrial areas are at each end of the space community. The flat surfaces are to radiate away waste heat of the habitat into space. The concept is a result of a 1976 Study on Space Manufacturing at NASA's Ames Research Center.

TWENTY-FIRST CENTURY SPACE COLONY
A resident of a 21st century space colony might view this vista of Earth-like landscape from inside his home in space. All the materials used to construct such a space colony would come from the Moon or the Astroid Belt and be manufactured in Space using solar power.
A concept of a space colony orbiting between the Earth and Moon is suggested by Dr. Gerard K. O'Neill of Princeton University who, with a group of university and NASA experts, have studied such colonies at NASA Ames Research Center, Moffett Field, California. In this settlement proposed by Dr. O'Neill Earth-like gravity would be produced by centrifugal force of rotation of the large wheel around its axis. At the hub of the wheel, an inhabitant would be weightless. Sunlight coming through the glass "windows" would be controlled by mirrors outside so that days, nights and seasons would result.

for those whose tastes, abilities, and rate of communication match with it, and unhealthy for others. High-communication individuals suffer in a low-communication community, and low-communication individuals suffer in a high-communication community. The same holds true for the matching of individuals to jobs, or individuals to individuals.

Successful matching requires availability of variety, and availability of variety depends on the number of different types of communities as well as the degree of heterogeneity within a community.

Certain types of facilities require a certain size of population. For example, a symphony orchestra cannot exist in a small town. A university cannot be built in a very small village.

There is also the problem of size vs. number. For example, many areas of the American midwest have a large number of small colleges, each with 1,000 or 2,000 students. The colleges all have libraries with more or less the same basic books. In a way this large number of small colleges creates heterogeneity. But, in another sense, a small number of large universities can create more heterogeneity, especially in the variety of library books or in the variety of departmental subjects. The planning of extraterrestrial communities involves the same problem. Certain types of heterogeneity can be maximized by having a large number of small communities. Other types of heterogeneity can be maximized by building a small number of large communities.

Self-Sufficiency of an Extraterrestrial Community

One of the most frequently asked questions regarding the idea of extraterrestrial communities is whether they can be self-sufficient. Before answering this question, let us list several different criteria for self-sufficiency:

1. Can survive and develop without any interaction with other communities.

2. If isolated, can survive at a reduced level.

3. Cannot survive without interaction with other communities, but is financially self-sufficient in the sense that the "export" and the "import" balance out.

4. Has a surplus.

Self-sufficiency in the sense of 3 is necessary and in the sense of 4 is desirable. *However, self-sufficiency in the sense of 1 is undesirable*, because it is conducive to isolationism, individualism, ethnocentrism, do-your-own-thingism, if-you're-poor-it-is-your-faultism, and eventually to cut-throat competition, don't-give-a-sucker-an-even-breakism, and exploit-or-you-will-be-exploitedism, in a way similar to the development of the American middle-class puritan ethic.

Turnover of Personnel

There are three kinds of people who go to work in Alaska: those who like adventurous life or like to challenge harsh, inconvenient environments; those who have a romantic but unrealistic notion of adventurous life, find themselves incapable of living in Alaska, and return from Alaska as soon as the first contract period is over; and those who go there for money, even though they hate the life in Alaska. The percentage of the second and third categories is very large. The same three types might be attracted to space communities.

The material conditions in extraterrestrial communities will be very comfortable, and even more comfortable than living in Washington, D.C., in summer or in Boston in winter. What would make life in an extraterrestrial community "harder" than life in Minnesota or California is probably mostly isolation from the earth and smallness of the environment. In these two aspects, an extraterrestrial community would resemble Hawaii rather than Alaska, as will be discussed below.

In any case, high monetary incentive should not be used because it attracts the wrong people. Furthermore, it would be unhealthy for the community as well as for the individuals concerned to make efforts to retain "misfits" in the extraterrestrial community. It would be healthier to return them to earth, even though this might seem more "expensive."

The Shimanagashi Syndrome

During the feudal period in Japan, political offenders were often confined on small islands. This form of punishment was called "shimanagashi." In many American prisons today, there are "isolation units" or "segregation units" where inmates considered to be troublemakers are confined for a length of time.

To a smaller degree, the "mainlanders" who spend a few years in Hawaii feel a strange sense of isolation. Announcements of conferences or manuscript deadlines often arrive in Hawaii long after the conferences have taken place or the deadlines have passed. You feel left out and intellectually crippled. Even though physically the life in Hawaii is very comfortable, mentally you suffer from the shimanagashi syndrome, unless you were born in Hawaii or have lived there long enough. For many people, life in Alaska has more challenge and excitement than life in Hawaii. Often the daily life in Alaska seems to consist of emergencies, which test your resourcefulness and your ability to cooperate with other individuals.

Furthermore, Hawaii is a group of small islands. Alaska is not only a part of a continent, but in winter the travel possibilities are unlimited due to snow on land and ice on the ocean, both of which serve as limitless highways for sleds and skis. In Hawaii, you cannot go beyond the shoreline. In Alaska, you can go far beyond the visible horizon.

Would the immigrants to extraterrestrial communities suffer from the shimanagashi syndrome? Technologists assure us that journals and books will be transmitted electronically between the earth and extraterrestrial communities. Therefore, the extraterrestrial communities will not be isolated in terms of communication. However, in terms of physical travel they will be isolated from the earth because the earth is at the bottom of a deep gravity hole. But travel between extraterrestrial communities will be quite inexpensive because the transportation system will not have to fight against a strong gravitational field.

Esthetics, Architecture and Landscaping

There are two levels of esthetics: *sensory esthetics* and *epistemological and philosophical esthetics*. Correspondingly, there are sensory aspects and epistemological aspects of architecture. Furthermore, there are spatial aspects and proxemic aspects of architecture.

The sensory aspects of architecture include color, light, shape, texture, and variety. The spatial aspects include people's movement, relative scale, and connectedness. The prox-

A Comparison of Space Community Designs

In order to avoid the solipsism syndrome (a feeling of unreality caused by prolonged exposure to an alien environment), Maruyama suggests that the following four design criteria be considered:
1. There must be a large macro-geometry in which you can see beyond the "theater stage" vicinity.
2. Something must exist beyond human manipulation.
3. Something must exist which grows.
4. There must be "something beyond the horizon" which gives the feeling that the world is larger than what you can see.
Below, Maruyama compares the effectiveness of five structural designs in meeting those criteria.

criteria	cylinder	sphere	circular torus	bundle torus	necklace
1.	excellent	excellent	medium	poor	very poor
2.	excellent	excellent	medium	poor	very poor
3.	excellent	excellent	medium	poor	very poor
4.	very poor	very poor	excellent	medium	medium

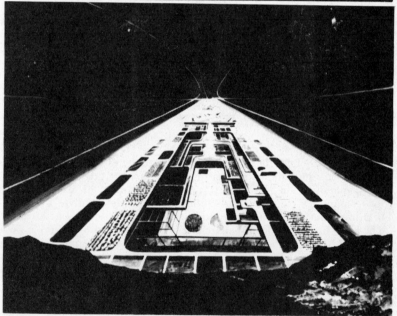

SPACE COLONY AGRICULTURAL AREA—An artist's conception of the agricultural area of a space colony, designed by the NASA-Ames/Stanford 1975 summer study. The area is shown situated between two parks. On the top four levels of the farm, soybeans, wheat, sorghum and some other crops would be grown. The bottom level is a drying facility. Water would be supplied directly from the river and indirectly through the fish tanks that line the sides. Altogether, these tanks could hold about 260,000 fish. The half-mile long farm would also be inhabited by rabbits and 2800 cattle. Since moisture, sunlight and heat conditions are controlled, the farm could yield far more than a comparable size farm on Earth. With three of these agricultural areas covering a total of only around 110 acres the colony would be able to produce enough food to be self-sufficient.

emic aspects relate to cultural variations (for example, what is considered to be a comfortable distance between conversing individuals); spatial patterns related to kinship; and spatial

configurations related to social structure (circular for non-hierarchical social structure, linear or vertical for hierarchical social structure).

The epistemological aspects relate

Social Organization, Architecture Should Be Complementary

In the following table, author Maruyama shows the effect various community designs would have on three basic, and very different, types of space communities.

community type	cylinder	sphere	circular torus	bundle torus	necklace
Type A: hierarchical homogenistic	favorable	favorable	medium	unfavorable	unfavorable
Type B: individualistic isolationistic	unfavorable (less privacy)	unfavorable (less privacy)	medium	favorable (more privacy)	favorable (more privacy)
Type C: heterogenistic mutualistic symbiotic	favorable	favorable	medium	unfavorable	unfavorable

to the underlying world view of the designer and the users. For example, if the philosophy is that humans are intimately connected with nature and that people have a need to be directly in touch with nature—visually, olfactorily and otherwise—then the design may include removable walls, large windows, and removable partitions. On the other hand, if the philosophy is that humans should be as independent as possible from nature, then the design will intend to separate the dwellers from their surroundings. If the philosophy is that humans should conquer and dominate nature, the design will stand out against nature. If the philosophy is that humans are a part of nature, then the architecture will be inconspicuous, blend in to the surroundings, and even act like a "black hole" which sucks light in.

Similarly, if the philosophy is that humans are intimately connected with other humans, then visual and acoustic openness and connectedness become more important than insulation and privacy. Some people might prefer to hear the noises of the street. Some people might prefer a communal or familial sleeping room rather than private bedrooms. The philosophy of togetherness may be related to the philosophy of having no secrets.

The philosophy of specialization and categorization is architecturally expressed by specialized rooms such as the dining room and the bedroom, which tend to be dominated by specialized furniture. On the other hand, non-categorical, relational and situational philosophy is architecturally expressed by non-specialized and flexibly convertible rooms, and even connectable rooms. Such rooms have removable furniture, and consequently most of the space can be used by people rather than occupied by furniture.

The philosophy of sharing is expressed by a communal or exchangeable kitchen, laundry room, dining room, etc. The philosophy of self-sufficiency is expressed by self-contained castle-like units.

There are also certain techniques which can facilitate some philosophies. For example, trees planted outside each window of a tall building have two effects: to those inside the building, they appear to be a forest; for those outside the building, they make the building look like a tree-covered mountain. The exterior of a building may also be made to look like a cliff or a waterfall. The interior of a building may contain a miniature landscape or use a recess to create an optical illusion of a large garden around the corner of a corridor. Cassette landscapes may be used which can be changed from season to season.

Choice of the type of landscape may reflect philosophy and personality. Some have the need to feel the immense expanse of grassland, deserts, ocean, cultivated fields or even sprawling cities. Others prefer a smaller, cozy corner at the bottom of a cliff with a small waterfall or in a misty forest. On the other hand, there are those who need to feel secure by being isolated from outside. In the future, there may be persons who need to feel independent by being suspended in midair.

International Participation

When there are many extraterrestrial communities, some of them may belong to individual nations, some may be international, and some may even form new extraterrestrial nations.

We cannot assume that the first extraterrestrial communities will be purely American: The U.S. may no longer be a major world power or a major technological center by the time the first extraterrestrial community materializes. Even if the U.S. remains a major world power, many nations, including non-western nations and African nations, will be highly technological by then, and it seems to be a waste of human resources if we do not internationalize the first extraterrestrial community.

The present technological nations are not necessarily advantaged because the technology they possess is earth-bound as well as culture-bound. They may have to first *unlearn* the forms, the assumptions, and the habits of the earth-bound technology before they can learn the new forms and assumptions of technology useful in extraterrestrial communities.

More important is the question of culture-boundness. We have the possibilities of developing new types of cultures in extraterrestrial communities, free from physical constraints such as climate and gravity, which restrict life on earth. So far, the "rich" nations have assumed that the European or the American way of living is more "advanced" and "scientific" than other ways. It might well be that some other ways of living—not necessarily those found in other existing cultures, but possibly entirely new ways of living which do not yet exist— may turn out to be more desirable under extraterrestrial conditions, and these ways of living may be based on epistemologies and logics different from the one prevailing in European and American cultures. Many so-called underdeveloped nations have an advantage not so much because their logics and epistemologies are non-European, but because they have experienced what may be called "trans-epistemological processes" (i.e., exposure to several epistemologies), and therefore know what is meant by different epistemologies, while most Americans do not quite know what different epistemologies or philosophies are.

There will be 15 or 20 years between now and the completion of the first extraterrestrial community in which to prepare the first immigrants for the experience. What we need is not merely technological training, but also much broader education, including different logics and epistemologies. There is no ready-made educational system for this, and we must begin from scratch. Therefore, all nations are on an equal footing. If we begin now, in 15 or 20 years all nations will have produced potential immigrants to the first extraterrestrial community.

239

Paolo Soleri's Cities of Tomorrow

ENVIRONMENTS FOR THE FUTURE

Charles Hillinger

All cities everywhere are absurd, unworkable, obsolete—sprawling megalopolises eating up the surface of the earth, their pollutants menacing the total geophysical and biochemical balance of the planet. So insists Paolo Soleri, architect-philosopher, prophet-visionary, who has spent the past quarter-century sketching revolutionary cities of the future.

Soleri calls his futuristic cities arcologies—architecture plus ecology. They are unlike any metropolitan area on the face of the earth. They soar skyward instead of spreading sideways.

Soleri envisions the Homo sapiens of tomorrow living in concrete anthills, in concrete beehives. His cities would stack hundreds of thousands of people in mile-high, nonpolluting, single structures which would hold everything necessary for human development—factories, commercial enterprises, shopping centers, apartments, schools, cultural centers.

People would walk through corridors, over bridges, ride escalators and elevators to their destinations within the single structure city. Every place would be reachable by foot within 15 minutes from any other given place.

Soleri's cities of concrete cubes, squares and apses stacked one atop another would be civilizations floating on the

Hexahedron, a city for 170,000;

seven seas, crown seashore cliffs or nestle in mountain canyons.

His Asteromo would spin through space, an asteroid housing 70,000 scientists (and their families) doing research in astronomy, physics and space biochemistry.

Is this just one man's fantasy? Perhaps. But the 56-year-old

Italian-born architect living in Scottsdale, Arizona, is not content with merely scrawling his imaginative urban centers on reams of butcher paper. The elfin-like prophet is moving the first of his cities of tomorrow from drawing board to reality.

On the edge of a towering mesa 70 miles north of Phoenix in a sweeping arena of sparsely

populated mountains and mesas, Soleri is building his first arcology. Looking like something out of the pages of science fiction, Arcosanti is rising from the rim of a steep, spectacular red-rock cliff.

Soleri pads around his remarkable project in sandals, shorts and T-shirts, supervising the efforts of an army of vi-

Arcvillage, an arcology for 30,000.

sionaries who idolize the architect as their master and guru whose ideas are not of today but of tomorrow.

During the five years Arcosanti has been under construction, more than 2000 young people from throughout the nation and from many foreign countries, fascinated by Soleri's philosophical and environmental perceptions, have come to the mesa to join the master in building his first arcology. They pay Soleri for the privilege of working beside him, digging ditches, pouring concrete, laying pipe, toting heavy beams and doing a hundred and one other difficult, tiring, dirty jobs necessary in building a city.

Arcosanti is planned as a complete, self-contained unit for 3000 men, women and children who would live in this first concrete beehive, work in it, play in it, relax and study in it. They would also be able to do all of these things without the need of automobiles except on the rare occasions when they would need to leave the arcology.

An arcology presents a vision of life in the future as Soleri sees it: "Multilevel. An aesthetocompassionate phenomenon. Its advent will be the implosion of the flat megalopolis of today into an urban solid of superdense and human vitality. Urban structures so dense as to host life, work, education, culture, leisure and health for hundreds of thousands of people per square mile."

Arcologies will be oases in the midst of wilderness. Untouched countryside will be at everyone's fingertips. Unspoiled, unlittered, uncluttered open land will embrace the spectacular single structure cities. According to Soleri, "The compactness of arcology gives back to farming and to land conservation 90 percent or more of the land that megalopolis and suburbia are engulfing in their sprawl."

With open space minutes away by foot for every city dweller, the metropolitan man of tomorrow will be both city dweller and country person at one and the same time. He will be able to partake fully of both city and country life.

"The car," continues Soleri, "will follow the horse to pasture. The car is dividing things more and more by scattering them all over. Antiswiftness inherent to scatterization makes high speed urban transportation a perpetual illusion.

"In arcology, distances are measured again by walks and in minutes. Within an arcology the car is nonsensical. It has nowhere to go."

Efficiency is the key to everything in an arcology. To quote Soleri: "The squandering in land, in time, in energy and in the wealth of megalopolis and suburbia, now well entangled in their increasing contradictions, is rejected as obsolete. In arcology the ratio of efficiency to energy becomes many times greater.

"Thus, pollution will be manyfold smaller. Pollution is a direct function of wastefulness. The elimination of wastefulness is the elimination of pollution.

"The obstacles of time and space are minimized, miniaturized. All of arcology can be called a marketplace. All of it a learning organism. All of it

5. URBAN FUTURES

a productive mechanism and a playground." Too many things in present-day cities, insists Soleri, "are spent cartridges. Too little is of nonbrittle nature."

In Soleri's arcologies, "Home nursing becomes as feasible and as professional as hospital care. But far less costly and far more personal. Nurses and doctors move from home to home, as from ward to ward, making the family doctor real again. Infirmaries, clinics and hospitals are always at walking distance."

Soleri's cities of tomorrow move "From haphazardness and dislocation to coordination and fitness."

What is to become of Paolo Soleri's first arcology if and when completed? "A research center. A university, perhaps," says the visionary.

How soon will the 25-story Arcosanti be completed? "Hopefully in 20 years," the prophet replies. Then, gazing out over the steep red-rock cliff and sweeping canyon below, muses: "Here a man can find harmony with both the urban setting and the natural environment. Here there is no suburban blight spreading out for miles and insulating the populace from nature.

"In its new, contracted form, the city can now offer its inhabitants what they seek from urban life: a true and vital richness of activities free from the fatiguing problems dictated by existing cities."

In his definitive book about arcology, *The City in the Image of Man*, published by the Massachusetts Institute of Technology, are printed detailed diagrams of 30 Soleri arcologies, including Novanoah, a mile-high, 6900-acre, floating ocean arcology designed for 2.4 million people. Such arcologies, "like enormous digestive systems would ingest the mass of water, extract from it the elements designated by the function of the diverse plants and eliminate the used water in an uninterrupted cycle.

"The different materials, vegetable and animal, chemical and mineral—once trapped, would be processed and/or stored in them [the arcologies], in part consumed, in part exported as food, fertilizer and so on, or used as material for production of goods.

"Novanoah could drift with the currents or be slowly propelled on short or long journeys. . . ."

Soleri's marvelous imagery is detailed page after page in *The City in the Image of Man*, describing arcologies with designations such as Arcoforte, Arcvillage, Logology, Babel, Babel Canyon, Arckibuz, Arcodiga, Babeldiga. . . .

The ultimate arcology, Babelnoah, holds a population of six million living in the complex of mile-high skyscrapers spread over 18,000 acres.

Soleri calls today's cities "inefficient systems bogged down with pollution, frustration and irritation." He is convinced his super single-structure cities are the logical answer in the bridge from today to tomorrow.

Below left and right: young people come from all over the world to pay for the privilege of working with Soleri. Bottom photo: an artist's view of Arcosanti, a city for 3000.

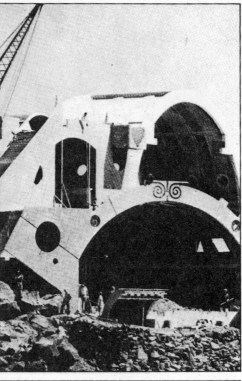

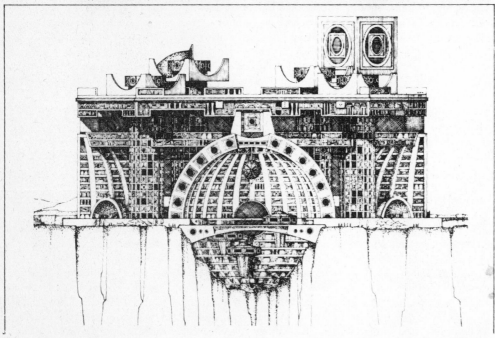

ae

We want your advice.

Any anthology can be improved. This one will be—annually. But we need your help. Annual Editions revisions depend on two major opinion sources: one is the academic advisers who work with us in scanning the thousands of articles published in the public press each year; the other is you—the person actually using the book.

Please help us and the users of the next edition by answering the questions on the last page of this book and returning it to us.

Thank you.

photos by Robert Tobey

INDEX

Credits/Acknowledgments

Cover design by Charles Vitelli

1. **Urbanization**
    Facing overview— © David Attie 1975.

2. **Varieties of Urban Experiences**
    Facing overview— © David Attie 1975. 56, 58—Reprinted by permission of the Social Policy Corporation. 87—Photograph by Terry Clough.

3. **Urban Problems**
    Facing overview— © David Attie 1975. 106-110—*The Futurist,* published by the World Future Society, P. O. Box 30369 (Bethesda), Washington, D.C. 20014. 161-162—UPI Photos. 164—Wide World Photo. 165—UPI Photo.

4. **Urban Social Policies**
    Facing overview— © David Attie 1975. 188—Mary Anne Shea

5. **Urban Futures**
    Facing overview—Courtesy Paul Rudolph, New York. Reprinted by permission. 236-238—Photos: NASA. 240-242—Photos by Irving Pintar/Cosanti Foundation.

We want your advice.

Robert Tobey

Any anthology can be improved. This one will be—annually. But we need your help. Annual Editions revisions depend on two major opinion sources: one is the academic advisers who work with us in scanning the thousands of articles published in the public press each year; the other is you—the person actually using the book.

Please help us and the users of the next edition by answering the questions below and then returning it to us.

Thank you.

What do you think of this Book?

1. What do you think of the Annual Editions concept?

2. Which article(s) did you like the most? Why?

3. Which article(s) should we drop from the next edition? Why?

4. Have you read any articles lately that you think should be included in the next edition:

What basic text did you use with this Annual Editions reader?

Title _____

Author(s) _____

If you didn't use a text, what did you use?

Was it a good combination?

(continued on back)

About you

I am a student ☐ an instructor ☐

Name _____ School _____

Term Used _____ Date _____

Address _____

City _____ State _____ Zip _____

Telephone _____ Office Hours _____

To Order a copy of Annual Editions

To order a copy, simply check off the volume you want on the list below and send this order form along with your check to us. We will take care of the postage. All orders are automatically filled with the latest edition—should you wish an older edition please indicate which edition you want. We will contact you should that edition be no longer available.

Volumes now available in the Annual Editions series:

__ AE Aging	$5.75		__ AE Human Development	$6.25
__ AE American Government	$6.25		__ AE Human Sexuality	$5.75
__ AE American History Pre-Civil War	$5.75		__ AE Macroeconomics	$5.75
__ AE American History Post-Civil War	$5.75		__ AE Marketing	$6.25
__ AE Anthropology	$6.25		__ AE Marriage & Family	$5.75
__ AE Biology	$5.75		__ AE Microeconomics	$5.75
__ AE Business	$5.75		__ AE Personality & Adjustment	$5.75
__ AE Criminal Justice	$5.75		__ AE Psychology	$6.25
__ AE Unexplored Deviance	$5.75		__ AE Social Psychology	$6.25
__ AE Early Childhood Education	$6.25		__ AE Social Problems	$5.75
__ AE Economics	$6.25		__ AE Sociology	$6.25
__ AE Education	$5.75		__ AE Urban Society	$5.75
__ AE Health	$5.75			

**First Class
Permit No. 84
Guilford, Ct.**

Business Reply Mail

No Postage Stamp Necessary if Mailed in the United States

Postage will be paid by

Attention: Annual Editions Service
The Dushkin Publishing Group, Inc.
Sluice Dock
Guilford, Connecticut 06437